1890-1900 POLITICS,
REFORM AND
EXPANSION

hARPER ✦ ɔORChBOOKS

EDITORS' NOTE: *A check-list of Harper Torchbooks, classified by subjects, is printed at the end of this volume.*

THE NEW AMERICAN NATION SERIES

Edited by HENRY STEELE COMMAGER and
RICHARD B. MORRIS

* In preparation

1890-1900 POLITICS, REFORM AND EXPANSION

BY HAROLD U. FAULKNER

HARPER TORCHBOOKS
The University Library
HARPER & ROW, *Publishers*
New York, Evanston, and London

Contents

Illustrations

vii

Maps and Charts

Editors' Introduction

THE decade of the nineties was the watershed of American history. On the one side stretches the older America—the America that was overwhelmingly rural and agricultural, that devoted its energies to the conquest of the continent, that enjoyed relative isolation from the Old World, that was orthodox in religion, optimistic in philosophy, and romantic in temperament. Over the horizon, on the other side, came the new America—an America predominantly urban and overwhelmingly industrial, inextricably involved in world politics and world wars, experiencing convulsive changes in population, economy, technology, and social relations, and deeply troubled by the crowding problems that threw their shadow over the promise of the future.

Already by the nineties the generation that had fought the Civil War was passing from the scene, and a generation that knew Pickett's charge and Missionary Ridge only as history and tradition was coming to the fore. Majors and colonels in faded blue or gray still strutted the political stage, but the most memorable politician of the decade— William Jennings Bryan—was born the year of secession, and his great rival, Theodore Roosevelt, was but a baby when the flag came fluttering down from Ft. Sumter. The issues that had agitated the postwar generation—reconstruction, the tariff, public lands, railroads—took on a faded and old-fashioned character. Politicians, notoriously the victims of the cultural lag, still waved the bloody shirt of the rebellion or invoked the memory of the stars and bars, but to little avail, and soon a new war united North and South where an old war had divided them. Even the statesmen of the previous decades, the bearded Blaines and Conklings, Mortons and Lamars came to seem alien and archaic when contrasted with new men like Bryan and La Follette and Theodore

Roosevelt or—perhaps more to the point—with new masters of industry and captains of finance like Rockefeller, Carnegie, and Morgan.

The problems that pushed so urgently to the fore in the nineties were economic and social, and did not seem to be illuminated by traditional political debates or yield to familiar party resolutions. The key issues of the new age, as Professor Faulkner makes clear, were reform and expansion, and about these issues the old political orthodoxies had little to say. The late eighties had brought hard times to the farmer, the workingman, and to many businessmen as well, and with hard times doubts and disillusionment; in the nineties came open revolt, a challenge to old beliefs, a repudiation of old shibboleths, a fragmentation of old parties. There was almost everywhere a feeling that somehow the promise of American life was not being fulfilled. The Union had been saved, but sectional animosities had scarcely abated, and the Negro was not much better off than he had been in slavery. The continent had been conquered, and the frontier was no more, but the cost of exploitation and waste was a sobering one. Industry flourished, and the new nation was rapidly forging ahead of her Old World competitors, but at the price of recreating those class conflicts from which the United States had heretofore been thought immune. Cities had grown and flourished, but with them slums and poverty, crime and vice, and Jefferson's warnings seemed to be justified within less than a century of his death. In 1890 Americans were reading *How the Other Half Lives;* they had not supposed that there was, in America, an Other Half, except among the Negroes. The ruthless exploitation of natural resources made the nation rich beyond the imaginings of its founders, but the riches were gravitating into the hands of the few, and the power of wealth in politics caused the gravest misgivings. Slavery had been ended, but not the inhumanity of man to man—and to women and children, as well: children of ten or twelve labored in factory and in mine; women stood twelve hours at the loom; absentee corporations foreclosed mortgages on distant farms; Negroes were denied both civil and political rights; the immigrant was cruelly exploited; the treatment of the dangerous and perishing classes outraged not only justice but decency. Millions flocked into the schools, but the census counted six million illiterates. Democracy flourished, and with it corruption.

These conditions might have led to revolt; instead they led to reform.

The process of federal centralization which was to be so important in the twentieth century was already under way, and some of the issues that agitated public life were fought out on the national stage—both in Congress and in the Supreme Court. More, perhaps, were debated and disposed of on the local and state level: at no time in our history have local and state politics been more significant or contributed more to the working out of ultimate solutions to major problems. It is one of the most valuable features of Professor Faulkner's book that he gives adequate attention to state and local affairs, and makes clear their connection with national.

The decade that had been ushered in so grimly ended on a note of confidence. Prosperity returned, to business, to factory, and to farm. Businessmen took heart, and hastened to create ever bigger combinations. The Klondike and Australian gold fields went far to settle the money question; farm prices increased and the farm problem all but disappeared. A "jolly little war" ended with America as a world power and with the ebullient Roosevelt as the first world statesman since Jefferson. With the new century, the spring of hope succeeded the winter of discontent. If few of the problems that had agitated the nineties were solved, the nature of the problems themselves had been made clear and some solutions formulated: that was a notable achievement.

This volume is one of the New American Nation Series, a comprehensive, co-operative survey of the history of the area now embraced in the United States from the days of discovery to the second half of the twentieth century. Since the publication by the House of Harper of the American Nation Series, over half a century ago, scholars have broadened the scope of history, explored new approaches, and developed new techniques. The time has come for a judicious reappraisal of the new history, a cautious application of the new techniques of investigation, and a large-scale effort to achieve a synthesis of new findings with familiar facts, and to present the whole in attractive literary form.

To this task the New American Nation Series is dedicated. Each volume is part of a carefully planned whole, and fitted as well as is possible to the other volumes of the series; at the same time each volume is designed to be complete in itself. From time to time the same series of events will be presented from different points of view: thus the volumes dealing with foreign affairs, constitutional history, and cultural history will in some ways retrace ground covered in this volume. Repetition is less regrettable than omission, and something is to be gained by looking at the same period and the same material from different and independent points of view.

HENRY STEELE COMMAGER
RICHARD BRANDON MORRIS

Preface

THIS volume, one of a long series of studies in American history, deals almost exclusively with the years 1890 to 1900. It is essentially concerned with the politics of the decade, with the economic history of the period, with efforts to reform and improve many areas of the existing society, and finally with the new burst of territorial expansion resulting in part from the Spanish-American War. Other volumes in this series will emphasize the constitutional and the cultural development of the decade in greater detail than the present author has attempted.

To those brought up in the tradition of "the gay nineties," it may be surprising to discover that the phrase is misleading. Except for the few exciting months of the Chicago World's Fair, there was little gaiety in the decade. On the contrary, five years of deep depression pushed agriculture to its lowest depths, demoralized industry and transportation, and brought with them various economic problems which became irretrievably interwoven with politics. The long and dreary battles over trusts, the control of interstate commerce, "free silver," and tariffs dominated the political life, but hardly raised the morale of the citizens. Nor did the efforts to solve these problems bring any immediate solutions to a harassed people.

To explode the myth of the nineties is not difficult. But I found it complicated, as is often the case, to point up the dominant characteristics of a single decade when the activities of the period started before the decade and continued in subsequent years. The nineties were restless, full of questioning and pioneering, when people were intent on reforming many aspects of social, economic, and political life. Thinking people of the nineties knew the weaknesses of existing society

as well as did the muckrakers of the next decade. But, unlike the muckrakers, they were not content with facts alone; they pioneered in many
efforts to better conditions. In a sense it was an introduction to a new
century where this work would be carried on and widened. Curiously,
all of this happened in a period during which the national government
was controlled by extremely conservative administrations.

This author is grateful for the help of the two editors of this series,
Henry S. Commager and Richard B. Morris, but particularly he is
indebted to Professor Commager, who assumed the responsibility of
supervising and criticizing this volume. Much credit is also due to
Christopher Lash of Williams College, who contributed a great deal
in suggesting chapter reorganizations in the original text, in emphasizing certain interpretations, and in giving some lift and spirit to the
book.

HAROLD U. FAULKNER

Northampton, Massachusetts
December 12, 1958

POLITICS, REFORM AND EXPANSION

CHAPTER 1

The Restless Decade

THE 1890's separated not only two centuries but two eras in American history. These years saw the gradual disappearance of the old America and the rather less gradual emergence of the new. They witnessed the passing of the frontier and the rise of the United States to a position of world power and responsibility which was to make any return to her old isolation increasingly difficult, if not impossible. Old issues were dead or dying; sectional tension was no longer a force of much importance in politics, and efforts to revive it proved unavailing. Most important of all, the triumph of industry over agriculture was now assured. The Industrial Revolution, if not completed, had gone so far as to make turning back to the ways of a simpler agrarian society out of the question. Yet by no means all Americans—perhaps not even a majority—were able to recognize or willing to acknowledge the significance of these momentous changes. The face of life was being perceptibly altered; thought, in many cases, had yet to accommodate itself to the fact. The American people, Henry Adams said, "were wandering in a wilderness much more sandy than the Hebrews had ever trodden about Sinai; they had neither serpents nor golden calves to worship. They had lost the sense of worship. . . ."[1] In their uncertainty they looked to the past for guidance and reassurance, but the past was of little assistance in confronting the problems of a new era.

The Industrial Revolution pushed the great questions of slavery and sectionalism into the past; by 1900 the Civil War belonged to a bygone age seen now through the filter of romance. Veterans on both sides cherished memories of the war, but they could now celebrate their

[1] *The Education of Henry Adams* (Modern Library ed., New York, 1931), p. 328.

I

reunions together. A few professional politicians might still wave the bloody shirt and revive old issues, but their efforts increasingly failed to interest the voters. During the Harrison administration Henry Cabot Lodge and other Republicans advocated a "Force Bill" to protect the right of Negroes to vote by federal supervision of congressional elections; it never even reached a Senate vote. Cleveland in his second administration appointed two Southerners to his cabinet, one a former Confederate officer. McKinley was the last Civil War veteran to be elected President. Reunion was essentially complete.[2]

The passing of the frontier signified more dramatically the waning of the old order. The historic census of 1890 officially declared the frontier to be closed—somewhat prematurely, for in actual fact the westward movement continued for years thereafter. Four times as many acres were homesteaded under the Act of 1862 after 1890 than before that date. After the usable land in this country had been occupied, almost 1,250,000 American pioneers moved into western Canada to take up fresh land there. The statement that "the unsettled area has been so broken into by isolated bodies of settlement that there can hardly be said to be a frontier line" was rather a notice of an impending future than an actual fact, but the mere imminence of a frontierless future was enough to cause widespread apprehension. This apprehension ran through Turner's celebrated essay of 1893; it was even more explicit in Theodore Roosevelt's *The Winning of the West*, in which Roosevelt again and again expressed the fear that the old American virtues, nurtured by the frontier, were in peril now that the frontier was no more than a memory. Indeed, so persistently did Americans of the nineties call attention to the disappearance of the frontier that it seemed at times to be exercising a greater influence on history as a memory than it ever had as a fact.[3]

Serious Indian troubles ended in the "Ghost Dance" War of 1890, and by the middle of the decade most of the good land on the Indian reservations had been opened to white settlers. Oklahoma was thrown open to settlement in 1889 after a decade of agitation and border incidents. Time and again "boomers" invaded the area and had to be ejected by federal troops. At length the government gave in to popular pressure; in March, 1889, President Harrison announced that the Oklahoma District would be opened to settlement on April 22. From

[2] Paul H. Buck, *The Road to Reunion, 1865–1900* (Boston, 1937).
[3] See Henry Nash Smith, *Virgin Land* (Cambridge, 1950), ch. XXII.

late March until the day of invasion adventurers, speculators and bona fide settlers gathered by the thousands on the southern border of Kansas and the northern border of Texas.

A few days before the announced date the prospective settlers were allowed to enter the Cherokee Outlet and the Chickasaw reservation. One hundred thousand settlers in every type of vehicle, including fifteen trains, crowded along the border line of the Oklahoma District waiting for the army to give the signal to advance. At eleven o'clock on the appointed day, wrote Edna Ferber in *Cimarron*,

they were crowding and cursing and fighting for places near the Line. They shouted and sang and yelled and argued, and the sound they made wasn't human at all, but like thousands of wild animals penned up. The sun blazed down. It was cruel. The dust hung over everything in a thick cloud, blinding you and choking you. . . . It was a picture straight out of hell. . . . Eleven-forty-five. Along the Border were the soldiers, their guns in one hand, their watches in the other. Those last five minutes seemed years long; and funny, they'd quieted till there wasn't a sound. Listening. The last minute was an eternity. Twelve o'clock. There went up a roar that drowned the crack of the soldiers' musketry as they fired in the air as the signal of noon and the start of the Run. You could see the puffs of smoke from their guns, but you couldn't hear a sound. The thousands surged over the Line. It was like water going over a broken dam. The rush had started, and it was devil take the hindmost. We swept across the prairie in a cloud of black and red dust that covered our faces and hands in a minute, so that we looked like black demons from hell.[4]

Within a few hours Guthrie was a tented city of almost 15,000 people and within a hundred days it had banks, a hotel, stores, newspapers, and an electric light plant. Oklahoma City, it was asserted, also had a tent population the first night of 10,000. Quite as rapidly the homesteaders were laying out their quarter sections in the surrounding country.[5] The thousands who swarmed into the District on that day were but the vanguard of many others who followed. Operating under the Dawes Severalty Act (1887), Congress extinguished Indian claims

[4] Edna Ferber, *Cimarron* (New York, 1929), pp. 23–25.

[5] H. S. Wicks, "The Opening of Oklahoma," *Cosmopolitan*, VII (Sept., 1889), 460–470, by one of the first settlers; J. S. Buck, "The Settlement of Oklahoma," *Wisconsin Academy of Science, Arts and Letters, Transactions* (Madison, Wis., 1907), XV, 325–380; Roy Gittinger, *The Formation of the State of Oklahoma* (Berkeley, Calif., 1917); V. E. Harlow, *Oklahoma, Its Origins and Development* (Oklahoma City, 1934); Carl C. Rister, *Land Hunger: David L. Payne and the Oklahoma Boomers* (Norman, Okla., 1942).

and opened one reservation after another to white settlers. The boomer invasion of 1889 was re-enacted in September, 1893, when 6 million acres of the Cherokee strip were opened.[6] By 1900 the population of Oklahoma numbered almost 400,000. The last great opening occurred in 1901.

By 1890 the last and greatest of the ranching frontiers had ended. Overproduction and depression hurt the industry; they were followed by severe winter storms in the late eighties which decimated the herds. At the same time farmers, aided by the railroads, barbed wire, and metal windmills, pressed on the heels of the retreating ranchers. By the late nineties farmers had taken over most of the land west of the 100th meridian which was suitable for crops. Barbed wire, which was utilized earlier by the farmers to protect their fields from roving cattle, was now used by ranchers to pen in their herds.[7] As with ranching, the early miners' frontier had also disappeared. The mining industry had come into the hands of large corporations, and prospecting was chiefly done under their direction. The individual prospector thrived only in literature—in the pages of Bret Harte and Mark Twain, or the songs and stories of the Gold Rush.

The changing character of immigration was another striking manifestation of the disappearance of the older America. In the first place, the number of immigrants was increasing. More than three and one half million immigrants (not counting Canadians and Mexicans) came to the United States between 1891 and 1900—more than during any previous decade except the one just past. In the second place, and more important, an increasing proportion of immigrants came from southeastern Europe and a steadily diminishing proportion from northwestern Europe. This shift began in the late seventies and gained momentum during the eighties; in 1896 migration from southeastern Europe surpassed that from northwestern Europe for the first time.[8] After that migration from the new source, from Russia, Poland, Austria-Hungary, and Italy, was consistently greater than that from the British Isles and Western Europe. By 1900 there were something over ten million people of foreign birth living in the United States, of whom more than seven million came from southeastern Europe.

[6] Marquis James, *The Cherokee Strip* (New York, 1945).
[7] Walter P. Webb, *The Great Plains* (Boston, 1931), pp. 205–318; Ernest S. Osgood, *The Day of the Cattleman* (Minneapolis, 1929), pp. 83–113, 213–258.
[8] *Reports of the Immigration Commission* (Washington, 1911), III, 8–12.

There was a much larger number of second-generation immigrants; 26 million Americans in 1900—34 per cent of the whole population—were born of foreign-born parents. Germans, Irish, Canadians, English, and Swedish, in that order, still made up the bulk of this population; but it was clear that if recent trends continued, they would soon be outnumbered by Slavs, Czechs, and Italians.[9] The Germans were concentrated in New York, Illinois, Wisconsin, and Pennsylvania; the English Canadians in Massachusetts, Michigan, and New York; the French Canadians in New England; the British in Pennsylvania, New York, and Massachusetts; and the Scandinavians in Minnesota, Illinois, Iowa, and Wisconsin. The newly arriving Slavs migrated to New York, Pennsylvania, and Illinois, and the Italians to New York and Pennsylvania.[10] The proportion of foreign-born to the total population was highest, in 1890, on the Pacific Coast, in New England, and in the Middle Atlantic states. More striking, however, was the fact that the foreign-born population tended to be concentrated increasingly in cities (partly, of course, because most of them first arrived there, and their dispersal took time)—a fact that added to the apprehension with which Americans of older stock viewed the rapid urbanization of the country.[11]

The new immigration gave rise to a demand for ending it. Farmers and laborers were loudest in this demand, but the fact that all three leading parties in the campaign of 1892—Republican, Democratic, and Populist—adopted planks favoring curtailment of immigration indicates that to some extent the demand was general. In 1894 an Immigration Restriction League was organized in Boston. Objections to immigration were largely on economic rather than on ethnic grounds, although the latter were by no means absent from the argument. The decline of immigration during the depression years 1894 and 1895 and again in 1897 and 1898 somewhat softened the competition of immigrant with native labor, and the demand for restrictive legislation consequently abated. On the whole sentiment still seemed to favor large-scale immigration with minor, if not nominal, restrictions, but there were many portents of a less liberal policy.

A House Committee on Immigration appointed in 1888 and later a

[9] *Abstract of the Twelfth Census*, 1900, pp. 7–10.
[10] *Statistical Atlas of the United States, 1900* (Washington, 1903), pls. 70–75.
[11] Walter F. Wilcox, *Studies in American Demography* (Ithaca, 1940), pp. 159–174.

Senate committee made reports which led to the Act of March 3, 1891.[12] To those already excluded under an Act of 1882—convicts (except those convicted for political offenses), the insane, and those likely to become public charges—four new categories were added: paupers; persons suffering from dangerous, contagious, or loathsome diseases; polygamists; and those whose passage had been paid for by others than friends or relatives. The same act strengthened the anti-contract labor law and set up the office of Superintendent of Immigration (made Commissioner General in 1895) in the Treasury Department. In 1897 a bill sponsored by Henry Cabot Lodge providing for a literacy test, aimed at the "new immigration," passed both Houses of Congress. There, according to *The Nation,* it "was most ostentatiously urged and defended . . . by Jingoes, protectionists, and labor demagogues,"[13] but the evidence points to its general support. President Cleveland, however, vetoed the bill two days before he left office.[14]

Negroes were numerically a smaller group than immigrants; there were seven and one-half million in 1890. Like the immigrants, they were drifting to the cities in larger and larger numbers.[15] Nevertheless, six out of every ten Negroes gainfully employed in 1890 were in agriculture and three out of ten in domestic service.[16] The movement of Negroes to northern cities was stimulated by the growing determination of the South to undo the work of Reconstruction through Jim Crow laws, terrorism, and systematic evasion of the Fifteenth Amendment. More than one thousand Negroes were lynched between 1890 and 1899, most of them in the South.[17]

Even before 1890 the South had practically extinguished the rights

[12] 26 *U.S. Statutes at Large,* 1084; *House Report 3992,* 50th Cong., 2d sess.; *Senate Report 1095,* 51st Cong., 1st sess.

[13] *The Nation,* LXIV (March 4, 1897), 153.

[14] Allan Nevins, *Grover Cleveland* (New York, 1933), pp. 724–726.

[15] Department of Commerce, Bureau of the Census, *Negro Population in the United States, 1790–1915* (Washington, 1918), pp. 25, 33, 65; Louise W. Kennedy, *The Negro Peasant Turns Cityward* (New York, 1930), pp. 41–57.

[16] Lorenzo J. Greene and Carter G. Woodson, *The Negro Wage Earner* (Washington, 1930), pp. 36–47 and Appendix; Bureau of the Census, *Special Report on Statistics of Occupations in 1890* (Washington, 1896), p. 19; Special Reports, *Occupations at the Twelfth Census* (Washington, 1904), pp. 14–15.

[17] Walter White, *Rope and Faggot* (New York, 1929), pp. 327–332; C. Vann Woodward, *Origins of the New South* (Baton Rouge, 1951), pp. 321–395, and his *The Strange Career of Jim Crow* (New York, 1955), *passim.*

of the Negro. After that date new constitutions or new legislation completed the process. The Mississippi constitution of 1890 was framed to discriminate against the ignorant and illiterate colored man, while the illiterate white man was hardly affected. Every elector, said the document, "shall be able to read any section of the constitution of this State, or he shall be able to understand the same when read to him, or give a reasonable interpretation thereof." A somewhat similar provision was adopted in a new South Carolina constitution of 1895. Two years later a new constitution in Louisiana provided that voters must be able to read and write or be the owners of property valued at not less than $300. This, however, was qualified by a provision that every person entitled to vote January 1, 1867, and his sons and grandsons twenty-one years of age or over in 1897 might vote.[18] By 1900 few southern Negroes could cast a ballot. It was not until 1915 that the franchise portion of an Oklahoma constitutional amendment was examined by the Supreme Court and the "grandfather clause" declared unconstitutional.[19]

All of this was done in plain sight and without compunction. Ben Tillman openly declared in the Senate in 1900:

We took the government away. We stuffed ballot boxes. We shot them. We are not ashamed of it. The Senator from Wisconsin would have done the same thing. I see it in his eye right now. He would have done it. With that system—force, tissue ballots, etc.—we got tired ourselves. So we called a constitutional convention, and we eliminated, as I said, all of the colored people whom we could under the fourteenth and fifteenth amendments.[20]

Northern liberals, with a few exceptions, did not come to the Negro's rescue as they had before, perhaps because it was no longer politically profitable to do so. Tillman charged the North with having forgotten "your slogans of the past—brotherhood of man and the fatherhood of God."

The brotherhood of man [he continued] exists no longer, because you shoot

[18] Francis N. Thorpe, *Federal and State Constitutions* . . . (7 vols., Washington, 1909), III, 1563; IV, 2121; VI, 3310–3311; Walter C. Ham, "The Three Phases of Colored Suffrage," *North American Review*, CLXVIII (Mar., 1899), 285–296.

[19] Guinn *v.* U.S., 2384 U.S. 347.

[20] Quoted in George Frisbie Hoar, *The Lust of Empire* (New York, 1900), p. 9.

negroes in Illinois, when they come in competition with your labor, as we shoot them in South Carolina when they come in competition with us in the matter of elections. You do not love them any better than we do. You used to pretend that you did, but you no longer pretend it, except to get their votes.[21]

.Nobody rose to deny the charge.

The Indians, now a mere remnant of one quarter million, fared no better than other minorities, although the federal government had at least made an effort to improve their condition. Living on reservations, chiefly west of the Mississippi, they had been reduced by this time to wards of the government and were supported largely by its bounty. Indian affairs had been inefficiently managed and the system was full of abuses. By the late eighties the demand for reform had become so great and the pressure of white men to occupy Indian lands so strong that Congress in 1887 passed the General Allotment Act sponsored by Henry L. Dawes of Massachusetts. It empowered the President, when he believed a tribe had reached a sufficient stage of development, to divide the reservation and allot to each head of a family 160 acres, with lesser amounts to bachelors, women, and children. Each Indian was given the privilege of citizenship except the right, for twenty-five years, of selling or encumbering his land. What was left reverted to the public domain after fair payments for the land. It was the first systematic effort to provide for Indian welfare and marked a revolution in the handling of Indian affairs.

The purpose of the Dawes Act was obviously to break up the tribal status and make the Indian a self-supporting citizen, as well as to open land for the white man. Between 1887 and 1906, when new legislation was passed, the federal government disposed of 75 million acres, over 50 million of which were acquired by the government to sell to white settlers. Much of the latter was in Indian Territory, later to become the state of Oklahoma in 1907. For the Indians, however, the Dawes Act was a failure. Legislators and reformers had provided a plan for the Indians' future, but their expectations were never fulfilled. Most of the Indians were unable or unwilling to change their way of life, pressure on their land was too great, and the land reserved for them was hardly adequate for decent living. Modifications of the act during the nineties were of little value, and it was soon clear that it had not solved the problem. It was not until the administration of

[21] *Ibid.*

Franklin D. Roosevelt, however, that the plan was discarded and efforts made to save the Indians' cultural traditions.[22]

In the eyes of most Americans the enormous growth of cities presented problems far more important than the condition of Indians, Negroes, or immigrants. In 1890 the population of the United States was about 62 million; by 1900 it had reached nearly 75 million. Of this increase of 13 million considerably more than half was confined to the North Atlantic and North Central states, and that six and one-half million was divided about equally between those two areas, whereas in the three preceding decades the North Central states had consistently outstripped the North Atlantic states. During the 1890's the increase was heaviest in New York, Pennsylvania, Illinois, Massachusetts, and Wisconsin, all states with a large urban population. Texas also gained heavily.[23] Only one state, Nevada, declined in population between 1890 and 1900, and her decline was caused by the exhaustion of the Comstock lode; but within certain areas of other states, all of them agricultural, population also declined. The retreat of settlement in western and central Kansas, Nebraska, and South Dakota and in eastern Colorado reflected a specific event—the great drought of 1887, which persisted for five years. The decline of eleven counties in California was caused by a decline in mining as well as by difficulties in farming. But the ebbing of population in rural New England and in parts of New York, Pennsylvania, Ohio, and Michigan reflected a decline of agriculture in general and a movement to the cities. Other parts of those states, as we have seen, were growing rapidly.[24] At the same time some nonurban areas opened up for settlement in Oklahoma, Wisconsin, Minnesota, and North Dakota, where lumbering or the opening of Indian reservations provided opportunity for expansion.[25]

The movement to cities, although growing steadily, was only one of

[22] J. P. Kinney, *A Continent Lost—A Civilization Won* (Baltimore, 1937), pp. 214–248; L. B. Priest, *Uncle Sam's Stepchildren* (New Brunswick, 1942), pp. 248–252; John Collier, *The Indians of the Americas* (New York, 1947), pp. 243–287; Oliver LaFarge (ed.), *The Changing Indian* (Norman, Okla., 1942).

[23] *Abstract of the Twelfth Census of the United States* (Washington, 1914), pp. 7, 34.

[24] *Supplementary Analyses and Derivative Tables* (Twelfth Census, Washington, 1906), pp. 44–45.

[25] *Statistical Atlas of the United States* (Twelfth Census, Washington, 1903), p. 36.

several movements undertaken by a migratory people, and the mobility of the people as a whole still conformed to an older pattern. Each census as far back as 1850 showed that more than one-fifth of the nation's whites had moved from the state of their birth.[26] The surplus of people who migrated to a state over those who left it generally reached a maximum about three decades after the first settlement. Then after three more decades of declining surplus a deficit appeared; that is, more people left the state than entered it. By 1890 Indiana, Illinois, Wisconsin, and Louisiana had become deficit states. Agricultural migration was pretty consistently westward, but migration caused by industry might pull population in any direction. Michigan, for example, never showed a deficit and New Jersey has had a surplus since 1890. The same is also true of Florida since 1850, but for quite different reasons.[27] The center of population in 1890 was twenty miles east of Columbus, Indiana; in 1900 it was six miles southeast of that city, a westward movement of about fourteen miles.

But the growth of cities remains the most arresting demographical development of the period. In 1880 about one-fifth of the population lived in towns or cities of 8,000 inhabitants or more; in 1900, one-third. Forty per cent lived in towns of 2,500 or more.[28] Some areas became overwhelmingly urban during these years. By 1900 six out of ten people in the North Atlantic area lived in cities of 8,000 or more. In Rhode Island the proportion of urban to rural population was 61.2 per cent, in Massachusetts 76, in New York 68.5, in New Jersey 61.2, and in Connecticut 53.2. These were the only states in the country in which over half the population lived in cities of at least 8,000 people, but in Pennsylvania, Delaware, Maryland, Illinois, and California over 40 per cent lived in such places. The total number of cities of that size increased during the decade by about one hundred.[29] In the North Central states, which contained one-third of the population in 1900, cities also grew rapidly. Three out of ten people in that area lived in cities by 1900. Eighteen of the fifty largest cities in the country were

[26] Charles J. Galpin and Theodore B. Manny, *Interstate Migration among the Native White Population as Indicated by Differences between State of Birth and State of Residence* (Washington, 1934), pp. 6–7.

[27] C. Warren Thornthwaite, *Internal Migration in the United States* (Philadelphia, 1934), pp. 9–12.

[28] W. H. Tolman, *Municipal Reform Movements in the United States* (New York, 1895), pp. 27–44.

[29] *Twelfth Census of the United States, 1900* (Washington, 1901), I, lxxxii–lxxxvii.

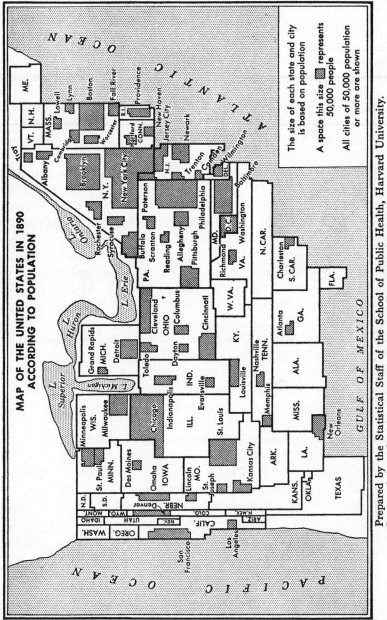

MAP OF THE UNITED STATES IN 1890
ACCORDING TO POPULATION

The size of each state and city is based on population

A space this size ▨ represents 50,000 people

All cities of 50,000 population or more are shown

Prepared by the Statistical Staff of the School of Public Health, Harvard University.
By permission of Arthur M. Schlesinger and The Macmillan Company.

located there as against ten in 1890, and two of the five largest cities, Chicago and St. Louis. (The others were New York, Philadelphia, and Boston.) It should be noted in passing that rapid urbanization in the late nineteenth century was not limited to the United States; it was a phenomenon common to most parts of the western world. Some areas of the United States, however, were even then in advance of Europe. Massachusetts had a larger proportion of its people in towns of ten thousand or over in 1890 than any nation in Europe, while Rhode Island, New York, and New Jersey had a larger proportion than any European country except England and Wales.[30]

While all of the states in the North Atlantic and North Central divisions showed an increase in population for the decade and in all but three (Vermont, Kansas, and Nebraska) a substantial increase, there were many areas in both divisions where rural depletion, as noted, was significant. In many areas this was attributable to a continued westward movement, but generally it was the lure of the city that drew off the more ambitious. The number of those who moved from the country to the village, from the village to the small city, and from the small city to the large one is unrecorded, but it was large. Even by 1890 the number of wage earners in industry almost equaled that of farm owners, tenants, and farm laborers combined.[31] The growth of cities, of course, was dependent not alone on rural migration; the tendency of immigrants, at least in the beginning, to live in cities was an important cause of growth. The foreign-born both of New York and Chicago in 1900, for example, amounted to one-third of the population; and the number of foreign-born and native-born of foreign parentage, to over three-fourths in both cities.[32]

Every cause for city growth, in fact, operated in America during this decade. In spite of the Panic of 1893 and the depression which followed, manufacturing continued its spectacular growth, although not as rapidly as in the eighties. In this growth the shift from water power to steam played an important part. Improvement in farm machinery

[30] Adna F. Weber, *The Growth of Cities in the Nineteenth Century* (New York, 1899), p. 153.

[31] Alvin H. Hansen, "Industrial Class Alignments in the United States," *Quarterly Publication of the American Statistical Association,* XVIII (Dec., 1920), 417–422.

[32] *Twelfth Census,* I, clxxix, clxxxvi–clxxxviii. "Foreign parentage," as used in this census, means "all persons, either of native or foreign birth, who had one or both parents foreign born."

increased specialized farming, released a surplus of farm labor, and produced a greater surplus of food for city consumption. At the same time machine-made products were displacing those formerly processed on the farm and releasing more farm labor. Wherever the population may have come from and whatever the causes may have been, the United States by 1900 had become a nation of cities, largely led and dominated by them.

In this rapidly changing economic order numerous problems clamored for attention. Most of them were by no means new. The fantastically high tariff rates imposed during the Civil War had continued with slight alleviation; efforts to reduce them revived in the eighties and the battle continued during the nineties. The problems of currency and the demand for inflation had been continuous since the war, and reached a climax in the nineties. Federal control of interstate railroad transportation was theoretically established in the Interstate Commerce Act of 1887, but it was sixteen years before new legislation made the act effective. The movement toward industrial consolidation and monopoly had begun in railroads with various pooling devices, and in manufacturing with "trusts" in oil, whisky, sugar, and lead. By the end of the eighties the problem of monopoly had moved from state to federal legislation.[33] The problems of the tariff, currency, railroads, and monopoly, which had pressed upon the nation in the eighties and earlier, had not, of course, been solved by the end of that decade, but persisted through the following years as urgent issues.

To many Americans of the late eighties, harassed by railroad abuses, high tariffs, high prices of many manufactured goods but declining prices for farm commodities, such legislation as the Interstate Commerce Act and the Sherman Antitrust Act of 1890 seemed to point, at least for the common man, to a brighter future. The brighter future did not soon develop, but this legislation did mark a turning point from "social Darwinism" and the philosophy of laissez faire. For years the rich and middle classes had found justification and satisfaction for their own fortunate position in Darwin's "survival of the fittest," now given social and moral connotations by Herbert Spencer, John Fiske, William Graham Sumner, and a host of others. These popular writers applied Darwin's interpretation of biological life directly to the study of social and economic life and used it to explain and justify the

[33] H. R. Seager and C. A. Gulick, Jr., *Trusts and Corporation Problems* (New York, 1929), pp. 49–51.

misfortunes, the irregularities, and the injustices that existed in American society. Social Darwinism seemed a made-to-order philosophy for the rising capitalists in the postwar period; it glorified laissez faire whether the result was unbridled competition or consolidation.[34]

Social Darwinism was too convenient a theory to be easily forsaken, but it was already being weakened before the eighties had far advanced. Henry George in his *Progress and Poverty* (1879) denied that social evils resulted from the working of "fixed laws, inevitable and eternal," but held that they came rather from a rationalization of greed. He insisted that it was the "injustice of society, not the niggardliness of nature," that was the cause of want and misery.[35] George was not the only critic of Spencer's social Darwinism. To William James, America's great philosopher and pioneer in psychology, Spencer's slick determinism was anathema; his pragmatism, already evident with the publication in 1890 of his famous *Principles of Psychology,* challenged, and went far to undermine, the philosophical underpinnings of social Darwinism. Nine years later, when John Dewey, a young but already noted philosopher, wrote *School and Society,* the Spencerian dogma had been not only questioned but repudiated and the paths to development through control pointed out. The works of James and Dewey, together with that of G. Stanley Hall at Clark University, founded in 1889, incidentally marked the beginning of the study of experimental psychology in American education and of the process of modernizing education.

While social Darwinism exerted its hold over all areas of American thought, it gripped the developing field of sociology with particular tenacity. Here Spencer's elaboration of Darwinism remained dominant for decades; it was to William Graham Sumner at Yale and Franklin Giddings at Columbia the core of their theories. But while the dogma reigned at Yale and Columbia, an obscure government scientist, Lester F. Ward, published his epochal *Dynamic Sociology* (1883), followed in 1893 by *The Psychic Factors of Civilization* and in 1898 by *Outlines of Sociology.* Like James and Dewey, Ward wrote out of a sense of

[34] Richard Hofstadter, *Social Darwinism in American Thought* (Boston, 1955), *passim;* Henry Steele Commager, *The American Mind* (New Haven, 1950), pp. 82–90; Thomas C. Cochran and William Miller, *The Age of Enterprise* (New York, 1942), pp. 119–128.

[35] Henry George, *Progress and Poverty* (Modern Library Ed., New York, 1929), pp. 141, 482; Eric F. Goldman, *Rendezvous with Destiny* (New York, 1952), pp. 97–100.

profound impatience with "the essential sterility," as he put it, "of all that has thus far been done in the domain of social science."[36] A government worker during most of his life, he knew from experience that laissez faire was both vicious and impractical. Nor did he find great difficulty in debunking the theory of the survival of the fittest. Years passed, however, before the negative and obsolete sociology then in vogue began to break down before his attacks. Nevertheless, by the end of the nineties many of the younger sociologists were turning from Sumner to Ward.

The pragmatic and realistic method made more rapid gains in economics. Indeed, institutional economics can be said to have originated in the United States, with the emergence in the mid-1880's of the group of young economists who founded the American Economic Association—Richard T. Ely, Henry C. Adams, Simon N. Patten, and Edmund J. James. These scholars vigorously criticized the classical economics; Ely declared in the manifesto of the new group, "While we recognize the necessity of individual initiative in industrial life, we hold that the doctrine of *laissez faire* is unsafe in politics and unsound in morals; and that it suggests an inadequate explanation of the relations between the state and the citizens."[37] The discussions and the resolutions which preceded the founding of the American Economic Association indicated a recognition of economics as an inductive and pragmatic science, of the relevance of ethical considerations in its study, and of the "necessity of state intervention in the economic processes." A declaration of independence from the English classical school, these discussions pointed to the road followed by most American economists during the next half-century.[38]

Thorstein Veblen was more explicit than Ely in his denunciation of orthodoxy and more open in his condemnation of contemporary society. His manner was studiedly iconoclastic and often seemed almost deliberately designed to offend the reader, apparently in the hope that enlightenment would follow. In *The Theory of the Leisure Class*

[36] Introduction to *Dynamic Sociology* (New York, 1883).

[37] Richard T. Ely, *Ground under Our Feet* (New York, 1938), p. 136; *Publications of the American Economic Association*, I (1887), 6–7.

[38] The first volume of the *Publications of the American Economic Association* in 1887, for instance, contained an article by Henry C. Adams on the "Relation of the State to Industrial Action." *Publications of the American Economic Association*, I, 471–549; Commager, *American Mind;* Joseph Dorfman, *The Economic Mind in American Civilization* (New York, 1949), III, 205–212.

(1899), his first book, he brought his peculiar powers to bear on the problem of "conspicuous leisure" and "conspicuous consumption"; both his method and his conclusions opened worlds to other students.[39] The book had a tremendous impact in shattering the façade of respectability behind which, according to Veblen, predatory wealth had ensconced itself, and in undermining the entire Spencerian philosophy.

Those who read *The Theory of the Leisure Class* half a century after it was written may find it dated. If this is true, it is because the book was an attack on conditions and ideas which, thanks partly to Veblen's own attacks, have either disappeared or been obliged to assume a somewhat more gracious aspect. At the turn of the century, however, conspicuous waste and conspicuous leisure were more obvious than at any other time in American history. Extravagance was tasteless, blatant, and unremitting. In New York, in the suburbs of the great cities, at Newport and at Tuxedo, the marble palaces of the new rich jostled those of the older business aristocracy in a display of waste that shocked the sensitive onlooker. Veblen merely articulated the accumulated indignation of his generation. In each of his subsequent books, as in *The Theory of the Leisure Class,* Veblen singled out a particular institution for criticism and attack. Their titles are self-explanatory: *The Theory of Business Enterprise* (1904), *The Instinct of Workmanship* (1914), *The Higher Learning in America* (1918), *The Engineers and the Price System* (1921). Always he held to the theory of development, that is, the evolution of economics. By his inductive method he intended to lessen the gap between theory and reality. The total result of his work was to weaken still further the sacrosanct position of laissez faire.[40]

New methods, imported from Germany, were also revitalizing American study of history and politics. From Germany American graduate schools imported the seminar, the thesis, the doctor's degree, and a concern for "scientific" accuracy. The scientific historian eschewed, among other things, theories of history such as had prevailed earlier in the century, notably in Germany itself; he confined himself to the facts in the belief that facts, once the historian had gathered enough of them, would "speak for themselves." It is true that some of

[39] Allan G. Grimsby, *Modern Economic Thought* (New York, 1947), particularly pp. 31–132 on "The Institutional Economics of Thorstein Veblen."
[40] Joseph Dorfman, *Thorstein Veblen and His America* (New York, 1934), and *The Economic Mind,* III, 434–455.

the historians of the period, including Henry Adams and his brother Brooks, were later to offer theories of history, but their theories had little influence. Henry Adams's effort to interpret history in terms of mathematical physics was particularly unsuccessful. More important at the moment was Captain Mahan's *Influence of Sea Power upon History* (1890), which expounded the theory that only nations with sea power could obtain a high standard of economic well-being and achieve an important place in world affairs. Sea power meant colonies and with the possession of colonies a strong navy to protect them.

Mahan's neo-mercantilism had considerable influence on historical writing and, in fact, upon history itself. But Henry Adams, John Bach McMaster, Frederick Jackson Turner, and Edward Eggleston influenced the writing of history more permanently. When in the early 1880's McMaster began to publish his multivolume history of the people of the United States, he weakened, at least in America, the antiquated idea that history was merely past politics. He "discovered the American social past."[41] The fact that McMaster was trained as an engineer, not as a historian, may explain his unconventional approach to the subject. Before McMaster completed his great work, Henry Adams had finished his *History of the United States*.[42] Except in the first six chapters of Volume I and the last three of Volume IX, Adams emphasized politics and diplomacy, but in those nine chapters he brilliantly described the economic, social, and intellectual life of the United States in the early years of the nineteenth century. These chapters were a striking example of what might be done in social history.

Two years after Adams published the last volume of his history, Frederick Jackson Turner read in 1893 at the World's Fair his famous paper on "The Significance of the Frontier in American History."[43] Whatever this and his subsequent essays may have contributed to an understanding of the importance of the frontier, they made clear that in the future America must be interpreted from the viewpoint of economics, sociology, and physiography as well as that of politics and diplomacy. Eggleston also drew upon related disciplines. A minister, novelist, and magazine editor, Eggleston turned to history only late in life, and published before his death only two fragments of a projected

[41] Eric F. Goldman, *John Bach McMaster* (Philadelphia, 1943), p. 144.
[42] Henry Adams, *History of the United States of America* (New York, 1889–1891), covers only the administrations of Jefferson and Madison.
[43] Cf. *The Frontier in American History* (New York, 1921), pp. 1–38.

study of the American people; but these, together with many magazine articles and lectures, gave some indication of further possibilities of social history.[44] All four of these historians were presidents of the American Historical Association; all four made their greatest contribution before the end of the century. They left a goodly heritage and the fault was not theirs if the writing of social history was slow to develop.

While the pragmatic approach turned some historians to social history, it won many more to an economic interpretation. To political scientists pragmatism had perhaps a deeper significance. The notion that the American Constitution represented the final word in constitutional government began to give way as political science concerned itself less with theory and more with experience. This movement was led by such men as Woodrow Wilson of Princeton University; Henry Jones Ford, newspaper editor and later professor at the same institution; and the pioneers at Johns Hopkins, Frank J. Goodnow and Weston W. Willoughby. Although J. Allen Smith was already active in the nineties, his well-known volume, *The Spirit of American Government,* did not appear until 1907, while the published work of Charles E. Merriam and Charles A. Beard also waited for the new century. But these men had been trained in the nineties, when the pattern of the new political science was taking shape.[45]

This intellectual atmosphere, compounded of pragmatism, skepticism, and restlessness, nourished muckraking, which was to blossom forth in the first decade of the new century. The techniques of muckraking, indeed, were already understood; the weaknesses in American political, economic, and social life stood out as glaringly in the nineties as in the next decade. Writers were already calling attention to the corruption of city governments, the bartering of franchises, the fantastic cost and inefficiency of city services, the conditions in slums, the prevalence of commercialized vice and organized crime, and the control of ignorant and illiterate voters by political bosses. They knew of the corruption of many of the railroads, of the growth of monopoly, and of the almost unbelievable inequality in the distribution of wealth. Many protested with the same vehemence as the later muckrakers.

It was in 1894 that Henry Demarest Lloyd exposed the Standard Oil

[44] *The Beginners of a Nation* (New York, 1896) and *The Transit of Civilization* (New York, 1901) are the fragments referred to. See *Dictionary of American Biography.*

[45] Commager, *American Mind,* pp. 310–358. See also Morton G. White, *Social Thought in America: The Revolt against Formalism* (New York, 1949).

Company in his *Wealth against Commonwealth,* perhaps the most bitter and telling attack ever made on monopoly in this country. In the same year William T. Stead published *If Christ Came to Chicago,* a realistic and disturbing picture of Chicago's underworld. In New York the Reverend Charles E. Parkhurst's attack on vice led to a sweeping legislative inquiry, headed by Clarence Lexow, which resulted in the temporary overthrow of Tammany and the appointment of Theodore Roosevelt as police commissioner.[46]

The decade of the nineties, in fact, was the first since the Civil War in which there appeared a group of social reformers large enough to be labeled as such. Jane Addams, Washington Gladden, and Josiah Strong; such forward-looking teachers as the Christian socialist George D. Harron; Edward W. Bemis, an advocate of city-owned utilities; Benjamin Andrews, president of two universities and one-time advocate of free silver; Frank Parsons, a champion of settlements and municipal public utilities; the great sociologist Edward A. Ross; and many others pioneered aggressively in the fight for better conditions. By the middle nineties W. D. P. Bliss could find enough material to edit an *Encyclopedia of Social Reforms.* The *Arena* and *The Forum* already functioned as patrons of reform. The *Arena,* published under the leadership of the "editorial dean of democracy," Benjamin O. Flower (1889–1896), and later under Charles Clark Ridpath (1897–1898), printed as many articles of criticism and exposure as the muckraking journals published in the next decade.

Other influences active in the nineties encouraged the rise of muckraking. Sensational journalism, best exemplified by Joseph Pulitzer's New York *World,* thrived on crusading forays into the underworld of vice and scandal; its rapid development, therefore, under the guidance of men who were admittedly more interested in good copy than in good government, nevertheless worked to the incidental advantage of reform. Such staid papers as Godkin's New York *Evening Post* and Nelson's Kansas City *Star* campaigned more consistently against corruption, but their effectiveness was limited not only by their editors' refusal to indulge in questionable journalistic practices but by their deep-dyed conservatism on economic issues. Hence it was Pulitzer's *World* that took the leadership in fighting vice and municipal corruption, in opposing Cleveland's jingoism in the Venezuela incident, and

[46] *New York State Committee Appointed to Investigate the Police Department of the City of New York, Report of Proceedings* (Albany, 1895).

in criticizing his close alliance with the Morgan syndicate in the bond sales. The *World* for many years was the most ably edited newspaper and the most important in the East.[47]

William Randolph Hearst, who acquired the New York *Journal* in 1895 and the *Evening Journal* in 1896, also campaigned upon occasion against municipal corruption.[48] His bitter rivalry with Pulitzer, however, led him into measures which in the long run contributed very little to the advancement of American journalism. Under the pressure of this competition, sensational journalism soon went to extremes; in their efforts to whip up war spirit against Spain, Hearst and Pulitzer discovered journalistic depths hitherto unexplored. But "yellow journalism," as it came to be called, was not without its benefits as well as its evils.[49] It brightened newspapers, widened their coverage, and increased their circulation. Between 1890 and 1900 the circulation of daily newspapers almost doubled. The combined circulation of American dailies was over 15 million in 1900 and that of weekly or semiweekly papers over 42 million.[50] Finally, the rise of yellow journalism reinforced the dependence of Americans on newspapers for enlightenment and entertainment—already a long-standing habit. Many Americans read little else.

News agencies, syndicates, and newspaper chains also originated in this period. The news-gathering agencies—the Associated Press and the Scripps-McRae Press Association—gave even rural weeklies access to news that previously had been monopolized by large metropolitan dailies, which alone could afford to maintain batteries of correspondents in distant places. Special features distributed by syndicates and the growth of newspaper chains had the same effect—standardization of subject, style, and even of editorial opinion. The newspaper, as a result

[47] James W. Barrett, *Joseph Pulitzer and His World* (New York, 1941); Don C. Seitz, *Joseph Pulitzer, His Life and Letters* (New York, 1924); Rollo Ogden, *Life and Letters of Edwin Lawrence Godkin* (New York, 1907); Edwin Lawrence Godkin, *Reflections and Comments 1865–1895* (New York, 1895).

[48] Ferdinand Lundberg, *Imperial Hearst: A Social Biography* (New York, 1936); Cora M. Older, *William Randolph Hearst, American* (New York, 1936).

[49] The term "yellow journalism" derives from the first effort to print colored pictures on fast newspaper presses in the Sunday editions of the *World* and *Journal*. R. F. Outcault, depicting child life for the *World*, did the leading figure, "The Kid of Hogan's Alley," in yellow. Hearst later captured the services of Outcault, whereupon Pulitzer engaged George B. Luks to continue the series. The "yellow kid" thereafter appeared in both papers. W. G. Bleyer, *Main Currents in the History of American Journalism* (Boston, 1927), p. 339.

[50] W. S. Rossiter, "Printing and Publishing," *Twelfth Census*, 1900, IX, 1046.

of these innovations, became broader in scope. It printed not merely news but fiction, with the result, as cynics observed, that the two categories occasionally tended to be confused with each other; it printed recipes, household hints, and advice to the lovelorn. All of this had a profound effect on popular culture.

The same influences that were playing on American newspapers also affected magazines. The low-priced magazine came into its own; *McClure's*, founded in 1893, sold for fifteen cents a copy, and within a few months *Munsey's* and *Cosmopolitan* reduced their prices to ten cents. Frank A. Munsey estimated in 1898 that reduction of prices had increased the sale of the cheap magazines by 500,000 during the previous years and the number of readers by three million.[51] The circulation of *McClure's* jumped in four months in 1895 from 120,000 to 250,-000.[52] Like the newspapers, magazines became sprightlier and less pedantic, while the polite essay and the travel sketch gave way to short stories and timely reports.[53] The new magazines accordingly reached a wider reading public; they influenced, but were themselves influenced by, mass opinion. The stream of muckraking carried the new magazines with it.

The changing character of journalism reflected, among other things, the shifting status of women. The popularization of the press was clearly dictated in part by a desire to reach feminine readers, a fact which suggests that women were becoming more important than they had been in setting standards of taste. Women had been demanding greater freedom and legal equality for a long time, and the battle was still far from won. There were many indications, however, that women were breaking out of what many of them had come to regard as the tyranny of the home. The number of women wage earners increased from over two and one-half million in 1880 to four million in 1890 and to five and one-third million in 1900. Although about 40 per cent of women workers at the last date were in domestic service, about one-

[51] F. A. Munsey, "Advertising in Some of Its Phases," *Munsey's*, XX (Dec., 1898), 480; George Britt, *Forty Years—Forty Millions: The Career of Frank A. Munsey* (New York, 1935); S. S. McClure, *My Autobiography* (New York, 1914).

[52] Louis Filler, *Crusaders for American Liberalism* (New York, 1939), p. 37.

[53] Arthur R. Kimball, "The Invasion of Journalism," *Atlantic*, LXXXVI (1900), 119–124; Arthur M. Schlesinger, *The Rise of the City* (New York, 1933), pp. 182–185; Harold U. Faulkner, *The Quest for Social Justice* (New York, 1931), pp. 257–259.

quarter were in manufacturing and many by this time had entered trades or professions. Women's clubs broadened the life of the middle- or upper-class woman in the same way that employment broadened the life of the working girl; both provided a relief from the monotony of domesticity. The women's clubs of America were loosely joined in 1889 in the General Federation of Women's Clubs, an organization boasting a membership of over 50,000 by 1898. It is true that by the end of the century only four states (Wyoming, Colorado, Utah, and Idaho) had granted equal suffrage to women, but the influence of women had long since reached out of the social into the cultural, political, and economic world. The more literate and energetic of the wealthy women had grown restless in the vapid competition for social success and were throwing their energies into causes already opened to women.[54]

The emergence of the New Woman was not the most important development of the 1890's, but it was characteristic of a period in which the new was to be seen on all sides, contending for domination with the old. The 1890's were indeed a "watershed," as one historian has called the period, on one side of which all streams of life and thought ran down into the past, on the other side of which lay the world of the twentieth century, baffling in its complexity, forbiddingly unfamiliar, yet not without a peculiar promise of its own.[55]

[54] Lloyd Morris, *Postscript to Yesterday* (New York, 1947), pp. 3–63; Schlesinger, *Rise of the City,* pp. 121–159; Faulkner, *Quest for Social Justice,* pp. 153–176.

[55] For the conception of the period as a "watershed," see Commager, *American Mind,* pp. 41 ff.

CHAPTER 2

The Revolt of the Cities

"THE government of cities," wrote Bryce in 1893, "is the one conspicuous failure of the United States."[1] He might have added that failure in this respect was not confined to the United States; in the last analysis it was the result neither of shortcomings in American democracy nor of any absence of civic pride but of the Industrial Revolution—a western European, not only an American phenomenon. The very novelty of the problem accounted for the failure to solve it.

The growth of cities since the Civil War had been rapid and chaotic. New York grew from two to almost three and one-half million between 1880 and 1900, Chicago from half a million to a million and a half. Cities like Detroit, Cleveland, and Milwaukee doubled in size. Inevitably the amenities of life lagged behind; "the problem in America," as Seth Low put it, "has been to make a great city in a few years out of nothing."[2] In meeting this problem everything was sacrificed to speed. Streets went unpaved; garbage and sewage removal were left to accident and time; water supplies were allowed to become polluted; and conditions in slums rapidly sank to appalling depths of human degradation. The correction of these conditions, as Bryce suggested, would be a test of democratic government, all the more demanding because the problem was not merely material but political as well. The fact was that all elements did not have an equal interest in reform; some people, indeed, had a positive stake in perpetuating the evils attacked by reformers. Rising businessmen profited handsomely through utility franchises or construction contracts; most of them, whether they ap-

[1] James Bryce, *The American Commonwealth* (new ed., 1917), I, 642.
[2] *Ibid.*, p. 658.

proved of it or not, did not hesitate to acquire them through bribery. Nor were city officials immune to corruption; where there were bribe-givers there were bribetakers.

The normal agencies of law enforcement could no longer be depended on to enforce the law; they found it more profitable to acquiesce in its violation. The investigations of the Lexow Committee, for example, revealed wholesale corruption in the New York Police Department. The police, it appeared, tolerated prostitution, allowed saloons to stay open illegally, and engaged in blackmail, extortion, and petty thievery. Operators of houses of prostitution testified to having paid large sums for protection; one had paid out $4,300 in regular payments, plus an "initiation fee" of $500 every time a new precinct officer took over, while another had paid $50 a month for ten years. Saloonkeepers paid $50 a month for the privilege of doing business on Sunday. Even more shocking was the disclosure that police officers themselves were being forced to buy their very jobs. One sergeant, desiring promotion, had passed the civil-service examination three times, once with a grade of 97.8, but had not been promoted. Finally he paid $15,000 into the coffers of Tammany Hall for promotion to captain's rank. Since he could not pay off such a debt out of his regular salary, he was obliged to resort to irregular sources of income—that is, to bribes. The circle of corruption appeared unbreakable.[3]

Part of the difficulty was the absence, in most cities, of a trained body of disinterested public servants. Civil-service reformers worked endlessly to remedy this deficiency, but the movement for reform made little headway against the persisting notion, a legacy of Jacksonian days, that special training was not required for public service and was in fact positively undemocratic.

The large immigrant population in many cities was an even more formidable obstacle to reform. By the nineties a large proportion of these immigrants came from countries where they had experienced little or no training in democratic government. Jane Addams's description of West Chicago could have applied, with minor alterations, to any number of cities:

[3] New York State Committee Appointed to Investigate the Police Department of the City of New York, *Report and Proceedings* (Albany, 1895); C. H. Park-hurst, *Our Fight with Tammany* (New York, 1895); W. T. Stead, *Satan's Invisible World Displayed* (New York, 1897); M. R. Werner, "That Was New York," *New Yorker,* XXXI (Nov. 19, 1955), 189–210 (Nov. 26, 1955), 99–139.

Between Halsted Street and the river live about ten thousand Italians—Neapolitans, Sicilians, and Calabrians, with an occasional Lombard or Venetian. To the south on Twelfth Street are many Germans, and side streets are given over almost entirely to Polish and Russian Jews. Still farther south, these Jewish colonies merge into a huge Bohemian colony, so vast that Chicago ranks as the third Bohemian city in the world. To the northwest are many Canadian-French, clannish in spite of their long residence in America, and to the north are Irish and first-generation Americans. . . .

The idea underlying our self-government breaks down in such a ward. The streets are inexpressibly dirty, the number of schools inadequate, sanitary legislation unenforced, the street lighting bad, the paving miserable and altogether lacking in the alleys and smaller streets, and the stables foul beyond description. Hundreds of houses are unconnected with the street sewer. The older and richer inhabitants seem anxious to move away as rapidly as they can afford it. They make room for newly arrived immigrants who are densely ignorant of civic duties.[4]

The presence of these masses made the problem of city government many times more difficult than it already was. As Seth Low declared, "an American city is confronted not only with the necessity of instructing large and rapidly growing bodies of people in the art of government, but it is compelled at the same time to assimilate strangely different component parts into an American community."[5] It is no wonder that reformers sometimes despaired of democracy itself.

The immigrants were important in another respect: their votes sustained the power of the political machines. They found in America opportunities in education, politics, and economic life beyond what they had known in Europe, but it was years before they learned how to take advantage of them. In the meantime they fell under the control of the machines. The ward boss, often a second-generation immigrant himself, was the one individual to whom the newcomer could turn for sympathy and understanding. "I think that there's got to be in every ward," said one immigrant, "a guy that any bloke can go to when he's in trouble and get help—not justice and the law, but help, no matter what he's done."[6] Reformers, on the other hand, with their high-sounding platforms and their crusades for temperance and women's rights, baffled and sometimes disgusted the immigrant; he felt much safer in the hands of the friendly machine.

[4] Jane Addams, *Twenty Years at Hull-House* (New York, 1911), pp. 98–99.
[5] Quoted in Bryce, *American Commonwealth*, I, 657.
[6] Oscar Handlin, *The Uprooted* (Boston, 1951), pp. 212–213.

The reformers on their part did not understand the immigrant. "The immigrant," one of them said, "lacks the faculty of abstraction. He thinks not of the welfare of the community but only of himself."[7] E. A. Ross regarded immigrants as "squalid" people whose tendency to raise large families proved that they cared nothing for the traditional American virtues—a decent standard of living, education, and self-advancement.[8] Some immigrants, of course, learned the arts of government, good and ill, and took advantage of them. The German-American Reform Union, for example, played an important part in the Parkhurst crusade against vice. On the other side of the picture, some immigrants became political bosses in their own right, like Tammany's Richard Croker. Such men, however, were in the minority.

Leadership in the struggle for municipal reform, in the absence of any solid working-class support, clearly had to come from the old governing class. Unfortunately many of the most talented members of that class were now absorbed in the scramble for gain, while the majority had drifted into political apathy from which they were roused only occasionally by national campaigns, which as a rule had little relevance to local issues. Nevertheless the reform efforts of the 1890's were led by members of the solid, respectable, educated middle class—men like Low, George William Curtis, and R. Fulton Cutting of New York, Edwin U. Curtis and Thomas Wentworth Higginson of Boston, Lyman J. Gage of Chicago, and Joseph W. Folk of St. Louis.

Still another obstacle to reform was the failure of reformers themselves to agree on what needed to be done. There were many varieties of reformers, each with its own program. One variety stressed the importance of "good government," which was to be achieved simply by eliminating corruption. The City Club of New York, founded by Edmund Kelly in 1892, was the first of at least twenty Good Government Clubs in this city and the prototype of many others elsewhere. Boston had its Municipal League led by Samuel B. Capen and Edwin D. Mead, Philadelphia its comparable league under Clinton R. Woodruff, Chicago its Civic Federation under Lyman J. Gage. By 1896 there were two hundred such organizations throughout the country, loosely affiliated with the National Municipal League founded in 1894.[9] The

[7] Ibid., p. 219.

[8] Eric Goldman, Rendezvous with Destiny (New York, 1952), pp. 77–79.

[9] Albert Shaw, "Our Civic 'Renaissance,'" Review of Reviews, XL (Apr., 1895), 416–427; W. D. P. Bliss (ed.), The Encyclopedia of Social Reforms

program of the good-government men—the "goo-goos," as Theodore
Roosevelt later scornfully referred to them—was hardly earth-shaking,
yet even these mild reformers soon discovered that corruption in city
governments was more than a moral issue, that it was inextricably
bound up with the growing influence of big business on the state and
national as well as on the municipal level, and that reform therefore
demanded a great deal more than merely a purification of the civil
service.

Six years after its foundation the National Municipal League offered
a "Municipal Program" for American cities, in two parts: a series of
proposed amendments to state constitutions designed mainly to free
municipal affairs from state control, and a model Municipal Corporations Act.[10] This program indicated the direction reform was to follow
in practically every major city. Everywhere the first battle was the
struggle for "home rule." Not only did representation in most states
heavily favor the country districts over the cities, but many purely
municipal matters fell under state jurisdiction, thus enabling an
absentee minority—often under business domination—to control the
affairs of large and growing cities. The winning of independence from
outside control often took years and was accomplished in the face of
bitter resistance. Once it had been achieved, the problem became a
matter chiefly of regulating grants of municipal franchises and of pre-
serving the city's public property in land. The fight against corruption
inevitably involved the fundamental question of public regulation of
private enterprise, and most municipal reformers eventually came to
recognize the need for a greater degree of public control than most
people (including the reformers themselves) would have sanctioned a
few years before.

The Municipal League also stressed the simplification of governmental machinery and the need for trained and experienced public
officials to handle city administration. Many reformers increasingly

---

(3rd ed., New York, 1897), article on "Municipal Reform," pp. 907–910.
William H. Tolman, *Municipal Reform Movements in the United States* (New
York, 1895), pp. 47–219, describes many of these organizations.

[10] A distinguished committee revised this program in 1915. For the original
program, see Horace E. Deming, *The Government of American Cities* (New
York, 1909), pp. 201–304; Deming was chairman of the committee which prepared the report. The revised version of 1915 is given in C. R. Woodruff (ed.),
A New Municipal Program (New York, 1919), pp. 297–364. Later revisions
came in 1925, 1933, and 1941.

favored the commission type of government adopted by the city of
Galveston in 1901. In 1900 a tidal wave and storm swept the city,
drowning one-sixth of the population and destroying a third of the
property. In this crisis the citizens threw aside the unwieldy government and in its place set up a commission of five. This was made
permanent by a new charter in 1901. In open meetings the commissioners would enact municipal ordinances, make appropriations, award
contracts, and determine appointments. One commissioner acted as
mayor-president; each of the other four supervised one of the main
city departments. Many cities adopted the Galveston plan; others
favored a single city manager aided by one or more commissioners.[11]

A second variety of reformer held that action more drastic than any
proposed by the Municipal League was necessary. Men of this view—
men like Hazen S. Pingree of Detroit, Samuel M. Jones of Toledo, and
Thomas L. Johnson of Cleveland—advocated municipal ownership of
public utilities, a remedy later espoused by many leaders of the League
itself. Whereas many middle-class reformers identified corruption with
the political machines and their lower-class constituents, and believed
that if only the "best people" were elected to office corruption would
disappear, men like Pingree, Jones, and Johnson made the discovery
that some of the worst corruptionists were among the "best people"
themselves. The researches of Lincoln Steffens did much to advance
that discovery; in city after city, Steffens found that the political
machines worked hand in glove with "respectable" business interests.
Of Boss Ed Butler of St. Louis, for instance, Steffens wrote:

His business was boodling, which is a more refined and a more dangerous
form of corruption than . . . police blackmail. . . . It involves, not thieves,
gamblers, and common women, but influential citizens, capitalists, and great
corporations. For the stock-in-trade of the boodler is the rights, privileges,
franchises, and real property of the city, and his source of corruption is the
top, not the bottom, of society.[12]

Other reformers saw the problem in religious rather than in political
terms. During the eighties and nineties many forward-looking clergy-
men, under the influence of such men as Washington Gladden, Josiah
Strong, and William D. P. Bliss, laid less stress on theology and the
hereafter and more on the need of a better environment. They

[11] Brief discussions with bibliography are given in H. U. Faulkner, *The Quest
for Social Justice* (New York, 1931), pp. 100–102.

[12] Lincoln Steffens, *The Shame of the Cities* (New York, 1904), pp. 105–111.

preached the "social gospel," insisting that Christianity must address itself not only to anticipation of future rewards but to making life more bearable in this world. The social gospel won most of its converts in the cities, where religious leaders began to develop the "institutionalized" church with its many philanthropic enterprises—organized charities, paid welfare workers, athletic clubs, study classes, forums, social halls, and hospitals. The failure of city governments and private organizations to perform these services threw them on the shoulders of men of God and good will. Later, when city governments entered more actively into welfare services and when other private organizations took up the work, the importance of churches in social work declined. But the social gospel, which reanimated religion at the turn of the century, permanently affected the Protestant churches. It also colored the entire reform movement, lending it the moral urgency which was to be so characteristic of progressivism.[13]

The founding of settlement houses was one result of the work of the "institutionalized" church. At least three settlement houses, inspired by the example of Toynbee Hall in London, had been founded in this country before 1890. These included the Neighborhood Guild of New York (1886) and the New York College Settlement on Rivington Street, founded in 1887 by Smith College students. In the same year Jane Addams and Ellen Gates Starr started Hull House. By 1895 there were at least fifty settlements in the cities of the North and East.

Jane Addams, writing of the founding of Hull House, made clear the connection between the social gospel and settlement work; she explained her work as grounded in "the impulse to share the lives of the poor, the desire to make social service, irrespective of propaganda, express the spirit of Christ—an impulse as old as Christianity itself."[14] Hull House was at first simply the expression of a humanitarian impulse. It ran clubs and kindergartens and a day nursery for working mothers; eventually it added a gymnasium, courses in arts and crafts, an employment bureau, and an orchestra. It was not long, however, before Jane Addams—like other reformers—discovered that without

---

[13] Faulkner, *Quest for Social Justice*, pp. 218–219; Henry F. May, *Protestant Churches and Industrial America* (New York, 1949), pp. 170–234; Charles H. Hopkins, *The Rise of the Social Gospel in American Protestantism* (New Haven, 1940), pp. 149–170; Arthur Mann, *Yankee Reformers* (Cambridge, 1954), pp. 72–101.

[14] Quoted in Charles A. and Mary R. Beard, *The Rise of American Civilization* (New York, 1933), II, 421.

state and national action individual efforts would fail. She and her associates led the first fight in Illinois against child labor and sweatshops. Their campaign led finally to the passage of legislation regulating conditions in sweatshops and forbidding the labor of children under fourteen.

Lillian D. Wald, who set up the Henry Street Settlement in New York, was another pioneer in the field. Miss Wald and Mary Brewster, both of them trained as nurses, were instrumental in initiating public health nursing in New York and in providing for the appointment of school nurses.[15] Andover House in Boston's South End, founded by Robert A. Woods in 1891, was more definitely a "university settlement," with greater emphasis on education than either Hull House or the Henry Street Settlement, but like the others it sprang initially from a religious motive. Woods had studied at Andover Theological Seminary and had later gone to England to study the work at Toynbee Hall —the center of the whole settlement movement.[16]

Beyond the immediate effort to improve the lot of slum dwellers, the settlements made other important contributions. Their workers were called upon by city and state governments and even by Washington to make surveys and studies of slums. Mayor Quincy of Boston appointed Woods to a committee to consider how the city might improve slum conditions; in studying the problem, Woods again profited from his English experience when he followed the model of Charles Booth's studies of London. Lillian Wald first suggested the Children's Bureau to the federal government, and the first two heads of that bureau, Julia Lathrop and Grace Abbott, came from Hull House. From Hull House also came Florence Kelley, the leading force in the National Consumers League, an organization dedicated to the elimination of sweatshop labor in tenements; the elimination of child labor, long hours, and night labor for women; and the promotion of minimum-wage laws. These settlements "produced an extraordinary group of women whose vitality and compassion reshaped American liberalism" and "educated a whole generation in social responsibility."[17]

The well-publicized activities of settlement houses brought the problem of slums forcibly to the nation's attention. In 1892 Congress

[15] Lillian D. Wald, *The House on Henry Street* (New York, 1915).

[16] Mann, *Yankee Reformers*, pp. 114–123.

[17] Arthur M. Schlesinger, Jr., *The Crisis of the Old Order* (Boston, 1957), pp. 23–25; C. R. Henderson, *Social Settlements* (New York, 1899), pp. 43–45.

directed the Commissioner of Labor to make a full investigation "relative to what is known as the slums of cities," the results of which, when published in 1894, shed more light on the matter.[18] It was Jacob Riis, however, more than any other individual, who dramatized the deplorable conditions in which millions of Americans were living. Riis came from Denmark to America at the age of twenty-one. After working at various jobs for seven years, he became a police reporter on the New York *Tribune*. Ten years in that job made him an expert on slums, and he spent the rest of his life crusading for improvements. His first great success as a reporter had been to prove the contamination of the city water supply in the Croton watershed. Later, with the help of others, he promoted the building of small parks and school playgrounds, the reform of schools, and the physical improvement of tenement houses. As a result of his labors Mulberry Bend, a notorious slum, was torn down and replaced by a park.[19]

Riis exerted his greatest influence, however, as a writer. *How the Other Half Lives,* which appeared in 1890, caused a sensation; it moved a callous generation to feelings of pity and guilt. No amount of legislative investigations and reports could have had an impact equal to Riis's sustained rhetoric:

Cherry Street. Be a little careful, please! The hall is dark and you might stumble over the children pitching pennies back there. Not that it would hurt them; kicks and cuffs are their daily diet. They have little else. Here where the hall turns and dives into utter darkness is a step, and another, another. A flight of stairs. You can feel your way, if you cannot see it. Close? Yes! What would you have? All the fresh air that ever enters these stairs comes from the hall-door that is forever slamming, and from the windows of dark bedrooms that in turn receive from the stairs their sole supply of the elements God meant to be free, but man deals out with such niggardly hand.[20]

Or take this passage, illustrating the plight of a woman working in a Broadway establishment:

She averages three dollars a week. Pays $1.50 for her room; for breakfast she has a cup of coffee; lunch she cannot afford. One meal a day is her allow-

---

[18] Seventh Special Report of the Commissioner of Labor, *The Slums of Baltimore, Chicago, New York and Philadelphia* (Washington, 1894).

[19] Jacob A. Riis, *How the Other Half Lives* (New York, 1890), *The Making of an American* (New York, 1901), and *The Battle with the Slums* (New York, 1902); Emma Louise Ware, *Jacob A. Riis* (New York, 1939), pp. 49–59, 77–115, 152–168.

[20] Riis, *How the Other Half Lives,* p. 43.

ance. This woman is young, she is pretty. She has "the world before her." Is it anything less than a miracle if she is guilty of nothing worse than the "early and improvident marriage," against which moralists exclaim as one of the prolific causes of the distress of the poor? Almost any door might seem to offer welcome escape from such slavery as this.[21]

The movement for municipal reform had yet another face. At some point the work of humanitarians like Riis broadened into the modern movement for city planning—which is to say that men like Riis called attention to problems which technology then had to solve and which the experts in turn eventually discovered could not be solved piecemeal but had to be considered as component parts of a larger entity. Merely calling attention to the problem was difficult enough in the face of profound public indifference; but by the mid-nineties Americans were at least conscious of the fact that appalling slums existed in every big city. Those of New York and Chicago were the worst; in New York more than two-thirds of the three and one-half million inhabitants lived in 90,000 tenement houses. The tenth ward in New York, where 747 people in 1898 lived on every acre of ground, was probably the most crowded place in the world. Vast areas in Chicago, Philadelphia, and other cities consisted of crowded jumbles of small ramshackle houses, inadequate to the number of families living in them and ill-equipped with sanitation or any other facilities for decent living. In such areas overcrowding bred illiteracy, poverty, crime, disease, and degradation. Saloons abounded. Arrests for infractions of the law were three times as great as elsewhere.[22] The slums appeared doubly deplorable when one reflected that in other parts of these cities, sometimes within a few blocks of the slums, stood the vast marble palaces of the newly rich. Just around the corner from tenements that harked back to the early days of the Industrial Revolution one saw hotels which vied with one another in opulent, wasteful display. The spectacle moved men like Henry George to meditate on the profound irony of modern progress.

How sadly all this contrasted with what might have been was dramatically revealed by the Chicago World's Fair in 1893; one student believed that "the great civic awakening dates from the year of the Chicago World's Fair."[23] Here for the first time in America an

[21] Ibid., pp. 237–238.
[22] Seventh Annual Report of the Commissioner of Labor, pp. 14–19.
[23] Charles Zueblin, A Decade of Civic Development (Chicago, 1905), p. 4.

entire artificial city was designed and built within a brief period. Architecturally—with the exception of Louis Sullivan's transportation building—the "White City" was not startling or new; it was built largely in the classic style. Its plan and grouping, however, were so skillful and its integration so effective as to amaze all with the beauty of the spectacle. Few could escape the fact that the World's Fair was a "miniature of the ideal city." Transportation was well planned; the roads macadamized and kept spotlessly clean; the water supply adequate; fire, police, and ambulance stations amply provided; and light, telephone, and telegraph wires carried in conduits. This small and ephemeral city, into which on some days about three-quarters of a million people crowded, represented the best that America could offer —a city intelligently designed for comfort, convenience, and beauty.

Men like Daniel H. Burnham, who supervised the building of the White City, had long appreciated the need for city planning, but the World's Fair gave the idea a new impetus. Frederick Law Olmsted, builder of parks, the New York architect Charles E. McKim, and the sculptor Augustus Saint-Gaudens contributed to the design of the model city and thereby helped to create the "city beautiful" movement, which supplemented the demand for planning. In these closely related movements emanating from the World's Fair, Burnham and Olmsted were for a long time the leading figures. Burnham had already headed an eminent committee which revived and simplified the early plans for the development of the city of Washington, the first of a long series of city plans; later he did the same thing for San Francisco, Cleveland, and even for Manila. Under his guidance the art of city planning came to be seen as more than the laying out of new streets; architects, landscape architects, and park planners, as well as engineers, were called in.[24] As for Olmsted, mere mention of some of his accomplishments will indicate his importance in the development of the modern city: Central Park and Riverside Parks in Manhattan; Prospect Park in Brooklyn; the capital grounds in Washington; the park systems of Boston, Hartford, and Louisville; and the grounds of Stanford University and the University of California. At his death in 1903, there was hardly a major city in America which remained untouched by his influence. "He

[24] Robert A. Walker, *The Planning Function of Urban Government* (Chicago, 1941), pp. 3–16; Charles Moore, *Daniel H. Burnham* (Boston, 1921).

had, without doubt," says Mumford, "one of the best minds that the Brown Decades produced."[25]

The Borough of Manhattan had over 1,140 acres of parks by 1900, most of them, however, in Central and Riverside Parks in the upper residential area. There were few parks in the tenement regions where they were needed most. A Small Parks Act had been passed in 1887, during the mayoralty of Abram S. Hewitt, but the first park built under that act—the Mulberry Bend Park—was not completed until 1896. It was a park of only three acres, but it did eliminate one of the most disgracefully crowded streets in the city.[26] The recommendations of a tenement-house commission appointed by the state in 1894 included the building of two small parks on the lower East Side and the establishment of suitable playgrounds for all new public schools. But not until six years later was the first of these parks, Hamilton Fish Park, opened to the public.

In the decade after 1898 great strides were taken in New York and in other cities as well. Park acreage in twenty-five cities more than doubled.[27] Earlier in the century large recreation centers had been provided in the outskirts of existing cities, but by the late nineties such areas as Central Park were surrounded by buildings. All that could be done was to clear away tiny plots in built-up areas in the hope of relieving congestion, and to connect existing parks by boulevards in a kind of chain. The latter idea may have come from a simultaneous effort of European cities to replace their fortified walls with encircling parks. Kansas City and Boston were the first cities to develop these chain systems. Kansas City after 1893 planned sixteen miles of boulevards connecting parks with a total area of 2,000 acres. Boston, with thirty-eight towns and cities within eleven miles of the State House, most of them with parks, began in the nineties to enlarge and integrate them. Under the leadership of Charles Eliot two commissions, a city and a metropolitan, were set up which planned and built a park system running from Middlesex Fells on the north to the Blue Hills Reservation on the south, with developments along the Charles, Mystic, and

[25] Lewis Mumford, *The Brown Decades* (New York, 1931), p. 93.

[26] Robert W. De Forest and Lawrence Veiller (eds.), *The Tenement House Problem* (2 vols., New York, 1903), II, 1–7; Jacob A. Riis, "The Clearing of Mulberry Bend," *Review of Reviews*, XII (Aug., 1895), 172–178.

[27] Charles M. Robinson, *The Improvement of Towns and Cities* (New York, 1901), p. 155.

Neponset Rivers. Chicago, Philadelphia, and other cities also began to execute elaborate plans of extension and "chain" connections.

Suburban areas began to build county parks at about the same time.[28] The best known of these was the Essex County Park System in New Jersey, authorized by the legislature in 1894. Extending along the Orange Mountains, it also included parks in Newark, the Oranges, and other cities.[29] As with tenement codes and other reforms, the inspiration for all these new parks came in no small degree from private citizens and civic organizations, not from municipal or state governments. Perhaps that is why the most critical problem—providing parks for slum districts—remained largely unsolved.

Progress in providing community playgrounds for children, a task intimately related both to parks and to slum clearance, was more rapid, precisely because municipal governments entered the field. Some of the early experiments—those of Hull House and Henry Street come to mind—were promoted by private organizations; so was the work of the Outdoor Recreation League in New York in the later years of the decade. But by 1900, municipal governments in most of the larger cities had begun to provide playground facilities. In 1898, Mayor Quincy of Boston opened twenty schoolyard playgrounds and the following year the Board of Education of New York opened no less than thirty-one.[30]

While progress in providing parks for slum districts was discouragingly slow, another problem of the slums, that of improving tenement houses and of drawing up new building codes, was being more vigorously attacked. In 1896 the New York Association for Improving the Condition of the Poor called a series of conferences to consider the construction of better tenements. It sponsored an architectural competition and organized a company to build model tenement houses. Two years later the Charity Organization Society, in part through the influence of Lawrence Veiller, turned its attention to the same problem. It drew up new tenement-house ordinances which won approval from professional and charitable organizations; in 1900 it held a tene-

[28] Andrew W. Crawford, "The Development of Park Systems in American Cities," American Academy of Political and Social Science, Annals, XXV (Mar., 1905), 218–234.

[29] Frederick W. Kelsey, The First County Park System (New York, 1905), and his "Park System of Essex County, New Jersey," American Academy of Political and Social Science, Annals, XXXV (Mar., 1910), 266–272.

[30] C. E. Rainwater, The Play Movement in the United States (Chicago, 1922), pp. 19, 31.

ment-house exhibition and a model tenement competition. So much interest was thus aroused that the state legislature in 1900 appointed another tenement-house commission and passed in the following year a full-length tenement-house law for cities over 250,000 based upon the commission's report. The new code required that all rooms and hallways be lighted and ventilated, and imposed strict regulations regarding size of rooms, running water, sanitation, and fire protection; no longer would the old "dumbbell" tenement, with its lack of light and air, clutter the cities of New York. The commission also recommended a separate tenement-house department for New York City, which was established under a revised city charter and went into operation under Mayor Seth Low in 1902.[31]

Transportation was almost as important as parks and housing in the functioning of the rapidly growing city. The nineties witnessed perhaps the greatest revolution in urban transportation in our history—the shift from horsecars to the electric trolley—but technological innovation merely complicated the problem. One might have expected the advent of electricity to thin city populations by allowing residents to escape into the suburbs. Instead it simply enabled more people to come into the city during working hours, thus adding to congestion rather than relieving it.

In 1890, about 5,661 miles of trackage in American cities were operated by horsepower; by 1902, horsepower was used on only 259 miles, electricity on 21,907 miles.[32] It was Frank J. Sprague, a graduate of Annapolis and a practical electrical engineer of unusual ability, who most clearly demonstrated the practicability of the electric street railway when he installed a system at Richmond, Virginia, in 1888, in which power was obtained from an overhead trolley wire fed from a central station. Street-railway men visited Richmond and read the future; within two years fifty-one cities had adopted the new system. By 1895 at least 850 companies were using electric power.

A new group of millionaires emerged: William L. Elkins and Peter A. B. Widener of Philadelphia, Henry M. Whitney of Boston, Charles Tyson Yerkes of Chicago, and Thomas Fortune Ryan, William C. Whitney, and August Belmont of New York. Not satisfied with covering the streets of these cities with a network of tracks and overhead wires

---

[31] De Forest and Veiller (eds.), *The Tenement House Problem*, I, xiii–xxv, 105–116; II, Appendix V.

[32] U.S. Bureau of the Census, *Street and Electric Railways, 1907*, p. 23.

(the wires later disappeared when engineers learned to run them underground), they built interurban trolleys and then, in order to promote business on Sundays and holidays, constructed spacious parks in the suburbs—their own distinctive contribution to the city beautiful. Such enterprise was warmly applauded; just as half a century earlier the prospects of future greatness seemed dependent on railroad communication with the outside world, so now cities large and small could see no future prospects without electric-powered street railways.[33]

Electric trolleys were not the only means of improving urban transportation, a problem that always seemed one jump ahead of solution. Experiments with overhead railways had begun in the sixties, and elevateds were in operation in New York, Brooklyn, and Kansas City by the eighties. Chicago opened her first elevated in 1892 and Boston in 1901. These were at first run by steam; but in 1897 Sprague introduced on the South Side Elevated Railway of Chicago a system of "multiple unit control"—that is, a system in which each car was powered, lighted, heated, and braked independently, but in which all could be operated by a master switch on any one of them. This improvement quickly replaced steam locomotion and other electric methods of running elevated trains.[34] But the elevated itself was destined in time to be replaced by the subway, work on which was already beginning. Boston had completed a mile and a half of her subway system in 1897; New York began work on hers in 1900.

While city transportation struggled to keep abreast of demand, a new cause of congestion appeared. Before the nineties few buildings stood higher than four or five stories. High land values, however, brought a demand for higher buildings and turned the attention of architects to the problem of designing buildings twenty and thirty, and eventually sixty and seventy, stories high. Two developments made the skyscraper possible. The first was the invention of the electric elevator; the second, the substitution of iron columns and skeletons for the massive masonry hitherto used. Practical hydraulic elevators had been in use for some years, but electric power was needed for the speed and

[33] Frank J. Sprague, "The Electric Railway," *Century*, LXX (July, Aug., 1905), 434–451, 512–527; Herbert H. Vreeland, "The Street Railway of America," in C. M. Depew (ed.), *One Hundred Years of American Commerce* (New York, 1895), I, 141–148; John Anderson Miller, *Fares Please* (New York, 1941), pp. 35–117.

[34] Harold C. Passer, "Frank Julian Sprague," in William Miller (ed.), *Men in Business* (Cambridge, 1952), pp. 229–237.

efficiency necessary for high buildings. The first such installation appears to have been made in a New York building in 1889. It was Sprague, again, who organized an electric elevator company and devised a method by which he could control either a single elevator or all of the elevators in a building by a single master switch.

In the eighties architects began to experiment with iron skeletons, particularly a group in the Midwest who were influenced by the functionalism of Henry H. Richardson—William LeBaron Jenney, Louis Sullivan, and Daniel Burnham. The Ames Building in Boston, the ten-story Tower Building in New York, both built in 1889, and the twenty-six-story World Building in New York in 1890 utilized iron skeletons. The twenty-story Flatiron Building in New York, constructed in 1902, was probably the most famous of the early skyscrapers. Later all of them were to sink into insignificance in comparison with newer structures which towered into the skies. But whatever their merits in allowing greater space for windows and in making office work more comfortable, these buildings, by furnishing space in the sky for more workers, added to the growing congestion below.[35]

Other innovations of the nineties contributed more immediately to greater comfort and health. In 1890, city streets were paved mostly with cobblestones and granite blocks—with wood blocks and bricks in the Midwest. Baltimore had 321 miles of cobblestones out of 371 miles of paved streets, largely because ships used cobblestones for ballast when returning without a cargo, and left the cobblestones behind when they sailed away. Chicago, on the other hand, had only two miles of cobblestones but 750 miles of wooden blocks.[36] After 1890, however, asphalt came to be used more and more extensively, mixed with heavy petroleum, sand, and other materials. Nevertheless, as late as 1900 about two-thirds of the streets of Chicago were not paved at all.[37]

Inadequate paving was only partly responsible for the filthy condition of city streets. Many streets were never cleaned; the collection of garbage and waste was a scandal, and corruption and ignorance perpetuated it. Americans who had never visited Europe did not even realize that cities could be kept clean, so accustomed had they become

[35] T. F. Hamlin, "Twenty-five Years of Architecture," *Architectural Record,* XL (1916); Fisk Kimball, *American Architecture* (Indianapolis, 1928).

[36] Department of Labor, *Statistics of Cities, No. 36* (September, 1901), p. 876.

[37] Nelson P. Lewis, "Modern City Roadways," *Popular Science Monthly,* LVI (Mar., 1900), 524–539.

to squalor. That relative cleanliness was a possibility, however, was made clear in New York during the reform administration of Mayor Strong, who appointed George E. Waring, Jr., as Commissioner of Street Cleaning. During his three-year term in office (1895–1898) Waring not only increased the number of street cleaners but raised their flagging spirits by putting them in white duck uniforms. By 1897 they were sweeping daily almost 1,000 miles of streets, compared with fifty a decade earlier. Waring also introduced the principle, then a novelty, of separating waste into garbage, ashes, and rubbish, and introduced new methods in the handling and disposal of garbage. It was no coincidence that the average New York City death rate of 26.78 in the years 1882–1894 dropped to 19.63 in the first half of 1897. So spectacular was the progress that other cities were inspired to new efforts.[38]

City streets improved in other ways. By the end of the decade New York had removed the maze of overhead telephone, telegraph, and trolley wires over its business districts and placed the wires in underground conduits. Chicago, Boston, and St. Louis were following its example. Meantime Charles E. Brush's carbon arc light and the Welsbach gas mantle brightened streets everywhere, and incandescent electric lights were in use in the smaller cities. Among the larger cities, only New York, St. Louis, and Providence extensively adopted the electric incandescent bulb before 1900, and New York and St. Louis still depended on the Welsbach burner, using arc lights for the larger streets and gas jets for the smaller. Philadelphia was the best-lighted city of the decade.[39]

As in other parts of the world, American cities generally appear on natural transportation routes, on rivers or harbors. This circumstance, together with increasing population, compelled a continued interest in bridgebuilding and the development of new techniques. The Brooklyn Bridge, completed in 1883 after thirteen years of construction, was the first suspension bridge using steel wire for the cables and steel for the

[38] George E. Waring, Jr., "The Cleaning of a Great City," *McClure's Magazine*, IX (Sept., 1897), 911–924, and "The Labor Question in the Department of Street Cleaning," *Municipal Affairs*, I (Sept., 1897), 515–524; see also his article in the supplement, *ibid.*, II (June, 1898). See also Charles Zueblin, *American Municipal Progress* (New York, 1917), pp. 73–86.

[39] Department of Labor, *Statistics of Cities, No. 36* (Sept., 1901), p. 886; Zueblin, *Municipal Progress*, pp. 87–95.

suspended structure.[40] Designed by John A. Roebling, who died before construction began, and supervised by his son, Washington Roebling, it shortly became the "most famous bridge in the world"; it taught engineers how to build enduring suspension bridges. From its example shortly sprang the Williamsburg Bridge over the East River in New York, which soon had the largest traffic of any bridge in the world; the Grand Avenue suspension bridge in St. Louis (1891), which carried a street over railroad yards; and the suspension bridge across the bay at Galveston, Texas, the longest highway bridge in America at that time.

Defects in city water supply, drainage, and sewage disposal, like slums and unclean streets, helped to make city life hazardous and disagreeable; they may explain, in part, why the death rate was so much higher in cities than in rural areas—18.9 per thousand in 1900 as against 15.2 per thousand in the country. For cities like New York, Boston, and Chicago the water problem could be summed up very simply: inadequacy of supply. New York and Boston attempted to find greater supplies in the back country, while Chicago, in an effort to purify the water of Lake Michigan, went to the extreme of reversing the course of the Chicago River so that the city's sewage would drain into the Illinois and Mississippi rivers—a feat which was not greeted with unmixed approval in St. Louis and New Orleans. Most cities at least had enough water; their problem was one of quality, not quantity. Methods of filtering and purification were primitive and contamination common. Nor were methods of sewage disposal more advanced. In 1900 Baltimore, New Orleans, and Mobile had practically no underground sewers; Philadelphia had but 886 miles of sewers to 1,400 miles of streets; and St. Louis only 495 miles to 875 miles of streets.[41]

But if dwellers in cities had to put up with badly paved and badly lighted streets, impure water, and inadequate sewage disposal, they could take pride in the advances that were being made in education; the philosophically inclined, seeking comfort, could ponder the impermanence of material things relative to those of the spirit. In education the cities were forging ahead of the countryside. City children were somewhat more likely to perish of cholera or diphtheria at an early age, but if they survived they would be better educated than their

[40] William C. Conant, "The Brooklyn Bridge," *Harper's New Monthly Magazine*, LXVII (May, 1883), 925–946.

[41] John A. Fairlee, *Municipal Administration* (New York, 1901), pp. 250–251; Zueblin, *Municipal Progress*, pp. 97–104.

country cousins—and that was some consolation, even in the Gilded Age.

The typical one-room rural schoolhouse was presided over by teachers whose average salary in 1898 was $217; the average pupil received eighty-three days of instruction a year. The city school, on the other hand, was sufficiently large for all purposes of grading and instruction. Attendance was more regular: the schools were in session 190 days out of the year; teachers were paid three times that of their rural colleagues; school libraries were better; buildings were more pleasant.[42] Moreover, the most significant advance of these years—the rapid development of secondary education—was confined almost entirely to the cities. Here the number of secondary schools, public and private, increased from about 4,158 in 1890 to 7,983 in 1900, and the number of pupils from 297,894 to 630,048.[43] During the nineties Utah, Pennsylvania, Kentucky, Indiana, and Oregon adopted compulsory school attendance, thereby bringing two-thirds of the states under such systems. The adoption of compulsory attendance benefited rural as well as city education.

Education in the cities was being revitalized in these years, as it was not in the country, by the ideas both of European and American educators—by Pestalozzi, Herbart, Froebel, and by the Americans William T. Harris, Francis Parker, and John Dewey. In the eighties and nineties the Americans devoted most of their attention to elementary education. Harris, U.S. Commissioner of Education from 1889 to 1906, "presided over the rearing of the structure" of the new public-school system. A political and economic conservative and one who looked dubiously upon many new ideas in education as mere "fads," he nevertheless pioneered in the kindergarten movement. (St. Louis, where he was long superintendent of schools, was the first American city to incorporate the kindergarten in the public schools.) For Harris the school was a social institution which would equip the young to live in the new industrial era.[44] Francis Wayland Parker also urged the importance of kindergartens, manual training, science study in elementary schools,

[42] *Report of the Commissioner of Education for the Year 1897–98* (Washington, 1899), II, 2343–2344.

[43] "Biennial Survey of Education, 1898–1930," *Office of Educational Bulletin* (1932), No. 20.

[44] Elwood P. Cubberley, *Public Education in the United States* (rev. ed., Boston, 1934), pp. 472, 474; Merle Curti, *The Social Ideas of American Educators* (New York, 1935), pp. 310–347.

physical education, and freedom of both child and teacher. As a teacher of teachers at the Cook County Normal School in Chicago, Parker stimulated his students with a new interest in childhood. Moved by an "intense devotion to freedom and individuality," he laid particular stress in his teachings on the "happiness of the individual and the beauty and spiritual value of democracy." "Francis Parker," one writer has said, "began the emancipation of the American child."[45]

John Dewey synthesized these early efforts. Believing that "democracy has to be born anew every generation"—an idea reminiscent of Jefferson—he sought to give the twentieth century a philosophy of education suited to its needs. He set up the University Elementary School at the University of Chicago in 1896 and in 1899 published *School and Society;* in both practice and theory he attempted to bridge the existing gap between the school and the social world—to "socialize" education. Social efficiency, he thought, not mere knowledge, should be the objective of education. The school should teach life by becoming a microcosm of society. Accordingly it should go beyond book learning and teach such things as the use of tools, a contact with nature, and even play; it should, in short, develop the student's "personality" as well as his mind. Harris and Parker had emphasized all these things, but Dewey welded them into a coherent philosophy of "progressive" education. Its impact immensely broadened American education, especially when it was buttressed by the work of G. Stanley Hall and William James in psychology. Their findings seemed to reinforce the central tenet of the advocates of the new education—that experience, not a set of preconceived absolutes, was the key to the growth and development of the mind.[46]

Like the schools, libraries, both public and private, were undergoing great changes during this period—another result of urbanization. The number of libraries with 1,000 volumes or more increased from 3,503 to 5,383 and the number of volumes from 25,977,000 to almost 45,591,000. During the nineties, six handsome new library buildings, each costing more than $1 million, were built or begun—the Library of Congress; public libraries in Boston, Chicago, New York, and Pittsburgh; and the Columbia University Library in New York City, as well as many others of lesser cost in smaller cities. The Boston Public

[45] Curti, *Social Ideas,* pp. 379, 385, 395; Cubberley, *Public Education,* pp. 474–475.

[46] Curti, *Social Ideas,* pp. 396–458, 499–541.

Library on Copley Square, a Roman Renaissance structure designed by Charles McKim, opened in 1895; the new Library of Congress, the largest and costliest library in the world, in 1897. In New York the Astor, Lenox, and Tilden libraries were united in 1895 as the New York Public Library.[47] A less spectacular development, but perhaps a more important one in the long run, was the greater efficiency with which libraries were being run. Librarians began to pay less attention to the mere accumulation of books and more to seeing that they were efficiently used. The tendency of libraries to be more closely affiliated with formal education was one indication of the new emphasis.

The cultivation of the arts was undergoing a similar expansion. New York, Boston, Chicago, Philadelphia, St. Louis, Washington, and even some smaller cities like Providence, Milwaukee, Syracuse, and Springfield, Massachusetts, already had notable art galleries and New York and Chicago could point with pride to their excellent museums of natural science. There were still few good orchestras outside Boston, New York, and Chicago, and American musicians still went to Europe to study. Nor was the American theater outstanding in this period. But whatever advances were being made in these fields were being made in the cities. Vaudeville artists, for instance, still toured the country, but few first-class performers ever reached the provinces; the heyday of the traveling companies was passing. It was in the cities that artists and scientists preferred to work and live; the cultural cleavage between metropolis and province, so familiar to European experience but previously almost unknown in America, was beginning to appear. The farmer was well on his way to becoming, in the eyes of the city dweller, a slightly inferior order of being, a "hayseed."

It was inevitable that cities should become centers of culture at the expense of the country, for wealth and leisure were increasingly concentrated there. Life in the city, to be sure, was often disagreeable and sometimes downright repugnant, but what struck the contemporary observer—and what strikes the student of the period—was the fact that vigorous efforts were being made to correct the worst evils. These efforts, of course, did not begin in the 1890's; they go back to earlier years, just as they continued in the progressive period. Even New York witnessed a reform election in 1886 when the able Abram S. Hewitt

[47] *Report of the Commissioner of Education, 1899–1900,* I, 923; Zueblin, *American Municipal Progress,* pp. 87–106; Arthur M. Schlesinger, *The Rise of the City* (New York, 1933), pp. 175–178.

won the mayoralty over two other reform candidates, Henry George and Theodore Roosevelt. His two years in office were a time of improvement and reform, marked by the formulation of his plan for the municipal construction of the Rapid Transit Railroad and by his break with Tammany Hall.

Nevertheless, if there was a decade in city affairs that could be called an "age of reform," it was the nineties. Lincoln Steffens's famous articles, later collected under the title *The Shame of the Cities,* did not begin to appear until 1902, but the evils he described were well known in the nineties, and reform was in the air. Unlike the muckrakers, the reformers of the nineties went beyond the exposure of evils; they were practical in their programs. They organized Municipal Leagues, drew up model city charters, opened settlements, laid plans for parks, drew up tenement-house ordinances, and attempted to reform the machinery of city government—in many ways the hardest task of all. In New York, for instance, the Parkhurst exposures of 1894 put William C. Strong in office. During Strong's two-year term, minor revolutions were effected by George E. Waring in the Department of Street Cleaning and by Theodore Roosevelt in the Police Department. The Board of Health enforced the new tenement-house law and the Department of Public Works more than doubled the water supply and laid twenty miles of asphalt pavement.[48] Evidently New Yorkers hesitated to indulge themselves with too much of a good thing, for they shortly returned Tammany to office. But the reformers under Seth Low were back again in 1902.

Reform enjoyed at least moments of triumph in nearly every city. Boston elected Edwin U. Curtis mayor in 1894. Curtis put each city department under a commissioner, appointed a board of commissioners to control the city electric railways, and revised the system of financing the public schools. In Chicago the Municipal Voters League, led by George C. Cole, had a clear majority in the City Council by 1899. Later, under the direction of Walter L. Fisher, the League succeeded not only in completely cleaning up the Council and improving many areas of city administration but in ending the power of the traction "boodlers." In 1899 the City Council, after a long struggle, forced Charles T. Yerkes, the Chicago traction magnate who had bribed the Illinois legislature into passing bills to make possible his renewal of franchises for one hundred years without payment to the city, to sell his interests in Chicago.[49]

In Toledo the famous "Golden Rule" Jones was elected mayor in 1897. Jones was a big sandy-haired Welshman with a ready smile and a rich gift of humor. Brought to this country at the age of three, he had earned a fortune in the manufacture of improved machinery for oil wells and a reputation for eccentricity in his relations with labor. He ran his factory according to the golden rule; that is, he treated his men like human beings. He introduced the eight-hour day and a minimum wage, gave vacations with full pay, and abolished child labor. His philosophy, if he could be said to have had one, was a curious mixture of Tolstoyan anarchism and a kind of "reform Darwinism," as Eric Goldman calls it; society, he insisted, produced the criminal, and it was society, therefore, not the individual, which must be reformed. "I don't want to rule anybody," he is reported to have said. "Nobody has a right to rule anybody else. Each individual must rule himself. He must decide for himself." This unconventional philosophy soon won him the enmity alike of politicians and of the "respectable elements," including the churches. "Everyone was against him," said Frederic C. Howe, "except the workers and the underworld." As Jones was re-elected four times, however, Howe may have exaggerated the extent of the opposition to his policies—or else Toledo had an uncommon number of thieves and gangsters.

Jones introduced the merit system in the police and public works departments and an eight-hour day for city employees. He opened kindergartens and playgrounds and introduced free concerts. He scrutinized street railway franchises with a wary eye. He took the clubs away from policemen and ended the custom of arresting on suspicion, and when the state legislature, deeply shocked by these humanizing innovations, passed an act putting the police in the hands of a commission appointed by the governor, Jones fought the act until the Ohio Supreme Court upheld him. This last struggle on behalf of home rule Brand Whitlock regarded as Jones's greatest contribution to the "science of municipal government," although Whitlock also mentioned his emphasis on "non-partisanship in local affairs."[50] The zeal for non-

[49] Max Lerner and Mary F. Halter, "Charles Tyron Yerkes," *Dictionary of American Biography*, XX, 609–611.

[50] Frederic C. Howe, *The Confessions of a Reformer* (New York, 1926), pp. 184–188; Brand Whitlock, *Forty Years of It* (New York, 1914), pp. 112–205.

partisanship, however, made it impossible to organize a permanent party of reform, in the long run a source of weakness. Jones's personal influence, which survived his death in 1904, maintained Whitlock in office until 1913; after that the reform movement in Toledo collapsed. But the example of Jones and Whitlock spread to other places.

Hazen S. Pingree of Detroit, like Jones, was a successful businessman who did not share the political opinions common to his class. Elected mayor in 1889, he was shocked at the corruption he found in the City Council. He himself repeatedly was offered bribes from the traction interests; once he was proffered $50,000 if he would refrain from vetoing certain franchises. The bribes completed his conversion to the principle of municipal ownership.

Good municipal government [he decided] is an impossibility while valuable franchises are to be had and can be obtained by corrupt use of money in bribing public servants. · . . . I believe the time has come for municipal ownership of street railway lines, water, gas, electric-lighting, telephone, and other necessary conveniences, which by their nature are monopolies.[51]

The mere fact that a man like Pingree could make such a statement probably did more good in the end than any concrete reforms, for the reforms could be undone by later administrations. But nothing could undo the fact that Pingree, a man who had proved his fitness in the Spencerian struggle for survival by making a great deal of money and who presumably should have been completely happy with life as he found it, found himself instead deeply dissatisfied with contemporary society, and said so. Such isolated displays of conscience pricked the complacency of the Gilded Age and led the way to progressivism.

Thus, although St. Louis and Minneapolis sunk to their lowest depths in the last years of the nineties, they were partially rehabilitated in the early years of the next century.[52] Cleveland under Tom Johnson enjoyed a civic renaissance after 1901.[53] Even Philadelphia and San Francisco, two of the most corrupt and boss-ridden cities in the country during the nineties, later breathed the purer air of progressivism.[54] In

[51] Edward W. Bemis (ed.), *Municipal Monopolies* (New York, 1899), pp. 657–658.

[52] Faulkner, *Quest for Social Justice,* pp. 90, 92, 96; Steffens, *Shame of the Cities,* pp. 29–97, 101–143.

[53] Lincoln Steffens, "Ohio: A Tale of Two Cities," *McClure's,* XXV (July 10, 1905), 302.

[54] Steffens, *Shame of the Cities,* pp. 193–229; Fremont Older, *My Story* (San Francisco, 1919).

the government of cities, as in so many other respects, the decade of
the 1890's was a period of transition. Not only were the cities of
America undergoing a startling physical transformation, but their
inhabitants were beginning to take pride in them; indifference and
apathy were on the wane.

CHAPTER 3

The Decline of Agriculture

WHILE the cities grew and prospered, rural America declined. The nineties marked in many ways the lowest status of the farmer in American history; progress seemed to be passing him by. In fact the farmer was as deeply involved in progress as anyone else; industrialism revolutionized and in the long run benefited agriculture. But the benefits of industrialism were not yet apparent, while its hardships were everywhere to be seen. Somehow the farmer had to accommodate himself to profound changes in his way of life, but the process was bound to be painful and the accommodation never quite complete as long as those changes threatened to reduce him to destitution. He could hardly be blamed if he failed to achieve a philosophical detachment in the face of adversity; peace of mind had to wait on rising prices.

By 1890 the day of the self-sufficing farm (if such a unit ever existed) had long since passed, and money payments had everywhere supplanted barter. Most farmers now raised little for their own use; most of what they produced they sold. The tiller of the soil had become a commercial farmer, and with that his outlook and psychology changed. He found himself in competition with other farmers, not only in his immediate neighborhood, but in other parts of the country and even in foreign countries. He was now a small entrepreneur, a speculator, a harassed businessman at the mercy of supply and demand as well as all of the uncertainties with which farmers normally had to contend. His ability to provide a living for his family came to depend on forces largely beyond his control.

The farmhouse no longer functioned as a manufacturing unit, since

the factories of many cities could produce all of the household commodities needed on the farm more cheaply than they could be made at
home. The farmer now bought from the cities commodities as varied
as those consumed by the cities themselves. At the same time the advent
of the railroad enabled him to send his products to distant markets. By
1900 the country was covered with a network of railroads, and the
effect on farming was apparent almost at once. In certain states—
Illinois was an example—nine-tenths of all farmhouses were located
within five miles of a railroad station.[1] One result of the commercialization of agriculture, to which such evidence attests, was to remove the
center of agriculture from the East to the vast areas of more fertile
land in the West. Neither East nor West benefited in the process;
industrialism decimated some areas and brought overproduction to
others.

During the great boom of the eighties, declared Senator Peffer, "a
territory larger than that of the thirteen original states was populated
in half a dozen years."[2] The Homestead Act was doubtless a factor in
this migration into the trans-Mississippi West, but its influence has
been greatly exaggerated. The government reserved much of the best
land to itself or granted it to states under the Morrill Act of 1862 and,
more important, to railroads. The railroads, with their huge land
grants to sell, contributed most to settlement. In order to attract settlers
they offered reduced railroad fares to the land of promise and reduced
prices and eased terms to those who arranged to buy their land. Their
agents left few spots east of the Mississippi or in western Europe untouched.[3] State land commissions also co-operated enthusiastically in
this advertising. The federal government greatly accelerated the settlement of the West, but not by means of the Homestead Act; its grants
to states and to railroads had far greater effect in promoting the boom.

If many farmers were moving further west, more were moving to
the city. This latter movement was not confined to the Northeast,
where it had been going on for decades; by 1890 it had spread to the
South and Middle West. The census of 1890 showed that two-fifths of

[1] Rodney Welch, "The Farmer's Changed Condition," *Forum,* X (Feb.,
(1891), 693.
[2] W. A. Peffer, "The Farmer's Defensive Movement," *Forum,* X (Feb., 1891),
693.
[3] For the activities of one railroad see J. B. Hedges, "The Colonization Work
of the Northern Pacific," *Mississippi Valley Historical Review,* XIII (Dec.,
1926), 311–342.

the area of Pennsylvania, one-fourth of New Jersey, almost five-sixths of New York State, and a good part of New England had declined in population during the previous decade, but it also showed a decline in 3,144 townships out of 6,291 in Ohio, Indiana, Illinois, Iowa, and Michigan.[4] Six hundred and ninety-one townships in Iowa and 800 in Illinois declined in population during the 1880's. Not all of this loss, however, either in the West or in the East, necessarily reflected a decline in agriculture. Much of it reflected the disappearance of small local industries—manufactories of agricultural implements, bricks and tiles, cooperages, flour and grist mills, and of sawmills.[5] In Vermont one student noted that "the proportion of abandoned wagon shops, shoe shops, sawmills and other mechanical businesses has far out-stripped the abandonment of farms."[6]

New England probably suffered more than any other section from the effects of a declining rural population. Certainly that section received more attention than others in the magazines and newspapers of the period. Of 1,502 townships in New England, 932 had a smaller population in 1890 than in 1880. Four-fifths of the townships of Vermont and two-thirds of those of New Hampshire lost population. In the twenty years from 1880 to 1900, the amount of improved land declined in Vermont and Maine by one-third and in New Hampshire by one-half—approximately a million acres in each state.[7] Thousands of abandoned farms were scattered throughout the region from Maine to Connecticut. As Howells' Silas Lapham said, "You can go through that part of the state [northern Vermont] and buy more farms than you can shake a stick at for less money than it cost to build the barns on 'em."[8]

The long winters, broken lands and hills, and large areas of unfertile land made large-scale farming impossible in New England. New England agriculture, one observer remarked, "cannot compete in cereals with the West, in fruit and vegetables with Delaware and New

[4] Arthur M. Schlesinger, *The Rise of the City* (New York, 1933), pp. 68–69.
[5] These local industries suffered from the concentration of industry and from railroad discrimination between places. Henry J. Fletcher, "The Doom of the Small Town," *Forum*, XIX (Apr., 1895), 214–223.
[6] Quoted in George F. Wells, "The Status of Rural Vermont," *Vermont State Agricultural Commission* (St. Albans, Vt., 1903), p. 6.
[7] Harold F. Wilson, *The Hill Country of Northern New England* (New York, 1936), pp. 97–108.
[8] William Dean Howells, *The Rise of Silas Lapham* (Boston, 1884), ch. XV.

Jersey; in cattle with men whose herds run summer and winter on the free ranches of the Government; in wool with the unhoused flocks of Texas and California, of New Zealand and Australia; in butter with Nebraska and Iowa; in dressed beef with the Armour syndicate; in the labor market with the local manufacturers." Agriculture in other areas also suffered from competition with industry or with other farming regions, from climate, and from a poor topography, but in no other area were these disadvantages to be found so completely and relentlessly combined.[9]

New England farmers, however, were at least able to leave their farms and find better jobs elsewhere. In the South, where agriculture also suffered from a prolonged depression, sharecroppers, tenant farmers, and small landowners remained on the land, cultivating their plots in increasingly unremunerative and hopeless fashion. One traveler wrote, "Apart from the New South, by which I mean the country around the region of the rapidly developing iron industries . . . the same wretched poverty prevails among the Southern people now, twenty-two years after the war, [as in 1865]."[10] "Since the red man left us the tobacco-seed," a Virginian said, "the farming interest has not been so depressed."[11] Southern agriculture, unlike that of New England, was expanding; 10 million bales of cotton were produced in 1894, 11 million in 1898 after new fields were opened up in Oklahoma.

Expansion, however, was as potent a cause of trouble in the South as contraction in New England. Although southern cotton enjoyed a virtual monopoly of the domestic market and encountered little competition abroad, the price of cotton fell steadily after 1870, reaching a low of six cents a pound in 1894 and again in 1898. Since cotton could hardly be raised profitably at less than eight cents, most cotton growers in the nineties were operating at a loss.[12] Tobacco brought an equally unsatisfactory return. Diversified agriculture, meanwhile, which might have brought some relief if pursued more assiduously, was declining relative to the growth of population; in the cotton belt it had practi-

[9] Charles C. Nott, "A Good Farm for Nothing," *Nation*, XLIX (Nov. 21, 1889), 406–408; Walter C. Frost, "Desolate Farm Sites in New England," *ibid.*, XLIX (Nov. 28, 1889), 431.

[10] William D. Kelley, *The Old South and the New* (New York, 1888), p. 121.

[11] Quoted in C. Vann Woodward, *Origins of the New South, 1877–1913* (Baton Rouge, 1951), p. 177.

[12] *Ibid.*, p. 186; Fred A. Shannon, *The Farmer's Last Frontier* (New York, 1945), pp. 112–117.

cally disappeared.[13] The condition of southern agriculture in 1890 was probably worse than at any other time in the region's history.

One of the most discouraging features of the situation was the growth of tenancy. Southern farms operated by tenants increased by 8.7 per cent between 1890 and 1900.[14] Since land sold slowly in the South and the value of crops was uncertain, mortgages were hard to get. Southern farmers carried on instead by means of a system whereby local merchants took a lien on the prospective crop, in the meantime selling the farmer food, clothing, farm implements, and hay at a credit price often 30 to 75 per cent or more above the cash price. Thus the farmer bought at the highest price and sold at the lowest. Under these conditions more and more farmers sank into debt and peonage—a fact which makes the growth of the Farmers' Alliances in the late eighties easy to understand.[15]

The West, during the nineties, was no better off. In that section farmers nursed grievances of long standing—low prices, transportation abuses, high interest rates on loans, and the high cost of commodities —but in the nineties they suffered more immediately from over-production and at the same time, paradoxically, from drought (particularly in Colorado, Kansas, Nebraska, and the Dakotas). The rapid opening of the western part of the Midwest had brought vast new lands under cultivation and greatly increased agricultural output. At the same time this expansion was accompanied by mounting debt. The proliferation of railroads in the West has already been noted; between 1880 and 1890 railroad mileage in Kansas, Nebraska, and the Dakotas increased from 5,135 to 18,943 while population was increasing by about 1,400,000, so that in Kansas, for example, there was a mile of railroad in 1889 for every nine and one-third miles of land and five and one-half miles of track for every thousand people in the state.[16]

[13] *Ibid.*, pp. 120–124.
[14] *Fourteenth Census Agriculture* (Washington, 1922), V, 133–134. The percentage of tenant farmers in the South Atlantic states increased from 24 to 29.6 per cent, in the East South Central states from 38.3 to 48.1 per cent, and in the West South Central states from 38.6 to 49.1 per cent.
[15] What was happening in the South is also reflected in the fact that although the number of farms and the total value of farm property both increased in the nineties, average acreage per farm steadily declined. *Abstract of the Twelfth Census of the United States, 1900*, pp. 288–293.
[16] R. C. Miller, "The Background of Populism in Kansas," *Mississippi Valley Historical Review*, XI (Mar., 1925), 470. Railroad mileage in Kansas increased from 3,102 to 8,810, in Nebraska from 1,634 to 5,407, and in the Dakotas from

Most of this railroad expansion had been financed by the East or by Europe, but counties, municipalities, and individual farmers in the West had also subscribed to the building of railroads; many areas were heavily indebted to them.[17] At the same time the new settler in the West, once he had succeeded in breaking soil on a few acres of land, had no difficulty in mortgaging his property; eastern investors were only too happy to lend him the money, and the farmer all too eager to borrow. Mortgage companies urged him to borrow amounts equivalent to the full value of his farm, and the farmers readily obliged in the heady expectation of bumper crops and great profits later on. "In Kansas and North Dakota," according to Hicks, "there was in 1890 a mortgage for every two persons, and in Nebraska, South Dakota, and Minnesota, one for every three persons—more than one to a family in all five states . . . throughout this region mortgages had multiplied in number and amount far beyond any reasonable limits."[18] In the boom years of the early eighties the railroad, the investor in mortgages, and the farmer all shared a boundless confidence in the future of the West, and good crops and rising land values seemed for a time to bear them out.

Speculation in farm lands—for the boom, like all booms, was speculative—was surpassed by speculation in city real estate. Omaha, Lincoln, Kansas City, Topeka, and Wichita swarmed with real-estate buyers who paid fantastic prices for favored locations and laid out new streets with utter abandon. Small towns and villages, falling under the spell of an optimism equally fatuous, recklessly voted bond issues to provide schools where there were no pupils to attend them, courthouses where there were no courts, and roads and bridges where there was no traffic to be seen for miles around. They issued franchises for streetcars and railroads which years later were still unneeded and unwanted. Nor was there any lack of eastern capital with which to indulge these follies. Speculation fed upon itself.[19]

Reckless overexpansion led eventually to collapse; the long drought of the late eighties hastened it. During the years of rapid settlement, annual rainfall averaged 21.63 inches in the western parts of Kansas,

---

399 to 4,726. J. R. Dodge, "The Discontent of the Farmer," *Century* (New Series), XXI (Jan., 1892), 452.

[17] *Ibid.*

[18] John D. Hicks, *The Populist Revolt* (Minneapolis, 1931), p. 24.

[19] *Ibid.*, pp. 25–28; Miller, "Background of Populism in Kansas," pp. 471–475.

Nebraska, and South Dakota—sufficient, if well distributed over the growing season, to insure good crops of corn and wheat. After 1887, rainfall in all but two years fell far below normal. In five of those years it was so low as to cause almost total crop failure. In 1894, the worst year of all, drought destroyed the crops in sixty-one of Nebraska's ninety-one counties. In half the state destruction was so complete that men did not even try to harvest their crops. Decline in production brought with it no compensating rise in price, because, while Kansas, Nebraska, and the Dakotas lay stricken, other states enjoyed fine years and produced large crops. Wheat prices plummeted from $1.19 per bushel in 1881 to 49.1 cents in 1894, corn from 63 cents a bushel in 1881 to 28 cents in 1890.[20] On few farms did the selling price equal the cost of production. It was cheaper to burn corn than to buy coal.

Further west nature also assumed the shape of a demon of destruction. In Wyoming, Montana, and elsewhere on the High Plains the severe winter of 1886–1887 decimated great herds of cattle and effectively ended the open-range industry of the West. Here too overexpansion had already cut profits sufficiently to discourage European and eastern investment. The bitter winter, following on the heels of other troubles, reduced many a cattle company to bankruptcy. It was years before the cattlemen recovered their prosperity.[21]

More prosperous farmers, it is true, survived all these disasters, and many of those who moved to the city or to other parts of the country were not farmers at all but land speculators. Nevertheless, the exodus of farmers was great. "In one season," wrote a Kansas editor, "eighteen thousand prairie schooners passed east over the Mississippi River bridge at Omaha—never to return." In the phrase then current, they "went back to the wife's folks."[22] One student estimates that 179,884 people, of whom a great many were doubtless genuine farmers, left Kansas between 1887 and 1891, with only seventeen out of 107 counties holding their own in population.[23] In 1897 the editor of the Topeka *Capitol* summed up the history of the last decade:

[20] Hallie Farmer, "Frontier Populism," *Mississippi Valley Historical Review*, X (Mar., 1924), 416–418.

[21] Ernest S. Osgood, *The Day of the Cattleman* (Minneapolis, 1929), pp. 218–258.

[22] Charles M. Harger, "New Era in the Middle West," *Harper's New Monthly Magazine*, XCVII (July, 1898), 277.

[23] Farmer, "Frontier Populism," p. 421.

In the boom period rival towns fought with weapons over the location of county seats. Today hillocks on the prairies mark their sites. Railroads paralleled each other. And then the buffalo grass crept up the grades and grew between the ties. It seemed as if the homesteads were to relapse into the original desert.[24]

As agriculture deteriorated in certain sections of the country, the morale of the rural population appeared visibly shaken. The rapid growth of cities, both in Europe and in America, the relative decline of the farming population, and the migration of tens of thousands of farm boys and girls to the cities shook the farmer's certainty that agriculture was, in Jefferson's words, "the most precious part of the state." The golden day seemed to have passed; rural America, prosperous, democratic, and egalitarian, seemed about to vanish altogether from the scene. It may be true, as Hofstadter suggests, that such an America had never existed in fact, but the vision of a "lost agrarian Eden" nevertheless continued to haunt the suffering farmer of the 1890's.[25] He found no consolation in the fact that growing cities provided a greater market for agricultural commodities and that with the use of new machinery farm products could be produced with fewer workers. These advantages might exist in theory, but they had yet to materialize.

The farmers were also disturbed by the increasing concentration of wealth in cities. By 1890 over three-fourths of the nation's wealth was concentrated in urban areas and the rate of this accumulation was increasing. There is little evidence, however, that urban wealth had been accumulated at the expense of the farmer any more than at the expense of the city dweller. The relevant fact was the marked trend toward concentration of wealth in the hands of a few individuals; the fact that these individuals lived in the city was of much less significance. Yet the farmer was becoming convinced that the city was "the enemy's country," as Bryan once unhappily referred to it during the campaign of 1896.[26] What angered the farmer was that the price he received for his products continually fluctuated with the market demand while the cost of transportation and the price of commodities which he had to buy, increasingly protected from competition, remained relatively stable. The farmer was thoroughly convinced, and there is a great deal of evidence to support his conviction, that he paid for these services

[24] Quoted *ibid.*, p. 421.
[25] Richard Hofstadter, *The Age of Reform* (New York, 1955), p. 62.
[26] Matthew Josephson, *The Politicos* (New York, 1938), p. 689.

and commodities a higher price than was warranted. Where he sometimes erred was in supposing that most of the people living in cities did
not share this grievance with him, but that they were indeed engaged,
as he sometimes seemed to think, in a far-flung conspiracy to subvert
the entire agricultural interest.

Farmers may have known that people from the cities as well as
farmers supported the Sherman Antitrust Act, but they paid little
attention to the fact. The farmers themselves, however, were not vitally
interested in the abstract question of monopoly. They were more
interested in the specific manifestations of monopoly, and even here
their interest in the problem was somewhat one-sided. On the question
of tariffs, for instance, they seemed confused, although some of them
doubtless realized that monopoly prices were made possible in part by
tariff protection.[27] The Populist platform of 1892 mentioned the tariff
only once and then in a political rather than an economic context:
"They [the major parties] propose to drown the outcries of a plundered
people with the uproar of a sham battle over the tariff, so that capitalists, corporations, national banks, rings, trusts, watered stock, the
demonetization of silver and the oppressions of the usurers may be lost
sight of."

The farmers concentrated most of their fire on more specific issues,
particularly on the railroads, the most bitterly hated of all monopolies
of the post-Civil War period. The Populist platform demanded that
"the government should own and operate the railroads in the interest
of the people." The significance of railroads in agricultural history can
hardly be overemphasized. The railroads not only helped to move the
center of agriculture westward and to stimulate agricultural production
by giving it access to new markets, but by doing so they virtually put an
end to the commercial cultivation of certain crops in many parts of the
East. As a result, farmers in the Northeast gradually had to substitute
truck and dairy farming for crops like wheat and corn. In every part
of the country the railroads doomed the self-sufficing farm to extinc-
tion and forced the commercialization of agriculture. The railroads
revolutionized American farming.

It was not these changes, however, that aroused the farmer. The
movement to curtail certain railroad practices and to bring the rail-

[27] Population trends, monopolies, and other factors in the farmers' discontent
are discussed in C. F. Emerick, "An Analysis of Agricultural Discontent,"
Political Science Quarterly, XI (Sept. and Dec., 1896), 432–463, 601–639.

roads under state and federal control centered in the Middle West, where the railroads had in general promoted agriculture, not in the East, where they had almost destroyed it. The rise of antirailroad sentiment in the Middle West is explained by the fact that railroads in promoting commercial agriculture at the same time rendered farmers excessively dependent on rail transportation. This very dependence in turn made it possible for the railroads to engage in all the practices to which the farmers objected at such length over the years: high rates, rebates, the long-and-short haul. It was to protest against such abuses that the Grangers had entered politics in the seventies. The Grangers also objected to the reckless financing of the railroads, which resulted in frequent bankruptcies (in which many farming communities suffered as railroad bondholders), to their corrupt influence in politics, and to the shift in land values resulting from railroad building. Many states, under the influence of the Grangers, passed laws directed against these evils, but Supreme Court decisions eventually weakened their effectiveness and forced a recourse to federal legislation. Neither the Interstate Commerce Act of 1887 nor the Sherman Antitrust Act of 1890, however, loosened the railroads' grip on the farmer. The ease with which the railroads thwarted the intention of those acts strengthened the farmer's conviction that a conspiracy of vested interests had seized control of the government and was bent on his utter destruction.[28]

In time, as farmers became more and more preoccupied with the simple fact of falling prices and growing indebtedness, the currency problem replaced the sins of the railroads as the center of their attention. By the early nineties currency inflation had become the outstanding demand of the embattled farmers; it was to be the great issue in the campaign of 1896. The origins of the monetary problem went back to the Civil War. During and after the war the suspension of specie payments and the widespread circulation of greenbacks having no metallic backing had caused a drastic inflation in which prices rose by as much as 100 per cent. In 1879 the government resumed specie payments and re-established the gold standard. In the resulting deflation farmers,

[28] *First Annual Report of the Interstate Commerce Commission* (Washington, 1887), reprinted in part in F. Flugel and H. U. Faulkner, *Readings in the Economic and Social History of the United States* (New York, 1929), pp. 609–618.

who had borrowed in order to expand production during a period of inflation, were now called upon to repay their loans in money worth far more than the money they had borrowed. The agrarian interests sought to raise prices through various inflationary schemes, of which the free coinage of silver was only one.

Silver had been demonetized in 1873 with very little comment or criticism because it had become so scarce, and consequently so expensive, that it had tended to go out of circulation. New discoveries of silver in the Rocky Mountains subsequently caused a fall in the price of silver and made it an ideal inflationary device, and as time went on agrarian agitators gave more and more prominence in their programs to the demand for silver coinage. In response to pressure from the agrarians Congress passed the Bland-Allison Act in 1878 and the Sherman Silver Purchase Act in 1890, both of which authorized the Treasury to buy a certain amount of silver for coinage. Both acts, however, left the Secretary with enough discretion to prevent much of this silver from circulating, if he chose to do so. He invariably did. Farm prices continued their calamitous decline, and the clamor of the farmers mounted.

As time went on the farmers evolved an explanation of their troubles, simple but not always accurate. The country, they came to believe, was divided into two groups.

There are but two sides in the conflict that is being waged in this country today [insisted a Populist manifesto]. On the one side are the allied hosts of monopolies, the money power, great trusts and railroad corporations who seek the enactment of laws to benefit them and impoverish the people. On the other are the farmers, laborers, merchants, and all other people who produce wealth and bear the burdens of taxation. . . . Between these two there is no middle group.

Or as Sockless Jerry Simpson put it, "It is a struggle between the robbers and the robbed."[29]

From this point of view a theory of conspiracy easily emerged: the "money power" had conspired to beat down and rule the rest of the country. The conspiracy was international in scope; it ran from Wall Street to Lombard Street and took in all the other financial capitals of

[29] Elizabeth N. Barr, "The Populist Uprising," in William E. Connelly (ed.), *A Standard History of Kansas and Kansans* (Chicago, 1918), II, 1170.

the world. The rise of this "Anglo-American Gold Trust" was sometimes attributed to the influence of "international Jews"; sometimes it
was associated in the farmer's mind with the influence of foreigners in
general—were not the cities populated largely by immigrants? But
whatever its origins, there was no question as to the success of this
movement to destroy the common man. "A vast conspiracy against
mankind has been organized on two continents," cried the Populist

Bullion value of 371¼ grains of silver (contents of one silver dollar)
in terms of gold at the annual average price of silver, 1866–1930.

platform, "and it is rapidly taking possession of the world." The proof
of this was the ease with which laws intended to protect the people had
been consistently evaded—the Interstate Commerce Act, the Sherman
Antitrust Act, and in particular the two silver coinage acts. The prominence of the money question in agrarian ideology was closely related to
the conspiracy theory; the image of gold and the image of Shylock
gradually merged, until gold became a symbol of all the unknown,
impersonal forces which were mysteriously working to drive the farmer
into poverty and debt. Currency reform became the reform of reforms.
"When we have restored the money of the constitution," declared
Bryan in his cross-of-gold speech, "all other necessary reforms will be

possible; but . . . until this is done there is no other reform that can be accomplished."[30]

In view of the growing desperation with which farmers contemplated their lot, it may be somewhat surprising to note that agriculture was not completely stagnant during the 1890's but continued to develop. The number of farms in the country, for instance, increased during the decade by more than a million, a greater advance than in any previous decade except the one between 1870 and 1880. Farm acreage, perhaps a more revealing indication of progress, increased by more than 200 million acres and the value of all farm property by over $4 billion. The value of implements and machinery increased by half. These statistics are subject to a few qualifications. Although the average number of acres per farm increased (except in the South Atlantic states, where subdivision of large holdings continued), the average number of *improved* acres declined. While the value of all farm property (land and improvements) increased considerably, the average value per farm remained about the same.[31] In all areas, particularly in the West and South, the depression following the panic of 1893 lowered agricultural prices and generally checked the advancing value of farm land. It was the upward movement of prices after 1897 that improved the situation, and it is this later improvement which is reflected in the statistics for the whole decade. Nevertheless, the picture even before 1897 was not uniformly black.

Real improvement began in 1897. Farmers proclaimed the arrival of a "new era." "It is doubtful," one western editor wrote, "if in all the history of the prairies there has been a year when the workers had so much to show for their efforts—both in material values and in enhanced credit."[32] Ray Stannard Baker heard a farmer remark in 1899 that "every barn in Kansas and Nebraska has had a new coat of paint." The observation moved Baker to write:

For any one who knew the West of 1895 and 1896, with its bad weather-stained houses, its dilapidated farms, its farm machinery standing out in the rain, its ruinous "boom towns," its discontented inhabitants crying out for legislation to relieve their distress, this bit of observation raises a picture of

[30] This Populist philosophy is well described in Hofstadter, *Age of Reform,* pp. 60–93.

[31] *Twelfth Census, Agriculture,* V, xvi, xviii, xxi, xxiii, xxix.

[32] Charles M. Harger, "New Era in the Middle West," *Harper's New Monthly Magazine,* XCVII (July, 1898), 278. He was speaking of Kansas and Nebraska.

improvement and smiling comfort such as no array of figures, however convincing, could produce. . . . The farmer has provided himself with food in plenty and the means for seeding his fields for another year; he has clothed himself and his family anew; he has bought an improved harvester, a buggy and a sewing machine, and now, with the deliberation which is born of a surplus and a sturdy confidence in himself and in the future, he is painting his barn.[33]

Other observers noted a general improvement in the South and Midwest. Even in the hill country of northern New England, readjustments and specialization were beginning to relieve distress; the New England farmer turned more and more to grain and to such perishable products as potatoes, milk, eggs, poultry, and fruit.[34] Other eastern states close to the great urban markets followed this example.

The Industrial Commission in its report of 1902 attributed the restoration of agricultural prosperity to four causes: (1) a rise in farm prices, (2) an increase of the circulating medium and extension of rural banking agencies, (3) a more general diffusion of manufacturing industries, and (4) the substitution of livestock production for cereals in the central West and, in general, the progress of diversified agriculture in various parts of the country.[35] Other causes can also be cited: the continued growth and diffusion of railroads and the opening of New Orleans as a port of export for foodstuffs, the decline of freight rates on agricultural products by water and rail, the rise in agricultural exports to an all-time high in 1898. Nor should one overlook the fact that farmers had grown in experience and wisdom during the bitter trials of the nineties. Finally, the country as a whole was prosperous at the turn of the century, and it was to be expected that agriculture would share, at least in part, in the general recovery.[36]

What caused the rise in prices? It is impossible to speak with entire certainty, but the importance of inflation is clear enough. Simultaneous discoveries of gold in Australia and in the Klondike, together with the invention of the cyanide process for extracting it from other ores, greatly enlarged the world's gold supply, decreased the value of gold,

[33] Ray Stannard Baker, "The New Prosperity," *McClure's*, XV (May, 1900), 86–94. For other evidences of recovery, see Charles M. Harger, "An Era of Thrift in the Middle West," *World's Work*, V (Feb., 1903), 3091–3093.

[34] Wilson, *Hill Country of Northern New England*, pp. 213–230.

[35] *Final Report of the Industrial Commission*, XIX (Washington, 1902), 149.

[36] H. U. Faulkner, *The Decline of Laissez Faire* (New York, 1951), pp. 22–30.

and inflated the currency. Per capita circulation of money in the United States increased from $22.82 in 1890 to $26.94 in 1900. Another cause of rising prices, stressed in the analysis of the Industrial Commission, was the growing tendency toward diversification of crops throughout the country and toward specialization in certain favorable areas. This specialization was made possible in part by the diffusion of small manufacturing based upon farm products—canning, the manufacture of cheese and butter, cotton spinning. Improved agricultural methods probably had some effect in raising prices. Whatever the causes, the condition of the farmer improved steadily from 1897 until the early twenties—one of the longest periods of sustained prosperity in the history of American agriculture.

By 1900, the westward movement having slowed somewhat, the productive agricultural areas of the United States were well defined. New York and New England specialized in dairying and mixed farming, the other North Atlantic and North Central states westward to the 104th parallel in corn and wheat, the South Atlantic and South Central states in cotton, the High Plains and Rockies in wool and livestock, and the West Coast in grain and fruits. After 1897, with exports and prices rising, prospects were especially bright in the twelve states of the North Central group. This area contained one-third of the nation's farm population, over one-third of all farms, half of all improved land, and half the total value of farm property. Specializing in the production of food crops and meat and draft animals, it was clearly the richest and most important farming region in the nation. In this rich area, even during the good years following 1897, as many as four-tenths of all receivers of farm income were wage laborers, and almost three-tenths of operating farmers were tenants. Tenancy continued to increase toward the end of the decade:

few producers [according to Fred Shannon] made in excess of a scant living. Money was amassed by holders of large areas farmed by tenants, and by other absentee landlords; money was gathered in by creditors; some money was made beyond the needs of a comfortable living by about one person in twelve engaged in agricultural occupations.[37]

The low income prevalent even in the most fertile farm areas after recovery had begun to set in was not the only persistently discouraging

[37] Fred A. Shannon, "The Status of the Midwestern Farmer in 1900," *Mississippi Valley Historical Review*, XXXVII (Dec., 1950), 506.

aspect of agriculture in the nineties. Equally discouraging was the slowness with which farmers embraced scientific farming. Not that they hesitated to use machinery; the fact that most of the fundamental inventions in farm machinery had been widely adopted by 1900 and that farmers continued to buy machinery throughout the bad years of the nineties shows that machinery was considered indispensable to successful farming. But farmers were careless and wasteful in using the soil. Man-power output more than doubled in this period, but yield per acre rarely increased. Land was subordinated to machinery; only its great fertility saved it from complete destruction. The few who did farm scientifically were regarded as cranks.[38] Whatever success the American farmer enjoyed, in the nineties as in other times, he certainly did not owe to his technical efficiency in making use of the knowledge available to him.[39]

Ignorance persisted in spite of the efforts on the part of government to encourage the use of scientific methods. In 1887 Congress passed the Hatch Act, which allotted $15,000 a year (a sum later increased) to each state and territory for the setting up of experiment stations. In 1889 the Commissioner of Agriculture was made a cabinet member. The Morrill Act of 1890 provided $15,000 for every state (to be gradually raised to $25,000) for instruction in agriculture, mechanical arts, and related subjects. By 1895 ten states had established departments of agriculture.[40] Meanwhile the federal government continued to aid education in agriculture through land grants; the stimulus given to education through such grants is immeasurable. Some institutions, like Purdue and the Massachusetts Agricultural College, were founded under the first Morrill Act of 1862. Many colleges, founded earlier, accepted and prospered under federal grants—Michigan State and Iowa State are examples. More important than the mere number of schools aided by the government, and harder to measure, is the

[38] Milburn L. Wilson et al., Agriculture in Modern Life (New York, 1939), pp. 223–224.

[39] In the words of two experts, written some years later, "The success and prosperity of the American farmer are due to the unbounded fertility of the soils, the cheapness of farm lands, and the privilege of utilizing modern inventions and machinery rather than to systematic organization and efficient farm management." Willet M. Hayes and Edward C. Parker, "The Cost of Producing Farm Products," U.S. Department of Agriculture, Bureau of Statistics, Bulletin No. 48 (Washington, 1906), p. 9; see also Shannon, Farmer's Last Frontier, p. 147.

[40] Ibid., pp. 272–280.

improvement in standards which resulted, but it is safe to say that many institutions by the end of the century could offer first-rate instruction in agriculture.

The government's interest in agriculture broadened when the Department of Agriculture was set up in the cabinet. Under Secretary Jeremiah M. Rusk (1889–1893), the Weather Bureau was moved from the Department of War to Agriculture, and a Division of Publications was established. Cleveland's Secretary of Agriculture, J. Sterling Morton (1893–1897), organized a Section of Foreign Markets, an Office of Public Road Inquiries, Division of Soils, and a Division of Agrostology. Morton was the father of Nebraska's Arbor Day. When James Wilson of Iowa became Secretary in 1897, the Department had a budget of almost $2.5 million, employed 2,444 persons, and operated through two bureaus (Weather and Animal Industry) and eighteen divisions.

The Department of Agriculture attracted brilliant and famous scientists. One of them was Theobold Smith, whose discovery in the 1890's that the tick transmitted cattle tick fever showed for the first time that an insect could act as an intermediary host in the transmission of a protozoan disease. This discovery, research leading to which cost $65,000, saved the cattle industry $40 million a year. Marion Dorset, another great scientist in the Bureau of Animal Industry, had already begun his research on hog cholera. He established for the first time that an animal disease, supposedly carried by a bacterium, could be caused by a "filterable" virus and controlled by means of serums and vaccines. Still another eminent scientist, Harvey W. Wiley, became Chief of the Division of Chemistry in the 1880's. During his long career he drew up methods of analyzing drugs, foods, and other agricultural products which became guides in every laboratory in the country. He was one of the early advocates of pure food and drug acts.

The Department also claimed the services of David G. Fairchild, who with many able assistants ransacked the world for new plants that might be usefully introduced in America. The successful introduction of tens of thousands of foreign plants revolutionized agriculture in many parts of the country, particularly in dry regions, which proved able to bear durum wheat. One of the Department scientists, the zoologist Charles W. Stiles, became interested in the hookworm disease, which he had learned of in Europe. One of his students, Major Bailey

K. Ashford, had discovered the disease in Puerto Rico and was convinced that it was responsible for the high incidence of anemia on the island. He brought samples of the hookworm to Stiles, who was then able to identify similar worms in the South. Finally the Department engaged Wilbur O. Atwater, who can rightly be regarded as the founder of the science of nutrition. No other country in the world carried on such extensive work in agricultural research and education as the United States. The Department of Agriculture, in fact, undoubtedly constituted at this time the finest scientific research organization in the world.[41]

The only practical achievement of these years in applied technology was the opening of arid land to cultivation by irrigation. Some early experiments in irrigation had been made by the Mormons in Utah and by farmers in Colorado and southern California, but the problem of dry areas was not systematically studied until 1878, when Major John Wesley Powell published his *Report on the Lands of the Arid Regions of the United States*. Powell was a naturalist, an ethnologist, and a geologist, achieving his greatest fame as Director of the United States Geological Survey. In his early years he was an enthusiastic explorer and was the first white man to lead a party some 900 miles down the Green and Colorado rivers.

In his report on the West, Powell set the line of twenty inches of rainfall—a line which approximately coincided with the 100th meridian—as the western limit of successful agriculture. Beyond that, however, agriculture might be undertaken in some areas with the aid of irrigation. The problem which the government faced in those areas, he said, was not the monopoly of land, which conservationists were beginning to worry about, but the monopoly of water.[42] He suggested plans for allotting land and distributing water, but he believed, as late as 1900, that the states, not the federal government, were the proper agencies to undertake the work.[43]

[41] Material on the Department of Agriculture during this period can be found in Alfred C. True, *A History of Agricultural Experimentation and Research in the United States 1607–1925*, including a *History of the United States Department of Agriculture* (U.S. Department of Agriculture, Miscellaneous Publications, No. 251, Washington, 1937), and in T. Swann Harding, *Two Blades of Grass* (Norman, Okla., 1947), pp. 45–48, 150–156, 174–178.

[42] Walter Prescott Webb, *The Great Plains* (Boston, 1931), pp. 348–356.

[43] J. W. Powell, "Institutions for the Arid Land," *Century*, XVIII (May, 1890), 111–116.

The drought of the late eighties, however, stirred action on the national level. Congress provided surveys in 1888, 1890, and 1891. Eight national Irrigation Congresses met at various times during the nineties, largely at the instigation of William E. Smythe, a conservationist who founded *Irrigation Age* in 1890. By 1900 irrigation was a national issue; both major parties in their platforms favored federal reclamation of arid lands. Congress had already passed the Carey Act of 1894, which attempted to stimulate state action by offering federal lands to any state which would reclaim and sell them to farmers. That act, however, failed in its purpose; nineteen years later the Public Land Office reported that of the seven million acres applied for, less than half a million had been reclaimed.

Captain Hiram M. Chittenden, in his report on reservoir sites in 1897, was the first individual to argue in an official document that since irrigation was an interstate problem it should be undertaken by the federal government.[44] Chittenden, like Powell, was thoroughly familiar with the West. A West Point graduate and army engineer, he had spent years on assignments in the West; later he became known as an authority on the history of the region.[45] His report, together with the agitation of Powell and others, moved Senator Francis G. Newlands of Nevada to introduce a bill in January, 1901, authorizing the federal government to build irrigation projects in sixteen western states, to be financed by sales of public lands. The reclaimed land was then to be sold to settlers, the proceeds to be applied to further projects.[46] The bill might have languished in Congress had not Theodore Roosevelt, an ardent conservationist, succeeded to the Presidency. Roosevelt threw the weight of his office behind the bill, which was passed on June 17, 1902. The Newlands Act was the cornerstone of the structure of federal reclamation.

So far as the progress of scientific farming was concerned, the somewhat belated assumption by the federal government of responsibility for the reclamation of arid lands was a bright place in an otherwise dreary landscape. In spite of the American farmer's reluctance to adopt more enlightened methods of cultivation, agriculture gradually re-

[44] "Preliminary Examination of Reservoir Sites in Wyoming and Colorado," *House Document 141*, 55th Cong., 2nd sess. See also Webb, *Great Plains*, pp. 359–361.

[45] See his *The American Fur Trade of the Far West* (1902).

[46] 32 U.S. Statutes at Large 388.

covered from the depression of the early nineties. Prosperity would in time help to close the gap between town and country which had widened so perceptibly during the depression years. Later developments, however, were vastly more important in eliminating cultural distinctions between the farms and the cities—the automobile, the radio, the telephone, rural electrification, rural free delivery, and the ultimate acceptance of scientific agriculture. Even in the nineties, however, when the distance between the urban and the rural parts of the country was wider than ever before, the character of rural life was already changing.

Even in the horse-and-buggy age, farmers' organizations were breaking down local isolation. The Patrons of Husbandry (the Grange), founded in 1867, grew to over 800,000 in the 1870's and still flourished in the nineties. Originally an exclusively social organization, the Grange never completely lost its social character. Hamlin Garland fondly remembered the Grange suppers in the winter, with their debates, songs, and prize essays, and the great annual picnic in July.

It was good [he wrote], it was inspiring—to us, to see those long lines of carriage wending down the lanes, joining one to another at the cross roads till at last all the granges from the northern end of the county were united in one mighty column advancing on the picnic grounds, where orators awaited our approach with calm dignity and high resolve. Nothing more picturesque, more delightful, more helpful has ever risen out of American rural life.[47]

The co-operatives sponsored by the Farmers' Alliances and by the Populists, although primarily economic in purpose, also served incidentally to bring farmers into closer contact with one another—the first step toward bringing them into closer contact with the life of the cities. By 1900 there were about 2,000 farmers' business organizations in the country, most of them in the Middle West. More than 1,600 of these were co-operative creameries or cheese factories, the rest mainly grain elevators or collective markets for fruit and livestock.[48]

Agitation for rural free delivery had already begun. Prodded by the

[47] Hamlin Garland, *A Son of the Middle Border* (New York, 1917), pp. 165–166; Solon J. Buck, *The Granger Movement* (Cambridge, 1913).

[48] Shannon, *Farmer's Last Frontier*, pp. 329–384; Theodore Saloutos and John D. Hicks, *Agricultural Discontent in the Middle West* (Madison, Wis., 1951), pp. 56–86.

Grange and in particular by Congressman James O'Donnell of Michigan, the Post Office, after conducting local experiments for some time, finally began to provide free delivery to rural areas in 1896. In 1897, eighty-four carriers operated 1,843 miles and served 44,280 people, at an expense of $14,840. Eleven years later thousands of carriers covered over 30,000 miles, serving 16 million people at a cost of $35,500,000.[49] The government lost money in the transaction, as critics had predicted it would, but by 1900 nobody questioned the need for such a system.[50]

One result of rural free delivery was a boom in the mail-order business. Both Montgomery Ward and Company and Sears, Roebuck and Company were already in operation; Montgomery Ward was founded in 1872 expressly to deal with the Grangers. By the early nineties both companies were aggressively urging the farmer to buy anything from men's socks to parlor organs and from patent medicines to reaping machines. The advent of rural free delivery and, somewhat later, of the parcel post system (1913) greatly facilitated their operations. The importance of the mail-order houses lay not in the proportion of the nation's total retail business which they conducted, which was small, but in the fact that in rural areas they provided the only alternative to the stores operated by local merchants. In many cases the local merchant discovered that he could not compete with their lower prices and glittering catalogues.[51] The mail-order houses, which emanated from the cities, brought urban tastes to the country and thus contributed to the standardization of American life. Rural free delivery had other effects. It stimulated improvement of rural roads and in time led to the revival of the almost forgotten constitutional power of the federal government to establish post roads. It became "the backbone of the argument in Congress for national aid in road building."[52]

The most important agency in transmitting urban culture to rural areas at the turn of the century was doubtless the Chautauqua. Founded in 1874 by Lewis Miller, an Ohio manufacturer and the

[49] *Report of the Postmaster General* (1927), p. 136.

[50] Pao Hsun Chu, *The Post Office of the United States* (New York, 1932), pp. 63–68.

[51] Mark Sullivan, *Our Times: The United States, 1900–1925* (New York, 1926–1935), I, 401–410; David L. Cohn, *The Good Old Days* (New York, 1940), studies American manners and morals through Sears, Roebuck catalogues.

[52] Wayne E. Fuller, "Good Roads and Rural Free Delivery of Mail," *Mississippi Valley Historical Review*, XLII (June, 1955), 67–83; N. S. Shaler, "The Common Roads," *Scribner's Magazine*, IV (1889), 477; Charles L. Deering, *American Highway Policy* (Washington, 1941), p. 221.

father-in-law of Thomas A. Edison, and John H. Vincent, a Methodist minister, the Chautauqua was originally intended to serve as a camp meeting for the training of Sunday-school teachers. It soon began to concern itself with instruction in more mundane subjects. It became a "university," as its devotees loved to exclaim, "of the people." From its center on the shores of Lake Chautauqua in southwestern New York it ramified throughout rural society. In 1878 it organized the Chautauqua Literary and Scientific Circle to supplement the annual summer sessions on the home ground; the Literary Circle offered a four-year course of reading in matters both polite and useful. By 1895 at least 225,000 readers had been enrolled at one time or another in one of the Chautauqua's thousand literary circles. "Many a frontier cabin, Southern plantation, ship on the seas," wrote a commentator with a gift for understatement, "has felt the influence of the Chautauqua."[53]

The organization continued to grow. In 1880 it began to publish its own magazine, *The Chautauquan;* in 1888 it founded the Chautauqua College of Liberal Arts. The latter offered a four-year course of resident and home study with required courses and a degree awarded after examination by the regents of the University of the State of New York. Summer assemblies like the one at Chautauqua sprang up all over the country; there were at least seventy by 1900.[54] In 1889 the movement broadened still further with the founding of the International Lyceum and Chautauqua Association. This association of "chain Chautauquas" grew out of the earlier lyceum movement as well as out of the Chautauqua itself. Local associations spread rapidly. In a good year as many as 10,000 of them met in tents all over the country.

The town of a thousand [wrote a lifelong participant], or even one as small as five hundred inhabitants, during its annual Chautauqua week will rally from the farms and hamlets two thousand people to hear a popular lecturer, five or seven thousand during the week.[55]

[53] Quoted in Henry B. Adams, "Chautauqua: A Social and Educational Study," U.S. Commissioner of Education, *Report, 1894–1895,* I, 1001. Arthur E. Bestor, Jr., *Chautauqua Publications* (Chautauqua, N.Y., 1934), is a guide to source materials and contains also a brief history of the organization and a bibliography.
[54] W. W. Willoughby, "The History of Summer Schools in the United States," U.S. Commissioner of Education, *Report, 1891–1892,* II, 921–952.
[55] Jesse L. Hurlbut, *The Story of Chautauqua* (New York, 1921), pp. 386, 387.

Many of the ablest educators in the country participated in the movement. For two decades the Chautauqua offered to the rural adult who thirsted after culture his last, best hope.[56]

The Chautauqua and the mail-order catalogue helped to break down the distinctive character of rural life. Nevertheless, there was still a sameness about life on the farm, from the rocky hillsides of New England to the prairies of the Dakotas—a sameness which at the same time set it apart from life in the city. Farming was everywhere a ceaseless round of hard physical labor from sunrise to sunset: plowing, sowing, harvesting, tending livestock as season followed season and year followed year. It was everywhere an unending and often uneven combat with uncertain weather, with insect pests that destroyed the crops, and with diseases that carried off the stock. In the older, settled parts of the country farmers lived in well-built frame or brick houses, whereas the first dwellings on the prairie were often mere cabins or sod houses, but the difficulties and uncertainties in each case were the same. New farm machinery increased productivity, but it did little to shorten the hours of arduous toil.

Women shared the physical strain of farming and probably suffered even more than the men from the loneliness of life. Time and distance imposed a solitude unbroken for days and weeks at a time. The church supper and the Grange picnic were only occasional diversions, while the county fair and the annual circus stood out sharply in the year's monotony as events of great and solemn magnitude, anticipated months ahead of time and cherished months after. In August and September there was the extemporaneous society of harvesttime. On the broad western prairies not even these amusements were to be found; there, isolation was complete.

The farmer enjoyed certain compensations, of course. Unlike the wage earner in the city, he escaped the hazards of industry. He rarely faced starvation, even in the worst of times. Often he owned title to his land. He had a security and independence inaccessible to the city worker. In spite of declining prices, the farmer who owned good land in developed areas could live on a scale which compared favorably with that of the urban masses. All this was changing, however, during the nineties; these were advantages associated with a simpler age. The Industrial Revolution made the farmer into a reluctant businessman,

[56] *Ibid.*, p. 386; see also H. A. Orchard, *Fifty Years of Chautauqua* (Cedar Rapids, Iowa, 1923); Schlesinger, *Rise of the City*, pp. 172–174.

exposed him to the vicissitudes of the market, and involved him in a brutal competition. At the same time, by breaking down his independence it also broke down his isolation. He was involved in a wider and more complicated society, one that held blessings as well as evils, but one that he was increasingly to share.

CHAPTER 4

Progress and Poverty

DURING the nineties Americans as a whole grew wealthier. The total wealth of the nation increased from $65 billion in 1890 to $88.5 billion in 1900, the national income from $12 billion in 1890 to $18 billion in 1900.[1] These gains, spectacular enough in themselves, were not as great as those of previous decades. Considering that over four of the years between 1890 and 1900 were years of deep and prolonged depression, the wonder is that any gains were made at all. That the American economy made such rapid strides in the face of what was one of the worst depressions in its history testifies to the great vigor of industrial capitalism in its formative years.

That industry was outstripping agriculture was evident by the 1880's, when the total value of manufactures for the first time exceeded that of agricultural commodities. By 1894 it was evident that American industry was rapidly outstripping industry in other countries; already the value of American manufactures was believed to be twice that of Great Britain and more than half that of European manufactures.[2] During the 1890's American industrial capital increased from $6,525,-000,000 to $9,813,000,000, an increase of more than $3 billion; the total value of manufactured products increased by an even greater amount. Yet in all categories of the industrial census—capital, value of products, value added by manufactures, cost of materials, number of wage earners, wages, and number of industrial establishments—the gains of the 1890's, except in the last category, were smaller than those

[1] Wilford I. King, *The Wealth and Income of the People of the United States* (New York, 1915), pp. 13, 129.
[2] *Twelfth Census* (Washington, 1902), VII, liv–lvi.

of the 1880's—another indication of the phenomenal rate at which industry had been growing since the Civil War.[3]

In this growth all sections of the country and almost all industries shared, and in about the same proportion as before. The events of the 1890's disturbed neither the geographical distribution of industry nor the supremacy of certain leading manufactures. The industrial center of the country remained in the East; during the decade it moved only 39.35 miles west and 6.63 miles south, to a point about seventeen miles southeast of Mansfield, Ohio. The five most important manufactures, according to the value of their products, remained, as in 1890, slaughtering and meat packing, flour and gristmill products, lumber and timber products, iron and steel, and foundry and machine-shop products. The order of their importance, however, shifted, and the shift indicates the direction in which industry was going. In 1900 they stood in the following order: iron and steel, slaughtering and meat packing, foundry and machine-shop products, lumber and timber products, and flour and gristmill products. Iron and steel almost doubled. In earlier years American manufacturing consisted mainly of the processing of products of the farm and the forest. By 1900 the raw materials of manufacturing were, increasingly, the products of the mines. The machine age had arrived.

A number of lesser industries showed great increases, and a list of them is instructive. The production of women's factory-made clothing, leather goods, pottery, rubber goods, wines, gas and oil stoves, lamps, and optical goods doubled during the ten years after 1890. Patent medicines, millinery custom work, the canning of vegetables and fruit, and the processing of cheese, butter, condensed milk, and sugar nearly doubled in value. Photographical apparatus tripled; electrical apparatus and supplies increased more than four times; bicycles and druggists' preparations increased at an even greater rate. These developments indicate, among other things, a considerable increase in the production of metal goods, a movement of many manufactures from home to factory, an increasing production of luxury goods which were fast becoming necessities, and the development of new industries, such as electrical appliances.[4] American industry was not only growing; it was becoming more diverse.

[3] *Abstract of the Census of Manufactures, 1914* (Washington, 1917), pp. 17–18.

[4] *Abstract of the Twelfth Census* (Washington, 1904), pp. 302–331.

The tremendous railroad construction of the previous years gave basic industries a national market. The rapid progress of invention was as much a reflection of new demands made on American industry as it was a cause of expansion, but there is no doubt that technological improvements enhanced industrial productivity. Steam had long since displaced water as a source of power in manufacturing, but steam itself was about to be challenged by electricity. The amazing electrical effects produced at the Chicago World's Fair dramatized the possibilities of electric power and turned engineers to the study of its practical application. In 1895 the first of three 5,000-horsepower alternating-current generators was completed at Niagara Falls. In the production of electric power, however, as in other fields, steam was destined in the long run to be more widely used than water. In 1896 George Westinghouse bought the American rights to build steam turbine operating generators; and in the years following, the use of steam in generating electricity grew steadily more efficient.[5]

In the manufacture of steel the Bessemer process was still in the ascendancy, but the more efficient open-hearth method was soon to outdistance it. At the same time progress was being made in the manufacture of machine tools which would eventually benefit all industries. Frederick Winslow Taylor and J. Maunsel White, after a series of experiments in the late nineties at the Bethlehem Steel Company, designed a high-speed carbon tool steel with a cutting edge so superior that it more than doubled the productivity of machine tools. In textile manufacturing the Northrup loom, one of the most amazing inventions of the period, made its appearance. Developed by James H. Northrup, George O. Draper, and others, the machine greatly increased the efficiency of workers by automatically ejecting empty bobbins and inserting fresh ones in the brief time (one-twentieth of a second) in which the shuttle was at rest between trips across the loom. Later Northrup introduced a mechanism which instantly stopped the loom when a single warp broke.[6]

Industry was not only growing both in value and in productivity; it was also becoming more concentrated. Neither the state laws of the

---

[5] At the same time engineers were turning increasingly to the use of alternating current. Cf. E. B. Alderfer and H. E. Michl, *Economics of American Industry* (New York, 1942), pp. 512–514; H. T. Warshow, *Representative Industries in the United States* (New York, 1928), pp. 307–309.

[6] Harold U. Faulkner, *The Decline of Laissez Faire* (New York, 1951), p. 122; Alderfer and Michl, *Economics of American Industry*, pp. 49, 115, 305.

1870's and 1880's nor the Sherman Antitrust Act arrested the movement toward consolidation. Between 1887 and 1897, eighty-six corporations capitalized at one million dollars or more were organized, forty-six of them in the years between 1890 and 1893, with a total capitalization, however, of only $1,414,294,100. The depression interrupted consolidation; but in the three years from 1898 to 1900, 149 such combinations were effected with a total capitalization of $3,784,-010,000. Only in these last years of the century did consolidation really begin to dominate American industry. Even so, only a third of the combinations organized in the nineties could be called "trusts" in the popular sense—that is, consolidations large enough to monopolize an industry.[7] Monopoly, nevertheless, was clearly the direction in which American industrialists were heading. This trend was promoted by the prosperity in the early and later years of the decade, by the lax corporation laws of certain of the states, and, presumably, by the failure of the Supreme Court in the Knight case of 1895 to halt consolidation in the sugar industry.

Nowhere was the movement toward consolidation more striking than in the case of the railroads. By 1890 the railroads had come to dominate all other forms of transportation. Inland transportation by water was practically obsolete except on the Great Lakes and a few other waterways.[8] Not only had railroads absorbed other modes of transportation; they had for some time earned an increasingly greater share in the national wealth. By 1900, valued at slightly less than $10 billion, they represented one-tenth of the total wealth of the country.[9] Railroad mileage increased from 163,597 in 1890 to 193,346 in 1900—an increase of less than 30,000 as compared with an increase of 70,000 miles

[7] Of the eighty-six such corporations organized between 1887 and 1897 only 20 to 25 per cent could be called monopolies. Cf. Luther Conant, Jr., "Industrial Consolidations in the United States," *Quarterly Publications of the American Statistical Association*, VII (Mar., 1901), 207–226; Eliot Jones, *The Trust Movement in the United States* (New York, 1929), pp. 38–45; Henry R. Seager and Charles R. Gulick, Jr., *Trust and Corporation Problems* (New York, 1929), p. 60; John Moody, *The Truth about the Trusts* (New York, 1904), p. 453 n.

[8] *Final Report of National Waterways Commission*, 62nd Cong., 2nd sess., Senate Document 469 (Washington, 1912), pp. 66–72, 511.

[9] *Final Report of the Industrial Commission* (Washington, 1902), XIX, 261–262; Interstate Commerce Commission, *Thirteenth Annual Report on the Statistics of Railways in the United States* (Washington, 1901), pp. 34, 52–53; Emory R. Johnson, *American Railway Transportation* (New York, 1903), pp. 29–32, 84–86.

in the previous decade. Since nearly 47,000 miles were built in the decade 1900–1910, it is clear that the decline of construction during the 1890's was the result not of approaching saturation of the market but simply of the depression, which by 1894 had thrown railroads owning one-fourth of the total mileage of the country into the hands of receivers—"a record of insolvency," said the Interstate Commerce Commission, "without parallel in the previous history of American railways, except it be in the period from 1838 to 1842."[10] The Reading, Erie, Northern Pacific, Union Pacific, and Atchison, Topeka and Santa Fe, among others, were all operated by receivers during the depression. Under such conditions it is not surprising that railroad construction fell to less than 2,000 miles annually in the five years from 1894 to 1898.

The depression profoundly influenced the structure of the railroads. Adversity speeded consolidation, and the reorganization of distressed railroads put them under the control of bankers. During the depression railroad reorganization became the most important activity of J. P. Morgan and Company; of its affiliate, Drexel, Morgan and Company; and of its rival, Kuhn, Loeb and Company. Morgan reorganized, among others, nearly all the southern railroads, the Reading, the Erie, and the Northern Pacific, which thereby passed under his dominion. To his later regret he left the Union Pacific to Kuhn, Loeb and Company, which, with Edward H. Harriman, picked up the dilapidated system and with it as a base became the great rival of Morgan.[11]

Widespread bankruptcy and reorganization, by bringing so many of the country's railroads under the control of a few firms in Wall Street, brought the process of consolidation to a new efficiency. At the same time consolidation was achieved by more conventional means—by merger, purchase, and lease. Whatever the means, the scale of consolidation in these years was unprecedented. In 1900 the Interstate Commerce Commission estimated that in sixteen months between July 1, 1899, and November 1, 1900, over 25,000 miles of railroads—more than one-eighth of the nation's railroad mileage—had been absorbed

[10] Interstate Commerce Commission, *Seventh Annual Report of the Statistics of Railways in the United States for the Year Ending June 30, 1894* (Washington, 1895), p. 10.

[11] Lewis, Corey, *The House of Morgan* (New York, 1930), pp. 198–215; Frederick Lewis Allen, *The Great Pierpont Morgan* (New York, 1949), pp. 81–98.

by other railroads in one way or another.[12] By 1906 at least two-thirds of the total mileage was controlled by no more than seven groups of financiers. The Vanderbilt interests controlled the northern routes from New York to Chicago, the Pennsylvania interests the roads to the Mississippi emanating from Philadelphia and Baltimore, the Morgan interests the South, and the Gould-Rock Island interests the Mississippi Valley. Beyond the Mississippi the Hill interests monopolized the Northwest and the Harriman interests the central and southern routes to the Pacific. Owing to the mysterious workings of the "community of interest," these seven groups were in reality only four, since the Morgan, Hill, Vanderbilt, and Pennsylvania interests were in essential agreement on all important matters of practice and policy.[13]

Whether consolidation was a more efficient form of enterprise than competition was a hotly debated question. The ardor with which consolidation was pursued by the railroad giants of the 1890's, however, could not be explained only as a businesslike search for superior efficiency. It could not be explained even as a search for greater profits. By the turn of the century it was clear that men like Morgan, Hill, and Harriman pursued consolidation for its own sake. For them, empire building was its own end and its own justification. As Harriman told the Interstate Commerce Commission in 1907:

. . . . If you will let us, I will go and take the Santa Fe tomorrow. . . . I would go on as long as I live.

Q. Then after you had gotten through with the Santa Fe and had taken it, you would also take the Northern Pacific and Great Northern, if you could get them?

A. If you would let me.[14]

The Interstate Commerce Act of 1887 had no discernible effect in preventing railroad consolidations. The Commission in calling for new legislation in 1898 summarized the failure of the old:

Tariffs are disregarded, discriminations constantly occur, the price at which transportation can be obtained is fluctuating and uncertain. Railroad managers are distrustful of each other and shippers all the while in doubt as to rates secured by their competitors. . . . Enormous sums are spent in purchas-

---

[12] *Fourteenth Annual Report of the Interstate Commerce Commission* (Washington, 1900), pp. 11–12.

[13] Faulkner, *Decline of Laissez Faire,* pp. 191–198.

[14] Quoted in Harold F. Williamson (ed.), *The Growth of the American Economy* (2nd ed., New York, 1951), p. 379 n.

ing business and secret rates accorded far below the standard of public charges. The general public gets little benefit from these reductions, for concessions are mainly confined to the heavier shippers. All this augments the advantages of large capital and tends to the injury and often to the ruin of smaller dealers. These are not only matters of gravest consequence to the business welfare of the country, but they concern in no less degree the highest interests of public morality.[15]

The reason for the failure of the Interstate Commerce Act was no mystery. Federal regulation of railroads was a new phenomenon; procedures had to be worked out and precedents established. Regulation, moreover, involved the most complex and intricate problems. These impersonal factors, however, were minor compared with the unremitting hostility of the railroads to regulation and the sympathy which they received from the courts. Although Congress in writing the Interstate Commerce Act had obviously meant to give the Commission power to enforce it, that body found itself blocked at every turn by its powerful antagonists. When the railroads refused to obey its decisions, the Commission had to appeal to the courts. Congress had probably intended the courts to pass only on the procedure by which the Commission arrived at its decisions, but the courts insisted on passing on the substance of each case. Ignoring the Commission's presentation of the facts, they reviewed the facts for themselves. In short, they simply heard each case again, spending an average of four years in deciding each of the numerous cases which came to them. Sixteen of these, in the first ten years of the act's operation, reached the Supreme Court, and fifteen were decided in favor of the railroads.

Two decisions of the Supreme Court in 1896 appeared to herald a better day. In one of these the Court upheld a congressional law giving the Interstate Commerce Commission power to compel the railroads to testify before it;[16] in the other, attempting to avoid long hearings, it admitted (Social Circle case) that the law had intended the courts to pass only on procedure.[17] Having gone so far, the Court suddenly relented and in the following year rendered the Interstate Commerce Commission completely powerless by declaring, quite simply, "that

[15] *Twelfth Annual Report of the Interstate Commerce Commission* (Washington, 1898), pp. 5–6.

[16] Brown *v.* Walker, 161 U.S. 591 (1896).

[17] Cincinnati, New Orleans and Texas Pacific Railway Company *v.* Interstate Commerce Commission, 162 U.S. 196.

Congress had not conferred upon the Commission power of prescribing rates either maximum, minimum or absolute."[18] Any shred of prestige or power remaining to the Commission after this devastating decision in the Maximum Rate case was speedily torn from it by the Court's decision in the Alabama Midland case, which effectively nullified its power to enforce the long-and-short-haul clauses of the Interstate Commerce Act.[19]

That the Supreme Court knew, when it robbed the Commission of all power to enforce the act, that it had nullified an overwhelming desire on the part of the people to regulate interstate commerce and eliminate long-standing abuses there can be no doubt. Said Justice Harlan, dissenting in the Alabama Midland case:

Taken in connection with other decisions defining the power of the Interstate Commerce Commission, the present decision, it seems to me, goes far to make that Commission a useless body for all practical purposes, and to defeat many of the important objects designed to be accomplished by the various enactments of Congress relating to interstate commerce. The Commission was established to protect the public against improper practices of transportation companies engaged in commerce among the several states. It has been left, it is true, with power to make reports, and to issue protests. But it has been shorn, by judicial interpretations, of authority to do anything of an effective character.[20]

Aside from the consolidation of railroads into a few huge clusters centered in Wall Street, the most notable development in transportation, although a much less spectacular one, was the rapid disappearance of horse-drawn vehicles in the cities and their replacement by electric trolleys.[21] The growth of cities made rapidly obsolete such primitive expedients as had previously provided adequate if not comfortable conveyance. Larger cities had already begun to build elevated railroads powered by steam; on many of these electricity now super-

[18] Interstate Commerce Commission v. Cincinnati, New Orleans and Texas Pacific Railway Company, 167 U.S. 511.

[19] Interstate Commerce Commission v. Alabama Midland Railway Company et al., 168 U.S. 144 (1897).

[20] Ibid., 168 U.S. 176.

[21] During the depression, street railways were the only major business which not only did not suffer from the hard times but showed an enormous advance in value—330 per cent. Street railways were the only boom industry of the depression years.

seded steam. Subway systems, the first of which was built in Boston in the last years of the decade, also used electric power.

Already, however, experiments in motor transportation were being conducted which would soon work still another revolution in surface transportation. By 1900, "horseless carriages" were in factory production and hundreds of them were to be seen on the streets. They had not yet progressed to the point of practicality, unless their owners were prepared to spend as much time repairing the vehicle as driving it, but the advantages of such transportation, if perfected, were already obvious. Most of the early experimentation leading to the development of the automobile was conducted in Europe; America's only contribution was George B. Selden's internal combustion engine. Although Selden applied for a patent in 1879, it was not granted until 1895, by which time the automobile industry had already begun to make rapid strides quite independently of Selden's invention.[22]

It was during the early nineties that American mechanics, hearing of the progress that had been made in Europe, turned their minds to the automobile. They experimented with a variety of sources of power —electricity, steam, gasoline, compressed air, carbonic acid gas, and alcohol—but all except the first three were quickly discarded. Most early engineers favored electricity. At the first important automobile show held in this country, the New York show in 1900, one-third of the space was devoted to various electric cars and most of the rest to steam-driven vehicles. Few mechanics were yet convinced of the superiority of the gasoline motor, in spite of its demonstrated efficiency. As early as 1893, Charles E. Duryea, a bicycle designer of Springfield, Massachusetts, and his brother constructed a gasoline engine, mounted it on wheels, and demonstrated it successfully on the road. Duryea won most of the races held in the United States during the mid-nineties and for a time was the leading figure in the field. His victory in a race at Chicago in 1895 gives some indication of the state of the automobile industry at that time: six cars entered the fifty-three-and-one-half-mile course and only two finished.[23]

---

[22] Ralph E. Epstein, *The Automobile Industry* (Chicago, 1928), pp. 227–235; Allan Nevins, *Ford: The Times, the Man, the Company* (New York, 1954), pp. 284–322.

[23] Other pioneers, whose services the National Automobile Chamber of Commerce officially recognized in 1925, included John B. Maxwell, Edgar L. Apperson, Andrew L. Riker, John S. Clarke, Rollin H. White, H. H. Franklin,

Henry Ford put his first car on the road in 1896. Ford had deserted life on the family farm in Michigan for an electric powerhouse in Detroit and had shortly succumbed to the lure of the automobile. His first car, which he built in a barn behind his house in Detroit, achieved a speed of twenty-five miles an hour.[24] It was several years, however, before Ford outstripped the field. Two years before, Elwood Haynes, somewhat inaccurately described as the "father of the automobile in America," had achieved a notable success in Kokomo, Indiana. A field superintendent of a natural-gas company, moved by the eminently practical desire to cut down the amount of time he spent traveling about the countryside, Haynes bought a gasoline motor and with the help of two local mechanics, Elmer and Edgar Apperson, mounted it on wheels. The three mechanics were so confident that it would run that they arranged to make its first test before a large Fourth of July crowd in which there were, needless to say, many skeptics. There was general amusement when Haynes began strenuously to turn a crank which protruded between the spokes of a rear wheel. To the consternation and amazement of the crowd, however, the engine roared and the car with a shudder lurched off at twice the speed a man could walk.[25] Still another pioneer in the field was Ransom E. Olds, who built a three-wheeled horseless carriage in 1887, a practical four-wheeled automobile in 1893, and a gasoline-driven car in 1896. By 1900, Olds was turning out 1,400 gasoline-driven vehicles a year.[26] The persistence of the preference for electricity and steam is difficult to understand.

Until 1898, probably no more than three hundred cars had been built in the United States. Factory production did not begin on a significant scale until the following year. Although Ray Stannard Baker in 1899 claimed that eighty companies with a capitalization of $388 million produced two hundred different types of vehicles "with nearly half as many methods of propulsion," it is doubtful that so many companies existed. Nor was the total capitalization of the industry indicative of its actual size; that figure represented hopes, not cash. The industry itself later estimated that not more than $5,760,000 was

Charles B. King, Elwood Haynes, Ransom E. Olds, and Alexander Winton. Epstein, *Automobile Industry,* frontispiece.

[24] Nevins, *Ford,* pp. 150–161.

[25] Mark Sullivan, *Our Times* (New York, 1926–1935), I, 486–487.

[26] Epstein, *Automobile Industry,* p. 209, calls Olds the "pioneer exponent of quantity production."

actually invested in automobiles in that year. The federal census of 1899 did not consider it important enough to list under a separate heading.[27]

After 1899 the industry grew by leaps and bounds. Five thousand cars were turned out in 1900, and a total of eight thousand were registered (as compared with a mere four in 1895). The manufacture of automobiles was still widely scattered, and there were a great many companies in the field, since the manufacturer merely assembled in a central plant parts built in many other factories. If the industry had a center in any single part of the country, it was in the Northeast, where skilled mechanics were to be readily found and where a high-price market existed. When Olds and Ford set up their factories in Detroit, and when their success with the gasoline engine finally forced engineers to abandon other types of engines, the industry gravitated to that city, which also had the advantage of proximity to raw materials. By 1903 Michigan had already assumed leadership. The rubber industry followed its principal market.[28]

One of the first problems faced by the automobile builders was the sad condition of the nation's roads.[29] Others had already complained of the roads, but the advent of the automobile gave their complaints a new validity. In 1890, there were two million miles of rural roads in the country, hardly a mile of which was improved. Road administration, left to local governments, was antiquated. Work on the roads was haphazard and irregular and roads were badly engineered. The leaders of the "Good Roads Movement" called for state supervision, state taxes for the upkeep of roads, trained engineers, and national co-operation in state road building. By 1900 the champions of good roads had succeeded in bringing about improvements in some areas. Money taxes had generally replaced the old system of "statute labor," and states were displacing towns in the supervision of roads. Led by New Jersey, Connecticut, and Massachusetts, five states had passed laws providing state aid for local construction, five states had established state highway

[27] Ray Stannard Baker, "The Automobile in Common Use," *McClure's*, XIII (July, 1899), 195–208; Epstein, *Automobile Industry*, Appendix 316 (from tables in various editions of the annual publications of the National Automobile Chamber of Commerce).

[28] Nevins, *Ford*, p. 223.

[29] Sullivan, *Our Times*, I, 475–505, esp. n. 483.

administrations, and at least one (Massachusetts) had begun to lay out a system of state highways.[30]

The railroads, as noted, had already displaced water transportation in many parts of the country, and the automobile was to displace it in many others. By 1890, transportation by canal (except on those connecting the Great Lakes) and by river was no longer of much importance. At the same time shipping in some places was steadily advancing. Coastwise shipping remained as important as ever—by this time the United States operated the largest coastal fleet in the world—and the rapid industrial development of the Great Lakes region caused a shipping boom in those waters. By 1900 the pattern of shipping on the Great Lakes was set: fleets of vessels owned chiefly by railroads and by mining or manufacturing companies brought iron ore or grain from the head of Lake Superior to the lake ports of Illinois, Indiana, and Ohio and returned with coal and oil. Such a fleet was operated by Mark Hanna of Cleveland.[31]

If coastwise and Great Lakes shipping prospered, ocean shipping rapidly declined. By 1898, tonnage registered in foreign trade had dropped to the lowest point (726,213) in the history of the American merchant marine. Whereas American ships at the beginning of the nineteenth century had carried over nine-tenths of the nation's foreign trade, by 1901 they carried no more than 8.2 per cent. Compared with manufacturing, foreign shipping no longer offered tremendous possibilities of profit, and capital no longer hastened into its development. Nor could American ships, which enjoyed no help from the government, any longer compete with those of nations which lavished handsome subsidies on their merchant fleets. As long as the subsidized ships of other nations were able to carry American commodities at low cost, Americans did not greatly concern themselves over the decline of their once proud merchant marine.

A minority, however, deplored it, arguing that a large and efficient

[30] Charles L. Dearing, *American Highway Policy* (Washington, 1941), pp. 46–47, 222–249; U.S. Bureau of Public Roads, U.S. Department of Agriculture, and Connecticut State Highway Department, *Report of a Survey of Transportation of the State Highway System of Connecticut* (Washington, 1926), pp. 9–13.

[31] *Report of the Commissioner of Corporations on Transportation by Water in the United States* (Washington, 1909–1913), Part IV, pp. 85–87; John G. B. Hutchins, *The American Maritime Industries and Public Policy, 1789–1914* (Cambridge, 1941), pp. 542–581; Herbert Croby, *Marcus Alonzo Hanna* (New York, 1923), pp. 56–59.

merchant marine would increase foreign trade, add to the national wealth by diverting freight profits to American shippers, aid the ship-building industry, and strengthen the national defense. Such arguments appealed neither to the captains of industry nor to the farmers. When Senator William P. Frye of Maine introduced bills calling for direct subsidies and for mail contracts, both the industrialists and the agrarians denounced it, and the railroads, which themselves had received enormous subsidies, professed to be horrified at such extravagance. Senator Frye's subsidy bill was voted down, but Congress did approve his proposed mail contracts after greatly reducing the proposed rate of pay. This Merchant Marine Act of 1891, inadequate as it was, was enough to induce the International Navigation Company to start a weekly service from New York to London in 1895 and to build two new ships. It also helped to maintain American ship service to Cuba, Mexico, and Venezuela. In 1898 Senator Hanna, who certainly had nothing personally to gain from the subsidy of ocean shipping, generously introduced a bill to subsidize all such shipping, not just mail carriers, but it was voted down.[32]

While the merchant marine declined, foreign trade itself increased, notwithstanding the high tariffs levied by Congress and a growing disposition in western Europe to retaliate. Exports of merchandise and specie increased from $909,977,000 in 1890 to $1,499,462,000 in 1900, and imports from $823,287,000 to $929,771,000. Imports of merchandise exceeded exports only in 1893; combined imports of merchandise and specie exceeded exports in no year during the decade. The balance of this excess was in part evened by freight payments to foreign ship-owners, by payments to foreign marine and fire insurance companies, by immigrant remittances abroad, and by expenditures of American tourists in Europe. Whatever balance remained was met by remittances of interest and by dividend payments on European foreign investments in this country.

Agricultural products made up three-fourths of the value of American exports in 1890, three-fifths in 1900; the year 1898 marked the highest point to that date in the value of agricultural exports. Cotton,

[32] See below, p. 264; Hutchins, *American Maritime Industries*, pp. 533–537; and "One Hundred and Fifty Years of American Navigation Policy," *Quarterly Journal of Economics*, LIII (Feb., 1939), 240–246; Royal Meeker, "History of Shipping Subsidies," *Publications of the American Economic Associates*, 3rd series, VI (New York, 1905), 166–171.

grain, packinghouse products, tobacco, beef, and dairy products in that order constituted the leading exports; two-thirds of the American cotton crop was normally exported, half of the tobacco crop, and a third of the grain crop. Nine-tenths of all these exports went to Europe, and half of these to Great Britain; Germany was second in order of importance as a market for American farm products. Occasionally as much as 20 per cent of the American wheat exported was sent to areas outside Europe, but even then Great Britain consumed more than half of the total. She consumed more American cotton than any other country and far more meat products, with tobacco exports more evenly distributed among European countries. Except for the United States itself, Great Britain was the American farmer's best market.[33]

The slightly declining importance of farm products in the total value of American exports was made up by exports of manufactures, which increased from 18 per cent of total exports in 1890 to 32 per cent in 1900. The leading manufactures exported were structural materials, builders' hardware, locomotives and engines, electrical machinery, rails, and finer wares such as typewriters, cash registers, and sewing machines. Exports of refined oil were rapidly growing in importance, and by 1900 half of the illuminating oil produced in the United States was sent abroad. The growing importance of copper exports reflected the expanding use, in Europe as in the United States, of electricity.

Of American imports, sugar was the most important single item. As a group, raw materials used in manufacturing—rubber, wool, hides and skins, raw silk, fibers, and uncut diamonds, the last of which amounted to 32 per cent of the value of imports in 1900—comprised the bulk of imports to this country. Foodstuffs, except for tropical or subtropical commodities like sugar and coffee, and manufactures were declining in importance as both agriculture and industry in the United States continued to expand. Half of all these imports came from Europe, the bulk of these from Great Britain. The proportion of imports coming from Britain, however, increased very little during the decade; even if American tariffs had not kept her manufactures out, the growth of American manufacturing would have had the same result. The proportion of imports from North and South America

[33] Edwin J. Nourse, *American Agriculture and the European Market* (New York, 1924), pp. 239–250.

declined slightly, while that from Asia and the Pacific islands increased.[34]

The shifting pattern of foreign trade in these years reflected the changing character of the American economy. Trade in agricultural commodities was beginning to decline, even as the industrialization of western Europe created a greater demand for them. But Europe had other sources of supply. In the 1880's and 1890's she continued to buy American products because those products, being overproduced, had to be sold at ruinously low prices. "The European market," one authority has said, "absorbed the quantities of American farm products that it did largely because we were conducting the most stupendous bargain counter in the history of agriculture."[35] The decline of agricultural exports in the 1890's was one indication that all this was very shortly to change. European tariffs and competition from new areas—the Ukraine, for instance—were to combine to restrict the market for American exports, while agriculture itself continued to grow proportionately less important in the American economy. By 1912 agricultural products had fallen to less than half of all American exports for the first time since 1860. Manufactures took their place. The import trade likewise showed the impact of industrialization. Whereas Americans had long imported large quantities of manufactures from Europe, they now produced them at home. Instead of finished manufactures they imported greater and greater amounts of raw materials. The Industrial Revolution in America left no aspect of economic activity untouched.

If industrialism altered the face of America, if it revolutionized transportation and changed the character of foreign trade, it still more profoundly altered the relations between capital and labor; nowhere else was its impact so unsettling. In 1890, more than 23 million Americans over ten years of age, including farmers, were gainfully employed; in 1900, the number had grown to 29 million—about half the total number of people over ten years of age. Of these about 4 million in 1890 and more than 5 million in 1900 were women.[36] Six hundred thousand of them in 1890 and 1,750,000 in 1900 were children from ten to fifteen years old.[37] Although the size of the labor force increased,

[34] Emory R. Johnson et al., History of Domestic and Foreign Commerce in the United States (Washington, 1915), II, 64–85.

[35] Nourse, American Agriculture and the European Market, p. 28.

[36] Fifteenth Census, Population, V, 37.

[37] The figure for 1890 includes children from ten to fourteen; that for 1900 includes children from ten to fifteen. Cf. Dan D. Lesohier and Elizabeth Bran-

the proportion of farm owners and tenants, of servants, and of "unclassified" workers declined, while the proportion of industrial wage earners and of farm laborers, as well as that of proprietors and professionals, and lower-salaried workers, grew.[38] By 1900 the 10,264,000 industrial wage earners in the country comprised 35.3 per cent of the labor force.

Of the industrial workers considered "organizable," only about 3.5 per cent belonged to unions, and the proportion did not change between 1890 and 1900. The Knights of Labor, which numbered over 700,000 in 1886, had dwindled to 100,000 in 1890 and only 74,635 in 1893. The disastrous strikes of 1886 crippled it, but it already suffered from its diffuse membership, which included farmers and shopkeepers as well as industrial workers; from its extremely unstable organization; from its weak leadership; and from the dissipation of its energies in politics. The American Federation of Labor, founded in 1886, superseded the Knights of Labor, but it numbered only 225,000 in 1890 and grew to only 548,000 in 1900. The four Railway Brotherhoods, all organized before the A.F. of L., counted 100,000 members in 1900.[39]

Until 1898 the A.F. of L. was a small, weak association of about forty national organizations, about three-fourths of which paid dues and sent delegates to the annual conventions. The largest and strongest of these were the United Brotherhood of Carpenters and Joiners, the Cigar Makers' Union, the Iron and Steel Workers' Union, the Iron Molders' Union, and the Typographical Union. These organizations had achieved some coherence and unity and had inaugurated sick benefits and strike funds; in a few plants they had won an eight-hour day. Their influence in most industries was slight. Some of them were led by energetic and able men—Adolph Strasser of the cigar makers, John Mitchell and John McBride of the miners, and Patrick J. McGuire of the carpenters and joiners.[40] Gompers, however, only forty-two years old in 1892, as president of the Federation already outshone

---

deis, *History of Labor in the United States, 1896–1932* (New York, 1935), III, 40.

[38] Alvin H. Hansen, "Industrial Class Alignments in the United States," *American Statistical Association*, XVII (Dec., 1920), 417–425.

[39] George E. Burnett, "The Growth of Labor Organizations in the United States, 1897–1914," *Quarterly Journal of Economics*, XXX (Aug., 1916), 780; Selig Perlman, *A History of Trade Unionism in the United States* (New York, 1922), pp. 180–186.

[40] Mark Starr and Harold U. Faulkner, *Labor in America* (new ed., New York, 1957), pp. 120–122.

them all; he was to remain president with the exception of one year until his death in 1924. The emerging labor movement, for better or worse, bore the unmistakable stamp of his character and temperament, his policies and philosophy.[41]

For labor the decade of the nineties was a period of storm and stress. No other group suffered more severely from the effects of the depression. Between 1893 and 1898, 7,029 strikes were called, an average of 1,171 a year.[42] The average of workers on strike in each of these years was 280,708. The number of unemployed tripled between 1894 and 1898; in 1894 and 1896, at least 15 and possibly 20 per cent of the nation's industrial workers were out of work.[43] In the spring of 1894 probably 10,000 unemployed workers in various parts of the country were on the road to Washington to petition Congress for relief.[44] Considering these conditions, it is a wonder that organized labor survived the depression at all. As Gompers said, the unions had for the first time weathered adversity: "It is noteworthy that while in every previous industrial crisis the trade unions were literally mowed down and swept out of existence, the unions now in existence have manifested, not only their power of resistance, but of stability and permanence. . . ."[45]

The unions suffered not only from the depression but from internal dissension. The point most violently disputed was whether organized labor should refrain from active participation in politics. Since socialism was the mode of political participation most frequently advocated, the familiar debate over politics boiled down, in the nineties, to a debate over the merits of socialism. In 1890 Daniel De Leon brought the dispute to a head by insisting that the A.F. of L. consider his Socialist Labor party a workers' party and support it. Gompers and McGuire used their efforts to defeat this suggestion. The failure of the Homestead strike in 1892, a dramatic illustration of the entrenched power of corporate wealth, gave new weight to the demand for political action; its advocates could point to the strike as proof that ordinary methods of action were unavailing against such power as capitalists

[41] Cf. Samuel Gompers, *Seventy Years of Life and Labor* (New York, 1925); Rowland H. Harvey, *Samuel Gompers* (Palo Alto, 1935).

[42] U.S. Commissioner of Labor, *Twenty-First Annual Report* (1907), pp. 13–15.

[43] See below p. 142.

[44] Lescohier and Brandeis, *History of Labor in the United States,* pp. 124–126; Donald L. McMurry, *Coxey's Army* (Boston, 1929), pp. 241–242.

[45] Quoted in Perlman, *Trade Unionism,* pp. 135–136.

could wield against the unions. Furthermore, the formation of the Populist party in the same year seemed to indicate widespread popular dissatisfaction with the old parties upon which labor might capitalize. In 1892 De Leon actively advanced these arguments before the conventions of both the Knights of Labor and the A.F. of L. His followers managed to unseat Terence V. Powderly as Grand Master of the Knights of Labor and to install in his place James R. Sovereign, whom they believed to sympathize with their policy. Sovereign, however, ignored them. The Socialists also ousted Gompers for one year as president of the A.F. of L. and helped to elect John McBride of the United Mine Workers, but they failed to convert the Federation to their program.

In 1895 the conservatives in the Federation pushed through a resolution that "party politics, whether they be democratic, republican, socialistic, populistic, prohibition or any other, should have no place in the conventions of the A.F. of L."[46] De Leon thereupon abandoned his campaign to control the Knights and the Federation and sought instead to weaken them by setting up a rival union of his own, the Socialist Trade and Labor Alliance. This maneuver led to still more unfortunate results for his cause. Not only did it strengthen Gompers in his conservatism but it aroused the opposition of many Socialists, who were not ready to sacrifice the gains already made by the older unions in the hope that their leaders would some day embrace socialism. These dissenters from De Leon's leadership seceded from the Socialist Labor party in 1900 and organized the Social Democratic party (called after 1901 simply the Socialist party of America).

Notwithstanding the Federation's declaration of abstention in 1895, many members continued to advocate political intervention. In 1896 pressure for intervention again became almost irresistible. Since the Federation had gone so far as to endorse free silver in three successive conventions, the interventionists argued with some consistency that it could hardly refrain from supporting a candidate pledged to silver. It required all Gompers' talents to beat down the demand for the endorsement of Bryan. In an atmosphere of accusation and recrimination, he triumphed and was re-elected president.[47]

[46] *Report of the Proceedings of the Fifteenth Annual Convention of the American Federation of Labor* (1895), pp. 79–80.
[47] Selig Perlman and Philip Taft, *History of Labor in the United States, 1896–1932* (New York, 1935), IV, 214–229; Perlman, *Trade Unionism*, pp.

These intrafraternal battles, won at length by the conservatives, were of great importance for the subsequent history of trade unionism. Until 1890, labor had identified itself with the antimonopoly agitation of various parties of reform or with European socialism. After 1895, most American labor leaders turned away from such a course and denounced all efforts to draw labor into class politics. Understanding the American commitment to capitalism and the difficulty of organizing a separate labor party, Gompers preached a policy of what he called "voluntarism," under which labor would concentrate on day-to-day bargaining with management for limited gains. Such a policy, however, did not preclude political activity. As long as strikes could be broken up by injunctions or unions prosecuted under the Sherman Act, there was little prospect that day-to-day bargaining would win many gains for labor. It was necessary, therefore, for the A.F. of L. to campaign for favorable legislation, while at the same time refusing to become allied with any political party. As Gompers said, "I have always sought to use political situations for labor's advantage."[48] But hope of a millennium through any panacea or party had been abandoned.[49]

If the reaching of agreements with employers was any indication, "voluntarism" in the nineties was not a spectacular success. The disastrous strikes of the depression years wrecked unionism in some industries and weakened its bargaining power in others. If any notable improvement in working conditions took place, it came about not through bargaining but through state legislation. Since the courts nullified most of this legislation, however, it had little effect. In 1895 the Supreme Court of Illinois declared invalid a law providing an eight-hour day for women, and in 1899 the Supreme Court of Colorado rejected a law limiting hours in the smelting industry to eight, on the grounds that it was "an unwarrantable interference with the right of both employer and employee in making contracts." The latter decision foreshadowed the ground which the Supreme Court was to take six years later in the celebrated Lochner case.[50] Meanwhile the courts upheld the use of injunctions in labor disputes. At the turn of the

---

140, 141, 208–213; Lewis L. Lorwin, *The American Federation of Labor* (Washington, 1933), pp. 24–54; Nathan Fine, *Labor and Farmer Parties in the United States, 1828–1898* (New York, 1928), pp. 147–183.

[48] Gompers, *Seventy Years*, II, 77.

[49] Cf. Perlman and Taft, *History of Labor*, pp. 3–12.

[50] Ritchie *v.* People, 155 Ill. 98. *In Re* Morgan, 26 Colo. 415; 58 Pacific 1071.

century the prospect for labor, all things considered, was not bright. The labor movement seemed to have gained inner solidarity, but the course upon which the A.F. of L. had now set itself had not yet brought most workers any tangible benefits; it had yet to prove itself. Trade unionism had survived the depression, but there was no guarantee that trade unionism in any form would improve the miserable condition of industrial workers. For the worker himself the future in 1900 appeared no brighter than the immediate past had been.

The distribution of wealth in 1900 was shockingly unequal. One writer estimated in 1889 that 200,000 people controlled 70 per cent of the nation's wealth.[51] Seven-eighths of the families of the country, on the other hand, controlled only one-eighth of the national wealth in 1890.[52] An appraisal of estates probated in five Wisconsin counties both rural and urban revealed in 1900 that the poorest two-thirds of the population owned only 5 per cent, the poorest four-fifths only 10 per cent, and the richest 1 per cent over half of the property probated. Similar studies made in Massachusetts disclosed the same pattern of distribution. It is safe to conclude that 80 per cent of Americans lived in 1900 on the margin of subsistence while the remaining 20 per cent controlled almost the entire wealth of the country.[53]

Recognition of this inequality lay beneath the widespread resentment against the McKinley tariff, strengthening the Farmers' Alliances, and the rise of Populism; it contributed to the Democratic victory in 1892. Even conservatives protested. The New York *Tribune* was moved in 1892 to undertake a study of American millionaires, the sources of their income, and the relation of their wealth to the tariff.[54] It dis-

[51] Thomas G. Sherman, "The Owners of the United States," *Forum*, VIII (Nov., 1889), 262–273.

[52] Charles B. Spahr, *The Present Distribution of Wealth in the United States* (New York, 1896), p. 69.

[53] King, *Wealth and Income*, pp. 72–87. George K. Holmes, a contemporary economist, estimated that at least "sixty-seven per cent of the wealth is owned by nine per cent of the families." George K. Holmes, "The Concentration of Wealth," *Political Science Quarterly*, VIII (Dec., 1893), 593.

[54] New York *Tribune*, May 1, 8, 12, 22, 29, and June 5, 1892. Shortly thereafter the *Tribune* published this material with corrections in a pamphlet, *American Millionaires*, reprinted in Sidney Ratner, *New Light on the History of Great American Fortunes* (New York, 1953). Although the work may have shown "a slight bias in . . . minimizing the importance of protected industries as the source of great fortunes," it "appears to have been carefully and honestly done," according to George P. Watkins, "The Growth of Large American Fortunes," *Publications of the American Economic Association*, 3rd series, VIII (1907), 141–142.

covered that there were 4,047 millionaires in the country, 71.4 per cent of whom made their fortunes in trade, transportation, manufacturing, or mechanical pursuits. The *Tribune's* financial specialist believed that only one-fourth of them made their fortunes in protected industries.[55] Ten years later the *World Almanac* published a similar list. Forty-two and two-tenths per cent of American millionaires, according to the *Almanac,* made their fortunes in trade, transportation, manufacturing, and mechanical pursuits and 47.8 per cent in other occupations. The remaining 10 per cent made their money in agricultural, mining, lumbering, professional, or personal service.[56]

These lists show that in spite of the vast areas of farm land in the United States and the pre-eminence of agriculture for two and a half centuries, farming was not a source of great personal wealth. The few millionaires listed in agriculture had made their fortunes in cattle ranching or in land speculation. The lists show further that speculators were generally displacing entrepreneurs as the richest men in the country; or, to put the matter in more polite language, finance capitalism was displacing industrial capitalism as the greatest source of wealth. These early surveys show, finally, that many millionaires by the turn of the century had inherited their money. Thus it appeared that the moneyed oligarchy which apparently ruled the nation would perpetuate itself.[57]

It might be argued that the unequal distribution of wealth alone does not indicate that most Americans were living in poverty. Prices were not generally high, nor did the cost of living advance during the decade of the nineties.[58] But hours of work were long and wages were low. According to one estimate, weekly hours of work in manufacturing industries averaged sixty in 1890 and fifty-nine in 1900, and annual earnings of all wage earners except farm laborers averaged only $486 in 1890 and $490 in 1900.[59] Workers in a few highly organized trades —bricklayers, masons, railroad conductors and engineers, plumbers—

[55] *American Millionaires,* pp. 91–93, reprinted in Ratner, *New Light on American Fortunes.*

[56] *World Almanac,* 1902, pp. 135–146; Watkins, "Growth of Large American Fortunes," *op. cit.,* VIII, 145–146.

[57] Watkins, "Growth of Large American Fortunes," pp. 145, 147. The millionaires listed under professional service were mostly corporation lawyers.

[58] Prices were highest in 1891 and 1893, then declined until 1896, when they began to rise again, until by 1900 they were slightly higher than in 1890. Douglas, *Real Wages,* pp. 36, 41.

[59] *Ibid.,* Table 147 opposite p. 392.

made as much as $4 a day, but such affluence was extremely un-common. Only a few workers earned as much as $18 a week, according to the census of 1900; two-thirds of the male workers over sixteen years of age earned less than $12.50.[60] The Interstate Commerce Commission estimated in 1900 that 82 per cent of all railroad workers earned less than $2.05 a day.[61]

Prices, of course, were also low. In Massachusetts, where prices were relatively high, wheat flour could be bought for $5.80 a barrel, sugar for 5¾ cents a pound, coffee for 28 cents a pound, roasting beef for 14⅔ cents a pound, butter for 24⅓ cents a pound, and milk for less than 6 cents a quart. Coal cost $6 a ton and men's heavy shoes $2 a pair, and the best ready-made suits sold for $20 or less.[62] Even with prices so low, however, the income of many American families was meager and that of some was barely adequate to survival. In the fifty years after 1900, the cost of living rose about four times. Wages rose at least five times, and most wage earners in 1950 were working only five days a week instead of six or even seven, and only eight hours a day instead of twelve. It may be unfair to judge the conditions of 1900 by the standards of the present day. Even by the standards of the time, however, the condition of vast numbers of Americans in 1900 bordered on poverty.

[60] *Bulletin of the Department of Labor,* No. 18 (September, 1898), pp. 670–682; Bureau of the Census, *Employees and Wages* (Special Report, 1900), pp. ci–civ.

[61] Interstate Commerce Commission, *Thirteenth Annual Report of the Statistics of Railways for the Year Ending June 30, 1900* (Washington, 1901), pp. 34, 40.

[62] *Bulletin of the Department of Labor,* No. 18, p. 696.

CHAPTER 5

Billion-Dollar Politics

O N NOVEMBER 6, 1888, the American people went to the polls
to decide whether Grover Cleveland or Benjamin Harrison
should be entitled to occupy the White House during the next four
years. The result was curious; an observer not familiar with the American democratic process would have found it thoroughly baffling. When
the votes were counted it was discovered that Cleveland had received
a bare plurality—5,540,050 votes to Harrison's 5,444,337. About
100,000 more American citizens preferred Cleveland than preferred
Harrison. Yet Harrison, strangely enough, was declared to be the new
President because his votes, as it happened, were cast in places like
Binghamton, New York, or Terre Haute, Indiana, instead of in
Atlanta, Nashville, or Baton Rouge. Victory in certain populous states
of the North, and particularly in New York and Indiana, gave Harrison
an electoral total of 233 to a mere 168 for Cleveland. The strangest
thing of all was that nobody questioned the justice of a system which
could produce such a bizarre triumph of geography over numbers.
Nobody proposed overthrowing it by force.

Many Democrats did protest that Harrison owed his victory in New
York to illegal means; his managers, they said, had traded the state
government to Tammany in return for Democratic support in the
presidential election. They also called attention to wholesale bribery in
Indiana. Many people did not find it difficult to believe these charges,
although they were never conclusively proved; but in the end everybody acquiesced cheerfully enough in the decision of the minority.[1]

---

[1] Ellis Paxson Oberholtzer, *A History of the United States since the Civil
War* (5 vols., New York, 1917–1937), V, 71–73. Cleveland himself did not
believe the charges of corruption in New York; he said in 1906 that he had no

This acquiescence was no doubt a heartening indication of the stability of American institutions. On the other hand it could also be regarded, less charitably, as a comment on the essential similarity of the two parties and their candidates. The fact is that a voter with an intelligent interest in such questions as civil-service reform, economy in government, or the tariff would have found it difficult to choose between Cleveland and Harrison on the basis of any of these issues, since both candidates worked heroically to avoid explicit reference to them. Cleveland, it is true, had recently asked Congress to lower tariffs, but during the campaign he repented of this folly and said no more about it.[2] He refused to campaign at all, in fact, on the ground that it would be undignified for the President to go about soliciting votes. Harrison at least appeared before the voters and declared himself in favor of a high tariff, but on other issues he too was silent. The keynote of the Harrison campaign was the suggestion made by Chauncey Depew, president of the New York Central and one of the chief Republican strategists, to Harrison's advisers. The candidate's grandfather, he reminded them, had made "one of the most picturesque campaigns in our history. There are enough survivors of that 'hard cider and log cabin' canvass to make an attractive contribution on the platform at every meeting, and thus add a certain historic flavor to General Harrison's candidacy."[3]

With the air filled with "historic flavor" and both candidates silent on most of the major issues, it is not surprising that the vote was so close. As for the question of what the voters wanted done or not done, no reasonable person would have dared to say on the basis of the election returns. The only safe conclusion was that the voters wanted a policy of caution and prudence. Since they elected 39 Republicans to 37 Democrats in the Senate and 166 Republicans to 159 Democrats in the House, they evidently regarded the party of Harrison as slightly

---

"idea or impression that the Presidential ticket was the victim of treachery in New York in the election of 1888." George F. Parker, *Recollections of Grover Cleveland* (New York, 1909), p. 342. There does not seem to be much doubt, however, that corruption was used in Indiana, although historians differ on the question of whether it influenced the decision. See Allan Nevins, *Grover Cleveland* (New York, 1932), pp. 435–442; Horace Samuel Merrill, *Bourbon Leader: Grover Cleveland and the Democratic Party* (Boston, 1957), pp. 131–132; Matthew Josephson, *The Politicos* (New York, 1938), pp. 429–433.

[2] Merrill, *Bourbon Leader,* pp. 123–128.

[3] Josephson, *Politicos,* p. 422.

more cautious and prudent—if that were possible—than the party of Cleveland.

These qualities, however, did not distinguish the policies of the new administration. Prudence, for instance, dictated some positive action on the tariff. James G. Blaine, who was to be the new Secretary of State, urged Harrison before his inauguration to call a special session of Congress to deal with the question. Otherwise, he asserted, it would again be the bone of contention in the congressional election of 1890.[4] Harrison, however, refused this advice and spent the next nine months in what seemed to him the more congenial work of finding jobs for loyal Republicans. The manner in which the faithful were accommodated was neither cautious nor prudent. Offices under the civil-service law, of course, could not be tampered with, but all the other offices were cleared of Democrats with a ruthless efficiency which astonished even a nation long accustomed to such practices. James S. Clarkson, an avowed opponent of civil-service reform, was appointed First Assistant Postmaster General, and he quickly re-established that department as the center of the spoils system. During a year and a half in office Clarkson cleared out over 32,000 of the 55,000 fourth-class postmasters. Party fidelity became the criterion of fitness for office; nepotism was not uncommon. Many newspaper editors were appointed to government positions, presumably in reward for their services during the campaign; Clarkson himself was one of these. Taken all in all, the administration's performance was a bitter blow to civil-service reformers who had severely criticized Cleveland for some of his appointments and who had voted for Harrison in hopes of an improvement.

The administration's lavish expenditure of public funds also disappointed some of its supporters. Ever since 1866, except for one year, there had been a surplus in the federal treasury. Cleveland had cited the growing surplus as an argument for lowering the tariff. Harrison, however, had already suggested another means of reducing the surplus when he remarked that the present time "was no time to be weighing the claims of old soldiers with apothecary's scales."[5] This offhand suggestion served as the basis of administration policy. The Commisioner of Pensions, James Tanner—one of Harrison's worst appointments—

[4] Nathaniel W. Stephenson, *Nelson W. Aldrich* (New York, 1930), pp. 77; 435, n. 3.

[5] Quoted in Davis R. Dewey, *National Problems* (New York, 1907), p. 184.

did all he could to get rid of the embarrassing surplus. He once told a group of veterans, "I tell you frankly that I am for 'the old flag and an appropriation' for every old comrade who needs it."[6] He was as good as his word; his liberality added millions to the pension budget. Tanner lasted only six months in office.

But in 1890 the Dependent Pension Act further increased these expenditures. Under that act all Civil War veterans of ninety days' service who found themselves unable to provide for themselves were to receive pensions of from $6 to $12 a month, according to incapacity. Widows of veterans of ninety days' service, if they had no means of support other than their own manual labor, were to receive $8 a month during widowhood and $2 for every child. This legislation doubled the number of pensioners by 1893. In that year over 966,000 individuals received government allowances; expenditures had risen from $89 million in 1899 to $157 million—a heavy price to pay, some thought, for the support of 450,000 actual veterans of the war.[7]

In his message to the Fifty-first Congress, which convened in December, 1889, Harrison suggested other means of reducing the surplus.[8] He proposed that the tariff be revised so as to extend the free list while at the same time applying duties to farm products as well as manufactures; that excise taxes on tobacco and on spirits used in arts and manufacturing be lifted; and that subsidies be voted for the merchant marine and Navy, for more adequate coastal defenses, for improvement of rivers and harbors, and for further purchases of Indian lands. Harrison's program, readily enacted by Congress, proved to be a brilliant success; by 1894 the surplus had become a deficit.

In the same message Harrison recommended federal antitrust legislation and legislation to guarantee fuller protection of Negroes in federal elections. He avoided the currency problem except to say that he was opposed to free coinage of silver. In actual fact, however, these recommendations of the President had slight effect. In the absence of strong presidential leadership, power had already passed to Congress,

---

[6] *The Nation,* XLIX (Aug. 1, 1889), 81.

[7] 26 U.S. Statutes at Large, 182; G. A. Weber, *Bureau of Pensions* (Baltimore, 1923), p. 16; W. H. Glasson, *Federal Military Pensions in the United States* (New York, 1918), pp. 238, 248–250; James Ford Rhodes, *History of the United States from the Compromise of 1850* (New York, 1892–1922), VIII, 344–346.

[8] J. D. Richardson, *Messages and Papers of the Presidents, 1789–1897* (Washington, 1897–1899), IX, 32–58.

which in turn was dominated by a small group of Republican leaders who knew what they wanted. In the House, Thomas B. Reed of Maine, the new Speaker, and William McKinley, of Ohio, appointed by Reed to the chairmanship of the Committee on Ways and Means, bent the majority to their will. McKinley, handsome, urbane, and gracious in manner, is remembered as a vacillating and spineless President, but as a Republican leader in the House he acted with forcefulness and vigor. The leading figure in the House, however, was Czar Reed. Huge of bulk, keen of mind, bland of expression, Reed ruled the House more by means of his sharp wit than by threats of force and reprisal. Serene and imperturbable, he was a benevolent despot rather than a tyrant, a fact which made his rule easier to bear but no less effective.

The only obstacle to Republican control of the House was the narrowness of their majority. Reed quickly came to the conclusion that his party could operate successfully only if existing parliamentary rules, under which a minority of members could delay action for weeks, were revised. He proposed that actual attendance, not votes, should determine a quorum, and that the Speaker should not be obliged to entertain dilatory motions. He referred to the existing method as a "system of metaphysics whereby a man could be present and absent at the same moment . . . who had disappeared from every place except the Capitol at Washington."[9] McKinley, supporting

never fancied that sullen silence was a statesmanlike way of stopping public business. The later generation of statesmen have inaugurated it. We have done it—all of us. I am not saying that you gentlemen on the other side are doing differently from what we have done for fifteen or twenty years past. I have sat here and filibustered day after day in silence, refusing to vote, but I cannot now recall that I ever did it for a high, or a noble or a worthy purpose.[10]

To this the opponents of revision replied with arguments no less lofty and high-minded. The rules of the House, declared Roger Q. Mills of Texas, were intended for a higher purpose than merely to secure the orderly procedure of business. They were "intended to cause the House to halt, to pause, to reflect, and in some instances, where it may become necessary, to go back and inquire of the sober second thought of

[9] William A. Robinson, *Thomas B. Reed* (New York, 1930), p. 206.
Reed's revisions, argued that the framers of the Constitution
[10] *Congressional Record*, 51st Cong., 1st sess. (January 30, 1890), p. 983.

the people again. It is on the sober thought of the people our Government rests."[11]

The showdown came on January 29, 1890, when the Committee on Elections awarded one of several contested seats to the Republican candidate. The importance of revising the procedures of the House now became clear. Unless the Republicans could seat members of their party in cases of contested elections, they could not control the House; and unless they succeeded in revising the rules, the Democrats could prevent the seating of contested members by interminable delays. When they now attempted to ratify the decision of the Committee on Elections, the Republicans found themselves two votes short of a quorum. Reed then ordered the clerk to record as present forty Democrats who had refused to vote. Pandemonium broke out; the Democrats, as one, bitterly protested. The debate—if such it could be called—lasted three days. In the end Reed had his way. A committee hand-picked by him drew up the new rules, and the House confirmed them on February 14. Up and down the land Democrats and mugwumps denounced Reed as a tyrant, despot, and "czar." Under the new rules, *The Nation* protested, "the caucus, the lash, and the gag have been substituted for debate and deliberation to a rather alarming extent."[12] A week later the same journal cried, in greater alarm, "The only question as to any Republican measure proposed in the House of Representatives is, whether Speaker Reed wants it to pass. If he does, it will go through; if he does not, that is the end of it."[13] But the usages introduced by Reed remained on the books. The Democrats, who controlled the next two Congresses, found them indispensable.[14]

Harrison, as we have seen, had recommended antitrust legislation in his annual message, in response to mounting public clamor against the trusts. Fourteen states had already forbidden trusts and monopolies in their constitutions; at least thirteen had prohibited them by statute. Six states—Kentucky, North Carolina, North Dakota, South Dakota, Tennessee, and Texas—not content with merely a constitutional or a statutory prohibition, had enacted both. The federal government itself had prohibited pooling in the Interstate Commerce Act—one type of

[11] *Ibid.*, pp. 1177–1178.

[12] *The Nation,* L (June 12, 1890), 459.

[13] *Ibid.* (June 19, 1890), p. 479.

[14] One of the best accounts of this episode is James A. Barnes, *John G. Carlisle* (New York, 1931), pp. 164–174.

restraint on trade. Both parties had called for government action to prevent monopoly in their platforms in 1888.[15] English common law had always recognized certain contracts as "reasonable" unless they were held to be in restraint of a third party. Contracts in restraint of a third party were not illegal but simply void and unenforceable. What the state laws and constitutional prohibitions in this country did was to make such contracts not only unenforceable but "illegal, actionable and indictable."[16] State action alone, however, proved ineffectual; the most notorious monopolies operated across state lines. In December, 1889, Senator John Sherman of Ohio therefore introduced in Congress a bill prohibiting combinations in restraint of trade. The bill was referred to the Judiciary Committee, where, according to George F. Hoar, it was "totally reconstructed" by Hoar, George F. Edmunds, and others.[17] It was then debated at length and finally passed in the Senate by a vote of 52 to 1 and by the House unanimously, becoming law in July, 1890.[18]

The principle and theory of the act was stated in Section I: "Every contract, combination in the form of trust or otherwise, or conspiracy, in restraint of trade or commerce among the several States, or with foreign nations, is hereby declared to be illegal. . . ." Violators were to be fined as much as $5,000 and imprisoned for as long as a year, and the injured person might recover three times the damage sustained. The circuit courts of the United States were invested with jurisdiction to prevent or restrain violations and the Attorney General directed to institute proceedings.

Perhaps Senator Hoar expressed the purpose of the bill as well as

[15] Henry R. Seager and Charles A. Gulick, Jr., *Trust and Corporation Problems* (New York, 1929), pp. 341–343; Jeremiah W. Jenks and W. E. Clark, *The Trust Problem* (5th ed., New York, 1929), pp. 211–213. By 1900, twenty-seven states had statutory prohibitions of monopolies and fifteen had constitutional prohibitions.

[16] Seager and Gulick, *op. cit.,* pp. 339–340.

[17] The original bill, for instance, vested the enforcement of the act in an executive commission; the act as passed left enforcement to the courts. Josephson, *Politicos,* p. 459.

[18] Senator Edmunds wrote Sections 1 (except seven words), 2, 3, 5, and 6; Senator George, Section 4; Senator Hoar, Section 7; Senator Ingalls, Section 8; and Senator Evarts, the seven words in Section 1, "in the form of trust or otherwise." Seager and Gulick, *Trust and Corporation Problems,* p. 370; A. H. Walker, *History of the Sherman Law of the United States of America* (New York, 1910), p. 28; George F. Edmunds, "The Interstate Trust and Commerce Act of 1890," *North American Review,* DCLXIII (Dec., 1911), 801–817.

anyone. Asked why, if monopoly was prohibited by common and statute law in the states, federal action was necessary, Hoar replied:

The common law in the States of the Union of course extends over citizens and subjects over which the state itself has jurisdiction. Now we are dealing with an offense against interstate or international commerce, which the State cannot regulate by penal enactment, and we find the United States without any common law. The great thing that this bill does, except affording a remedy, is to extend the common-law principle, which protected fair competition in trade in old times in England, to international and interstate commerce in the United States.[19]

Although many members managed to be absent when the vote on the Sherman Act was taken, the virtual unanimity of the decision seems clear proof of the overwhelming demand for action and of the absence of political factionalism. Nor is there much to the oft-repeated charge that the law was made intentionally ambiguous in order to satisfy the voters without hurting business.[20] The ambiguity of the act seems to have been the subsequent contribution of the Supreme Court. Senator Cullom, who defended the law as "one of the most important enactments ever passed by Congress," had to admit that "it was never seriously enforced until the coming of Theodore Roosevelt's administration."[21] Neither Harrison, Cleveland, nor McKinley showed any real interest in enforcing it. Cleveland himself disliked the law, thinking that a stronger one might have brought better results, while his Attorney General confessed that he had never believed in it from the beginning. "You will observe," said Olney, "that the government has been defeated in the Supreme Court on the trust question. I always supposed it would be, and have taken the responsibility of not prosecuting under a law I believed to be no good."[22]

[19] *Congressional Record*, 51st Cong., 1st sess., p. 3152.

[20] Both contemporaries and historians made this charge. Senator Orville Platt of Connecticut, for example, said during the debate on the bill, "The conduct of the Senate . . . has not been in the line of the honest preparation of a bill to prohibit and punish trusts. It has been in the line of getting some bill with that title that we might go to the country with." Josephson, *Politicos*, p. 460. Historians who have endorsed this view include Josephson himself; Charles A. and Mary R. Beard, *The Rise of American Civilization* (rev. ed., New York, 1930), II, 327; and Samuel E. Morison and Henry Steele Commager, *The Growth of the American Republic* (4th ed., New York, 1951), II, 144.

[21] Shelby M. Cullom, *Fifty Years of Public Service* (Chicago, 1911), p. 254.

[22] Quoted in Nevins, *Cleveland*, p. 671, from the Olney Papers, January 22, 1895.

Even without this executive indifference, enforcement would have been difficult in the atmosphere of the 1890's when the spirit of laissez faire pervaded all political thought. The novelty of the trust and corporate forms and the uncertainty surrounding many aspects of their legal status also hindered decisive and clear-cut action. Whatever the reasons, the fact remains that down to 1901 the government instituted only eighteen suits under the Sherman Antitrust Act.[23] In one of them, the E. C. Knight case (1895), the Supreme Court, by defining "commerce" so narrowly as practically to exclude all forms of interstate enterprise except transportation, almost consigned the law to oblivion. "The fact that an article is manufactured for export to another State," Chief Justice Fuller solemnly declared, "does not of itself make it an article of interstate commerce. . . ."[24]

This doctrine still left room for the Sherman Act to be invoked against railroads, combinations of which were successfully broken up in the Trans-Missouri Freight Association case (1897), the Joint Traffic Association case (1898), and, later, in the Northern Securities case (1902). In the first of these, however, the court brought up a new question, which if pursued far enough would enable even railroads to escape punishment under the act—the question of whether Congress had meant to prohibit *all* restraints on trade or merely "unreasonable" restraints. In this instance the Court held that all restraints were prohibited.[25] Fourteen years later, however, it reversed itself on this matter in the Standard Oil case, Chief Justice White arguing that Congress had intended "that the standard of reason which had been applied at the common law . . . in dealing with subjects of the character embraced by the statute, was intended to be the measure used" in determining whether combinations in restraint of trade should be punished under the law. What was reasonable and what was not, the Court alone might decide.[26]

Twelve days after Harrison signed the Sherman Act, Congress

[23] Walton Hamilton and Irene Till, *Antitrust in Action* (Washington, 1941), Appendix G; Temporary National Economic Committee, *Investigation of Concentration of Economic Power,* 76th Cong., 3d sess., Senate Committee Print, Monograph No. 16.

[24] U.S. *v.* E. C. Knight Company, 156 U.S. 1 (1895). In the Swift case the Supreme Court overruled this doctrine in favor of the broader "stream of commerce" doctrine. Swift and Co. *v.* U.S., 196 U.S. 375 (1905).

[25] U.S. *v. Trans-Missouri Freight Association,* 166 U.S. 290 (1897).

[26] Standard Oil Company of New Jersey *et al. v.* U.S., 221 U.S. 1 (1911).

passed another important bill bearing the name of the venerable Senator from Ohio, the Sherman Silver Purchase Act. This law was designed to supersede the Bland-Allison Act of 1878, which had provided for limited silver coinage in order to appease the agrarian element in both parties. Under that act the Treasury had in twelve years put $378,166,000 in silver dollars into circulation without causing any of the dire consequences that had been predicted. The injection of silver into the circulating medium had neither driven gold out of circulation, as Gresham's law insisted it had to, nor caused inflation. Industry was rapidly expanding and could absorb additional amounts of money without difficulty. Moreover, the surplus enjoyed by the government during most of these years enabled the Treasury to redeem notes in gold instead of in silver and to retire Civil War bonds, a measure which also had a deflationary effect by reducing circulation of national bank notes (secured by government bonds) by $126 million between 1886 and 1900. Although conservative financiers continued to distrust the Bland-Allison Act and Presidents Arthur and Cleveland urged its repeal, its operation had not endangered the gold standard, in spite of the fact that by 1889 silver stood at only 72 cents in relation to the gold dollar.

Neither party had given any special prominence to the money issue in the campaign of 1888. The Republicans, hoping to capitalize on Cleveland's opposition to the Bland-Allison Act, condemned "the Democratic Administration in its efforts to demonetize silver," but the Democrats hardly mentioned silver in their platform. Neither did Harrison in his inaugural address. He was apparently taken by surprise, therefore, when his Secretary of the Treasury, William Windom, proposed in his first annual report to expand the use of silver.[27] Harrison mentioned the matter in his first message to Congress only to say warily that he had "always been an advocate of the use of silver in our currency," but that he had not had time to give Windom's complicated plan more than a hasty examination.

Windom was neither a financier nor an economist; his proposal, in fact, was in the realm of the fantastic.[28] He proposed that the government buy at the market price all the silver offered for sale, the

[27] *Treasury Report, 1889,* pp. lxxiv–lxxxii.
[28] Alexander D. Noyes, *Forty Years of American Finance* (New York, 1909), pp. 139–146.

silver to be stored in bulk and paid for in notes of the United States. These notes were to be redeemable "on demand, in such quantities of silver bullion as will equal in value, at the date of presentation, the number of dollars expressed on the face of the notes at the market price of silver. . . ." The notes might also be redeemed in gold at the option of the government. This plan met the approval neither of the gold men nor of the silver men. The former opposed it because it set no fixed limits on the amount of silver which the Treasury was committed to buy; in effect, it made the government a speculator in metals. The silverites opposed it because it did not make silver the equal of gold by establishing a fixed ratio between them. Silver certificates, under the Windom plan, would fluctuate in value with the market price of silver.

Windom's motives were political rather than economic. By enlarging the circulation of silver he hoped to propitiate the demand for inflation, and by creating an artificial market for silver he planned to win the support of representatives from the silver-mining states, who wanted "to do something for silver." In view of the narrow Republican majority in Congress their support was necessary, particularly in maintaining high tariff duties for which there was little enthusiasm in the West. Many advocates of silver did indeed vote for the McKinley tariff on the understanding that something would be done for silver. In the end, however, both the Windom plan and a free coinage bill passed at one point by the Senate were discarded (the latter through the stubborn resistance of Speaker Reed in the House), and a new measure enacted which represented still another compromise. Under the Sherman Silver Purchase Act the Secretary of the Treasury was to purchase 4,500,000 ounces of silver bullion every month and to issue in payment treasury notes of full legal-tender value. These notes were to be redeemed in gold or silver at the discretion of the government. At the same time the bill declared it to be "the established policy of the United States to maintain the two metals on a parity with each other upon the present legal ratio or such ratio as may be provided by law."[29] Both Houses passed the measure by a strict party vote, the Democrats unanimously opposing it. Something of its nature can be gathered from the fact that Sherman himself supported it only to prevent the enactment of a bill providing for free coinage. "The day

[29] 26 U.S. Statutes at Large, 289 (1890).

it became law," he later wrote, "I was ready to repeal it, if repeal could be had without substituting in its place absolute free coinage."[30]

Sherman's reasoning was to be the line taken by Republicans in defending the bill. (Privately they also reminded their protectionist constituents that it was the price paid for the McKinley tariff.) The argument that the Sherman Act had saved the country from free coinage, however, was spurious; there was not enough strength in Congress to pass a free-silver bill over Harrison's probable veto. Nor is it likely that many Republicans shared Senator Platt's fear that a veto would tend to "break up the Republican party, and, worse than that, to array the West and Southwest against the East."[31] It was weak and vacillating statesmanship that produced the bill. Nor did it even satisfy the demand for silver, for in practice it proved no more inflationary than the Bland Act. Under the latter the government had to buy silver to the amount of a fixed value of dollars; if the price of silver declined, as it did, the government found itself required to buy greater and greater amounts of silver. The Sherman Act substituted ounces for dollars. When the price of silver continued to fall, after a brief spurt upward, the government found itself able to buy the required amount of silver for fewer dollars. The amount of money thus injected into the currency soon fell below even the amount provided by the Bland Act. Moreover, both Harrison and Cleveland interpreted the stated intention of the act to maintain gold and silver on a parity with each other as binding the government to redeem notes only in gold.[32]

The Sherman Silver Purchase Act was one half of a sectional bargain within the Republican party. The other half was the McKinley tariff. Ever since Cleveland's message of December, 1887, the tariff had been the leading political issue before the country and the only one on which there was even a semblance of disagreement between the two parties. Both parties had many allies in the business world, but the Democrats tended to be more closely tied to bankers and railroad men, who had nothing in particular to gain from a high tariff, while the Republicans found their best friends among the manufacturing in-

---

[30] John Sherman, *Recollections of Forty Years* (Chicago, 1895), II, 1070–1071, 1188.

[31] Letter to Hartford *Post*, quoted in *The Nation*, L (May 8, 1890), 365.

[32] Davis R. Dewey, *Financial History of the United States* (6th ed., New York, 1918), pp. 436–438; see also his *National Problems*, pp. 220–228.

terest, which demanded protection.[33] The Republicans owed their
victory in 1888 in large part to their skill in "frying the fat" out of
protected manufacturers, and they had accordingly committed themselves to still further advances in the schedules. They interpreted the
election of a Republican Congress as a popular vindication of their
stand on the tariff.

In his message of December, 1889, Harrison urged revision both of
the administrative features of the present law and of its schedules. As
a sop to the farmers, who were becoming restive under a system that
seemed to benefit industry alone, he recommended that "the inequali-
ties of the law should be adjusted, but the protective principle should
be maintained and fairly applied to the products of our farms as well
as of our shops."[34] Within a week after Congress assembled, the House
Ways and Means Committee took up the high-tariff bill passed by the
Senate in 1888 and began to consider ways of making it still higher.
The committee, appointed by Reed, was one of the strongest ever to
sit in Congress. Presided over by McKinley, it included Nelson
Dingley, Jr., Joseph E. McKenna, Sereno E. Payne, and Robert M.
La Follette, Republicans, and John G. Carlisle and Roger Q. Mills,
Democrats.

For several weeks it heard a long series of distinguished guests testify
as to the merits of the protective system. In reply to the argument that
if rates were not lowered the Treasury surplus would grow to un-
manageable proportions, the exponents of protection ingeniously replied that if only duties were made high enough to discourage *all*
foreign imports, there would be no revenue at all. For the first time in
history protectionists abandoned the ancient pretense that protection
was only a stage in the development of "infant industries"; they now
argued openly that these progeny ought to be sheltered from the harsh
outside world even after they had reached manhood.[35] The Mc-
Kinley bill, which passed both houses after extended debate and became law on June 10, 1890, clearly embodied the most advanced
thought on the subject of tariffs. The general level of rates was higher
than ever before. Duties on raw sugar were repealed and those on
some kinds of iron and steel reduced, but those on a bewildering variety

[33] Horace Samuel Merrill, *Bourbon Democracy of the Middle West, 1865–
1896* (Baton Rouge, 1953), and his *Bourbon Leader,* pp. 44–45, 50–51, 72–78.
[34] Richardson, *Messages and Papers,* IX, 39.
[35] Dewey, *Financial History,* p. 438; Josephson, *Politicos,* pp. 450–451.

of other commodities were greatly increased, often to the point of outright prohibition. The duty on tin plates, for instance, was made so high that many foreign manufacturers of plate actually moved to this country rather than go out of business. Protection could have been no more efficient.[36] The orthodox were shocked to the core, and Mr. Cleveland ranted like a Populist demagogue, calling the McKinley Act "an unjust tariff which banishes from many humble homes the comforts of life, in order that in the palaces of wealth luxury may more abound."[37]

Following President Harrison's recommendation, the McKinley Act was the first tariff to contain a complete schedule of protective duties on agricultural products. It increased existing duties on barley, butter, hams, and bacon and laid duties for the first time on a number of other commodities, such as eggs. These duties probably did very little to help the farmer except insofar as they cut competition from Canada in barley, hay, eggs, and livestock, but they were of some value to the Republican party. Together with the Sherman Silver Purchase Act, the tariffs on farm products probably won a few friends for the party among the farmers. Both, however, were mere gestures, and it was not long before the farmers began to see that the Republicans were more interested in their votes than in their well-being.

Two features of the McKinley Act were novel. In the first place the duty on sugar was eliminated; to compensate domestic producers for any loss they might thereby sustain they were granted a bounty of two cents a pound for fourteen years. McKinley defended the free admission of sugar on the grounds that American growers produced only one-eighth of the sugar consumed in the United States and that long years of protection had not stimulated the industry. The elimination of the duty would benefit the consumer by lowering the price of sugar, while the bounty would protect what capital was already invested in domestic production. The Democrats sneered that the provision would benefit neither the growers nor the consumers but the American Sugar Refining Company, which, after all, was the largest single consumer of raw sugar in the country.

[36] During the fiscal years 1892–1894 the average customs rates were over 49 per cent, or a 4 per cent increase on dutiable goods. *Statistical Abstract of the United States, 1918,* p. 783. For the text of the act see 26 U.S. Statutes at Large, 131 (1890); see also Frank W. Taussig, *The Tariff History of the United States* (7th ed., New York, 1923), pp. 251–279.

[37] Nevins, *Cleveland,* p. 464.

In the second place, the principle of commercial reciprocity was incorporated in the act at the bidding of Secretary of State Blaine, who was conducting a campaign of his own to promote closer diplomatic and commercial relations with Latin America.[38] Blaine was disturbed by the inclusion of sugar on the free list. Eighty per cent of Latin American goods were already admitted free, he pointed out, while many American exports to Latin America had to pay high duties. The removal of the duty on sugar tipped the scales of trade decisively against the United States; it threw open the American market to Latin American countries while their own products remained sheltered from competition. "There is not one section or line in the entire bill," Blaine wrote to Senator Frye of Maine, "that will open the market for another bushel of wheat or barrel of pork."[39] To correct this imbalance of trade he proposed to give the President power to levy duties by proclamation on sugar, molasses, tea, coffee, and hides if he considered that any country exporting these commodities to the United States was imposing "unequal and unreasonable" duties on American goods. Senator Aldrich added to the bill an amendment incorporating Blaine's views.

If this was reciprocity, it was reciprocity of a curious type. Far from a movement toward lower tariffs which might increase trade and benefit both the United States and its neighbors to the South, it was a threat to raise tariffs in this country if other countries did not lower theirs. William L. Wilson later denounced the plan before the Democratic convention as a fraud. "It is not reciprocity at all," he said. "It is retaliation, and, worst of all, retaliation on our own people."

Already [he went on] we are regaled with pictures of Benjamin Harrison clad in armor and going forth to battle for reciprocity on a plumed steed. Simple Simon fishing for whales in his mother's rain barrel, and in great triumph capturing an occasional wiggle-waggle, is the only true, realistic picture of the reciprocity of the McKinley bill.[40]

Under the Aldrich amendment to the McKinley Act the United States subsequently signed ten reciprocal agreements, including those with Germany and Austria-Hungary, with Great Britain and Spain for their Caribbean colonies, and with Brazil, Santo-Domingo, and

[38] David S. Muzzey, *James G. Blaine* (New York, 1934), pp. 437–454.
[39] Quoted in Edward Stanwood, *American Tariff Controversies* (Boston, 1903), II, 276; see also *The Nation*, LI (July 17, 1890), 41.
[40] *Campaign Text Book of the Democratic Party* (New York, 1892), p. 12.

four Central American countries. Although the results of the agreements with Germany and Austria-Hungary were not unfavorable, trade with only one Latin American country, Cuba, showed any increase.[41] John W. Foster, who negotiated all of the agreements, insisted that they "proved highly satisfactory during the period they were in force."[42] Unfortunately there was not much evidence to test his hypothesis, as the agreements were discontinued under the Wilson-Gorman Act of 1894.

Whatever might be said for or against the McKinley tariff—and much was said on both sides—all parties agreed that it had helped to reduce the Treasury surplus; high rates caused imports, and therefore revenue, to decline. The elimination of the tariff on sugar, combined with the bounty paid to American producers, worked to the same end.[43] The McKinley Act, however, was only one of several influences which turned the surplus into a deficit. The depression beginning in 1893 led to a decline in foreign trade. Naval appropriations almost doubled between 1888 and 1893. The liberality of the "billion-dollar Congress," particularly in the matter of pensions, helped to dispose of surplus income. The continuous purchase of silver bullion also drained money from the Treasury. All these factors contributed to the speedy solution of the problem that had seemed so critical to Grover Cleveland—the problem of what to do with too much money. After 1894 the country would never again be able to indulge in the luxury of regarding a surplus in the Treasury as an alarming matter demanding vigorous action. Nobody could deny, however, that if vigorous action was demanded, the Harrison administration proved equal to the emergency.

Having enacted the Sherman Antitrust Act, the Sherman Silver Purchase Act, and the McKinley tariff, and having spent unprecedented quantities of money, the first session of the Fifty-first Congress deserved to be known as one of the most active on record. Whether any of its actions could be described as accomplishments was another

[41] Emory R. Johnson et al., History of Domestic and Foreign Commerce of the United States (Washington, 1915), II, 342–343; Taussig, Tariff History, pp. 279–282.

[42] John W. Foster, Diplomatic Memoirs (2 vols., Boston, 1909), II, 16.

[43] Congress had estimated that the McKinley tariff would cut revenue by $43 million. During the first fiscal year of their operation the new schedules cut revenue by $52 million, two years later by nearly $100 million. See Noyes, American Finance, pp. 135–138.

question—a question, however, which no amount of oratory could prevent people from asking. Even hardened believers in the spoils system might wonder whether the Republicans had not gone too far in pleasing their constituents. The Sherman Antitrust Act could conceivably be defended as a bipartisan effort to deal with a serious problem, and even the Silver Purchase Act, although clearly a vote-getting measure, had some merit; but the wholesale dismissal of Democratic officeholders, the innumerable pensions, the extravagant expenditures on rivers and harbors, and finally the tariffs granted with complete abandon to all whose contributions might prove useful in future campaigns—all these raised doubts as to whether the Republicans were guided by anything but a spirit of narrow partisanship. Nor were these doubts dispelled by the rather feeble efforts of the Republican Congress to revive the old issues of reconstruction in the interests of political advantage.

Harrison himself had recommended a bill empowering the federal government to supervise congressional elections in the South. The partisan advantages of such legislation were obvious. Cleveland had been elected in 1884 partly through the disfranchisement of southern Negroes; in 1888 he had again swept the solid South. Unless the Republicans could restore their old control of the South, they would find themselves at a permanent disadvantage in federal elections. Many of them began to murmur, with Congressman McKinley, that "the people of the North will not continue to permit two votes in the South to count as much as five votes in the North."[44] Henry Cabot Lodge sponsored the bill in the House. Aided by Reed, it passed by the close vote of 155 to 149. Many Republicans opposed it. Although they still believed that their party's reconstruction policy had been correct, they understood that it had failed and hesitated to revive sectional and racial animosity, particularly in view of the reviving prosperity of the South (aided by northern investments). Some Republicans feared that long debates on the Force Bill would delay the passage of silver and tariff legislation, which was still pending when the bill was introduced. In the Senate eight Republicans deserted the party and voted against the bill, in return for southern support of the Sherman Silver Purchase Act. The leadership of Sherman and Hoar, for once, was unavailing; the Senate voted to remove the bill from the calendar and later in-

---

[44] *Congressional Record,* 51st Cong., 1st sess., p. 6934.

definitely to postpone consideration.[45] Thus died the last real effort—until 1957—to enforce the Fifteenth Amendment.

The second session of the Fifty-first Congress, compared with the first, was distinctly anticlimactic. The Senate resumed debate on the Force Bill, but nothing came of it. It once again passed a free-silver bill, and the House once again defeated it. The Fifty-first Congress had to stand on its amazing record of 1890. Aside from its more spectacular achievements, it had enacted some other minor but useful bills: a Forest Reserve Act empowering the President to withdraw timber land on watersheds, a bill to prevent export and import of adulterated food products, an international copyright act. It created a Federal Circuit Court of Appeals to relieve the Supreme Court of some of its burdensome duties. It arranged for the World's Fair to be held in Chicago in 1892. On the other hand, more characteristically, it refunded to the states the entire tax levied in 1861 and after, a sum of $15,387,234. Cleveland had earlier vetoed a similar raid on the Treasury; Harrison was more liberal. This gift to the states, however, was a mere fraction of what Congress managed to spend in two sessions—almost a billion dollars. The thrifty railed at this "billion-dollar Congress." Speaker Reed was reported to have replied, "This is a billion-dollar country." He made no claim to authorship of the remark but confessed that it had "both wit and wisdom."[46] That many people, however, found it unconvincing was demonstrated by the results of the mid-term elections.

One other accomplishment of this period should be cited—the opening of new land to settlement. Between 1889 and 1893 Harrison detached 23 million acres from Indian reservations and made them available for settlement.[47] Eleven million acres in the Sioux country of South Dakota were thrown open in February, 1890, to a crowd of waiting boomers, who rushed across the border in a manner reminis-

[45] Rhodes, *History of the United States*, VIII, 358–364; Oberholtzer, *History of the United States*, V, 116–117; Paul H. Buck, *The Road to Reunion, 1895–1900* (Boston, 1937), pp. 278–281; George F. Hoar, *Autobiography of Seventy Years* (New York, 1903), II, 150–171; Henry Cabot Lodge and T. V. Powderly, "The Federal Election Bill," *North American Review*, CLI (Sept., 1890), 257–273; Robert Smalls, "Election Methods in the South," *ibid.* (Nov., pp. 1890), 594–600; A. W. Shaffer, "A Southern Republican on the Lodge Bill," *ibid.* (Nov., 1890), pp. 601–609.

[46] Robinson, *Reed*, p. 251; "Spending Public Money," *North American Review*, CLIV (Mar., 1892), 319.

[47] Richardson, *Messages and Papers*, IX, 203.

cent of the settlement of Oklahoma a year earlier. Oklahoma itself was organized as a territory on May 2, 1890. The same year witnessed a final episode in the long conflict between white men and Indians. The Teton Sioux of South Dakota, their reservation diminished by a recent treaty with the government and faced with famine and drought (partly because the government had failed to meet its treaty obligations), turned against a group of cavalry and disarmed them at Wounded Knee. The cavalry lost twenty-five killed and others wounded, in retaliation for which they massacred about two hundred Indian warriors, women, and children.[48]

The elections of 1890 did not go well for the Republicans. In the Maine election in September, Speaker Reed won hands down, but the result in other states holding early elections indicated widespread disapproval of the administration and foreshadowed a Democratic victory in November.[49] Nor was Harrison the man to rally his party's flagging spirits. Genial and cordial in his household and in the company of a few personal friends, he impressed strangers as ungracious, unsympathetic, and frigid. He spoke in public with dignity, ease, and tact, and in a manner remarkably free of banality, but in private conversation with politicians these very virtues became liabilities. One western Senator said: "Harrison can make a speech to ten thousand men, and every man of them will go away his friend. Let him meet the same ten thousand in private, and everyone will go away his enemy."[50] He gracefully adorned a platform, but in closer relations with political cohorts he failed to convey the enthusiasm necessary to campaign successfully.

If Harrison's leadership did not enhance the party's chances of winning the election, the administration's record made that event still more unlikely. Mugwumps were disturbed by the failure to advance the cause of civil-service reform. Harrison himself, it was true, was a man of personal integrity, and he had observed the Civil Service Act to the letter and even widened its application. His integrity, however, had to contend with the generous impulse to reward his followers. Generosity usually prevailed. *The Nation* finally threw up its hands

[48] Oberholtzer, *History of the United States,* V, 120–126; R. A. Billington, *Westward Expansion* (New York, 1949), p. 667.

[49] *The Nation,* LI (Sept. 11, 1890), 201.

[50] H. J. Peck, *Twenty Years of the Republic, 1885–1905* (New York, 1907), p. 170; Hoar, *Autobiography,* I, 414.

1. BENJAMIN HARRISON

2. JAMES G. BLAINE

3. Tariff Reform and Civil Service Reform seem in danger of going overboard. Cleveland uses knife to veto Bland free-silver bill. (W. A. Rogers cartoon in *Harper's Weekly*, April 14, 1894.)

5. President Cleveland with his second cabinet. Left to right, the President, John G. Carlisle, Richard Olney, Judson Harmon, Hilary A. Herbert, Daniel S. Lamont, J. Sterling Morton, William L. Wilson and Hoke Smith. (From *Cabinet Diary of William L. Wilson*, courtesy of F. P. Summers.)

Culver Service

4. GROVER CLEVELAND

6. WILLIAM L. WILSON

7. RICHARD OLNEY

8. JOHN G. CARLISLE

9. JOHN SHERMAN

10. THOMAS B. REED

11. A perilous situation—an Eastern view of free silver. (W. A. Rogers in *Harper's Weekly*, December 28, 1894.)

12. Interior of Electrical Building, Chicago World's Fair, 1893.

13. Entrance, Transportation Building, Chicago World's Fair.

14. "General" Coxey on his way to Washington.

15. Coxey's Army entering Allegheny, Pennsylvania.

16. JOHN P. ALTGELD

17. JAMES B. WEAVER

18. EUGENE V. DEBS

19. A typical cartoon of the agrarian crusade. (Reproduced from *The Pageant of America*, Copyright Yale University Press.)

20. Jane Addams

21. Samuel Gompers

22. American Peace Commission in Paris, October, 1898. Left to right, Whitelaw Reid, Senator Gray, John Bassett Moore, Judge Day, Senator Frye, Senator Davis.

23. "Reflections—Night," 1896, by Alfred Stieglitz. (With permission of Georgia O'Keeffe for the Alfred Stieglitz Estate.)

24. WILLIAM JENNINGS BRYAN

Culver Service

25. COLONEL THEODORE ROOSEVELT of the "Rough Riders." (From *Harper Pictorial History of the War With Spain*.)

26. WILLIAM McKINLEY

27. MARCUS A. HANNA

28. "The Terminal," 1892, by Alfred Stieglitz. (Permission Georgia O'Keeffe for the Alfred Stieglitz Estate. Photo courtesy The Museum of Modern Art, New York.)

29. "Tammany Street Cleaning before Waring's day in front of 9 Varick Place." (Jacob A. Riis Collection, courtesy of Museum of the City of New York.)

and denounced Harrison as the "most subservient disciple of the spoils doctrine who has occupied the Presidential chair since the Civil-Service law was enacted."[51] Nor did the reformers approve of the pensions dispensed so freely by the administration. Americans believed in principle that their soldiers' services to the nation should be recognized, but to provide for all those who had at any time suffered disabilities of whatever sort seemed a perversion of principle. To support the man who lost a leg at Bull Run was one thing, but to send a monthly check to the man who survived Bull Run unscathed and then fell downstairs one night twenty years later was quite another. When compared with the standards which Cleveland had so laboriously maintained, there was little to recommend the Dependent Pension Act or the work of Tanner. Pensions and jobs at least satisfied the recipients of them; the Sherman Silver Purchase Act satisfied nobody, not even the silver miners, for although the government now bought large amounts of silver, increased production kept the price down. More serious, however, was the failure of the act to satisfy the demand for cheap money. Farmers were more numerous than mugwumps or silver miners; their votes might in the end decide the election.

The farmers, as we have seen, suffered from a prolonged depression. As prices fell, they found it increasingly difficult to borrow money. Long-term interest rates rose to as high as 8 or 10 per cent in some parts of the West, while short-term rates were sometimes twice as high. Meanwhile prices went down and down; from 1886 to 1888, wheat averaged 73 cents a bushel, corn 36 cents, oats 28 cents. Drought drove prices up in 1890, but the poor crop made the total return smaller than before.[52] In the next year prices declined more precipitously than ever. In this extremity the farmers began to demand sweeping federal action. The Southern Alliance, meeting at St. Louis in 1889, advocated the abolition of national banks and the substitution of greenbacks for national bank notes, free and unlimited coinage of silver, prohibition of speculation in the futures of agricultural and mechanical products, prohibition of alien ownership of land, reclamation of public lands from the railroads, reduction and equalization of taxation, and government ownership of all means of transportation

[51] *The Nation,* L (Mar. 13, 1890), 211.
[52] *Historical Statistics of the United States, 1789–1945* (Washington, 1949), pp. 106–107; Solon J. Buck, *The Agrarian Crusade* (New Haven, 1920), pp. 104–106.

and communication.[53] As a means both of meeting the farmer's chief problem, overproduction, and of inflating the currency, the St. Louis convention also proposed the "subtreasury" plan. Under this plan government funds would be removed from the private banks in which they were now deposited and deposited instead in government subtreasuries. These would be set up in every county which produced $500,000 worth of agricultural products. At each subtreasury office, warehouses would be built in which farmers might store their surplus crops, receiving against the deposit a loan of United States legal tender equivalent to 80 per cent of the current local value of the crops. Loans would be made at the rate of 1 per cent and the debtor allowed a year in which to redeem them. If he failed, his crops would be sold at auction to satisfy the debt.[54]

To say that the Harrison administration had failed to meet any of these demands would be an understatement; it had not even tried. The feebleness of its single gesture, the silver legislation, was evident by 1892. Nor had the Sherman Antitrust Act—nor, for that matter, the Interstate Commerce Act of 1887—brought any discernible relief. The leaders of the Alliance, much against their will, for the alliances had originally been nonpolitical in intent, became more aggressive in their demands for political action. In some southern states they captured the Democratic state conventions, wrote their demands into the state platforms, and in the election of 1890 won control of eight legislatures. Led by Leonidas L. Polk in North Carolina, Benjamin F. Tillman in South Carolina, and Thomas Watson in Georgia, the agrarians elected governors in South Carolina, Georgia, and Tennessee. They elected forty-four Alliance candidates to Congress, where they could already count on the support of some members sympathetic to Alliance views.

In the West the election of 1890 took on the quality of a social and political revolution. In Kansas the campaign resembled "a religious revival, a crusade, a pentecost of politics in which a flame sat upon

[53] *Ibid.*, pp. 129–130; Carl C. Taylor, *The Farmers' Movement, 1620–1920* (New York, 1953), pp. 229–230.

[54] John D. Hicks, *The Populist Revolt* (Minneapolis, 1931), pp. 186–204, and "The Subtreasury: A Forgotten Plan for the Relief of Agriculture," *Mississippi Valley Historical Review*, XV (Dec., 1928), 355–373; Taylor, *Farmers' Movement*, pp. 243–246. On the Alliance Movement, see William A. Peffer, "The Farmers' Defensive Movement," *Forum*, VIII (Dec., 1889), 464–473.

every man, and each spake as the spirit gave him utterance."[55] Mary Ellen Lease went up and down the state urging the farmers to "raise less corn and more Hell."

Wall Street [she cried] owns the country. It is no longer a government of the people, by the people and for the people, but a government of Wall Street, by Wall Street and for Wall Street. The great common people of this country are slaves, and monopoly is the master. The West and South are bound and prostrate before the manufacturing East. Money rules, and our Vice-President is a London banker. Our laws are the output of a system which clothes rascals in robes and honesty in rags. The parties lie to us and the political speakers mislead us . . . the politicians said we suffered from overproduction. Overproduction when 10,000 little children, so statistics tell us, starve to death every year in the United States, and over 100,000 shop-girls in New York are forced to sell their virtue for the bread their niggardly wages deny them![56]

Whereas the southern Democracy had capitulated to the Alliance and had been taken over by Alliance men, Midwestern Democrats stood firm against all innovations. The agrarians therefore met at Topeka in June, 1890, and organized a new party, called simply the People's party. It was a colorful gathering. Mrs. Lease and "Sockless Jerry" Simpson, with his flowing black beard and lowering brow, represented Kansas. Minnesota sent Ignatius Donnelly, the "sage of Nininger," who had begun political life as a lobbyist for Jay Cooke and who now denounced the railroads with the fervor of a convert. From Iowa came James E. Weaver, already the veteran of many battles on behalf of the common man. In addition the convention attracted many people who simply loved a good fight, especially when it involved a clear-cut moral issue. Many of these were fanatic temperance advocates, more interested in abolishing alcohol than in abolishing monopoly and privilege. Their presence was a source of embarrassment, and in some places of actual weakness, to the party, on which the Democrats were quick to capitalize.

The party regulars, under the direction of the eminent Bourbons William F. Vilas of Wisconsin and J. Sterling Morton of Nebraska, early in the campaign hit upon the strategy of diverting the issue from the Topeka platform to the prohibition issue. By identifying the tem-

[55] Elizabeth N. Barr, "The Populist Uprising," in William E. Connelly (ed.), *A Standard History of Kansas and Kansans* (Chicago, 1918), II, 1148.
[56] *Ibid.*, p. 1150.

perance movement with political nativism, they hoped to win the support of minorities in certain Midwestern states. Thus they not only ridiculed prohibition as it had been put into force in parts of Nebraska, Iowa, and Minnesota but attacked laws passed in Illinois and Wisconsin requiring that schools teach most subjects in English. Catholics especially hated this legislation, which seemed to threaten the parochial schools; and since the regular Democrats fared best in the most urbanized states of the Middle West—Minnesota, Wisconsin, and Illinois—it would appear that they were generally successful in confusing the issue.[57]

Nevertheless, Populists and independents everywhere polled an impressive number of votes. In Kansas "Sockless" Jerry Simpson, running against the "silk-stockinged" James R. Hallowell for governor, won a decisive victory, and the agrarians captured the lower house of the legislature. William A. Peffer defeated the veteran demagogue John A. Ingalls in the race for the Senate. In Nebraska the radicals won control of the legislature; in several other states they cut deeply into Republican majorities. In the country as a whole, ten congressmen and two senators (Peffer and James H. Kyle of South Dakota) were elected on platforms favoring agrarian reform. Democrats and Republicans alike viewed the election returns with mounting agitation.[58] The results of the election, in fact, were worse than the most pessimistic Republicans had predicted. In the House the Republican majority was swept away: 235 Democrats and 10 Populists and independents were elected to a mere 86 Republicans. In the Senate the Republicans retained a majority of eight, through the recent admission of Montana, North Dakota, South Dakota, and Washington in 1889 and of Idaho and Wyoming in 1890. Many Republican notables lost their seats, including McKinley, Ingalls, Joseph G. Cannon, and John Henry Gear.[59] Each part of the country, including New England, saw a

[57] Merrill, *Bourbon Democracy*, pp. 203–206. On the Wisconsin law, see W. L. Vilas, "The Bennett Law in Wisconsin," *Forum*, XII (Oct., 1891), 196–207; on the Illinois law, see John Bascom, "A New Policy for the Public Schools," *ibid.*, XI (Mar., 1891), 59–66.

[58] Hicks, *Populist Revolt*, pp. 153–185. On the agrarian leaders, see also Hamlin Garland, "The Alliance Wedge in Congress," *Arena*, V (Mar., 1892), 447–457; Annie L. Diggs, "The Women in the Alliance Movement," *ibid.*, VI (July, 1892), 161–179; Hicks, "The Political Career of Ignatius Donnelly," *Mississippi Valley Historical Review*, VIII (June–Sept., 1921), 80–132.

[59] McKinley was defeated largely because the Democratic legislature gerry-

Republican decline. Voters returned a majority of Democrats or Populists, even such normally Republican strongholds as Michigan, Massachusetts, Iowa, Illinois, Minnesota, Wisconsin, Kansas, and Nebraska. The defeat was overwhelming.

Opinion was divided as to what issues were chiefly responsible for the downfall of the Republicans. Many politicians at the time, and many historians later, attributed the defeat to the tariff. The agrarians thought otherwise. "People who believe that the issue was won on tariff lines are mistaken," said Leonidas Polk. "It was financial reform that caused the sweep."[60] In parts of the South and West the currency issue may indeed have been paramount. There can be no doubt, however, that rising prices contributed to the demand for a change, and that many people attributed higher prices to the tariff. The McKinley tariff was vehemently denounced throughout the campaign, often unjustly; bad as the act was, the campaign against it was in some ways worse. "In hundreds of cases," said Speaker Reed, "the 'drummers' [traveling salesmen] were, intentionally or unintentionally, missionaries to preach Democratic doctrine. They went all over the country with their stories of advances in prices that were to be made next week or next month on account of the McKinley Bill."[61] Clerks in the stores lost no time marking up prices.

There is some evidence that the Democrats systematically set out to create the impression that prices were shooting upward as a result of the tariff.

In McKinley's own district [writes his biographer], a few days before election, tin peddlers were hired to go into rural districts. They offered coffee pots at $1.50 and tin cups worth about five cents, for twenty-five cents or more. Everybody was horrified. Of course, no sales were made, but the lesson was well impressed that the dreadful McKinley Act had greatly increased the cost of living.[62]

In actual fact, foodstuffs were not sufficiently protected under the McKinley Act to have caused any marked rise in price, nor was there

---

mandered his district. Charles S. Olcott, *The Life of William McKinley* (2 vols., Boston, 1916), I, 82–85.

[60] Chicago, *Inter-Ocean* (Nov. 22, 1890), quoted in Frank M. Drew, "The Present Farmers' Movement," *Political Science Quarterly*, VI (June, 1901), 309.

[61] Interview in the New York *Sun*, Nov. 15, 1890, quoted in Peck, *Twenty Years of the Republic*, p. 215 n.

[62] Olcott, *McKinley*, I, 180.

much danger that clothing would go up. Certainly the act had not been in effect long enough for anyone to predict its consequences with any accuracy. The Democrats, however, did not hesitate to give out the impression that the nation was about to be reduced to destitution.[63]

Their insistence on the tariff issue committed the Democrats themselves to take action when they assumed control of the House. With Charles F. Crisp, a Georgia silverite and low-tariff advocate, in the Speaker's chair in place of Reed, the prospects for action seemed favorable. In selecting a chairman of the Ways and Means Committee, however, Crisp passed over the one man in the House who might have led a vigorous fight for tariff reduction, Roger Mills of Texas, and appointed instead William M. Springer, a nonentity. The House voted only minor reductions and added a few items to the free list (for "educational purposes," they said); but with the Senate still Republican, the Democrats could argue plausibly that revision was impossible in any case. Having disposed of the tariff, the Fifty-second Congress devoted the rest of its time to preparations for the impending presidential election. Both parties could make good use of the time— the Republicans in order to restore harmony and discipline after their recent disaster, the Democrats to rally support around the massive, impenetrable figure of Grover Cleveland, whose candidacy was anticipated with growing misgivings by the agrarian wing of the party.

[63] *The Nation*, LI (Oct. 9, 1890), 275; Edward Stanwood, *American Tariff Controversies in the Nineteenth Century* (Boston, 1903), II, 292.

CHAPTER 6

The Election of 1892

WHEN Cleveland left the White House in March, 1889, he took up residence in New York City, where he joined the law firm of Bangs, Stetson, Tracy and MacVeagh, and in his conscientious and methodical manner carried on a busy practice, chiefly as a referee appointed by the courts. His friends and enemies alike believed that his public life was at an end; his enemies greeted his departure with delight. Henry Watterson said contemptuously, "Cleveland in New York reminds one of a stone thrown into a river. There is a 'plunk,' a splash, and then silence."[1]

Watterson's optimism was premature. By 1892 Cleveland was far from silent. At first he had enjoyed the relief from his presidential duties, and for about ten months after his defeat he remained in complete political retirement. Then he began to make public addresses on nonpolitical subjects. After 1890, however, moved by resentment over the McKinley tariff and encouraged by the Republican defeat in the congressional elections, he plainly signified his willingness to re-enter public life—always providing, of course, that he was called by the people once again to take up the onerous duties of office.[2] It is true that he insisted, in a letter of March, 1891, that he was "in a miserable condition—a private citizen without political ambition trying to do private work and yet pulled and hauled and importuned daily and hourly to do things in a public and semi-public way which are hard

[1] Quoted in Harry Thurston Peck, *Twenty Years of the Republic* (New York, 1916), p. 252.
[2] Allan Nevins (ed.), *Letters of Grover Cleveland, 1850–1906* (Boston, 1933) p. 201.

and distasteful to me."[3] At the same time he did nothing to discourage the pulling and hauling.

In December, 1889, Cleveland spoke before the Merchants Association in Boston on political honesty and on ballot reform, then only beginning to be an issue in this country. The speech, his first since leaving office, was so well received that admirers began to talk of Cleveland for the Presidency in 1892. Two of his devoted followers, Daniel S. Lamont, his private secretary, and the journalist George F. Parker, began almost at once to work for his nomination. "There was no organization," Parker later recalled, "no plan, no money, for promoting the third nomination, and yet, somehow, the movement began to take on something like form—not from any open approval on the part of the man chiefly involved, but by the silence which is said to give consent."[4] Cleveland continued to make frequent appearances, emphasizing in his speeches the issues which he had already made peculiarly his own—civil-service reform, economy in government, a reduction of tariffs. He was rapidly building up a following, particularly among the mugwumps in the party, who had already forgotten that Cleveland's own record on questions of patronage had not always conformed to their notions of honor and decency.

Cleveland immeasurably enhanced his appeal to the Bourbon element—with which, indeed, he had always identified himself—by coming out strongly against free silver. In January, 1891, the Senate passed another free-coinage bill. Every Democrat except George Gray of Delaware voted for it, and throughout the country many Democratic leaders were veering into the silver camp. At this juncture Cleveland received an invitation to attend a meeting of the Reform Club in New York called to protest against free silver. He replied in a widely circulated letter:

I shall not be able to attend and address the meeting as you request, but I am glad that the business interests in New York are at last to be heard on this subject. It surely cannot be necessary for one to make a formal expression of my agreement with those who believe that the greatest peril would be invited by the adoption of the scheme, embraced in the measure now pending in Congress, for the unlimited coinage at our mints.

If we have developed an unexpected capacity for the assimilation of a

[3] Cleveland to L. Clarke Davis, Mar. 9, 1891, *ibid.*, p. 249.
[4] George F. Parker, *Recollections of Grover Cleveland* (New York, 1919), pp. 128, 132.

largely increased volume of this currency, and even if we have demonstrated the usefulness of such an increase, these conditions fall far short of insuring us against disaster if, in the present situation, we enter upon the dangerous and reckless experiment of free, unlimited, and independent silver coinage.[5]

Some of Cleveland's friends feared that by taking a definite stand on the silver issue he had repeated his mistake of 1887, in which he had committed himself to tariff reform immediately before an important election. The silver letter, however, had the opposite effect; it won Cleveland friends among conservatives all over the country who were in great need of reassurance. At the same time it did not altogether tie his hands, for there was nothing in the letter to preclude him from favoring the coinage of silver if it could be undertaken in a responsible and conservative manner—through international agreement. The letter condemned only "reckless experiment." Thus it brought gold-standard men like Vilas hastening to Cleveland's side but did not alienate the bimetallists.[6]

The silver letter and the encouragement which the response to it gave to Cleveland's candidacy had the incidental effect of eliminating minor candidates from the field, thereby clearing the field for Cleveland's chief rival, the powerful David B. Hill, Democratic governor of New York. Hill was the Tammany candidate. An able lawyer, he was also a consummate politician adept at intrigue; he delighted in playing off the upstate Democrats in New York against Tammany Hall. In this manner he had been elected governor in 1888, while Cleveland was losing the state, and again in 1890. The legislature then elected him senator, but he refused to relinquish the governorship until the election of the following November, clinging against precedent to two offices at the same time. In 1891, under his supervision, Roswell P. Flower was nominated for governor by the machine and elected on a platform which avoided approval of Cleveland's tariff principles and straddled the silver issue. Still in firm control of the state, Hill now believed himself in an excellent position to block Cleveland's nomination and to bring about his own.

Late in 1891 the Democratic National Committee announced that the national nominating convention would convene the following June

[5] Nevins, *Letters of Cleveland,* pp. 245–246.

[6] Horace S. Merrill, *Bourbon Democracy of the Middle West* (Baton Rouge, 1953), pp. 213–221, and *William Freeman Vilas, Doctrinaire Democrat* (Madison, Wis., 1954), pp. 174–175.

21. The New York state committee then called a state convention to meet on February 22 to elect delegates-at-large to the national convention.[7] It was customary for state conventions to be held at a much later date; none had met before April 20 in twenty years. It was increasingly evident to the moderate and reasonable men around Cleveland that Governor Hill had little use for precedent. This alone would have been enough to shock their rigorous sense of propriety, but they had a more practical reason for viewing this latest stratagem of the opposition with indignation. If the convention should be held in February, the roads would be choked with snow. Upstate farmers, the guardians of political virtue in New York State, would find it impossible to attend, and the delegates to the national convention would be selected by the Tammany forces and the small-town politicians under Tammany control. The selection of Hill men would not only give him the votes of the nation's largest state but would doubtless stimulate his candidacy elsewhere as well.[8]

In spite of the fury of the Cleveland men, the "snap convention," as it was called, met in February, and the delegates were duly instructed for Hill. The unseemly tactics of his rival, however, had stirred Cleveland to action. It was now perfectly clear to him that the election of Hill would endanger all the causes closest to his heart, for Hill cared not a fig for civil-service reform or for economy and efficiency in government, he was perfectly willing to be ruled by expediency when it came to tariff legislation, and he was not above a compromise on silver. On the very day on which the "snap convention" was meeting in New York, Cleveland delivered at the University of Michigan a vigorous, eloquent, and even moving statement of his principles. He was uncompromisingly high-minded. He did not stoop to attack Hill in person but urged his listeners to interest themselves "in public affairs as a duty of citizenship" and not to abandon the field "to those who discredit and debase politics." The next morning's papers gave Cleveland's address full coverage, along with the news of the "snap convention" in New York. The contrast between Hill's rigged victory and Cleveland's declaration of principle was not lost on people who

[7] Alfred Henry Lewis, *Richard Croker* (New York, 1901), p. 305, asserted that Gorman, not Hill, suggested the "snap convention." Robert McElroy, *Grover Cleveland, The Man and the Statesman* (New York, 1923), I, 326, endorsed that interpretation. John R. Lambert, *Arthur Pue Gorman* (Baton Rouge, 1953), p. 172, ridicules it.

[8] Nevins, *Cleveland*, pp. 483–486.

agreed with Cleveland that politics was, or ought to be, the art of applying moral precepts to the discussion of public affairs. Nor did the endorsement of Hill by the New York convention lead to the expected stampede for his nomination. Other states held firm for Cleveland. It became clear that New York alone could not bend the convention to the support of Hill. Even in New York there was a reaction against him. The Cleveland adherents met late in May and held their own convention, knowing that their delegates would not be seated, but wishing to protest the manner in which the Hill delegates had been chosen. This demonstration gave further comfort to Cleveland's supporters.

In the last weeks before the convention the direction of Cleveland's campaign was assumed by William C. Whitney, the New York traction millionaire. A close friend, Whitney had served as Cleveland's Secretary of the Navy. Energetic, able, and tactful, he represented that group of conservative businessmen who followed Cleveland because of his own honesty and his insistence on honesty as well as economy in government, and in particular because of his stanch defense of "sound money." Like Cleveland, Whitney believed that politics was a matter of principle. Unlike Cleveland, however, he saw that something more than principle was often necessary. He was practical enough to call a secret meeting of prominent Democrats at his New York mansion on June 9, which laid down basic strategy and organized an informal committee to work for Cleveland behind the scenes.[9] This committee, greatly enlarged, met at Chicago three days before the convention and quietly set about to prevent the coalescence of the various anti-Cleveland groups. When the convention convened on June 21, Whitney believed that Cleveland could be nominated on the first ballot.[10] But he also gave some thought to the problem of reuniting the party after the convention. Thus he persuaded Boss Croker to announce that Tammany would support Cleveland if he was nominated.

[9] Parker, *Recollections of Cleveland,* pp. 156–158. Among those present were Judge William G. Ewing of Illinois, William E. Harrity of Pennsylvania, Samuel R. Haney of Rhode Island, Bradley B. Smalley of Vermont, Samuel E. Morse of Indiana, Don M. Dickinson of Michigan, William L. Wilson of West Virginia, William F. Vilas of Wisconsin, Francis L. Stetson of New York, and John E. Russell, Nathan Mathews, and Josiah Quincy of Massachusetts. Parker was secretary.

[10] Mark D. Hirsch, *William C. Whitney* (New York, 1948), pp. 390–397.

Among the favorite sons, Governor Horace Boies of Iowa, Senator Gorman of Maryland, and Senator John G. Carlisle of Kentucky were the most prominent, but their supporters were confused and ineffective. They were more interested in denouncing the other candidates than they were in pushing their own. Watterson, for instance, who supported Carlisle, seems to have done so chiefly out of antipathy to both Cleveland and Hill. "If we go [to New York] for a nominee," he had written, "we shall walk through a slaughter house into an open grave."[11] The Hill men, on the other hand, tried to convince the delegates that it was their duty to stand by the Empire State; perhaps they felt that New York had priority in the matter through having been the first state to hold its nominating convention. Edward Murphy, Jr., said that he hoped the Democracy of other states would not "humiliate the Democracy of the state of New York by nominating a resident of that state whom the organizations there are positive cannot be elected."[12] His appeal, however, fell on deaf ears; prudent politicians sensed that the Hill movement had collapsed.

The only hope of blocking Cleveland's nomination lay in persuading Hill to relinquish his votes to Gorman. Gorman approached Hill in his own behalf, to no avail; he then gave up his canvass. Even Tammany was ready to throw Hill aside, and was impatient with his persistence in what now appeared a hopeless cause. "If the New York delegation could have gotten away from its instructions and dropped Hill," Croker later declared, "we could have beaten Cleveland and named Gorman."[13] Even this, however, was never a very likely possibility; it represented wishful thinking on the part of Croker rather than an intelligent appraisal of the mood of the convention. As Whitney said shortly after the convention opened, "I can't keep the votes back. They tumble in at the windows as well as the doors."[14] He was now so certain of victory that he advised the Cleveland delegates from New York not to contest the seating of the Hill delegates.

With William L. Wilson in the chair, the convention finally got around to the business at hand. Nominating speeches were surprisingly brief; they lasted only from five in the afternoon until two in the

[11] James A. Barnes, *John G. Carlisle, Financial Statesman* (New York, 1931), p. 197.

[12] New York *World,* June 17, 1892.

[13] Lewis, *Croker,* p. 308.

[14] Quoted in Peck, *Twenty Years,* p. 291.

morning. They did not appear to change any votes.[15] At two, Bourke Cockran, Tammany's great orator, stood up to request a recess until the following morning. The delegates, however, demanded a vote. Cockran then mounted the platform and for forty-five minutes held the rapt attention of the convention, but his arguments that Cleveland's nomination would only bring defeat to the party made little impression. Having failed to get an adjournment, and having failed to move the delegates with oratory, Cockran sat down.[16] The vote was taken immediately. Cleveland received $617\frac{1}{3}$ votes, Hill 114 (72 from New York), Boies 103, Gorman $36\frac{1}{2}$, Adlai E. Stevenson $16\frac{2}{3}$, and Carlisle 14. A few votes were scattered among five others. Cleveland had triumphed resoundingly on the first ballot. As a sop to the silverites, Stevenson was nominated for Vice-President.

The platform was a happy blend of expediency and principle. It denounced the Force Bill, which had not passed the Senate and was not likely to, at great length—one-fourth of the document was devoted to a discussion of this iniquitous proposal. The platform also attacked the McKinley tariff as a "fraud," as robbery of the many for the "benefit of the few," and as "the culminating atrocity of class legislation," and reiterated the traditional Democratic belief that a tariff for anything but revenue was unconstitutional.[17] It characterized the Sherman Silver Purchase Act as a "cowardly makeshift" but did not explain why; the rest of the money plank included so many shades of economic and political opinion as to be altogether meaningless. Trusts and combinations were warmly denounced; civil-service reform was upheld in Cleveland's own well-known words, "Public office is a public trust." Finally the convention declared itself to be in favor of the restoration of public land illegally held by corporations and syndicates, restriction of the immigration of certain groups, promotion of public education, improvement of internal waterways, construction of a Nicaraguan canal, and enactment of laws ameliorating the condition of labor.[18]

The Republicans meanwhile had renominated Harrison without

[15] Festus P. Summers, *William L. Wilson and Tariff Reform* (New Brunswick, N.J., 1953), pp. 136–139.

[16] James E. McGarren, *Bourke Cockran* (New York, 1948), pp. 118–129.

[17] This last was inserted at the insistence of Watterson and Tom Johnson; Vilas, Whitney, and Cleveland himself favored a more indefinite tariff plank. Merrill, *Bourbon Leader,* pp. 160–161.

[18] Kirk H. Porter, *National Party Platforms* (New York, 1924), pp. 173–177.

enthusiasm. The President had earned a certain grudging respect from members of his party and even from a few intellectuals—Henry Adams went so far as to say that "Mr. Harrison was an excellent President, a man of ability and force; perhaps the best President the Republican Party had put forward since Lincoln's death. . . ." But the majority regarded him as cold and aloof, and, at times, almost contemptuous of his fellows.[19] Moreover, at least three powerful Republican bosses detested him. Senator Thomas Collier Platt of New York believed that Harrison had broken a bargain to give him a cabinet appointment in return for his support in 1888. Matthew S. Quay of Pennsylvania, who had been forced to resign as chairman of the Republican National Committee because he was under suspicion of embezzlement, felt that Harrison, in readily accepting his resignation, had failed to come to the defense of a friend. Thomas B. Reed said simply, "I never had but two personal enemies in my life. One of these, Mr. Harrison has pardoned out of the penitentiary and the other he has just appointed Collector of the Port of Portland."[20]

The consensus was that Harrison was an "iceberg"; Platt called him "as glacial as a Siberian stripped of his furs."[21] Few thought he could be elected if he was nominated.[22] Reed wrote in a letter to Lodge in 1891, "Well, perhaps he is as good a man to get licked with as anybody. This may sound like repetition and if it does I can only add that I hope he won't get a chance to be even licked. It would be too good for him."[23] But in spite of this widespread indifference, Harrison was nominated. A number of influences worked in his favor. He was President, in the first place, and could not very well be repudiated openly if he sought the nomination. In the second place, as President, he controlled the South through the patronage and the southern delegates alone gave him almost a majority in the convention. In the third place, his only possible rival, Blaine, failed to make a vigorous fight for the nomination.

Platt, Quay, and other leaders spread before Blaine the rosy picture

[19] For Adams's remark, see *The Education of Henry Adams* (Boston, 1918), p. 321.

[20] Thomas Collier Platt, *Autobiography* (New York, 1910), pp. 206–207; W. A. Robinson, *Thomas B. Reed* (New York, 1930), p. 161.

[21] Platt, *Autobiography*, p. 252.

[22] Ellis P. Oberholtzer, *A History of the United States since the Civil War* (New York, 1917–37), V, 176–177.

[23] Robinson, *Reed*, p. 283.

of an easy victory. Blaine, however, although he was only sixty-two in 1892, was in bad health; he suffered from gout and chronic Bright's disease. (He died a year later, on January 27, 1893.) His illness, in fact, had prevented him from exercising the full duties of his office during his last year as Secretary of State, and Harrison himself had had to take over the job. Blaine retained the position, however, and as a member of the cabinet could hardly work against Harrison for the nomination. These considerations influenced Blaine in February, 1892, to write to J. S. Clarkson, chairman of the Republican National Committee, that he "was not a candidate for the Presidency" and that his "name would not go before the Republican National Convention for the nomination." Many of his friends took this as definite, but others, including Clarkson, assumed that it was merely the usual disclaimer and continued their efforts.

On June 4, three days before the Republican convention met at Minneapolis, Blaine suddenly and without warning resigned from the cabinet, sending a cold and formal letter to the President. Harrison accepted it with equal coldness. Blaine's resignation has never been adequately explained. Surely illness was not the reason. Blaine had been ill for a year without resigning and now that Harrison's term was almost over could certainly have continued in office for a little longer. Was it because he wished to be free to campaign for the nomination? In that case he should have resigned much earlier; nor is it likely that so astute a politician as Blaine could have seriously believed that a candidacy of three days would bring him the prize. It is possible, however, that he was misled by the optimistic predictions of his friends. Quay, for example, insisted that he would be nominated on the first ballot.[24] In any event, the fat was in the fire. Blaine's son represented him at the convention, and his friends worked frantically for the nomination. The speeches in his behalf won great applause, but Harrison, in the end, got the votes. McKinley also received a number of votes, although his name was not put formally in nomination; Mark Hanna hoped that a good showing for McKinley in 1892 would prepare the way for his nomination in 1896. One ballot only was necessary

[24] George H. Knoles, *The Presidential Campaign and Election of 1892* (Palo Alto, 1942), pp. 52–56, discusses possible explanations of Blaine's resignation. The closest he comes to any conclusion is that "the available evidence indicates that Blaine did not have a genuine desire for the nomination." On Blaine's campaign see *ibid.*, pp. 49–70, and David S. Muzzey, *James G. Blaine* (New York, 1934), pp. 459–488.

to nominate Harrison, who received 535⅙ votes to 182⅚ for Blaine, 182 for McKinley, four for Reed, and one for Robert Lincoln of Illinois. The nomination was then made unanimous, and Whitelaw Reid of the New York *Tribune* was named by acclamation for Vice-President.

The platform was not a distinguished document. It reaffirmed "the American doctrine of protection" and "the Republican policy of reciprocity" without specifically endorsing the McKinley tariff. It declared for "the use of both gold and silver as standard money, with such restrictions and under such provisions, to be determined by legislation, as will secure the maintenance of the parity of values of the two metals, so that the purchasing and debt-paying power of the dollar, whether of silver, gold, or paper, shall be at all times equal." It reaffirmed the Monroe Doctrine and endorsed a Nicaraguan canal. Pensions for veterans were mentioned with approval. The Republicans also demanded extension of the free-delivery postal service and more stringent immigration laws. Asking that every citizen be allowed "to cast one free and unrestricted ballot in all public elections," they denounced "inhuman outrages perpetrated upon American citizens for political reasons in certain Southern States of the Union."[25]

Both Republicans and Democrats, it will be noted, straddled the currency issue in their platforms—an indication of their growing concern over agrarian demands for inflation. These demands, along with many others equally terrifying to conservatives, had now led to the creation of a national third party, the appearance of which threatened to undo all the efforts of the major parties to keep explosive issues out of politics. The Populists had been active since the elections of 1890. When the Northern Alliance met at Cincinnati in May, 1891, many of them were ready to organize a national party at once, but were restrained by the cautious General Weaver, who advised postponing the decision until the election year.[26] If Weaver had any thought of heading off the third-party movement, he was to be disappointed. The movement was irresistible, and the failure of either of the major parties to commit themselves on a single issue important to the agrarians brought it to a head in July, 1892, when the nominating conven-

[25] Porter, *National Party Platforms*, pp. 173–177.
[26] John D. Hicks, *The Populist Revolt* (Minneapolis, 1931), pp. 211–217; Russell B. Nye, *Midwestern Progressive Politics* (East Lansing, Mich., 1951), p. 71.

tion of the People's party met at Omaha. There, Ignatius Donnelly mounted the rostrum to read the stirring preamble to the Populist platform:

We meet in the midst of a nation brought to the verge of moral, political, and material ruin. Corruption dominates the ballot-box, the Legislatures, the Congress, and touches even the ermine of the bench. The people are demoralized; most of the States have been compelled to isolate the voters at the polling places to prevent universal intimidation and bribery. The newspapers are largely subsidized, homes covered with mortgages, labor impoverished, and the land concentrated in the hands of capitalists. The urban workmen are denied the right to organize for self-protection; imported pauperized labor beats down their wages, a hireling standing army, unrecognized by our laws, is established to shoot them down, and they are rapidly degenerating into European conditions. The fruits of the toil of millions are boldly stolen to build up colossal fortunes for the few, unprecedented in the history of mankind; and the possessors of these, in turn despise the Republic and endanger liberty. From the same prolific womb of governmental injustice we breed the two great classes—tramps and millionaires.

There followed a list of demands. Silver, "which has been accepted as coin since the dawn of history," should be freely coined at a ratio to gold of 16 to 1, and the circulating medium should in this way be increased to not less than $50 per capita. Postal savings banks should be established. The "unperverted Australian or secret ballot" should be adopted; the initiative and referendum put into practice; the President limited to a single term; Senators elected by direct vote of the people. The subtreasury plan, "or a better system," should be instituted. A graduated income tax should be levied. All means of transportation and communication should be owned and operated by the government; for "the railroad corporations will either own the people or the people must own the railroads." Finally, alien ownership of land should be prohibited and "all land now held by railroads and other corporations in excess of their actual needs . . . should be reclaimed by the government and held for actual settlers only."

Scenes of frantic rejoicing greeted the reading of the platform. An eastern journalist wrote:

And when that furious and hysterical arraignment of the present times, the incoherent intermingling of Jeremiah and Bellamy, the platform, was adopted, cheers and yells . . . rose like a tornado from four thousand throats and raged without cessation for thirty-four minutes, during which women

shrieked and wept, men embraced and kissed their neighbors, locked arms
. . . leaped upon tables and chairs in the ecstasy of their delirium. . . .[27]

In the camp-meeting atmosphere the delegates sang, to the tune of the
"Battle Hymn of the Republic,"

> They have stolen our money, have ravished our homes;
> With the plunder erected to Mammon a throne;
> They have fashioned a god, like the Hebrews of old,
> Then bid us bow down to their image of gold.[28]

After this, the business of nominating a candidate seemed almost
irrelevant. Many of the Populists would gladly have nominated Walter
Q. Gresham, a liberal Republican believed to favor free silver, an
opponent of railroad extortion, and a friend of organized labor.
Gresham, however, declined to run. (Later he declared for Cleveland
and, after Cleveland's election, became Secretary of State.) His refusal
left the field to General Weaver and Senator James H. Kyle of South
Dakota. Weaver, the more experienced politician, won the nomination
995 to 275. James G. Field of Virginia, a Confederate veteran who
had lost a leg in the war, was nominated for Vice-President.[29] Field
was an excellent campaigner who was respected by Southerners. As
Weaver himself was a Union veteran, the ticket was not without
sentimental appeal.

Weaver, fifty-nine years old in 1892, had been leading third-party
movements since the late seventies. Born in Ohio, he grew up on the
frontiers of Michigan and Iowa. He displayed an aptitude for public
speaking and accordingly attended law school in Cincinnati. *Uncle
Tom's Cabin* converted him to Republicanism, and he was active in
the organization of the party in Iowa. When the war came, he enlisted in the 2nd Iowa Infantry, was elected a first lieutenant, and
ended his career in the Army as colonel of his regiment; later he was
brevetted a brigadier general. After the war he found advancement
within the railroad-controlled Republican party more difficult than it
had been in the Army, especially in view of his opinions on the money
question. He thereupon seceded from the party and became a Green-
backer, in which capacity he was three times elected to Congress. In

[27] F. B. Tracy, "Menacing Socialism in the Western States," *Forum*, XXV
(May, 1893), 352.

[28] Eric F. Goldman, *Rendezvous with Destiny* (New York, 1952), p. 45.

[29] He attained the rank of major in the Confederate Army. *Who Was Who
in America* (Chicago, 1942), p. 395.

1880 he ran for President on the Greenback ticket. From 1880 to 1892 he continued to agitate for action against the railroads and for inflation. Utterly incorruptible, his commanding presence and fiery oratory made him an excellent campaigner. His only weakness was that he was a moderate and, like all moderates, often found himself in a position displeasing to all.[30]

In spite of the excitement which surrounded the launching of the People's party, the ensuing campaign was one of the quietest and least spectacular since the Civil War, perhaps because the major parties were so appalled by the presence of the Populists that they refrained, as if by mutual agreement, from attacking each other in their usual fashion. Both major candidates, for the first time in history, were Presidents and, if not immune from attack on that account, at least had to be treated with respect. Nor did either care to drag the other into a contest of personalities. "I desire this campaign to be one of Republicanism and not one of personalities," said Harrison, and his words set the tone of the campaign.[31]

Senator Cullom, writing almost twenty years later, held that the campaign "was entirely fought out on the tariff issue."[32] If this was so, it was through no choice of the Republicans, who had already found the McKinley Act a liability in the campaign of 1890. The Democrats, however, insisted on making an issue of it, and the Republicans were obliged to come feebly to its defense. Using statistics from the unpublished Aldrich Report, they attempted to show that over a long period of time wages had increased while prices of manufactures had fallen. Unfriendly critics noted that they devoted most of their attention, however, to the period before the enactment of the McKinley tariff.[33] The fact remained that certain retail prices had risen during the last two years, nor could the Republicans successfully answer the argument that all prices might have been lower without the high tariffs.[34] As Cullom mournfully wrote to Harrison a few days after the election, "The people sat down upon the McKinley Tariff Bill

[30] Fred Haynes, *James Baird Weaver* (Iowa City, 1913); see also the sketch by John D. Hicks in *Dictionary of American Biography*, XIX, 568–570.
[31] Quoted in Peck, *Twenty Years*, p. 297.
[32] Shelby M. Cullom, *Fifty Years of Public Service* (Chicago, 1911), p. 257.
[33] See Nelson W. Aldrich, "The McKinley Act and the Cost of Living," *Forum*, XIV (Oct., 1892), 242–254.
[34] "Wholesale Prices, 1890–1915," *Bulletin of the United States Bureau of Labor Statistics, No. 200* (Washington, 1916), pp. 14–19.

two years ago, and they have never gotten up. They were thoroughly imbued with the feeling that the party did not do right in revising the tariff up instead of down. They beat us for it in '90 and now again."[35]

If the tariff was the leading issue, it was not the only one. Resentment against the lavish expenditures of the billion-dollar Congress persisted, and the Democrats had no trouble in exploiting it by reminding the voters that the Republicans, if they were so eager to reduce the surplus, could have done so by relieving the taxpayers. The Republicans suffered again, as they had suffered in 1890, on account of the Sherman Silver Purchase Act; nor was the Force Bill any more popular than it had been two years before. All the issues on which the Republicans had been defeated in the congressional elections now served to weaken them in the presidential campaign.

More recent events also injured the Republican cause. Late in June, 3,800 workers in the Carnegie steel mills at Homestead, Pennsylvania, walked out on strike when they failed to reach an agreement with Henry C. Frick, chairman of the Carnegie Company, on wages and working conditions. Frick, an implacable opponent of organized labor, hired 300 Pinkerton detectives—the "standing army" referred to in the Populist platform—to guard the plant while he broke the strike. On the morning of July 6, 1892, the detectives were loaded on barges near Pittsburgh to be towed up the Monongahela River to Homestead. The strikers, however, learned of this movement and when the Pinkertons arrived stood ready to give armed resistance. A pitched battle ensued. Three detectives and ten strikers were killed; thirty detectives and an indefinite number of strikers were wounded. Deserted by their tug and stranded in the river, the Pinkertons surrendered. The governor sent in militia; even then, the strikers held on until autumn. Their sufferings attracted widespread public sympathy, which not even an attempt on Frick's life by a New York anarchist, Alexander Berkman, entirely dissipated. Republican leaders urged Carnegie and Frick to recognize the union and come to an agreement; they refused. In the end the strike failed utterly. It broke the Amalgamated Association of Iron and Steel Workers, an organization of 24,000 men and one of the strongest unions in the country, and destroyed unionism in the steel industry for nearly fifty years.[36]

[35] Cullom, *Fifty Years,* p. 259.
[36] Henry David, "Upheaval at Homestead," in Daniel Aaron (ed.), *America in Crisis* (New York, 1952), pp. 133–170; John R. Commons *et al., History*

The Democrats attempted to draw a connection between the troubles at Homestead and the tariff. Daniel W. Voorhees of Indiana declared that "labor riots, battles, blood-stained fields . . . have sprung alone from the doctrine of protection." Cleveland in his acceptance speech of July 20 said:

[American workers] are still told the tale, oft repeated in spite of its demonstrated falsity, that the existing Protective tariff is a boon to them, and that under its beneficent operation their wages must increase, while, as they listen, scenes are enacted in the very abiding place of high Protection that mock the hopes of toil and attest the tender mercy the workingman receives from those made selfish and sordid by unjust governmental favoritism.[37]

The tariff, the Democrats insisted, did not protect the worker; it ground him down, while at the same time increasing the price of everything he had to buy. Democratic orators refrained from analyzing in any detail, however, the process by which the workingman was ground down by high tariffs. They did not, for instance, dwell on the relation of tariffs to monopoly. They left that to the Populists. There were too many monopolists in the Democratic party to make any detailed examination of the economics of the tariff question. The party speakers stuck to the issue of the high cost of living, an issue of tried and tested efficacy.

Other strikes during the summer—of silver miners at Coeur d'Alene, of railway switchmen in Buffalo, of soft-coal miners in Tennessee— redounded to the discredit of the Republicans. All of these strikes were defeated with the aid of federal or state troops. In each case the Democrats insisted that the McKinley tariff was ultimately responsible.

Victory fell to the Democrats not only because of the Republicans' vulnerability to criticism from all quarters but also through the Democrats' own strenuous efforts, particularly those of Whitney. The memory of 1888, in which New York and Indiana turned the balance against Cleveland, stirred Whitney to especially vigorous action in those states. Fearing that Cleveland would lose his own state without the wholehearted support of the machine, Whitney persuaded his

---

of Labor in the United States (New York, 1919), II, 495–496. Burton J. Hendrick, *The Life of Andrew Carnegie* (Garden City, 1932), I, 365–413, and George Harvey, *Henry Clay Frick* (New York, 1928), pp. 106–145, give the employers' side.

[37] Democratic National Committee, *Campaign Textbook of the Democratic Party* (New York, 1892), p. 17.

chief to reconcile his differences with Tammany. Cleveland reluctantly consented to meet Murphy, Croker, and boss William F. Sheehan of Buffalo at Whitney's house, but he would make no binding commitments; rather than do that, he said, he would withdraw from the race. The soft-spoken Whitney managed to smooth ruffled tempers, however, and Croker stood firm behind the national ticket.[38] Even Hill accepted the inevitable and announced his support of Cleveland. In spite of all this, Cleveland preferred to think that he was handicapped by the enmity of the machines. "It's a funny thing," he wrote, "for a man to be running for the Presidency with all the politicians against him."[39] Certainly there was no enthusiasm among the politicians for Cleveland, but neither did they wish to alienate him in the event of his winning the election.

Politicians may have had no love for Cleveland, but, to judge from the election returns, the voters had. They gave him 5,556,543 votes, and Harrison only 5,175,582. Cleveland polled 277 electoral votes, Harrison 145.[40] The geographical distribution of the vote surprised nearly everyone, including Cleveland himself. With the Republicans apathetic and dispirited, he had been expected to carry the "doubtful" states of New York, New Jersey, Connecticut, and Indiana, but nobody believed that he could win the Republican states of Illinois, Wisconsin, and California. The Democratic National Campaign Committee, in fact, did not even send funds to the Middle West, assuming that Cleveland's only hope of victory lay in the East.[41] Yet Cleveland not only carried Illinois, Wisconsin, and California, but missed carrying Ohio by only a thousand votes. His victory had reached landslide proportions.

The Populists had not held the balance of power in the election, as the more sanguine of their leaders had hoped, but they probably contributed to the magnitude of Cleveland's victory by drawing votes from the Republicans. All told, the Populists polled slightly more than a million votes. They carried five states—Kansas, North Dakota,

[38] Nevins, *Cleveland,* pp. 494–498; McElroy, *Cleveland,* I, 347–354.

[39] Cleveland to Bissell, July 24, 1892, Nevins, *Letters of Cleveland,* p. 296. Harrison had the same impression with regard to his own candidacy. On election day he noted that neither candidate had aroused "enthusiasm with the active men in politics." Quoted in C. R. Williams, *The Life of Rutherford Birchard Hayes* (Boston, 1914), II, 376.

[40] Edward Stanwood, *A History of the Presidency* (Boston, 1916), I, 515–518.

[41] Merrill, *Bourbon Democracy,* p. 230.

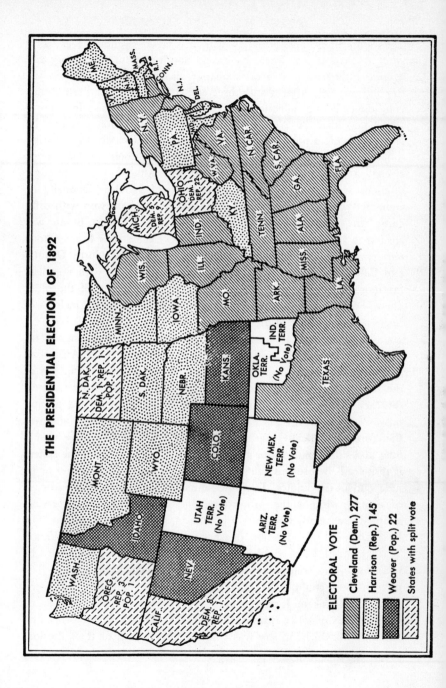

THE PRESIDENTIAL ELECTION OF 1892

ELECTORAL VOTE

Cleveland (Dem.) 277
Harrison (Rep.) 145
Weaver (Pop.) 22
States with split vote

Colorado, Idaho, and Nevada—with a total of twenty-two electoral votes. In Minnesota, Iowa, Nebraska, South Dakota, Wyoming, and Montana they made a good showing; all of these states fell to the Republicans only after a stiff three-cornered fight.[42] But the Populist vote alone did not adequately reflect the profound desire for reform which pervaded the West and South. In the South, for instance, the Populists made a poor showing, but the southern Democracy was itself shot through and through with Populism. In Illinois the Democrats elected a governor, but the governor was Altgeld, whose political opinions were no less radical than those of Ignatius Donnelly or General Weaver. In Nebraska, where the Republicans won with difficulty, an obscure Democrat named William Jennings Bryan was elected to Congress. Although the Populists elected only five senators, ten representatives, and three governors (in Kansas, North Dakota, and Colorado), the number of those who sympathized with Populism far more than they sympathized with the conservation of the older parties was far greater. Moderate men could not suppress feelings of uneasiness in the face of these painful facts.

Quite apart from its outcome, the election of 1892 was significant in another respect; it was the first election in which the Australian ballot was widely used. Thirty-three states adopted it, without any of the dire results that had sometimes been predicted. In order to grasp the fact that the Australian ballot was something new and an improvement over previous methods of conducting elections, and was therefore energetically resisted and despised and secured only after a long and surprisingly bitter struggle, it is necessary to recall the system it displaced. Before this time ballots were printed up by parties or by independent candidates, distributed outside the polling place, and cast, of course, without the protection of secrecy. That such a system adapted itself easily to fraud, intimidation, and bribery is obvious. The foreman could take due note of who voted for whom and who did not. The ward politician could ascertain which of his clients ought to be recipients of his continuing favor and which ought to be ignored. The political boss could know at a glance whether bargains were being fulfilled or broken. If any doubts of desirability of reform persisted in the minds of sober citizens, the elections of 1888 in New York and Indiana, in which bribery was rife, disabused them of their illusions

[42] Hicks, *Populist Revolt*, pp. 238–273.

and stirred them to action. Cleveland's speech in Boston late in 1889, in which he strongly urged adoption of the Australian ballot, gave added impetus to the movement for reform.

After the reform was accomplished, as is so often the case, many of those who had strenuously opposed it adapted themselves to it without difficulty, even conceding that it had been necessary all along. The Cincinnati *Commercial Gazette,* for instance, an opponent of the secret ballot, commented after the elections of November, 1891, in which it had been used for the first time in Ohio:

Our citizens can be congratulated on the general conduct of the momentous affairs of the day, offering so happy a contrast to the methods of a few years ago, when howling mobs surrounded many of the voting places, fighting within themselves, pulling and pushing voters about, and shamefully mal-treating some; when even police officers took a hand in unlawful and unruly proceedings, and clubbed and dragged unoffending citizens to the station houses in order to prevent them from voting. A reaction to better times has come. The political bummer and thug has been relegated to the background, where he is made to behave himself, while good citizenship, always the majority power when it chooses to assert itself, has come to the front.[43]

If the Populist successes were disheartening to men like Cleveland, the success which attended the introduction of the secret ballot was, in its smaller way, heartening; the reflection that good citizenship, "when it chooses to assert itself," would prove to be the majority power was reassuring in a year in which the masses were so unruly. Nevertheless, it was evident that to rely on the good citizenship of men like Jerry Simpson and Ben Tillman would be to clutch at straws. If the agitation for free silver and subtreasuries and government ownership of the railroads was to be turned back, strenuous efforts would be required on the part of conservatives, and with this thought in mind Cleveland turned to his first task—the choice of a cabinet. In this he seems to have encountered more than the usual difficulties; he complained in January, "I cannot get the men I want to help me."[44]

After much deliberation, he offered the position of Secretary of State to Walter Gresham. Gresham was reported to be not unkindly

[43] Quoted in Joseph B. Bishop, "The Secret Ballot in Thirty-Three States," *Forum,* XII (Jan., 1892), 594; see also Charles C. Allen, "Electoral Reform Legislation," *ibid.,* III (Dec., 1890), 91–96, and Charles A. Beard, *American Government and Politics* (New York, 1911), pp. 675–685.

[44] Nevins, *Cleveland,* p. 511.

disposed toward free silver, but he was a Republican who had bolted his party to support Cleveland and it was only politic to recognize his services in the campaign. So far as the conduct of foreign policy was concerned, Gresham's appointment was not a particularly happy one. A man of sound judgment, he was at the same time tactless and absent-minded. He also suffered from poor health, and was to die in office in 1895. His death was a deep blow to Cleveland.[45] To the Treasury Cleveland appointed John G. Carlisle, three-time Speaker of the House and senator from Kentucky. According to his biographer, Carlisle "must be ranked as the outstanding statesman of the South in that long stretch of years between the end of the Civil War and the end of the century."[46] Keen of intelligence, warm and kind in disposition, he was both popular and respected in Congress. What was more to the point, he was a sound-money man—to the dismay of many of his early friends, who had drifted into the other camp. Carlisle himself had once favored cheap money; when taxed with inconsistency, he replied sternly that he would rather be right than consistent.[47]

Richard Olney of Massachusetts, who became Cleveland's Attorney General and later his Secretary of State, was practically unknown at the time of his appointment. A corporation lawyer, Olney did not please liberals by his presence in the cabinet, nor was he to please them by his actions. Hot-tempered, pugnacious, and stubborn, Olney often exerted an unfortunate influence on Cleveland. The appointment to the War Department of Daniel S. Lamont, Cleveland's private secretary during his first term, was also criticized. More closely tied to Wall Street than any other member of the cabinet, he was criticized, and not unjustly, as the errand boy of magnates and tycoons. Two representatives of the "New South" served in the cabinet. Hoke Smith, owner of the Atlanta *Journal,* was made Secretary of the Interior and Hilary A. Herbert of Alabama, a Confederate veteran, Secretary of the Navy. The former had been of use in opposing the Hill movement in Georgia. The latter was known to represent the conservative elements in the South; he was "sound" on both the tariff and the currency. J. Sterling Morton, who was appointed Secretary of Agriculture, was also a respected repository of financial wisdom, having battled the

[45] Matilda Gresham, *Life of Walter Q. Gresham* (Chicago, 1919), II, 669–818, covers his career as Secretary of State.

[46] James A. Barnes, *John G. Carlisle* (New York, 1931), p. 517.

[47] *Ibid.,* pp. 513–522.

silverites to the death in Nebraska.[48] Strangely enough, he showed little interest in dispensing the patronage that fell to him as a member of the cabinet, but a good deal of interest in his job. His concern in reforesting the almost treeless western part of Nebraska, for instance, led to the institution in 1872 of Arbor Day, which is still observed in most states on the day of his birthday, April 22.

Cleveland's cabinet contained men of real ability, but with the exception of Carlisle it was not a distinguished one. With some changes, it perhaps improved before the end of Cleveland's term. After the death of Gresham, Olney, a more energetic man, was made Secretary of State and his post was filled by Judson Harmon, an able Ohio lawyer. In the same year Wilson S. Bissell retired from the Postmastership and was succeeded by William L. Wilson, who had led the fight for tariff reform in the House. It was while Wilson was Postmaster General that rural free delivery was instituted.[49] What chiefly distinguished Cleveland's cabinet, both before and after these changes, was not character or intellect so much as an unbending conservatism on economic issues. No representative of the agrarian wing of the party gained admittance to the select circle of Cleveland's advisers; Gresham was the only man tainted with the philosophy of radicalism, and he was put in the State Department where he could do little harm. No representative of labor sat in the cabinet, no man who even remotely sympathized with labor except in the abstract sense in which Cleveland referred to the "hopes of toil" which had been dashed at Homestead by the McKinley tariff. The cabinet, whatever its other merits, could hardly be said to represent the American people.

Nor was there any suggestion in Cleveland's brief inaugural, delivered on a chilly March day with the ground white with snow, that many Americans were becoming deeply dissatisfied with their lot and that a million of them had recently voted for the candidates of the People's party. Cleveland merely reiterated the principles which had long guided him. He promised to continue the work of civil service reform. He pledged his party to economy, honesty, and good government and declared that it would avoid all forms of paternalism from the protective tariff to "reckless pension expenditure" and the "de-

[48] Merrill, *Bourbon Democracy,* pp. 241–244. See also James C. Olson, *J. Sterling Morton* (Lincoln, Neb., 1942).

[49] See above, pp. 67–68. One other change occurred in 1896, when Hoke Smith, whose state had endorsed Bryan, went home to support him. David L. Francis of Missouri finished his term.

moralizing madness for spoils." He would restrain monopolies so far as the federal government had the power to do so. Condemning "protection for protection's sake," he promised tariff reform "undertaken wisely and without heedless vindictiveness." Finally he gave it as his opinion that nothing was more vital to American "supremacy as a nation" than " a sound and stable currency." Any danger to it "should at once arouse to activity the most enlightened statesmanship."

From these remarks conservatives could take heart; the return of the Democrats would lead to no rash and headlong descent into experimentation and novelty. As Henry Clay Frick had written to Carnegie shortly after Cleveland's election, "I am very sorry for President Harrison, but I cannot see that our interests are going to be affected one way or the other by the change in administration." To which Carnegie replied, "Well we have nothing to fear and perhaps it is best. People will now think the Protected Manfrs. will be attended to and quit agitating. Cleveland is a pretty good fellow. Off for Venice tomorrow."[50]

[50] Harvey, *Frick*, p. 157.

CHAPTER 7

Depression, Bonds, and Tariffs

"THERE has never been a time in our history," said Benjamin Harrison in his last message to Congress, "when work was so abundant, or when wages were as high, whether measured by the currency in which they are paid, or by their power to supply the necessaries and comforts of life."[1] Within months the worst financial panic in years broke over the country. Ten days before Harrison left office the Philadelphia and Reading Railroad, with no warning, suddenly went bankrupt. The volume of sales on the day of its collapse was the greatest in the history of the New York Stock Exchange. The air was filled with anxiety. The unfortunate Cleveland was installed in the White House. Then on May 5 the National Cordage Company failed in spectacular fashion, shortly after paying its regular dividend. The market collapsed abruptly. Banks called in their loans; the stream of credit dried to a trickle. Businesses failed daily. The Erie went down in July, the Northern Pacific in August, the Union Pacific in October, the Atchison in December.

Before the year was out, 500 banks and nearly 16,000 businesses had declared themselves bankrupt.

The month of August [wrote the *Commercial and Financial Chronicle*] will long remain memorable . . . in our industrial history. Never before has there been such a sudden and striking cessation of industrial activity. Nor was any section of the country exempt from the paralysis. Mills, factories, furnaces, mines nearly everywhere shut down in large numbers, and commerce and enterprise were arrested in an extraordinary degree . . . and hundreds of thousands of men thrown out of employment.

[1] J. D. Richardson, *Messages and Papers of the Presidents* (Washington, 1897), IX, 309.

By September, according to the *Banker's Magazine* of London, the American people were "in the throes of a fiasco unprecedented even in their broad experience." "Ruin and disaster run riot over the land."[2]

The panic broadened into a major depression. In the following year railroad traffic for the second time in history suffered an absolute decline. Railroad construction fell off drastically, reaching its lowest point since 1851. By 1895, new mileage shrank to 1,800 as compared to 4,700 in 1892. By the end of June, 1894, more than 40,818 miles and one-fourth of the capitalization of American railroads were in the hands of receivers. Three-fifths of railroad stock paid no dividends. Investment in all businesses declined sharply; new stock issues on the New York Exchange dropped from $100 million in 1892 to less than $37 million in 1894. Consumption of consumer goods fell in 1894 to 75 per cent of capacity, and wages and prices tumbled after consumption, both dropping at least 10 per cent. Unemployment mounted alarmingly, although in the absence of accurate statistics it was difficult to know exactly how many workers were out of a job at any given time. *Bradstreet's* estimated the unemployed in August, 1893, as about 850,000, but Richard T. Ely put the figure at 2 million. Gompers in December put it at 3 million. During the worst months of 1894 it is safe to conclude that as much as 20 per cent of the labor force was unemployed. In New York the police at one time estimated that 67,280 were out of work and 20,000 more were not only out of work but homeless and vagrant. In Chicago, more than 100,000 were jobless during the winter of 1893–94.[3]

[2] Ida M. Tarbell, *The Nationalizing of Business, 1878–1898* (New York, 1936), pp. 228–231; Samuel Rezneck, "Unemployment, Unrest, and Relief in the United States during the Depression of 1893–97," *Journal of Political Economy,* LXI (Aug., 1953), 324–325.

[3] Charles Hoffman, "The Depression of the Nineties," *Journal of Economic History,* XVI (June, 1956), 138–141, 152; Joseph A. Schumpeter, *Business Cycles* (New York, 1939), pp. 341–342, 388–389; Simon Kuznets, *National Product since 1869* (New York, 1946), p. 231; Rezneck, "Depression of 1893–97," pp. 327–328. In a longer study, "The Depression of the Nineties— An Economic History" (Ph.D dissertation, Columbia University, 1954), pp. 102–116, Hoffman estimates the total labor force, excluding agriculture, public service, and the professions, at 14½ million, and the number of unemployed during the winter of 1893–94 at from 2,450,000 to 2,750,000—that is, from 17 to 19 per cent of the labor force. He estimates the unemployed during the second trough of the depression, 1896–97, as 15 per cent of the labor force. See also Leah H. Feder, *Unemployment Relief in Periods of Depression* (New York, 1936), p. 79; Carlos C. Closson, Jr., "The Unemployed in American

The year 1895 brought a brief improvement, but in 1896 a second shock caused a further decline, and economic activity plunged to 75 per cent of capacity in 1897. By that time the number of bank failures since 1893 had reached 800. "Men died like flies under the strain," wrote Henry Adams, "and Boston grew suddenly old, haggard and thin."[4] Stock prices reached their lowest point in August, 1896, when they stood at 68 per cent of the level of August, 1892. Not until 1898 did recovery begin to be apparent; in that year the drain of gold from the country, continuous since 1889, finally ceased, and consumption of perishable goods regained its 1892 level. Not until 1901 or 1902 could the country be said to have been functioning normally, and even then many areas still suffered from the lingering effects of the depression.[5]

There was no agreement as to the causes of the depression; one's explanation depended on one's political predilections. Conservatives agreed with Cleveland in attributing it to the Sherman Silver Purchase Act, which they believed had undermined business confidence in the gold standard.[6] Beyond this, they blamed radical attacks on property. E. L. Godkin of *The Nation*, William Graham Sumner of Yale, and J. Lawrence Laughlin of Chicago University elaborated this view at great length. Godkin believed that the depression was the work

Cities," *Quarterly Journal of Economics*, VIII (Jan., 1894), 169–217, 257–258; Paul H. Douglas, *Real Wages in the United States, 1890–1926* (Boston, 1930), pp. 440, 447; Alvin H. Hanson, "Industrial Class Alignments in the United States," *Quarterly Publications of the American Statistical Association*, XVII (Dec., 1920), 417–422.

[4] *The Education of Henry Adams* (Boston, 1918), p. 338.

[5] There is no adequate full-length account of the causes of the depression of 1893–97. W. Jett Lauck, *The Causes of the Panic of 1893* (Boston, 1907), the standard work, is badly dated; so is Frank P. Weberg, *The Background of the Panic of 1893* (Washington, 1929). Far superior are the more recent treatments by Hoffman, "Depression of the Nineties," and Rezneck, "Depression of 1893–97"; but Rezneck does not treat the causes of the depression. Hoffman's dissertation, "The Depression of the Nineties—An Economic History," is more extensive, but is available only on microfilm. See also O. M. W. Sprague, *History of Crisis under the National Banking System* (Washington, 1910), pp. 153–216; Alexander Dana Noyes, *Forty Years of American Finance* (New York, 1909), *passim;* and Frank S. Philbrick, "The Mercantile Conditions of the Crises of 1893," Nebraska University, *University Studies*, II, No. 4 (1902).

[6] See Andrew Carnegie, "A Word to Wage Earners," *North American Review*, CLVII (Sept., 1893), 354; Charles S. Smith (president of the New York Chamber of Commerce) *et al.*, "The Business Outlook," *North American Review*, CLVII (Oct., 1893), 385–398; Henry C. Ager, "Causes of the Present Business Depression," *American Journal of Politics*, IV (Mar., 1894), 248.

of "socialists and labor agitators" who had been "filling the bellies of the poor with the east wind." "The craze against property that has been sweeping through the country," he said, sapped the national morale; what the country needed was respect for property, character, and authority. For Laughlin, the depression was "the inevitable manifestation of an idea strongly held by under-educated men."[7]

Labor leaders and agrarians took a very different view of the matter. Samuel Gompers laid the depression to capitalistic greed. For years, he said, "Production, production, production, faster, greater, was the impulse, the thought, and motive of the caiptalist class," even as the rights of the laboring man were being forgotten. The moral was clear: if labor's demands had been heeded, "it is safe to say that the panic of 1893 would have been averted, deferred, and certainly less intense."[8] The agrarian radicals likewise blamed the depression on the capitalists, but they emphasized the money issue, arguing that it was the failure to introduce free silver coinage that had caused the crisis.[9] It was left to Henry Adams, however, to carry the theme of conspiracy to its extreme; the panic, he wrote, was the result of a "dark, mysterious, crafty, rapacious, and tyrannical power . . . to rob and oppress and enslave the people."[10]

These were by no means the only explanations offered; everybody had his own interpretation of what had happened, in which his particular enemies were exclusively to blame. The Democrats blamed the depression on the Republicans, noting that Republican laws were still in effect when the panic began. The Republicans accused the Democrats of having frightened the business community with their reckless talk of lowering the tariff.[11] Only a few contemporary commentators penetrated the fog of political prejudice to show that the events of 1893 were part of a longer development and that no single party or program could be held responsible for a failure in which the whole country was directly or indirectly involved.[12]

---

[7] Quoted in Rezneck, "Depression of 1893–97," pp. 339–340.

[8] Quoted *ibid.*, p. 327.

[9] See, e.g., William M. Stewart, "Misrepresentation in the Senate," *North American Review*, CLVII (Nov., 1893), 513–522.

[10] W. C. Ford (ed.), *Letters of Henry Adams* (Boston, 1938), II, 30.

[11] William E. Russell, "Political Causes of Business Depression," *North American Review*, CLVII (Dec., 1893), 641–652; Thomas B. Reed, "The Political Situation," *ibid.*, CLVII (Sept., 1893), 256–257.

[12] See, e.g., Frederic C. Howe, "Commercial Depressions and Business Cycles,"

In retrospect it is possible to distinguish a number of deeper causes of the depression. In the first place, many industries, in particular the railroads, had expanded their activities far beyond the market demand. During the 1880's almost 74,000 miles of railroad were built, more than during any previous decade. Much of this expansion was dictated not by any reasonable estimate of traffic possibilities but by the pressure of competition; each road recklessly and hastily threw up lines that were not needed, through miles and miles of uninhabited wilderness, merely to insure that another road would not claim the territory first. Inevitably enterprises built on dreams and credit had to collapse; when the dreams failed to materialize, credit also evaporated. The fortunes of other industries, like steel, were bound up with those of the railroads, and when the railroads began to fail one by one in the summer of 1893, the failure quickly spread to other sectors of the economy; thirty-two steel corporations failed during the first six months of 1893. Economic activity in the United States had reached a new stage of interdependence, and a weakness in the very heart of the system unavoidably enfeebled the rest.[13] The same conditions characterized banking. Formerly failures in one part of the country had not necessarily caused failures in other parts. By 1890, however, banking had become centralized in New York, where a large proportion of the country's reserve capital inexorably gravitated. Moreover, these reserves had been freely used in speculation. When stocks fell, many city banks fell with them; and since the city banks held up to 60 per cent of the reserves of other banks throughout the country, the panic, once it had seized New York, almost immediately became nationwide.[14]

Like the greater depression of the 1930's, that of 1893 was preceded by several years of agricultural depression. In 1880 agriculture produced 26 per cent of the national wealth; in 1890 it produced only 21 per cent.[15] Such a decline in the value of agricultural commodities

American Journal of Politics, V (Nov., 1894), 449–460; George R. Gibson, "The Financial Excitement and Its Causes," Forum, XV (June, 1893), 483–493.

[13] See Schumpeter, Business Cycles, pp. 341–343, 388–389. The only industry which underwent any notable expansion in this period was the street-railway business, in which there was an increase of 330 per cent for the decade.

[14] George W. Dowrie, "Money and Banking since 1860," in Harold F. Williamson (ed.), The Growth of the American Economy (New York, 1944), p. 643.

[15] Tarbell, Nationalizing of Business, p. 220.

represented a considerable decline in purchasing power which was not made up elsewhere—what was lost in agriculture was made up in the expansion of industries which were already overexpanded. The farmer's real income had declined steadily since income, as we have seen, had declined steadily since 1888. When he pleaded for relief, he was told, in effect, that his troubles were no concern of the rest of the nation. The prolonged depression of the nineties gave the lie to that opinion. The fact was that agriculture, like practically everything else, had expanded rapidly in the 1880's, compelling expansion in many other industries as well. The railroads, the manufacture of farm machinery, and many other businesses thrived on the expansion of agriculture and could hardly help to escape eventual involvement in its decline.

Without these existing weaknesses in the American economy, it would not have been so vulnerable to blows which it began to receive from abroad. In 1890 the failure of Baring Brothers in London resulted in considerable liquidation of American securities by European holders. It caused a minor panic in this country, from which the Stock Exchange quickly recovered. European capital continued to leave the country, however; between 1890 and 1896, European repatriation of American investments averaged about $60 million a year. The withdrawal of foreign capital at a time when American industries were overexpanded was probably the immediate cause of the crash. In itself, however, the panic in Europe would not have caused a major depression in America. It merely exposed weaknesses that were already present.

None of these influences—the overexpansion of railroads and other industries, the weakness of the banking system, the agricultural depression and the decline of purchasing power, the European panic—appealed to the American people in 1893 as offering an explanation of their difficulties. Discussion fastened instead on the money question. No doubt the Democrats were correct in pointing out that widespread speculation in bullion and silver stocks had followed the enactment of the Sherman Silver Purchase Act, and that, together with the rush to purchase commodities in expectation of rising prices under the McKinley tariff, caused a severe money stringency. They were doubtless correct in claiming that the purchase of great quantities of silver had made conservative businessmen tremble for the safety of the gold standard. Where they erred was in supposing that these facts told the whole story. Cleveland, addressing a special session of Congress on August 8, 1893, reviewed the "unfortunate plight" in which the nation found itself and roundly declared, "I believe these things are principally chargeable to Congressional legislation touching the purchase and coinage of silver by the General Government." Accordingly, he asked for "prompt repeal" of the Silver Purchase Act of 1890.[16] This, it appeared, was the only immediate answer to the depression which the administration had to offer. That it was not enough the history of the next four years was to make painfully clear.

Cleveland had been under constant pressure ever since his election to deal with the money problem. His political friends, backed by leading financiers like Henry Villard, August Belmont, James Stillman, and J. P. Morgan himself, had repeatedly urged him to call a special session of Congress immediately after his inauguration to repeal the Sherman Act. Cleveland, partly on the advice of Carlisle, Gresham, and Lamont, declined at first to do so. He did not wish to seem to yield to pressure from Wall Street; nor did he believe that the country was ready for repeal.[17] He contented himself with announcing on April 23 that parity between gold and silver would at all costs be maintained.[18] When that announcement brought only momentary relief to the business community, Cleveland at last consented, on June 30, to call Congress into special session, to meet on the following August 7.

On the day following his call for a special session, Cleveland underwent an operation to remove a malignant growth from the roof of his mouth. The operation was performed in secrecy in New York Harbor on the yacht of Cleveland's friend, Elias C. Benedict. Although the surgery involved the removal of his entire left upper jaw, it required no external incision; nor were his eyes or his speech affected. The secret, therefore, was kept; it was two months before any outsider knew what had happened.[19] The operation was successful, and Cleveland shortly returned to his duties with an artificial jaw of vulcanized rubber, but otherwise intact. The reasons for the secrecy in which the entire business was clothed are clear enough. In the chaotic early months of the depression, the gold-standard men looked to Cleveland

---

[16] Richardson, *Messages and Papers,* IX, 401–403; *Congressional Record,* XXV, 53rd Cong., 1st sess., 205–206.

[17] Allan Nevins, *Grover Cleveland* (New York, 1932), pp. 523–524.

[18] Noyes, *American Finance,* pp. 186–187.

[19] Nevins, *Cleveland,* pp. 528–533.

as their only hope. Without his determination and without his control of the patronage, repeal of the silver legislation could not be effected, especially in view of the fact that the Vice-President, Adlai E. Stevenson, was notoriously soft on the money question. Everything seemed to hang by a thread. The news that Cleveland was even ill might hearten the radicals; the news that he was undergoing a major operation might endanger the very survival of the country.

When Congress convened in August, it was immediately clear that opinion on the silver question conformed to sectional rather than to party lines, and that party discipline would be difficult to maintain. During the extended debate on the administration's proposal to repeal the Sherman Act, southern and western members of both parties rose to denounce the outrage; Easterners of both parties rallied to the support of the administration. The arguments on both sides were by now thoroughly familiar. The agrarians reiterated their thesis that they were the victims of a sinister conspiracy of international bankers bent on plundering the people. They recapitulated the history of the last twenty-five years in support of their theory. Down to 1873, they argued, both gold and silver had served as money. Money had been plentiful and prices high. The farmer borrowed money to expand his operations, assuming that good times would continue. Then when nobody was looking Congress perpetrated the dastardly "crime of '73" and demonetized silver. The result, highly advantageous to the creditor, was disastrous to the debtor. The volume of money dwindled; prices fell. The debtor was asked to pay his loans in money of far greater value than he had borrowed, money which he did not possess; he mortgaged his house, his barns, his stock; he sank at last into tenancy, poverty, and despair. Even the act of 1890 had brought little relief, but what little relief it had brought the "bloated aristocracy" of Wall Street and the British bankers now proposed to take away. And as if all this were not enough, the East now had the effrontery to ask the West for help in furthering its vicious designs. It asked the West, in the words of Richard Bland, "to lay the blighting hand of confiscation upon the millions of people inhabiting that country to turn them out as tramps upon the land, merely to satisfy the greed of British gold."[20] As for the argument that silver purchases had caused the depression and that to end them would cure it, nothing, the West

[20] *Congressional Record*, 53rd Cong., 1st sess. (August 11, 1893), p. 252.

insisted, could be further from the truth. The prosperity of the rest of the country would never be restored so long as farmers went in rags.

Whatever the particular merits of this argument, the sincerity of its advocates could hardly be questioned. Nor could anyone successfully challenge the accuracy of their account of conditions in the West and South. The three-hour speech of William Jennings Bryan, easily the most stirring of the debate, left even his opponents with the sense that there was perhaps more to be said for his position than they had commonly assumed. After a long discussion of the problem, Bryan closed with words which were to become the keynote of the great struggle of 1896:

Today the Democratic party stands between two great forces, each inviting its support. On the one side stand the corporate interests of the nation, its moneyed institutions, its aggregations of wealth and capital, imperious, arrogant, compassionless. They demand special legislation, favors, privileges, and immunities. . . . On the other hand stands that unnumbered throng which gave a name to the Democratic party and for which it has assumed to speak. Work-worn and dust-begrimed, they make their sad appeal. . . . Although the ones who most deserve the fostering care of Government, their cries for help too often beat in vain against the outer wall, while others less deserving find ready access to legislative halls.[21]

In the House, the fight for repeal was led by William L. Wilson, aided by Bourke Cockran and Thomas B. Reed. After a long debate, the silverites attempted to substitute for the administration bill a free-silver bill and were defeated. On August 28 the House then voted, 239 to 108, to repeal the Sherman law. The administration had not dared to hope for such a victory.[22] The bill then went to the Senate, where opinion was more evenly divided. The Finance Committee reported the bill for repeal by a bare majority of one, and then with an additional paragraph declaring for some form of bimetallism in principle. The chairman of the committee, Daniel W. Voorhees of Indiana, a bitter opponent of Cleveland and a long-time inflationist, cast the deciding vote, a fact noted with curiosity by the opposition. As they suspected, the President had managed to win the support of Voorhees only by handing him the entire patronage of Indiana, although the fact that his state had previously declared itself overwhelmingly for repeal

[21] *Ibid.* (August 16, 1893), pp. 410–411.
[22] The Democrats voted 138 for repeal and 78 against it and the Republicans 101 to 22. The Populists cast eight negative votes.

doubtless facilitated Voorhees' conversion to gold. Nor was this the only occasion in which Cleveland made generous use of the patronage to whip his party into line.[23]

The closeness of the vote in the Finance Committee was an indication of the bitterness of the struggle which was to follow. The silverites were determined to resist repeal to the end, and they had nearly enough votes to do it. The recent admission of the Dakotas, Montana, Washington, Idaho, and Wyoming greatly strengthened their cause; all but two of the twelve senators from those states opposed repeal. Voorhees, Mills, Edward D. White, John R. McPherson, and John M. Palmer led the administration forces. They were joined among the Republicans by Allison, Aldrich, Morrill, and Sherman himself, after whom the original bill was named.[24] Isham G. Harris of Tennessee, Henry M. Teller and Edward O. Wolcott of Colorado, George G. Vest of Missouri, William M. Stewart and John P. Jones of Nevada, and the Populists Henry William V. Allen of Nebraska and William Peffer of Kansas all spoke passionately against repeal. Allen once held the floor for fifteen hours at a single stretch. The silverites, indeed, endeavored to kill the bill by talking it to death. The administration men invoked cloture on October 11, but, after a continuous session of thirty-eight hours, the silverites carried an adjournment. Thirty-seven of the forty-four Democrats in the Senate were now convinced that only a compromise could save the day. They brought a compromise plan before Cleveland. The President, however, refused to hear of it, and his insistence was enough to crush the compromise effort. A week later, on October 30, the Senate voted to repeal the Sherman Act, 43 to 32.[25]

[23] The statement in Harry Thurston Peck, *Twenty Years of the Republic, 1885–1905* (New York, 1907), on the use of patronage to effect repeal is, according to Nevins, "substantially true." James A. Barnes, *John G. Carlisle* (New York, 1931), p. 285, believes that money as well as "political pressure" were used to secure repeal, but notes that "the same methods were used by the opposition."

[24] In view of his part in the fight for repeal, it becomes somewhat difficult to credit Sherman's statement in his *Recollections of Forty Years* (2 vols., Chicago, 1895), II, 1189, that he had "never for a moment . . . regretted the passage of the Act of 1890, commonly called the 'Sherman Act.' . . ." He added that "I had no more to do with it than the other conferees."

[25] Including pairs, by 38 and 37. On the fight for repeal, see Barnes, *Carlisle*, pp. 250–286; Nevins, *Cleveland*, pp. 533–548; Noyes, *American Finance*, pp. 197–206.

Cleveland had achieved a brilliant but, as it turned out, a costly triumph. The conservative press sent up paeans of praise in his name. "To Mr. Cleveland," exclaimed *The Nation,* "and we might almost say to Mr. Cleveland alone, belongs the honor of putting an end to the deadlock in the Senate and securing the passage of the repeal bill."[26] "It was the President's victory that the law was at last repealed," wrote Woodrow Wilson in the *Atlantic,* "and everyone knew it."[27] The repeal of the obnoxious legislation, concluded the New York *World,* was a triumph for Cleveland, "for a sound and stable currency, for the credit of the government, for the rights of the people."[28] From this last statement, however, the people themselves dissented in increasing numbers.

Cleveland had staked his reputation on the repeal of silver purchases, insisting that they were the cause of the depression. If repeal failed to improve the condition of the country, he would find it difficult to explain to the country what had gone wrong. In fact, repeal brought no relief from the depression.[29] If it gave the bankers greater confidence in the future of capitalism, as the administration had insisted it would, they discreetly kept their confidence to themselves; no outpouring of confidence was visible on the Stock Exchange. Prices and wages continued to fall and unemployment to rise. Agriculture showed no improvement. Not only did repeal fail to bring about the miraculous prosperity which had been predicted; it did not even save the gold standard. That was saved only by the heroic labors of the House of Morgan.[30]

It had long been the general belief that unless the Treasury could show a gold reserve of at least $100 million at all times, the gold

[26] *The Nation,* LVII (Oct. 26, 1893), 297.

[27] *Atlantic Monthly,* LXXIX (Mar., 1897), 297.

[28] New York *World,* Oct. 31, 1893, p. 1893.

[29] Noyes, *American Finance,* pp. 201–202.

[30] It could be argued, of course, that the continuing decline of the gold reserve was to be attributed to the amount of silver certificates and greenbacks which had already been injected into the currency. In 1893 Carlisle pointed out that $346,681,016 in greenbacks and $155,930,940 in treasury notes had been issued under the Sherman Act which under the law had to be redeemed in coin on presentation. There had also been coined $419,332,550 in legal-tender silver upon which certificates had been issued to the amount of $334,-138,504. Since the Sherman Act itself declared it to be "the established policy of the United States to maintain the two metals on a parity with each other," the Treasury undertook to redeem all these notes in gold. *Treasury Report, 1893,* lxxi–lxxii.

standard could no longer be maintained. As Cleveland said, the hold-ing of a reserve of $100 million "came to be regarded by the people with a sort of sentimental solicitude."[31] When Cleveland entered office in March, 1892, the gold reserve had already fallen to $100,982,410. Even that figure had been achieved only by persuading the New York banks voluntarily to surrender some of their gold. By the same means Secretary Carlisle managed to maintain the reserve at slightly over the danger point for about a month. After that the struggle to shore up the Treasury's dwindling reserve was continuous and unremitting.

The administration, holding the Sherman Act responsible for the drain on the gold reserve as well as for the depression, expected its repeal to improve the situation. It is true that fear for the gold standard had caused hoarding of gold and unusual demands on the Treasury for redemption of paper. There were other influences, however, quite apart from the coinage of silver, which contributed to the decline of the gold reserve. The panic in Europe caused large withdrawals after 1890. An unfavorable balance of trade contributed to the same result. Under the McKinley tariff, moreover, customs receipts, and particu-larly customs receipts in gold, steadily declined.[32] None of these in-fluences had anything to do with the Sherman Act. After the crash of May 5, 1893, the demand for gold became frantic. Eastern banks fell under heavy pressure, not only from local creditors, but from banks in the interior, for the return of a total of more than $200 million de-posited in the East and payable on demand. For many banks the strain was too great; many, as we have seen, collapsed, dragging other busi-nesses with them. The strain on the Treasury was also great. By the end of July the gold reserve had fallen below the safety line. In

---

[31] Grover Cleveland, *Presidential Problems* (New York, 1904), p. 126.

[32] The decline of customs receipts in gold was, to be sure, related to concern over the gold standard, although it was chiefly a reflection of the decline of foreign trade. Before 1890, receipts in gold amounted to nine-tenths of all customs receipts. By the end of 1892, they amounted to only 4.4 per cent of the total. Greenbacks, silver certificates, and Treasury notes were substituted in their place. To some extent this was the fault of Treasury practice. Until 1890 it had been the custom of the subtreasury in New York to settle clear-inghouse balances chiefly in gold or in gold certificates. Beginning in 1890, the Treasury, frightened by the declining gold reserve, began to settle New York balances in Treasury notes and later in greenbacks. See Lauck, *Causes of the Panic,* pp. 85–88; Noyes, *American Finance,* pp. 168–172. For the withdrawal of gold to Europe, see A. B. Hepburn, *A History of Currency in the United States* (New York, 1915), p. 368.

January, 1894, it reached the incredible figure of $62 million. The day of judgment appeared to be at hand.

Carlisle in desperation asked Congress to allow him to float short-term loans at low rates of interest, presumably in gold—a procedure forbidden under an act of 1870.[33] When Congress ignored the request, he tried in January, 1893, to float a loan of $50 million in ten-year bonds bearing 5 per cent, to be payable in gold coin at a price yielding 3 per cent. The market for government bonds, however, was not good, and this particular offering rendered a return no better than that on any other government bonds, domestic or foreign. The deadline which Carlisle had announced approached, therefore, with less than $5 million subscribed. The Secretary then called a conference of bankers in New York, "which resulted," Cleveland later recalled, "in so arousing their patriotism, as well as their solicitude for the protection of the interests they represented, that they effectively exerted themselves, barely in time to prevent a disastrous failure of the sale."[34] The issue finally brought in about $58,661,000 in gold; but as subscribers first withdrew $24 million in gold from the Treasury through redemption of notes and then paid the same gold back to the Treasury to pay for the bonds, it could not be considered a complete success.

The political consequences of the bond issue were still more lamentable. Even the bankers doubted whether the President had the power to borrow money in order to redeem silver certificates in gold; the Populists were certain he did not. For them, the bond issue was merely one more manifestation of a bankers' conspiracy to contract the currency. Senator Peffer cried, "In the face of idleness, destitution, hunger, and desperation in every State and in every city of the Union, and with $250,000,000 in the public Treasury, the President is compelled to sell the people's credit to appease the clamor of these misers of Wall Street."[35] The Senate's reply to the bond issue was to pass a bill calling for the coinage of the silver seigniorage in the Treasury— that is, the money which represented the difference between what the government had paid for a dollar's worth of raw silver (something less than a dollar, at the low current price of silver) and the value of a silver dollar equivalent to a dollar in gold. The amount of money thus

[33] *Treasury Report, 1893,* pp. lxiv–lxxi.

[34] Cleveland, *Presidential Problems,* p. 140.

[35] *Congressional Record,* 53rd Cong., 2nd sess., p. 1176; Barnes, *Carlisle,* p. 291, admits the bond issue was of dubious legality.

put into circulation would not have been large—$55,150,000—and many moderate men in the administration camp urged the President that the time had come to compromise with the silverites. Cleveland refused, on the ground that to admit coinage of even the silver seigniorage would be to reopen the whole question which repeal of the Sherman Act had closed. The House passed the seigniorage bill. Cleveland vetoed it.[36]

Since the first bond issue had failed to relieve the situation, and since the administration stanchly refused to budge from its refusal to redeem all notes in anything but gold, there was nothing to do but to resort to another bond issue. In November Carlisle asked for another $50 million in 5 per cent ten-year bonds. This time he sought to discourage purchases made with gold withdrawn from the Treasury, and succeeded in obtaining $58,538,500 in gold.[37] Relief, however, was only momentary; those who had loaned gold to the government were soon clamoring at the Treasury to get it back again. "Thus we have an endless chain in operation," said Cleveland in his second annual message, "depleting the Treasury's gold and never near a final rest." He chided Congress for refusing to give him the power to issue short-term bonds, the only kind that would do any good, and noted with disapproval that there was even "a disposition in some quarters to deny both the necessity and power for the issue of bonds at all."[38] Meanwhile conservatives pressed him for more effective action. J. Lawrence Laughlin complained, "To push the reserve slightly above the $100,000,000 by a small issue of bonds, inevitably followed by its disappearance below the line, impressed no one very forcibly."[39]

By February 8, 1895, the gold reserve had fallen to less than $42 million, and Cleveland sent a special message to Congress asking for power to cancel notes as they came in for redemption and to require payment of all important duties in gold.[40] A bill embodying these provisions, however (the Springer bill), was overwhelmingly defeated. The administration decided to issue more bonds. But this time they would be sold privately instead of on the market. With this in mind, the administration opened negotiations with Morgan and with

[36] Nevins, *Cleveland,* pp. 600–603; Richardson, *Messages and Papers,* IX, 487.

[37] Barnes, *Carlisle,* p. 358.

[38] Richardson, *Messages and Papers,* IX, 553.

[39] "Our Monetary Programme," *Forum,* XX (Feb., 1896), 652–666.

[40] Richardson, *Messages and Papers,* IX, 561.

August Belmont, the American representative of the Rothschild interests. The bankers offered to buy $50 million of bonds bearing 3¾ per cent, an offer which the government declined. On the night of February 7, while the Springer bill was going down to defeat in the House, Morgan himself, with his counsel, Francis L. Stetson,[41] and his junior partner, Robert Bacon, arrived in Washington and demanded to see the President. He was not received until the following morning. Cleveland told him coldly that a public issue had been decided upon. Morgan recapitulated the arguments for a private issue, the most impressive of which was that only a private syndicate could obtain gold from Europe and guarantee that it would not leave the country. But Carlisle had doubts that a private sale could be legally negotiated. Then someone remembered an old Civil War statute which authorized the government to buy coin and pay for it in bonds. Lawbooks were sent for and examined, the passage discovered to be appropriate to the present crisis, and the deal closed. When the meeting broke up, someone noticed that Morgan had ground his cigar to ashes between his fingers onto the carpet.[42]

Under the contract signed that afternoon the bankers agreed to buy $62 million in 4 per cent bonds at 104½, thus providing the Treasury with 3,500,000 ounces of gold—about $65 million worth. They would obtain at least half the gold in Europe and would protect the Treasury from withdrawals, so far as lay within their power, during the period of the loan. If Congress within ten days would substitute the words "gold bonds" for the words "coin bonds" in the contract, they would reduce the interest charge from 3¾ per cent to 3 per cent. Cleveland sent the terms to Congress, pointing out that the substitution of "gold" for "coin" would save the country $18 million.[43] Congress, however, refused to act. The bond issue yielded $65,116,244 to the government. Morgan and Belmont disposed of the bonds at 112¼ in less than four hours. How much they made on the transaction was never divulged;

[41] Stetson was a partner in the law firm with which Cleveland had been connected after his first term. He was Morgan's chief specialist on railroads.

[42] The deal was not formally concluded until that afternoon, when Carlisle, Morgan, and Belmont signed a contract drawn up by Stetson and William E. Curtis, Assistant Secretary of the Treasury. According to Frederick Lewis Allen, the statute of 1862 was suggested by Morgan himself; Nevins gives Curtis the credit. See Nevins, *Cleveland*, pp. 661–662; Barnes, *Carlisle*, pp. 387–389; Frederick Lewis Allen, *The Great Pierpont Morgan* (Bantam ed., New York, 1956), pp. 87–90.

[43] Richardson, *Messages and Papers*, IX, 567–568.

Morgan, when asked by Congress to state the amount, said: "That I decline to answer. I wish to state that I am perfectly ready to state to the committee every detail of the negotiation up to the time that the bonds became my property and were paid for. What I did with my own property subsequent to that purchase I decline to state. . . ."[44]

The New York *World* in 1895 accused the bankers of having made at least $16 million on the deal. Lewis Corey, in his book *The House of Morgan*, published in 1930, put the figure at "from seven to twelve million dollars." Noyes called the terms "extremely harsh"; Nevins called them "exorbitant." Frederick Lewis Allen, on the other hand, who had access to some of the records of the transaction, estimated that the American syndicate made only $1,534,516.[45] Whatever the actual profits were, the fact that the government of the United States had been obliged to seek the aid of private bankers in order to save its credit appeared to many people as simply another illustration of the depths to which the government had fallen; that the bankers had profited at all was scandalous in itself. The people, said Bryan, were beholden to the President. They owed him the gratitude "which a confiding ward feels toward his guardian without bond who has squandered a rich estate," or "which a passenger feels toward the trainman who has opened a switch and precipitated a wreck."[46] Cleveland, also with irony, confessed "without shame and without repentance" his "share of the guilt."

> Though Mr. Morgan and Mr. Belmont and scores of other bankers and financiers who were accessories in these transactions may be steeped in destructive propensities, and may be constantly busy in sinful schemes, I shall always recall with satisfaction and self-congratulation my association with them at a time when our country sorely needed their aid.[47]

Morgan and Belmont could at least claim to have fulfilled their part of the bargain. They obtained half the gold in Europe, as they had promised, and successfully prevented it from leaving the country. But

---

[44] Quoted in Allen, *Morgan*, p. 95.

[45] *Ibid.*, pp. 96–97; Nevins, *Cleveland*, pp. 664–665; Noyes, *American Finance*, p. 234. Carlisle himself admitted that "the terms were hard for the Government." Barnes, *Carlisle*, p. 388.

[46] *Congressional Record*, XXVII, 53 Cong., 3rd sess. (February 14, 1895), Appendix, p. 285.

[47] Cleveland, *Presidential Problems*, p. 170. See also Bond Sales Investigation, *Senate Executive Documents*, No. 5, 54th Cong., 2nd sess., and Noyes, *American Finance*, pp. 234–250.

even Morgan and Belmont could not prevent people who still had legal-tender notes from presenting them to the Treasury for redemption—notes which the government, having failed to secure remedial legislation from Congress, was bound to redeem in coin (although not necessarily in gold). By January, 1896, the gold reserve had again sunk to a "dangerous level," and Secretary Carlisle announced still another bond issue—a public sale of $100 million of 4 per cent bonds. This time there was no difficulty in obtaining bids, most of them for 110 to 112. Of $111,166,232 realized from the sale, more than $97 million came from New York. Of the total amount, however, about $40 million were purchased with gold withdrawn from the Treasury by redemption of notes. The fourth issue was the least successful of all, but it was enough to tide the administration through its final unhappy year.[48]

The four bond issues brought in, all told, nearly $300 million in gold, of which at least a fourth had been originally obtained by redemption of greenbacks and treasury notes. None of them had been successful in arresting the decline of the gold reserve; yet the administration had, after all, realized its main objective—preservation of the gold standard. Considering the refusal of Congress to vote the administration adequate power to deal with the emergency, the administration could not be criticized for having failed to meet it. And the fact remains that when Cleveland left office, the United States was still on the gold standard. Whether the country would not have been more prosperous had it chosen to leave the gold standard was another matter. The bond sales had saved gold, but they had not cured the depression. They were an economic failure and a political disaster, as Cleveland was shortly to discover. He knew all along, in fact, that his course would split the party and perhaps enable the radicals to seize control of it, but he chose to abide by his principles at the cost of his popularity. There can be no question of his courage. The only question is whether his courage did not at times outrun his wisdom.

Meanwhile the administration had suffered a severe defeat in its efforts to revise the tariff. The battle over the tariff began long before Cleveland was even inaugurated, for the Democrats, by making an issue of it in the campaign of 1892, had bound themselves to take action if they were elected. When a reporter asked Cleveland in January, 1893, if he intended to recommend a reduction of duties, he

[48] Barnes, *Carlisle*, pp. 399–424, is the best discussion of the fourth issue.

asked, "What were we elected for?" At the same time, however, Cleveland had no intention of recommending a free-trade measure. In his letter of acceptance he had said:

We believe a readjustment can be accomplished . . . without disaster or demolition. We believe that the advantages of freer raw materials should be accorded to our manufacturers, and we contemplate a fair and careful distribution of necessary tariff burdens, rather than the precipitation of free trade.[49]

These sentiments were echoed by William L. Wilson when he reported his bill to the House on December 19, 1893: "With the tariff, as with every other long-standing abuse . . . the legislator must always remember that in the beginning temperate reform is safest, 'having in itself the principles of growth.' "[50] Safety, indeed, was to be the watchword of the administration's campaign for reform of the tariff.

The Wilson bill, which was passed by the House on February 1, 1894, by a vote of 204 to 140, removed the duties from many raw materials, including wool, coal, iron ore, hemp, and flax, and reduced the duties on most manufactures. Both Wilson and Cleveland could entirely approve it. As Roger Mills said, "The Wilson bill may be criticized because it does not go far enough in the line of readjustment and reform, but no fairminded man can attack it because it goes too far."[51] There was one feature of the bill, however, which the administration approved only with reluctance and misgiving—a provision that all incomes over $4,000 be taxed 2 per cent per annum. This revolutionary clause, as one might have guessed, was the work of the agrarians, who had long demanded that taxation be equalized. Mills himself declared that "the present system of taxation will not and cannot be endured."[52] The administration, however, claimed that the income tax had been inserted in the bill merely to compensate for the loss in tariff revenues which would result from the lower duties.

Having easily passed the House, the Wilson bill encountered bitter resistance in the Senate, where it was debated for five months. Forty-four Democrats, thirty-eight Republicans, and three Populists sat in

[49] New York *Daily Tribune,* September 27, 1892.

[50] *House Report* No. 234, 53rd Cong., 2nd sess., p. 2.

[51] Roger Q. Mills, "The Wilson Bill," *North American Review,* CLVIII (Feb., 1894), 238.

[52] *Ibid.* See also George Tunnell, "The Legislative History of the Second Income Tax," *Journal of Political Economy,* III (June, 1895), 311–337.

the Senate; even if the Populists voted with the Democrats, the bill would fail if only five Democrats voted against it. That defections were very likely to occur became apparent at once. Hill asserted that he would at no time vote for a bill containing an income tax. The two senators from Louisiana, Edward D. White and Donelson Caffery, said that they would vote for no bill under which raw sugar was admitted free. Calvin S. Brice of Ohio and Gorman of Maryland opposed the bill as injurious to the manufacturing interests which they represented. The senators from West Virginia and Alabama, solicitous of the mining and steel industries, objected to the absence of duties on iron and steel. Still other difficulties faced the administration. Hill and Murphy of New York and a number of other machine Democrats still resented Cleveland's triumph in the late campaign.[53] As for the western Democrats, they had been alienated by Cleveland's insistence on repeal of the Sherman Act, and many of them were in no mood to throw themselves into a fight over the tariff, even for the sake of the income tax. Finally, as if the antiadministration Democrats could not already muster enough support to defeat the bill, they received valuable assistance from the Republicans. Hoar, Sherman, Allison, Aldrich, and Quay willingly contributed their rhetorical talents to the debate; at one point Quay filibustered for twelve days with a speech covering 235 pages of the *Congressional Record*.[54]

Finding it impossible to proceed, the Senate Democrats compromised. A party conference approved no less than 408 amendments, which were reported early in May by James K. Jones of Arkansas. Jones took the responsibility for the new bill, but the administration attributed the changes to Gorman, whose subcommittee on finance considered the bill. The legislation accordingly became known as the Wilson-Gorman bill. Even the changes proposed by the Gorman committee, however, failed to mollify the advocates of protection. Two hundred more amendments were introduced before the Senate finally passed the bill on July 3 by a vote of 39 to 34.

While the bill was pending in the Senate, it began to be charged in the press that the American Sugar Refining Company had played a larger part in writing the new sugar rates than was altogether proper. It was further said that the "sugar trust" demanded the privilege of helping to shape legislation in Congress, in spite of the fact that none

[53] Nevins, *Cleveland*, pp. 567–572.
[54] Ida Tarbell, *The Tariff in Our Times* (New York, 1911), p. 228.

of its officers had been elected by the public to sit in that body, in compensation for its lavish contributions to the Democratic campaign chest in 1892. Not only that, but some senators had taken advantage of secret information in the matter to speculate freely in the stocks of the American Sugar Refining Company. These sensational charges led in due time to an investigation, in the course of which Senators Quay of Pennsylvania and McPherson of New Jersey were found to have bought sugar stocks while the bill was pending. A number of others were suspected of having done the same thing.

Neither Quay nor McPherson denied having speculated in the stocks of a company which was bound to be directly affected by legislation then pending in Congress, but they denied that in doing so they had done anything improper. Quay said flatly, "I do not feel that there is anything in my connection with the Senate to interfere with my buying or selling the stock when I please, and I propose to do so in the future." The investigation also made it clear that the sugar trust was in the habit of making campaign contributions to both sides, the largest contribution in each state going to the dominant party. "Then the sugar trust is a Democrat in a Democratic State, and a Republican in a Republican State?" Senator Allen asked Henry O. Havemeyer, president of the American Sugar Refining Company. His company, Havemeyer said in reply, pursued "only the politics of business." "It is a very suitable and proper thing to do," he added.[55]

Cleveland hoped that when the Gorman bill went back to the House, a stiff fight might be made there to eliminate some of the more obnoxious of Senator Gorman's amendments. In order to encourage the Democrats he allowed Wilson to read from a letter he had received from the President on July 2. "Every true Democrat and every sincere reformer," Cleveland wrote, "knows that this bill in its present form and as it will be submitted to the conference falls far short of the consummation for which we have long labored. . . . Our abandonment of the cause or the principle upon which it rests means party perfidy and party dishonor."[56] Gorman and Jones regarded the letter as a stab in the back; they believed that Cleveland had accepted their amendments as a necessary compromise.[57] They urged their colleagues

[55] *Senate Report,* No. 606, 53rd Cong., 2nd sess., pp. 352, 656–657.

[56] Nevins, *Cleveland,* p. 581; *Congressional Record,* 53rd Cong., 2nd sess. (July 19, 1894), p. 772.

[57] John R. Lambert, *Arthur Pue Gorman* (Baton Rouge, 1953), pp. 227–237.

in the House to stand firm. The administration finally surrendered on August 13, and the House passed the bill, 182 to 106, without changing a single amendment. Cleveland, profoundly disappointed, allowed the bill to become law without his signature.

The Wilson-Gorman Act, which finally emerged as the result of this prolonged struggle, bore little resemblance to the original Wilson bill. Only wool remained on the free list; the duties on cotton and silk goods, pig iron, steel, rails, coal, iron ore, chinaware, and tin plate were all reimposed, although the new rates were lower than those of the McKinley Act. The rates under the Wilson-Gorman Act averaged 41 per cent on dutiable goods and 21 per cent on all goods, as compared with 49 per cent on dutiable goods and 22 per cent on all goods under the McKinley Act.[58] The celebrated reformed tariff of the Democrats was barely distinguishable from the old unreconstructed Republican tariff.

Judged by almost any standard, the financial policy of the second Cleveland administration was a failure. Politically it split the party. It accomplished only one of the objectives Cleveland had set for himself; the gold standard, it is true, was successfully maintained, but not through repeal of the Sherman Act, which was designed to save gold by easing the drain on the Treasury reserve. So far as the Treasury reserve was concerned, the repeal of the Sherman Act was a conspicuous failure. As for reduction of the tariff, nothing of any importance had been accomplished. Nor did the policies of the Cleveland administration alleviate the depression; it deepened in 1894 and, after a brief upturn in 1895, again in 1896. Not until late in 1897 did recovery begin. To Cleveland's disgust, the Republicans then claimed credit for it; their victory in 1896, they argued, had saved the country from the horrible prospect of free silver and brought renewed confidence to the business world.

. . . A crushing weight has been lifted and rolled away [wrote *Dun's Review* immediately after the election], and the business world has begun to adjust itself to a state of freedom and security which it has not known for years. Dread of immeasurable disaster no longer locks up resources and paralyzes enterprise, and new contracts involving many millions have become binding since the election. . . .[59]

[58] U.S. Tariff Commission, *Dictionary of Tariff Information* (1924), p. 755; *Statistical Abstract, 1918,* p. 783; F. W. Taussig, *The Tariff History of the United States* (7th ed., New York, 1923), p. 318.

[59] *Dun's Review,* Nov. 7, 1896.

But if the Republicans believed that by restoring confidence in the gold standard they had restored prosperity, they had forgotten that Cleveland had spent four years trying to save the gold standard and had in fact succeeded in saving it—his one indisputable achievement. The gold standard was already secure by the time the Republicans came to office. Yet the country was no closer to recovery in 1896 than it had been in 1893. The defense of gold, in short, did not bring recovery, a fact which shows that other causes were far more important in bringing on the depression than excessive anxiety over the currency. If the currency had been the real issue, Cleveland would have left office acclaimed as a hero instead of defeated and forlorn, despised by half his party, discarded by the other half as a political liability, and regarded by large numbers of his countrymen as a man who had sold them out to the House of Morgan.

CHAPTER 8

1894

M ORE than two and a half million men walked the streets in search of work in the terrible winter of 1893–94.[1] The countryside was suddenly filled with tramps, wandering aimlessly from one town to the next, shabby and forlorn. On city street corners, little knots of hungry, sad-faced men appeared; passers-by averted their eyes to avoid the reproachful stare of poverty. In Chicago there were 100,000 such men. At night every precinct station in the city was crowded with anywhere from sixty to a hundred men who had no place else to sleep. Others sprawled in the corridors and on the stairways of City Hall. A reporter estimated that the city's saloon keepers furnished 60,000 free meals a day.[2] Ray Stannard Baker, a cub reporter for the *Record,* exclaimed with a curious mixture of enthusiasm and despair, "What a spectacle! What a human downfall after the magnificence and prodigality of the World's Fair which has so recently closed its doors! Heights of splendor, pride, exaltation in one month; depths of wretchedness, suffering, hunger, cold, in the next."[3]

Unemployment in such numbers revolutionized the problem of poverty. Americans had always believed that any man who did not have a job was either too lazy to get one or in some way disabled. Private charity housed and fed the latter; society condemned and ignored the former. Both classes, however, represented only a tiny minority. Now in 1894 men who were neither unable nor unwilling to work prowled the streets in vast numbers. Private charity could not possibly provide for them. City governments tried to fill the gap, but

[1] See above, p. 142, n. 3.
[2] Ray Ginger, *The Bending Cross* (New Brunswick, N.J., 1949), p. 99.
[3] Ray Stannard Baker, *American Chronicle* (New York, 1945), p. 2.

their efforts were necessarily makeshift. Detroit, under the direction of Mayor Hazen Pingree, turned over vacant land in the city to the poor so that they could support themselves by growing enough to eat. Many other cities imitated this Garden Plot Plan—the "Pingree Potato Scheme," as it was popularly known; it was attractive because it did not conflict with traditional ideas of self-help.[4] Nor did the "Indianapolis Plan," under which the city dispensed food in return for work.

Both of these plans, however, at least acknowledged the responsibility of government to provide for those who could not provide for themselves; the latter was a step toward public works of some kind. But men quickly discovered that any effective program of public work had to be supervised not by the cities but by the state governments, or, better yet, by the national government, and many who conceded the power of municipalities to act denied the same power to the states and most denied it to Washington. When the New York legislature drew up a state program of public works, Governor Flower rejected it. "In America," he said, "the people support the government; it is not the province of the government to support the people." A program of work relief would provide "a dangerous precedent for the future, justifying paternal legislation of all kinds and encouraging prodigal extravagance."[5] Even reformers and welfare workers feared that relief would sap the self-reliance of its recipients. "Relief work," said Josephine Shaw Lowell, "to be a benefit and not an injury, must be continuous, hard, and underpaid."[6]

Such doubts—doubts as to the effect of relief on character, doubts as to the power of government to undertake it—crippled all attempts to deal with the depression. It was only when government failed to act that angry men began to take matters into their own hands. In Massillon, Ohio, Jacob S. Coxey set about organizing a massive march on Washington. A self-made businessman of considerable affluence— he was said to be worth $200,000—Coxey had long been active in the service of reform, first as a Greenbacker, then as a Populist. The depression stirred him to new efforts. The federal government could end the depression, he insisted, simply by putting men to work on the

[4] Samuel Rezneck, "Unemployment, Unrest, and Relief in the United States during the Depression of 1893–97," *Journal of Political Economy*, LXI (Aug., 1953), 331; see also Leah H. Feder, *Unemployment Relief in Periods of Depression* (New York, 1936), pp. 98–188.

[5] Rezneck, "Depression of 1893–97," p. 332.

[6] *Ibid.*, p. 330.

public roads. The roads needed improvement in any case; at Coxey's instigation, in fact, members of Congress had already introduced a bill calling on the Secretary of the Treasury to issue $500 million in legal-tender notes for construction and improvement of roads. Now the Good Roads Bill took on new importance as a means of creating employment. Coxey also proposed to allow states or cities to issue noninterest-bearing bonds for public improvement, the bonds to be deposited with the Secretary of the Treasury as security for legal-tender notes to be issued for the improvements. Thus public works, internal improvements, and monetary inflation would all be promoted at the same time, and happiness and prosperity restored to the country.

The only obstacle to Coxey's program was the refusal of Congress to enact it. Coxey, as a veteran reformer, was not surprised at this indifference; he had a remedy for it. "We will send a petition to Washington with boots on," he said.[7] He thereupon announced that on Easter Sunday, 1894, an army of "commonwealers" would leave Massillon, on foot and with no weapons but the righteousness of their cause, to march on Washington, where they would present their plans to Congress. He predicted confidently that 100,000 men would turn out. On Easter Sunday, however, only 100 men set out for the Capitol, accompanied by half as many reporters, among them the skeptical Ray Stannard Baker, who sent back to Chicago dispatches ridiculing the leaders of the march as impracticable visionaries, at once dangerous and comic.

There was more than a little truth in the charge. Coxey had appointed as director of the march one Carl Browne, printer, painter, editor, rancher, politician, labor agitator—a "great, big, strong fellow with a hearty bass voice," as one observer described him, "part faker, part religionist, part Wild West cowboy, and withal a natural leader of men."[8] Browne liked to appear in a bizarre costume consisting of a fringed buckskin coat, the buttons of which were Mexican silver dol-

[7] There is some dispute as to whether Coxey himself coined this memorable phrase. See Henry Vincent, *The Story of the Commonweal* (Chicago, 1894), pp. 16, 49; Donald L. McMurry, *Coxey's Army* (Boston, 1928), p. 33. Vincent was the official historian of the movement.

[8] A. Cleveland Hall, "An Observer in Coxey's Camp," *Independent,* XLVI (May 17, 1894), 415. Samuel Gompers remembered him as "a man of parts, a bighearted lover of men, a dreamer and an idealist." *Seventy Years of Life and Labor* (New York, 1925), II, 11.

lars, a sombrero, high boots, and other adornments. He always rode a white charger. He had developed a highly original theology which he expounded on all possible occasions, according to which the soul of Christ and the souls of all the dead of the earth mingled, at some unspecified point in time, in a huge reservoir from which new souls emerged. Christ was thus reincarnated in all men, but especially in Coxey and Browne. Thus originated the "Commonweal of Christ." Browne managed to convert Coxey to this strange blend of pantheism and Neoplatonism—a fact which did not add to the "General's" prestige among the reporters who accompanied his army.

Leaving Massillon on March 24, the Commonwealers marched through Pittsburgh, Allegheny City, Homestead, McKeesport, and Uniontown, picking up followers along the way; by the time they reached Homestead, they numbered nearly 600. In all these places, where the shadow of hard times hung over everything, the men were greeted with sympathy and aided with donations of food and clothing. Large crowds turned out in the evenings and on Sundays to hear Coxey and Browne explain their mission. There was no trouble with the police. On the other side of the mountains the Commonwealers found people more skeptical, perhaps because more prosperous, but they met with no violence. By that time their number had shrunk to 140, after having crossed the Blue Mountains in a raging snowstorm. Although they were joined by other recruits, notably by one Christopher Columbus Jones and a contingent of 100 students from Lehigh University, they never quite regained their former size. When the army arrived in Washington on April 29, it counted in its ranks about 500 men.[9]

How Coxey would be received in Washington, no one knew. The Populists had tried to insure a friendly reception by reminding the government that peaceably disposed citizens had the right to petition Congress, and Coxey had been granted permission to stage a parade. At the same time the administration noted that the law prohibited parades or other demonstrations on the Capitol grounds. It was clear that the government intended to enforce the statute. When the Commonwealers entered the city on May Day morning, they found it

[9] The most detailed account of the march is in Vincent, *Commonweal,* pp. 56–124; see also McMurry, *Coxey's Army,* pp. 72–103, and "The Industrial Armies and the Commonweal," *Mississippi Valley Historical Review,* X (Dec., 1923), 215–252; Baker, *American Chronicle,* pp. 6–25.

guarded by enough police on duty, according to one observer, "to take every single Coxeyite into custody," and by large reserves of police and federal troops.[10] Coxey, however, was undismayed; he decided to defy the law and march his men to the Capitol. A large crowd—15,000 to 20,000 people—lined the streets. A cheer went up as the men marched by.

When the Commonwealers reached the Capitol grounds, they were stopped by a phalanx of police. Coxey, Browne, and Jones conferred with the police, who stood firm in refusing to let the men pass. The three men, however, slipped through the police guard and headed for the Capitol. Coxey reached the steps, where he was once again confronted by policemen, who forbade him to speak. Coxey had anticipated this; he gave to the reporters a statement protesting against the government's refusal to let him speak. Browne and Jones were then arrested and taken off to jail, but Coxey was released. As he climbed into a waiting carriage with his wife and child, the crowd, which had watched these events in silence, suddenly sent up a cheer. The cheering alarmed the nervous police, who began to fling about them with their clubs. About fifty people were beaten or trampled in the stampede set off by the action of the police, but the crowds continued to follow the Commonwealers as they marched back to their camp across the river, and to cheer them.

The unprovoked violence of the police did not escape criticism. Tom Johnson of Ohio demanded an investigation in the House of the whole day's activities, but he was soon squelched. The administration in the end had its way. On May 21 Coxey, Browne, and Jones were convicted of carrying banners on the Capitol grounds, and Coxey and Browne of walking on the grass—an even more heinous offense. Each was sentenced to twenty days and fined $5.

Coxey's was not the only "army" to attempt to march to Washington. The "industrial armies" of the West, indeed, were far larger than that of the Commonwealers, totaling about 5,000 men at one time or another. Lewis C. Fry of Los Angeles commanded 1,000 men, Charles T. Kelly of San Francisco at least 1,500 (including Jack London, who kept a journal of the march). Kelly's army forced the Union Pacific to carry them in boxcars as far as Council Bluffs; they traveled the rest of the way to Washington on foot. An army from Montana, refused

[10] Hall, "An Observer in Coxey's Camp," p. 616.

similar transportation by the Northern Pacific, captured a train and ran it themselves, pursued by another train of deputies. At Billings workers and deputies engaged in a battle, in which the workers, aided by sympathetic townspeople, momentarily defeated the forces of law and order. They were eventually surrounded and captured by federal troops.[11]

No less than seventeen armies set out for Washington in the spring of 1894; about 1,200 men eventually reached the Capitol. As a rule they preserved a strict discipline, excluded professional vagrants from their number, and sought to avoid collisions with the local authorities. Almost everywhere they were greeted with sympathy by the people of the country through which they passed. It was the fact of this sympathy, more than anything else, which disturbed sober and substantial citizens and strengthened them in their determination not to yield to what they considered a concerted attempt to substitute mob rule for the rule of law and virtue. Even moderate men like Grover Cleveland, terrified by these manifestations of popular discontent, determined to use the full force of federal authority to crush the spirit of rebellion.

Other men, however, were beginning to see the matter in a kinder light. Ray Stannard Baker, for instance, at first ridiculed the Coxeyites, predicting that they would never even reach Washington. When the army began to materialize and when he saw that most of the men were desperately in earnest, he changed his mind. Not that he came to admire the ragged marchers. But he no longer found it possible to dismiss them as mere eccentrics and cranks or, as many regarded them, as pathetic victims of foreign ideologies. By the end of March, 1894, Baker was writing to his editor, "I am beginning to feel that the movement has some meaning, that it is a manifestation of the prevailing unrest and dissatisfaction among the laboring class. When such an ugly and grotesque fungus can grow out so prominently on the body politic there must be something wrong."[12] Nor was the trouble with American society merely the fact that men were unemployed; the trouble lay deeper than that. The real difficulty lay in the refusal of the government to accept responsibility for aiding the suffering victims

[11] McMurry, *Coxey's Army*, chs. VIII–IX; Ida Tarbell, *The Nationalizing of Business, 1878–1898* (New York, 1936), pp. 241–243; W. T. Stead, " 'Coxeyism': A Character Sketch," *Review of Reviews*, X (July, 1894), 49, 56. For London's diary, see J. E. Briggs (ed.), "A Jack London Diary," *Palimpsest*, VII (1926), 129–158.

[12] Baker, *American Chronicle*, pp. 18–19.

of industrialism; it was this refusal to act, more than the mere fact of unemployment, against which Coxeyism was a protest. As Thorstein Veblen noted, what distinguished the Populists and the Coxeyites from earlier reformers was their appeal to federal authority for relief. Theirs was not the democracy of the town meeting but was, as he put it, an "appeal to Caesar." For them, "the classic phrase is no longer to read 'life, liberty and the pursuit of happiness'; what is to be insured to every free born American citizen under the new dispensation, is 'life, liberty and the *means* of happiness.'" [13]

It was not only the unemployed who suffered during the depression and desperately sought relief. Those workers who still had jobs considered themselves little better off—a fact which is reflected in the number of strikes which took place during 1894. At least 1,394 strikes were called during that year, a number surpassed in only four previous years, and never before had the number of men on strike—505,049— or the number of employees thrown out of work by strikes—660,425— been so high. [14] The year 1894 has well been called the *année terrible* of American history between 1865 and the First World War. In April about 125,000 United Mine Workers went out on strike when the mine owners refused to restore wages to the previous year's level. The owners broke the strike without difficulty. After eight weeks the miners went back to work, faced now with the problem not of restoring an earlier wage scale but of preventing further cuts in the small wages they already made. It should be noted that in Illinois Governor Altgeld, who sympathized with the strike, did not hesitate to call out the state militia to keep order. [15]

The railroad workers were more successful, at least at first. In 1893 Eugene V. Debs, secretary and treasurer of the Brotherhood of Locomotive Firemen, abandoned craft unionism and attempted, by founding the American Railway Union, to unite all workers in that

[13] Thorstein Veblen, "The Army of the Commonweal," *Journal of Political Economy,* II (June, 1894), 458.

[14] Commissioner of Labor, *Twenty-First Annual Report* (Washington, 1907), pp. 11–104; G. G. Groat, *Organized Labor in America* (New York, 1916), pp. 159–203.

[15] Waldo R. Browne, *Altgeld of Illinois* (New York, 1924), pp. 129–130; Harry Barnard, *Eagle Forgotten: The Life of John Peter Altgeld* (Indianapolis, 1928), pp. 274–279; *Report of the Proceedings of the Fourteenth Annual Convention of the American Federation of Labor* (1894), p. 10; Almont Lindsey, *The Pullman Strike* (Chicago, 1942), pp. 14–18.

industry, skilled and unskilled, in one union. Except for Negroes, every railway worker was invited to join, and dues were small enough—$1 a year—to make membership available to all. In spite of the hostility of the Railway Brotherhoods, Debs's union grew rapidly, numbering about 150,000 by the middle of 1893.[16] By April, 1894, the American Railway Union was ready to face its first test of strength. When James J. Hill slashed wages on his Great Northern Railroad to an average of less than $40 a month, Debs demanded that he confer with the union on the restoration of wages to the previous level. When Hill refused, Debs led his men out on strike. The Railway Brotherhoods refused to co-operate, and the government attempted to discourage the strikers by reminding them that interference with the mail was a federal offense. Nevertheless, every Great Northern train, except for mail trains, had to stop running. Hill sought to unite public opinion against Debs by arranging for him to speak to the St. Paul Chamber of Commerce. Instead Debs won the businessmen to his point of view, and they supported him in his demand that the strike be arbitrated. The dispute was thereupon submitted to arbitration, and the workers won most of their demands.[17]

The confidence which this quick and easy victory inspired in the leaders of the American Railway Union abruptly collapsed two months later in the Chicago railway strike. The Chicago strike originated not on the railroads but in the factories of the Pullman Palace Car Company. In the town of Pullman, a few miles south of Chicago, George M. Pullman over the years had built up a unique and highly successful business. The business consisted of two parts—the construction, rental, and maintenance of Pullman "palace cars" (that is, dining, parlor, and sleeping cars), and the manufacture and sale, on contract, of other cars. The first division provided most of the company's revenue, but 60 to 70 per cent of the working force was normally employed in the second division. In addition, Pullman in his capacity as head of the Pullman Land Association owned the town which he himself had built to house his working force. Pullman was not a town in any legal sense but only a subdivision of Hyde Park, but the company owned the land, the buildings, and all media of opinion. At its best, therefore, the

[16] United States Strike Commission, *Report and Testimony on the Chicago Strike of 1894* (Washington, 1895), pp. xxiii–xxv, 11–13; Ginger, *Bending Cross,* pp. 91–100.

[17] Ginger, *Bending Cross,* pp. 102–107.

town was a "philanthropic monopoly," as a New York *Sun* correspondent called it in 1885—or, as Pullman himself preferred to call it, a "model town."

Even the workers admitted that it was beautiful. It had parks, playgrounds, lakes, and gardens; it had churches and a library. At its worst, the town was simply a monopoly. Unrestrained by competition or control, Pullman charged rents 15 to 20 per cent higher than rents in neighboring towns. Even more galling to the workers was the fact that he ruled his domain as a kind of feudal manor, calling the men his "children." A minister of the town said, ". . . you are made to feel at every turn the presence of the corporation. . . . This is a corporation-made and a corporation-governed town, and is utterly un-American in its tendencies." Four years later the Supreme Court of Illinois came to the same conclusion and ordered Pullman to sell all his property in the town not essential to manufacturing. Company towns, the court declared, were "opposed to good public policy and incompatible with the theory and spirit of our institutions."[18]

In 1894 the Pullman Company, like nearly every other company, felt the pinch of hard times. The depression, however, did not affect all branches of the business in the same way. In the manufacture of palace cars, Pullman enjoyed an absolute monopoly; and although he leased no new cars to the railroads during the early months of 1894, the revenue from cars already leased and from their maintenance and repair continued undiminished. The palace-car division of the enterprise, therefore, continued to earn money. In the manufacture and sale of ordinary cars, however, Pullman had to compete with other companies. This part of his business suffered greatly from the depression; production had to be drastically cut, and employment fell from 5,500 to a mere 1,100 by November, 1893. Pullman then began to sell cars at a loss, a device which enabled him to secure enough business to put some of his men back to work. By the spring of 1894, employment had risen to 3,300. In order to put men to work, however, Pullman had reduced their pay five times within a year, without at the same time reducing rents in the town of Pullman. The income of the workers beyond their rent, barely enough to live on in times of prosperity, had dwindled by April, 1894, to a mere pittance. The workers, driven to

[18] U.S. Strike Commission, *Report,* pp. 444–454; Ginger, *Bending Cross,* p. 110; Lindsey, *Pullman Strike,* pp. 343–344.

the edge of desperation, joined the American Railway Union "because," they said, "it gave us a glimmer of hope." They sent a grievance committee to confer with the management. Several days later the members of this committee were suddenly dismissed by the company. On May 11 the Pullman workers went on strike.[19]

Pullman professed to be deeply wounded by this action; he accused his "children" of ingratitude. Had he not taken bids at a loss in order to give them jobs? The United States Strike Commission, however, appointed by Cleveland in July, 1894, to investigate the strike, had little difficulty in establishing that Pullman had other motives for taking bids at less than cost. Nor did the company lose money as a result of this policy. According to the Commission, the company lost $52,000 on a number of contracts early in the winter of 1893–94. At the same time the workers, through wage cuts, lost $60,000. The wage cuts more than made up for Pullman's losses. The continuing profits from the palace-car business, moreover, enabled the company as a whole to weather the depression without serious loss. It earned $9,600,000 in the year ending July, 1894, as compared with $11,400,000 in the previous year. The decline in revenue reflected, not the loss on bids, but the general slump in volume; nor were they serious enough to prevent the company from paying out $2,880,000 in dividends in 1894, a figure which was actually larger than that paid the year before ($2,520,000).[20]

When Carroll D. Wright of the Strike Commission asked Pullman why it was that the stockholders had not been asked to help share the company's losses in 1894, why it was only the workers who made less money as a result of the depression, Pullman answered that the workers did not contribute to the business any of the advantages which it enjoyed over its rivals. The managers contributed their superior business ability; the stockholders contributed their money. What did the workers contribute to the success of any enterprise? But Pullman himself had already admitted that only by lowering wages had he been able to sell cars during the depression. Did not the wage reductions, asked Commissioner Wright, represent a "contribution"? And might

[19] U.S. Strike Commission, *Report,* pp. xxxii–xxxix, 87–88, 578–580; Lindsey, *Pullman Strike,* pp. 90–123.

[20] U.S. Strike Commission, *Report,* pp. 566–569; Springfield *Republican,* July 11, 1894, quoted in William H. Carwardine, *The Pullman Strike* (Chicago, 1894), pp. 56–57.

is not have been wiser to restore wages than to provoke a strike which stopped production for weeks? Not if that meant bargaining with a union, the company answered. "There is a principle involved there," said Thomas H. Wickes, vice-president of the Pullman Company, "that the company felt in justice to itself it was bound to maintain: that was the control of its own business."[21]

Many eminent individuals urged Pullman to compromise. The Civic Federation of Chicago and the Common Council of the city recommended conciliation and arbitration. Mayor John P. Hopkins of Chicago and Mayor Pingree of Detroit called on Pullman with telegrams from mayors of fifty cities, all calling for arbitration. To all such suggestions Pullman answered simply that there was nothing to arbitrate; what a company paid its workers was something for the company alone to decide. His intransigence after a while began to annoy even conservatives: Mark Hanna, who also favored arbitration, said, "A man who won't meet his men half-way is a God damn fool."[22]

For the American Railway Union, the strike at Pullman raised a delicate question. Fresh from the successful strike on the Great Northern, Debs had no desire to be drawn immediately into another strike, in which defeat would certainly cancel the gains wrested from Hill. On the other hand, the Pullman workers were clamoring for help. Sympathy eventually prevailed over caution. Four thousand Pullman workers, not technically railroad workers, were admitted to membership in the American Railway Union. Debs and George W. Howard, vice-president of the union, continued to urge the Pullman workers not to strike, but they went ahead with their plans and then appealed to the union, holding its first annual convention in Chicago in June, for help. The convention, moved to sympathy, sent a delegation to confer with Pullman and Wickes, who refused to entertain any proposal of arbitration. Although Debs and Howard again advised caution, the convention then voted to refuse to handle any Pullman cars and to close the Pullman shops at St. Louis and at Ludlow, Kentucky, if the company did not accept arbitration by June 26. When that day arrived and the company still stood firm, the union declared a boycott of all Pullman cars. The railroads themselves, in theory, would not be affected. In fact, however, when the railroads came to the aid of Pullman and began to dismiss switchmen refusing to handle Pullman cars,

[21] U.S. Strike Commission, *Report,* pp. 604, 609.
[22] Thomas Beer, *Hanna* (New York, 1929), pp. 132–133.

the union had little choice except to retaliate by calling a strike against the railroads. By the end of June, 20,000 men on the railroads emanating from Chicago were on strike, and twice that number were striking throughout the country. A boycott declared in sympathy with the workers of a single plant had quickly developed into a great strike affecting the nation's entire railroad system.[23]

The strike was eventually defeated by the combined opposition of the Railway Brotherhoods, the American Federation of Labor, the General Managers Association, and the federal government. The Railway Brotherhoods had always resented the appearance of the American Railway Union as a rival. They now found a powerful ally in Samuel Gompers. When leaders of some of the Chicago trade unions urged Gompers to call a general strike in that city, he called instead a meeting of the executive council of the Federation. The council met at Chicago on July 12 and declared that "the best interests of the unions affiliated with the American Federation of Labor demand that they refrain from participating in any general strike or local strike which may be proposed in connection with the present railroad troubles." The council recommended "that all connected with the American Federation of Labor now out on sympathetic strike should return to work, and those who contemplate going out on sympathetic strike are advised to remain at their usual vocations." Gompers was willing to go no further than to wire President Cleveland to bring the crisis to an end and to raise $500 for the legal defense of Eugene Debs. He refused, however, to take any action which might jeopardize the power of the A.F. of L.[24]

The General Managers Association was a more formidable antagonist. Organized in 1886, the Association represented the twenty-four railroads centering in Chicago, which among them operated 41,000 miles of track and were capitalized at over $2 billion. By organizing the General Managers Association, these railroads hoped to eliminate destructive competition among them, particularly in the field of labor relations. In 1893, for instance, the Association laid down the "Chicago scale" of wages for switchmen, to which all the member rail-

[23] U.S. Strike Commission, *Report*, pp. 87–94; Lindsey, *Pullman Strike*, pp. 122–136.
[24] Samuel Gompers, *Seventy Years of Life and Labor* (New York, 1925), I, 404–416; see also his testimony in U.S. Strike Commission, *Report*, pp. 188–205; Ginger, *Bending Cross*, pp. 121–122, 144.

roads were expected to conform. The Association also helped its members to defeat the efforts of unions to alter wages and working conditions by furnishing strikebreakers and blacklisting discharged employees. As an organization clearly designed to eliminate competition among railroads, the General Managers Association was of dubious legality. The Strike Commission, in fact, asserted that it had no more standing in law than pools and rate agreements. "It cannot incorporate, because railroad charters do not authorize roads to form corporations or associations to fix rates for services and wages, nor to force their acceptance, nor to battle with strikers. It is a usurpation of power not granted." The Commission concluded, in no uncertain terms, "The Association is an illustration of the persistent and shrewdly devised plans of corporations to overreach their limitations and to usurp indirectly powers and rights not contemplated in their charters and not obtainable from the people or their legislatures."[25]

It was the General Managers Association which supervised the dismissal of men refusing to switch Pullman cars and the hiring of substitutes, which brought pressure on the authorities to use force to suppress the strike, and which, finally, invented the masterly strategy under which federal aid was finally justified on the grounds that the strike threatened the movement of mail. The American Railway Union itself took pains to see that the mails were not obstructed; it had already learned during the Great Northern strike that federal intervention might be justified on these grounds. It was the railroads who deliberately precipitated the issue by refusing to run any trains not carrying a full complement of cars. When the workers refused to move Pullman's palace cars, the railroads refused to move the government's mail, and then blamed the unions for obstruction of the mails.[26]

The federal government was only too willing to endorse the views of the General Managers Association. It is altogether likely, in fact, that even without the assistance of the railroads Attorney General Olney would have been able to think of some other pretext for intervention. Certainly he was more interested in crushing the strike than in protecting the mails. As he himself declared, his motive was to "make it [the strike] a failure everywhere." That a corporation lawyer and a director of the Santa Fe, Burlington, and New York Central railroads should have entertained such thought was not surprising or

[25] U.S. Strike Commission, *Report,* p. xxxi.
[26] *Ibid.,* pp. xxi, 581.

novel. The only surprising thing is that the President should have given him complete freedom to implement his opinions with all the force of the law.[27]

Long before any interference with the mails actually occurred, Olney instructed the United States district attorney in Chicago, Thomas E. Milchrist, to look for it. On June 30 he appointed a special federal attorney, Edwin Walker, to perform the same function. Walker happened to be general counsel for the Chicago, Milwaukee and St. Paul and also, by an even more extraordinary coincidence, for the General Managers Association. As Clarence Darrow later wrote, "The government might with as good grace have appointed the attorney for the American Railway Union to represent the United States."[28] Nevertheless, Walker became the real director of affairs for the Department of Justice in Chicago.

On June 30, although there had been no violence in the course of the strike, the General Managers Association requested the government to appoint deputies to preserve order. Walker obediently telegraphed the request to Washington, and Olney told him to appoint all the men that were needed. About 3,600 were selected by the General Managers Association, which armed and paid them. They deserved to be well paid, for they were expected not only to serve as United States officers but to run the trains as well, in the absence of the regular working force. They were hardly men of great refinement; they seem to have enjoyed provoking disturbances which they themselves then proceeded to quell. Walker himself described them as "worse than useless."[29] The railroads, however, were in no position to be discriminating in their choice of personnel.

Meanwhile Milchrist and Walker, with the assistance of the General Managers Association, were whipping up an injunction, which they served on the leaders and members of the American Railway Union on July 2. This instrument not only enjoined the union from interfering with the mails but suggested that the strike might actually be construed as a conspiracy in restraint of trade under the Sherman Act. The latter idea sprang from the fertile brain of Richard Olney. The Sherman Act, if it had any meaning at all, seemed to be designed to prosecute trusts, but Olney was not a man to stick at petty legal re-

---

[27] Henry James, *Richard Olney* (Boston, 1923), p. 47.

[28] Clarence Darrow, *The Story of My Life* (New York, 1932), p. 61.

[29] Lindsey, *Pullman Strike*, p. 167; Ginger, *Bending Cross*, pp. 138–139.

finements. He saw no reason why it should not apply to labor unions, and he instructed his dutiful subordinates to that effect. It needed no persuasion to convince lawyers of the soundness of his interpretation of the law.[30]

On the day after the injunction was served, a riot broke out in the Rock Island yards at Blue Island, Illinois. A mob, in which observers saw few striking railroad workers but many irate townspeople, ditched a mail train—a clear case, at last, of obstruction of the mails. The United States marshal, J. W. Arnold, read the injunction to the mob and commanded it to disperse. "The reading of the writ," he notified Olney, "met with no response except jeers and hoots." The mob threw several baggage cars across the tracks, thereby obstructing the mails still further. Arnold gave it as his earnest opinion that federal troops should be sent at the "earliest moment"; Walker, Milchrist, and Federal Judge P. S. Grosscup supported him.[31] In Washington the cabinet met. Secretary of State Gresham and General Nelson Miles opposed federal intervention, but Cleveland, speaking of the need to end the "reign of terror in Chicago," supported Olney in his demand for action. Ignoring the constitutional provisions requiring state application for federal aid, he ordered troops into Chicago. About 2,000 troops arrived early on the Fourth of July.[32]

Except for the riot at Blue Island, the city had been quiet until the arrival of the troops. From then on, however, the American Railway Union lost all control of the situation. Mobs, which the Strike Commission described as "composed generally of hoodlums, women, a low class of foreigners, and recruits of the criminal classes," took possession of railroad yards, upsetting, burning, and destroying cars and stealing whatever property they could lay their hands on.[33] Nevertheless it was difficult to accept the President's opinion that terror reigned in

[30] The injunction is given in Debs's testimony before the Strike Commission, *Report*, pp. 179–180, and reviewed in *In Re* Eugene Debs *et al.*, 158 U.S. 564–600 (1895).

[31] *Report of the Attorney General, 1896*, Appendix, p. 66; see also *Report of the Attorney General, 1894*, pp. xxxi–xxxiv. Debs later said that the injunction, in his opinion, "ended the strike." U.S. Strike Commission, *Report*, p. 143.

[32] Cleveland's account of the episode shows slight knowledge of the situation in Chicago, an utter disregard of the constitutional rights of Illinois, and the contempt which men who think they are right often show toward their opponents. See Grover Cleveland, *Presidential Problems* (New York, 1904), pp. 79–117.

[33] U.S. Strike Commission, *Report*, pp. xlv–xlvi.

Chicago. Few strikers were seen in the mobs or arrested, and none were killed by troops or deputies. The American Railway Union had no part in instigating mob violence. On the other hand, no one could deny that a great deal of property was destroyed. Twelve people were killed.[34]

In spite of the injunctions served on the American Railway Union, the strike continued. On July 10, therefore, Debs and three other union officials were arrested and indicted for conspiracy. On July 17 they were charged with contempt of court in having disobeyed the injunction; later five others were indicted on the same charge. The conspiracy proceedings were never completed, but the union leaders were tried for contempt in the same court which had issued the original injunction, convicted, and sentenced to imprisonment, Debs for six months, the others for three. In January, 1895, the prisoners appealed to the Supreme Court for a writ of habeas corpus. Clarence Darrow and Lyman Trumbull appeared on behalf of Debs, arguing not only that Debs had not interfered with the mails but that, even if he had, a court of equity was not the place to try such a case. Olney appeared for the government, and the opinion of the court bore the stamp of his logic. Justice Brewer, speaking for the court, reaffirmed the power of the federal government to prevent interference with the mails and with interstate commerce, and held that it might do so either by criminal action or by action in equity—that is, by issuing an injunction. Darrow and Trumbull denied that the government could resort to injunctions in such cases; in rejecting their contention, the Court gave the use of injunction in labor disputes a prestige which it had never before enjoyed.[35]

If the Chicago railway strike broke the power of the American Railway Union and provided enemies of labor with a new instrument of battle in the injunction, it also contributed to the decline of the Cleveland administration and thus gave radicals some comfort in the

[34] The Strike Commission estimated the total cost of the strike as more than $7 million. But this included not only damage to property, but the expenses of the railroads in hiring deputy marshals, loss of railroad earnings, and loss of wages to Pullman and railroad employees. *Ibid.,* p. xviii; see also Ginger, *Bending Cross,* p. 154.

[35] *In Re* Debs, 158 U.S. 564 (1895); Lindsey, *Pullman Strike,* pp. 274–305; Allen F. Westin, "The Supreme Court, the Populist Movement and the Campaign of 1896," *Journal of Politics,* XV (Feb., 1953), 27. The Court did not in this case attempt to decide whether the Sherman Act could be used against unions.

end. Cleveland, in dispatching troops to Chicago, had reckoned without the governor of Illinois, John Peter Altgeld. Altgeld, the son of
German immigrants, had been brought to the United States as an
infant. Without formal education he had risen, in the American
fashion, to eminence. After service in the Civil War he embarked on a
distinguished legal career that eventually carried him to the Supreme
Court of Cook County, of which he became chief justice. He also
made a fortune in real-estate speculation, which enabled him to
devote his full talents to politics. In 1892 he was elected the first
Democratic governor of Illinois since the Civil War. By 1894 he was
one of the most prominent leaders in the party. The equal of Cleveland in independence and courage, he never wavered in the face of
popular opposition to his policies. During his first year in office he had
pardoned three anarchists convicted of precipitating the Haymarket
riot of 1886, arguing that the jury which had convicted them was
packed, the judge prejudiced, and the defendants not proved guilty.
After this act of generosity Altgeld himself was denounced as an
anarchist throughout the land.[36]

Altgeld sympathized with the stirrings of labor, if that made him an
anarchist. But he was also governor, and the law required him to send
militia to any place in which riots and disturbances occurred and in
which local authorities asked for assistance in maintaining order.
During the miner's strike early in 1894 he had sent troops on request.
During the railroad strike he sent troops to Decatur, Danville, Mounds,
and Spring Valley, although he correctly suspected that some of the
requests for help were inspired by the desire to break strikes rather
than by any concern for order.[37] Finally he sent troops to Chicago,
when Mayor Hopkins finally asked for them on July 6. He did not send
them earlier because they were not asked for. Hopkins evidently felt
they were not needed; Altgeld in the end had to prod him to request
them.[38]

Convinced that he was doing all that was necessary to preserve
order, Altgeld was outraged when the federal government ordered
troops to Chicago. He immediately wired Cleveland that the sending

[36] Harvey Wish, "Altgeld and the Progressive Tradition," *American Historical Review*, XLVI (July, 1941), 813–831; John P. Altgeld, *Live Questions*
(Chicago, 1899), *passim*.
[37] Lindsey, *Pullman Strike*, pp. 181–182; Browne, *Altgeld*, pp. 128–134.
[38] Lindsey, *Pullman Strike*, pp. 197–198.

of federal troops was "unnecessary" and "unjustifiable," and he demanded their immediate withdrawals. Illinois, he said, was "able to take care of itself," and had indeed done so many times by sending military aid to the scene of disturbances. It was his opinion that the President had been "imposed upon" and misled by newspaper accounts of events in Chicago, accounts which were sometimes "pure fabrications" or "wild exaggerations." There was in fact no situation in Illinois which warranted the sending of federal troops; "it is not soldiers that the railroads need," he wryly remarked, "so much as it is men to operate trains." Finally, he suggested that there was no legal basis for the action of the government. It was true that an act of 1871 empowered the government to send troops into a state if federal laws could be enforced in no other way, but such a state of affairs, he insisted, did not exist in Illinois.[39]

Cleveland replied briefly that troops had been sent "upon the demand of the post office department that obstruction of mails should be removed, and upon representations of the judicial officers of the United States that the process of the Federal courts could not be executed through the ordinary means, and upon competent proof that conspiracies existed against commerce between the States." Altgeld again protested, at great length, that the government's action undermined the "far-reaching principle of local self-government." Cleveland dismissed Altgeld's second telegram with the blunt reminder "that in this hour of danger and public distress, discussion may well give way to active efforts on the part of all in authority to restore obedience and law and to protect life and property." For conservatives and for most of the nation's press, Cleveland's last telegram remained the final word on the legal aspects of the case.[40]

Altgeld, however, was not without support. Four state governors, including J. S. Hogg of Texas, wired Cleveland, "You are notified that you may not feel called upon by the plea of any alarmist to use United

[39] Altgeld incorrectly gave the date of this law as 1881. He probably had in mind the law of 1871, although he may also have intended to refer to a law of 1861 which empowered the President to suppress "unlawful combinations, or conspiracies" which interfered with the operation of federal laws. Both laws had reference to the sectional conflict between North and South. Altgeld referred to the law as "in reality a war measure," a remark which seems to point to the act of 1871, since it would not have been necessary to refer to the earlier law as "in reality" a war measure.

[40] The exchange of telegrams is given in Browne, *Altgeld,* pp. 153–156, and in Barnard, *Eagle Forgotten,* pp. 295–307.

States troops here unless requested by State authority."[41] Henry
Demarest Lloyd wrote:

The Democratic party for a hundred years has been the pull-back against
centralization in American politics. . . . But in one hour here last July, it
sacrificed the honorable devotion of a century to its great principle and surrendered both the rights of States and the rights of man to the centralized
corporate despotism to which the presidency of the United States was then
abdicated.[42]

If the elections of 1894 were any indication, Lloyd's comment was
probably more representative of the prevailing opinion of the government's action than the elaborate praise of the press.

The Pullman strike was of course not the only issue in the congressional elections. Politically, it only completed a process already far
advanced, for Cleveland had already weakened and divided his party
by insisting on repeal of the Sherman Silver Purchase Act and by
issuing bonds to save the gold service in preference to coining the
silver seigniorage. The internal weakness of the party, as much as any
strong preference for the Republicans, explains the Democratic de-
feats in 1894. The administration, however, had also antagonized many
of its supporters outside the party. The mugwumps, for instance, had
turned to the Democrats for tariff reform, and had suffered a cruel
disappointment. Cleveland vetoed a number of pension bills; appointed
William Lochran, a less open-handed man than the lavish Tanner, as
Commissioner of Pensions; retained Theodore Roosevelt, a Republican,
on the Civil Service Commission; and extended the civil-service list;
but none of these accomplishments could blind mugwumps to his failure to secure tariff reduction.[43] Finally, the Democrats went into the

[41] Quoted in Nevins, *Cleveland,* p. 626.
[42] Caroline Lloyd, *Life of Henry Demarest Lloyd* (New York, 1912), I, 146–
147.
[43] In 1894 Cleveland added 5,468 places to the classified service, largely in
the Government Printing Office, Internal Revenue Service, and pension
agencies. In 1896, too late for it to do him any good, he extended the classified
service again. This extension was one of the most important in civil-service
history, including the Post Office Department, long a target of reformers. When
Cleveland entered office in 1893, about 43,000 places were under civil-service
rules. When he left office in 1896, there were 86,932 out of a total of 200,000
civil servants. Cleveland indeed labored endlessly in the cause of civil-service
reform; the amount of time he and William L. Wilson spent on the matter
seems almost beyond belief. The following entry in Wilson's diary is typical:
"Received a note [Sunday, March 1, 1896] by a special messenger from the

election with a handicap greater than any of these. The depression alone was a formidable obstacle to their success; together with the administration's dismal record, it was insurmountable.

In the elections the Democrats maintained technical control of the Senate, but suffered heavy losses in the House which gave the Republicans a majority of 140. Such prominent Democrats in the House as Wilson, Springer, Holman, and Bland failed of re-election. In twenty-four states the Democrats failed to elect a single member to the House, and in each of six others only one Democrat was elected. Illinois, Wisconsin, and New York, captured by the Democrats in 1892, returned to the Republican camp, and Hill, running for governor in New York, was overwhelmingly defeated by Levi Morton.[44] "There is not a Northern State," gloated the New York *Daily Tribune*, "left to the proud party which swept the country in 1892."[45] Even Delaware, Maryland, West Virginia, and Missouri went Republican. In addition the Republicans carried four western states—Kansas, Colorado, North Dakota, and Idaho—which had been carried in 1892 by Populists or by a fusion of Populists and Democrats.[46]

The Populists polled 1,471,590 votes, an increase of about 400,000 votes, or 42 per cent, over 1892. Yet the results, for the Populist candidates, were disappointing. The silver states, which had either voted for Weaver in 1892 or given him a large percentage of the vote, returned to the Republican fold. In only two states—Nebraska and North Carolina—did the Populists poll more than 48 per cent of the vote, and in those states they achieved success only by fusing with the Democrats in Nebraska and with the Republicans in North Carolina. Only four senators and four representatives in the fifty-fourth Congress

---

President, that if I would come around a little after eight we could go over a 'few quiet, orderly, Sunday-like post office cases.' Was at the White House until near midnight, but we got through with only nine troublesome cases." Festus P. Summers (ed.), *The Cabinet Diary of William L. Wilson, 1896–1897* (Chapel Hill, 1957), p. 37.

For the administration of pensions under Cleveland, see William H. Glasson, *Federal Military Pensions in the United States* (New York, 1918), pp. 240–241.

[44] *The Nation*, commenting on Hill's defeat, reaffirmed its oft-expressed opinion that he was by all odds "the worst man in American politics." LIX (Nov. 15, 1894), 351. The election in New York was a defeat for Tammany and a victory for William L. Strong more than it was a defeat for the administration. Local issues predominated.

[45] Nov. 8, 1894.

[46] *Political Science Quarterly*, X (June, 1895), 370–371.

openly styled themselves Populists.[47] The party had failed to live up to its promise of 1892.

If discontent thrives on economic adversity, one might have expected the Populists to make a better showing in the depression year 1894 than they had in 1892, a year of general prosperity. The defeat of Populism, however, did not indicate any falling off in discontent; it was to be explained as the result of other causes. In the first place, although the Populist party made only minor gains, many Republicans and Democrats were elected who sympathized with Populist views. The radicalism of sections of the old parties, particularly of the Democrats, itself sapped the vitality of the Populist party, although not necessarily of Populism itself. This process was completed in 1896, when the Democrats simply absorbed much of what was left of the Populist party. In the second place, other issues clouded the political picture in several states, especially in the South, where the issue of white supremacy was used to persuade the electorate not to desert the Democrats. Finally, the Populists once again failed to attract the support of labor. In the Northeast they polled no more than 5 per cent of the vote in any state; in the industrial states of the Middle West, no more than 14 per cent. If they had managed to capitalize on the mounting discontent among laboring men, the results would have been very different. In any case no conservative could take much delight in the election returns. The Populists had been defeated, but the anti-Cleveland wing of the Democratic party was becoming stronger every day, and even the Republicans faced a possible split in the party over the money issue. The world had by no means been made safe for orthodoxy.

Nor did the two years following the election of 1892 make it any safer. Cleveland's negotiations with Morgan, his persistent refusal to compromise on the money question, and his reluctance to take positive action in dealing with the depression made his conservatism increasingly unattractive to his own party. The bitter experiences of recent years were beginning to push many sensitive men into a radicalism which made even Populism, so horrifying to conservatives, seem

[47] The senators were William V. Allen (Nebraska), Marion Butler (North Carolina), James H. Kyle (South Dakota), and William A. Peffer (Kansas). Of these only Butler was elected in 1894. *Congressional Directory,* 54th Cong., 2nd sess., pp. 189, 191. See also John D. Hicks, *The Populist Revolt* (Minneapolis, 1931), pp. 326–329.

mild in comparison. Eugene Debs went to jail and came out a Socialist. A creed of violent class conflict began to spread among the rank and file of workers in the western mines, who cherished the dark memory of Coeur d'Alene. Even moderates having little sympathy with unionism of any kind were revolted by the ruthlessness with which unionism was attacked by the self-constituted defenders of property rights. Even moderates noted with uneasiness the growing rigidity of conservative thought and began to believe that the country had more to fear from conservative intransigence than from the demand for reform.

Nowhere was this intransigence more clearly revealed than in the decisions of the Supreme Court. The Court had been intransigent for years; the Cleveland administration encouraged it in its battle against the forces of change. Attorney General Olney, for instance, frankly declared that the Sherman Antitrust Act was "no good," and prosecuted the Knight case only because he inherited it from his predecessor.[48] In view of his apathy it was not surprising that the Court was able to come to the strange conclusion that the American Sugar Refining Company, which refined 95 per cent of the sugar in the country, was not a conspiracy in restaint of trade.[49] Nor did Cleveland's appointments to the Court do anything to make it more liberal; both Edward D. White of Louisiana, appointed by Cleveland in 1894, and Rufus W. Peckham, appointed in 1896, were diehard conservatives.[50] Even without the assistance of the administration, however, the Court would have been able to hold its own, for it fought with the knowledge that both God and Darwin were on its side. Olney prosecuted no new antitrust cases during his term as Attorney General. His successor, Judge Harmon, instituted two cases, both of which were decided in favor of the government; these decisions somewhat revived the Sherman Act.[51] In other decisions, however, the Court took un-

[48] Quoted in C. B. Swisher, *American Constitutional Development* (Boston, 1943), p. 430.

[49] U.S. *v.* E. C. Knight Company, 156 U.S. 1 (1895).

[50] White, who became Chief Justice in 1910, voted with the majority in the Debs case and in the income-tax case; he voted against the dissolution of trusts in both the Knight case and the Trans-Missouri Freight Association case. Peckham took no part in any of these cases but the last, in which he upheld the dissolution of the Trans-Missouri Association and wrote the opinion of the court.

[51] U.S. *v.* Trans-Missouri Freight Association, 166 U.S. 290 (1897), and Addyston Pipe and Steel Co. *v.* U.S., 175 U.S. 211 (1898). In the second of these, the Court held that an agreement between two manufacturing firms dividing a certain territory between them constituted a restraint on the dis-

compromisingly conservative positions.[52]

By all odds the most notable of these, and one of the most unpopular decisions ever handed down by the Supreme Court, was the case of Pollock v. Farmers' Loan and Trust Company, in which the Court nullified the income-tax provision of the Wilson-Gorman tariff. The constitutionality of an income tax had already been upheld in *Springer* v. *United States* (1881); in 1895, five out of nine justices voted to reverse the earlier decision after hearing the case twice and listening at great length to the arguments of learned counsel, who described the income tax as class legislation, as socialistic, and as a vicious plot on the part of the poor to plunder the rich. Only occasionally did counsel refer to the Constitution in an effort to show that an income tax was a direct tax which could be levied only in proportion to population. The Court, in the absence of any real reference to constitutional precedent, seemed vacillating and confused. One of the justices was reported to have changed his mind in the middle of the deliberations. The opinion of the majority, delivered by Justice Field, reflected the circumstances in which the decision had been arrived at. Charged with class prejudice, it rested only on the contention that the income tax was an "assault upon capital," the "stepping-stone to others, larger and more sweeping, till our political contests . . . become a war of the poor against the rich."[53]

Coming on the heels of a long line of decisions which protected corporations and men of great wealth at the expense of everybody else, the income-tax decision was for many people only one more indication that the government had fallen into the hands of the plutocracy. But a national election was approaching, in which the government might be restored to the people. If all those who were dissatisfied with the state of the nation were to combine their efforts, victory might at last be theirs. The question was whether they could

---

tribution—and therefore on the transportation—of an article of commerce. It will be noted that this decision did not challenge the doctrine of the Knight case that manufacturing was not commerce. For Trans-Missouri Freight Association case, see Seager and Gulick, *Trust and Corporation Problems,* p. 378 ff.

[52] The case of Eugene Debs, one of the most important of these, has already been noted. See above, p. 178.

[53] Pollock v. Farmers' Loan and Trust Company, 157 U.S. 429, 158 U.S. 601 (1895). See also Swisher, *Constitutional Development,* pp. 436–452; E. R. A. Seligman, *The Income Tax* (2nd ed., New York, 1914), pp. 493–589; Nevins, *Cleveland,* pp. 667–671, 778–779; Sidney Ratner, *American Taxation* (New York, 1942), pp. 193–214.

find a leader who would unite them. Such a leader, in the early months of 1896, was nowhere to be seen; all the candidates available to head a movement for reform seemed to have disqualified themselves in one way or another. The leader, it seemed, would have to be a new man, almost an unknown man, who could bring to politics youth, vigor, and a commanding personality. The stage was set for the emergence of William Jennings Bryan.

CHAPTER 9

The Bryan Campaign

B ETWEEN the congressional elections of 1894 and the presidential
campaign of 1896, the money question came to obscure all other
political issues. Free silver seemed, for a time, the only issue on which
men who desired political change could unite. The Populists, distressed
by their poor showing in 1894, gradually abandoned their complicated
program of reform and concentrated on the simpler issue of monetary
inflation, which experience had shown to be the most effective means
of attracting votes, at least in the western states. General Weaver
declared, "I shall favor going before the people in 1896 with the
money question alone, unencumbered with any other contention what-
soever."[1]

Silver had other political advantages. For those Populists who now
believed that success could come only through collaboration with one
of the older parties, it offered the best hope of fusion, for both parties
abounded with inflationist sentiment. Radicals in the older parties,
hoping to attract Populist support, valued the issue for the same
reason. Moreover, it appealed to the silver miners, who were ready to
contribute large amounts to finance a campaign for silver legislation—
an immensely practical consideration in view of the difficulty of obtaining funds for campaigns. Above all, the money issue had about it a
deceptive simplicity which commended itself to reformers and politicians alike. If times were hard and people poor, surely the explanation must lie in the scarcity of money. Did it not stand to reason that if
more money were created there would be more of it to go around?

The latter argument was compellingly set forth by W. H. Harvey in

[1] John D. Hicks, *The Populist Revolt* (Minneapolis, 1931), p. 344.

a brilliant polemic, *Coin's Financial School,* published in 1894. Hundreds of thousands of copies of this pamphlet were sold between 1894 and 1896; it became the gospel of the silver movement. Harvey, a native of Virginia, had practiced law in Ohio, tried his hand at ranching, and prospected for silver in the West. The panic of 1893 wiped out his resources, and he returned East to edit a weekly newspaper in Chicago. The journal failed, but *Coin's Financial School* made its editor famous. His pamphlet purported to be a record of a series of classes conducted by a diminutive authority on currency known simply as "Coin." A number of well-known opponents of silver, as well as an audience of more sympathetic citizens, were said to have attended the lectures in order to hold Coin up to ridicule. Their views, however, were smartly confounded by the "smooth little financier," and most of his critics went away converted to his views. All this proved embarrassing to some of the men depicted as having attended Coin's lectures, who had to assure their irate followers that the classes had never actually been held. Influential as Harvey's book was, it "did not create the silver movement, but the strength of the silver movement created the market for that kind of literature."[2]

Defenders of gold replied to the arguments of men like Harvey that the coinage of silver would bring about none of the expected benefits.

The greater or less quantity of money there is roaming about in circulation [said J. Lawrence Laughlin] is no reason why any one gets more of it. Money, like property, is parted with for a consideration. No matter how many coins there are coming from the mint under free coinage and going into the vaults of the banks to the credit of the mine owners who own the bullion, there are no more coins in the pockets of Weary Waggles, who is cooling his heels on the sidewalk outside the bank.

This was logical enough, but the reference to "Weary Waggles" weakened the argument. In the end Laughlin, like nearly all defenders of the gold standard, could not conceal his opinion that the demand for silver coinage was "simply an attempt to transfer from the great mass of the community who have been provident, industrious and successful, a portion of their savings and gains into the pockets of those

---

[2] Fred E. Haynes, *Third Party Movements Since the Civil War* (Iowa City, 1916), p. 295; W. H. Harvey, *Coin's Financial School* (Chicago, 1894), and *Up to Date, Coin's Financial School Continued* (Chicago, 1895); see also Willard C. Fisher, "Coin and His Critics," *Quarterly Journal of Economics,* X (Jan., 1896), 187–208.

who have been idle, extravagant, or unfortunate." Here was only the uncompromising logic of laissez faire and social Darwinism.[3]

The trouble with Laughlin's argument was that it was clearly contrary to fact; to blame the plight of the farmers on their lack of enterprise or thrift ran counter to what every farmer knew from experience. As Harvey replied in his well-publicized debate with Laughlin:

You say people should work and turn out property, and they will get their money. They are working, but they can't get the money. [Applause.] They produce the property, and find the property costs them what they get for it; that they get what it costs them to produce. . . . The trouble is, when they have produced the property, you have destroyed the price. [Applause.][4]

Such arguments, repeated throughout the Middle West and South, became increasingly persuasive. The demand for silver, when added to the clamor of the silver miners, rose to a crescendo; and as the political campaign drew near, many politicians in both parties began to wonder whether the time had not come to give in to it, or at least to compromise with it. Among the Republicans, a bloc of senators led by Teller of Colorado and Pettigrew of South Dakota openly advocated free silver. Many others favored international bimetallism. When the Republican National Convention met in St. Louis in June, 1896, therefore, it appeared that the party would have to compromise with the silverites, particularly since McKinley himself, whose nomination was already a foregone conclusion, was a bimetallist who had voted for both the Bland-Allison and the Sherman Silver Purchase Acts. The gold men, however, terrified by fears of a violent social upheaval, desperately wished to commit the party to the gold standard.

The central figure in whatever decision was arrived at would clearly be that of Marcus A. Hanna, the Warwick who engineered McKinley's nomination. A Cleveland capitalist who had made a fortune in coal, iron, oil, and merchandising, Hanna had retired from business in 1895 to supervise the nomination of McKinley. In rounding up delegates he was incessantly active, and he himself bore almost the entire expense

[3] J. Lawrence Laughlin, *Facts about Money, Including the Debate with W. H. Harvey, May 17, 1895* (Chicago, 1895), pp. 223–224, 233.

[4] *Ibid.*, pp. 241–242. See also F. W. Taussig, *The Silver Situation in the United States* (American Economic Association, 1892), VII, 1–118; E. Benjamin Andrews, *An Honest Dollar* (Hartford, 1894); Francis A. Walker, *International Bimetallism* (New York, 1896).

of the effort.[5] His very success soon made him a symbol of the money power, working quietly behind the scenes to accomplish his evil designs; cartoonists caricatured him as a low-browed man with a bulldog face and a waistcoat covered with dollar signs. In reality Hanna was an intelligent and independent student of the political art. He shared neither the dogmatism nor the infatuation with money for its own sake that characterized the capitalists with whom he was confused by the public; later he attained the stature of real statesmanship during his years in the Senate. In 1896, however, Hanna, although he was not unsympathetic to the plight of the farmer and the workingman, believed that the safety of the country lay in a high tariff, in a close alliance between property and politics, and above all in the election of McKinley. To assure the latter, he was ready, as a practical man, to compromise on silver in order to keep it in the background during the campaign.

Hanna and McKinley at first approved a plank which straddled the money issue. It declared only for the "existing standard." Eastern and Middle West business interests, however, soon convinced them that the gold men would dominate the convention and force the party to promise to preserve the "existing gold standard." Hanna then made up his mind to acquiesce in this change in the wording of the plank, but in such a way as to make the gold men think that they had forced him to their position. In return for this "concession," Hanna then demanded that the Easterners support McKinley. "The whole thing," said Hanna, "was managed in order to succeed in *getting what we got,* and that was my only interest."[6]

In later years a number of other people claimed credit for having inserted the word "gold" into the Republican platform. Herman H. Kohlsaat, a Chicago publisher, claimed that he had been the one to win over Hanna and to introduce the word into the platform submitted to the Committee on Resolutions. Both James B. Foraker of the subcommittee on resolutions and Senator Orville Platt believed that they were responsible for the insertion of the magic word. Many believed that Henry Cabot Lodge had brought the change, and he did not deny it. In this welter of conflicting contentions, one can only conclude that the platform was the work of many men and that no one

[5] Herbert Croly, *Marcus Alonzo Hanna* (New York, 1923), pp. 183–184.

[6] *Ibid.,* p. 199; Thomas Beer, *Hanna* (New York, 1929), pp. 137–148; Matthew Josephson, *The Politicos* (New York, 1938), pp. 653–661.

could claim exclusive credit. If anyone could be said to have had the major share in the decision, it was Hanna, who might have blocked it. Since the gold men dominated the convention, however, they would probably have prevailed even over his opposition, if he had been foolish enough to oppose them.[7]

The central plank in the Republican platform finally read:

The Republican party is unreservedly for sound money. It caused the enactment of a law providing for the resumption of specie payments in 1879. Since then every dollar has been as good as gold. We are unalterably opposed to every measure calculated to debase our currency or impair the credit of our country. We are therefore opposed to the free coinage of silver, except by international agreement with the leading commercial nations of the earth, which agreement we pledge ourselves to promote, and until such agreement can be obtained the existing gold standard must be maintained. All of our silver and paper currency must be maintained at parity with gold, and we favor all measures designated to maintain inviolable the obligations of the United States, of all our money, whether coin or paper, at the present standard, the standard of most enlightened nations of the earth.[8]

When this plank was read to the convention, Senator Teller, speaking for a minority of the Committee on Resolutions, offered a substitute for it, which he supported in an earnest speech: "The Republican party favors the use of both gold and silver as an equal standard money, and pledges its power to secure the free, unrestricted, and independent coinage of gold and silver at our mints at the ratio of sixteen parts of silver to one of gold." The convention voted, 818½ to 105½, against Teller's substitute. At least 100½ of the votes cast for it came from the South and from the states west of the Mississippi. Led by Senators Teller, Pettigrew, Fred T. Dubois of Idaho, and Frank J. Cannon of Utah, twenty-two silver delegates then left the convention.[9]

The rest of the platform was accepted without disagreement. It contained the usual innocuous endorsements of civil-service reform, temperance, and the Monroe Doctrine, declared itself in favor of a high tariff and of pensions for veterans, and included a few banalities

[7] Croly, *Hanna*, p. 203; H. H. Kohlsaat, *From McKinley to Harding* (New York, 1923), pp. 33–40; Arthur W. Dunn, *From Harrison to Harding* (New York, 1922), I, 175–178.

[8] Kirk H. Porter, *National Party Platforms* (New York, 1924), pp. 203–204.

[9] Elmer Ellis, *Henry Moore Teller* (Caldwell, Idaho, 1941), pp. 241–264, and his "The Silver Republicans in the Election of 1896," *Mississippi Valley Historical Review*, XVIII (Mar., 1932), 525–557.

meant to appeal to labor. Nor was the nomination of a candidate any more controversial; Hanna had done his work well. McKinley was nominated by the temporary chairman of the convention, Charles W. Fairbanks; seconded by the permanent chairman, Senator John N. Thurston of Nebraska; and nominated on the first ballot by a vote of 661½ to 84½ for his closest rival, Thomas B. Reed. Quay of Pennsylvania, Morton of New York, and Allison of Iowa received a few votes from their own states. Garret A. Hobart, a New Jersey politician and corporation lawyer who was almost unknown outside his own state, was nominated for Vice-President.[10] The whole business lacked enthusiasm. William Allen White wrote:

Reporters who have attended national conventions say that this is the most listless convention they have ever reported. There is no life in it. The applause is hollow; the enthusiasm dreary and the delegates sit like hogs in a car and know nothing about anything.[11]

Hanna's thorough preparations left little room for spontaneity, and, as the Democrats could have told him, spontaneity is the life of any political convention. They were to prove it once again at their own convention in Chicago.

The Democrats, unlike the Republicans, had no idea who they ought to nominate. Opposition to the administration was steadily mounting, but the opposition seemed able to suggest no plausible candidate of its own. Altgeld would have been the logical choice, but he was disqualified by birth. Ever since the Pullman strike he had been working to steer the party away from the Cleveland policies. In 1895 he caused a state convention of Democrats in Illinois to declare for free silver, and other states promptly followed.[12] By the time the national convention met on July 7, the silver delegates were in the majority and were therefore in a position to write the platform. Whether they could muster the two-thirds necessary to nominate a candidate remained to be seen. William C. Whitney arrived with a special train of eastern

[10] Dunn, *Harrison to Harding*, I, 225, describes Hobart as a "business politician" "well liked by Senators" and "useful to the Senate and to the President." See also Croly, *Hanna*, p. 191.

[11] Emporia *Gazette*, June 23, 1896, quoted in Walter Johnson, *William Allen White's America* (New York, 1947), p. 89; see also *The Autobiography of William Allen White* (New York, 1946), pp. 273–278.

[12] Harvey Wish, "John P. Altgeld and the Background of the Campaign of 1896," *Mississippi Valley Historical Review*, XXIV (Mar., 1938), 503–518.

hard-money men to prevent the convention from falling into the hands of the forces of anarchy and mob rule, but it soon became evident that not even Whitney could swing the convention to a sound-money candidate.[13]

The National Committee recommends the temporary chairman of the convention, and its recommendation is usually followed. In 1896, however, Hill of New York, the choice of the National Committee, was defeated 556 to 349 by John W. Daniel of Virginia, a strong bimetallist. Another bimetallist, Senator Stephen M. White of California, was chosen permanent chairman. On the second day of the convention the silverites obtained a two-third majority on a proposal to unseat the gold delegation from Nebraska, seated by the National Committee, in favor of a silver delegation headed by Bryan. These events clearly showed that the silver forces completely controlled the convention. Altgeld then addressed the convention at length, declaring that the Democrats would make "no compromise on the currency issue." The delegates cheered him uproariously.[14]

On the third day the platform was brought in. Senator Jones of Arkansas read it. It sounded like a document from the pen of Altgeld, which in fact it was. It was quite unlike the usual party platform in containing no words of praise for the outgoing administration. On the contrary, it denounced the administration. One resolution read:

We are opposed to the issuing of interest-bearing bonds of the United States in time of peace and condemn the trafficking with banking syndicates, which, in exchange for bonds and at enormous profit to themselves, supply the Federal Treasury with gold to maintain the policy of gold monometallism.

Another plank pointedly referred to the Pullman strike:

We denounce arbitrary interference by Federal authorities in local affairs as a violation of the Constitution of the United States, and a crime against free institutions and we especially object to government by injunction as a new and highly dangerous form of oppression by which Federal Judges, in

[13] Allan Nevins, *Grover Cleveland* (New York, 1932), pp. 689–704.

[14] Harvey Wish, "John Peter Altgeld and the Election of 1896," *Journal of the Illinois State Historical Society*, XXX (Oct., 1937), 359. Carter Harrison, a delegate at the convention, later wrote: "Altgeld rather than Bryan or any other, was responsible for the clarion Chicago utterance. . . . [Bryan] was little more than the silver-tongued mouthpiece of the thinker." Carter H. Harrison, *Stormy Years* (Indianapolis, 1935), p. 70.

contempt of the laws of the States and rights of citizens, become at once legislators, judges and executives. . . .[15]

Elsewhere the platform demanded more vigorous enforcement of the Sherman Act, enlargement of the powers of the Interstate Commerce Commission, abolition of national bank notes, a tariff for revenue only, an income tax, and, most important, free coinage of silver. The party had openly repudiated its President; "sledge-hammer Altgeld," as Vachel Lindsay later called him, had "wrecked his power."

The goldbugs immediately offered amendments to the platform. Debate then began. Tillman of South Carolina led off with a bitter denunciation of the eastern money power in general and of Cleveland in particular. "We of the South," he said, "have burned our bridges behind us so far as the eastern Democrats are concerned."[16] Hill, Vilas, and former Governor Russell of Massachusetts answered him in more measured terms, but the tumultuous crowd barely heard them. As Russell's speech ended, the young and buoyant figure of Bryan could be seen rapidly making his way toward the platform. His audience could not know that he had been preparing for this moment for two years, polishing parts of the speech he was about to deliver before many a country audience.[17] In a sense he had been preparing for it all his life, ever since his college days, when he began to win prizes in oratory. He had always assumed that oratory was the key to political success, and history was now at last to bear him out.

He would be presumptuous, Bryan began, to challenge the "distinguished gentlemen" who had just addressed the convention, if the present contest were a contest of persons. Where principle was concerned, however, "the humblest citizen in all the land, when clad in the armor of a righteous cause, is stronger than all the hosts of error." These opening words set the tone of the speech; Bryan clearly believed himself to be voicing the inchoate thoughts of the people. His opponents, he said, spoke only for the business interests, complaining that the platform would disturb those interests. But the people had "business interests" of their own.

[15] Porter, *National Party Platforms,* pp. 181–187.
[16] *Public Opinion,* July 16, 1896, pp. 70–71.
[17] Mark Sullivan, *Our Times* (New York, 1920–1925), I, 120–131; William Jennings Bryan and Mary Bryan, *Memoirs of William Jennings Bryan* (Philadelphia, 1925), p. 103.

We say to you that you have made the definition of a business man too limited in its application. The man who is employed for wages is as much a business man as his employer; the attorney in a country town is as much a business man as the corporation counsel in a great metropolis; the merchant at the cross-roads store is as much a business man as the merchant of New York; the farmer who goes forth in the morning and toils all day—who begins in the spring and toils all summer—and who by the application of brain and muscle to the natural resources of the country creates wealth, is as much a business man as the man who goes upon the Board of Trade and bets upon the price of grain; the miners who go down a thousand feet into the earth, or climb two thousand feet upon the cliffs, and bring forth from their hiding places the precious metals to be poured into the channels of trade are as much business men as the few financial magnates who, in a back room, corner the money of the world. We come to speak for this broader class of business men.

Except for a reference to the Supreme Court's decision in the income-tax case, in which he denied that an income tax was unconstitutional and pointed out that it did not become so "until one judge changed his mind; and we cannot be expected to know when a judge will change his mind," Bryan passed briefly over most of the platform in order to dwell on the silver issue—the "paramount issue," he called it. Instead of dwelling on the technical aspects of the issue, he chided the Republicans for declaring for bimetallism, if it could be done intentionally, when they believed the gold standard to be such an excellent thing, accusing them of evading the issue. The issue could not be evaded, however; the lines of battle were drawn.

Mr. Carlisle said in 1878 that this was a struggle between "the idle holders of idle capital" and "the struggling masses, who produce the wealth and pay the taxes of the country"; and, my friends, the question we are to decide is: Upon which side will the Democratic party fight; upon the side of "the idle holders of idle capital" or upon the side of "the struggling masses"? That is the question which the party must answer first, and then it must be answered by each individual hereafter. The sympathies of the Democratic party, as shown by the platform, are on the side of the struggling masses who have ever been the foundation of the Democratic party. . . .

You come to us and tell us that the great cities are in favor of the gold standard; we reply that the great cities rest upon our broad and fertile prairies. Burn down your cities and leave our farms, and your cities will spring up again as if by magic; but destroy our farms and the grass will grow in the streets of every city in the country. . . .

If they dare to come out in the open field and defend the gold standard as a good thing, we will fight them to the uttermost. Having behind us the producing masses of this nation and the world, supported by the commercial interests, the laboring interests and the toilers everywhere, we will answer their demand for a gold standard by saying to them: You shall not press down upon the brow of labor this crown of thorns, you shall not crucify mankind upon a cross of gold.[18]

Bryan's stately peroration, rendered in his magnificent voice, electrified the convention. The delegates leaped to their feet, cheering wildly. Only in the morning did some of them, like Altgeld, pause to reflect, "It takes more than speeches to win real victories. Applause lasts but a little while. The road to justice is not a path of glory; it is stony and long and lonely, filled with pain and martyrdom." "I have been thinking over Bryan's speech," Altgeld said to Clarence Darrow. "What did he say, anyhow?"[19]

The speech did help to turn back the movement to amend the platform by introducing planks which affirmed the gold standard and praised the Cleveland administration for its "honesty, economy, courage, and fidelity." It united the silver forces and held them firmly against compromise. More than that, it practically guaranteed Bryan's nomination. Perhaps that is why Altgeld had certain reservations about it. No admirer of Bryan, Altgeld would have preferred to nominate "Silver Dick" Bland of Missouri, author of the famous Bland-Allison Act and a stalwart silverite of long standing. When the balloting began, Bland took the lead and held it for three ballots, followed by Bryan, Boies, and Robert E. Pattison of Pennsylvania, the only gold candidate. On the fourth ballot Bryan forged ahead. Altgeld called the Illinois delegation into conference. When they decided by a small majority to support Bryan, Altgeld endorsed him, and he was nominated on the fifth ballot.[20] Except for the backers of Pattison, few gold delegates bothered to vote. Most of them had left the convention by the time Arthur Sewall, a banker, shipbuilder, and railroad director of Maine who for some reason believed in free silver, was nominated for Vice-President.[21]

---

[18] William Jennings Bryan, *The First Battle* (Chacgo, 1896), pp. 199–206; H. S. Commager (ed.), *Documents of American History* (6th ed., New York, 1958), No. 342.

[19] Clarence Darrow, *The Story of My Life* (New York, 1932), p. 92.

[20] Wish, "Altgeld in the Election of 1896," pp. 357, 363–364.

[21] Edward Stanwood, *A History of the Presidency* (Boston, 1898), I, 541–

Respectable opinion in the East unanimously condemned the shocking developments in Chicago. Nothing too harsh nor bitter could fully express their feelings. Their vilification of the silver Democrats was complete. Their platform was rank Populism intensified with hate and venom. At Chicago the "Jacobins," they believed, were in full control. *The Nation* sounded the same theme, charging that Bryan's speech was "an appeal to one of the worst instincts of the human heart—that of getting possession of other people's property without the owners' consent."[22] As the news of the triumph of the Jacobins spread, the stock market faltered; men rushed to the Treasury to draw out gold. Lifelong Democrats announced that they would vote for McKinley.

Not all gold Democrats, however, could stomach the idea of voting for a Republican. Some, led by Vilas and other Midwestern leaders and supported by eastern financiers, organized a "National Democratic" party and nominated Senator Palmer of Illinois and General Simon B. Buckner of Kentucky. Cleveland sympathized with them, although he did not endorse them; so did most of his cabinet. Carlisle actively supported the separate ticket. In two states, Kentucky and California, the gold Democrats appear to have drawn enough strength from the regular Democrats to throw the election to McKinley.[23]

If the nomination of Bryan dismayed the gold Democrats, it presented the Populists with a dilemma equally cruel. If they endorsed Bryan, they would destroy the independence of their own party; if they refused to support him, they would jeopardize the success of a man who, whatever his party affiliation, was running on a Populist platform. Most Midwestern Populists found it possible to support Bryan in conscience. In the South, however, fusion with the Democracy was a vital issue, for the southern Populists had built up their party with the support of the Republicans. Fusion would destroy the precarious independence of the party. The cause of reform might temporarily

550; W. V. Byers (ed.), *An American Commoner: The Life and Times of Richard Park Bland* (Columbia, Mo., 1900), pp. 237–240; Bryan, *First Battle*, pp. 210–232; J. B. Kern, "The Political Career of Horace Boies," *Iowa Journal of History*, XLVII (July, 1949), 241–243.

22 *The Nation*, LXIII (July 16, 1896), 42.

23 Horace S. Merrill, *Bourbon Democracy of the Middle West* (Baton Rouge, 1953), pp. 269–272; Nevins, *Cleveland*, pp. 705–707; James A. Barnes, *John G. Carlisle* (New York, 1931), pp. 465–475; Festus P. Summers (ed.), *The Cabinet Diary of William L. Wilson, 1896–1897* (Chapel Hill, 1957), pp. 109, 111, 114, 116; Edgar E. Robinson, *The Presidential Vote, 1896–1932* (Palo Alto, 1934), pp. 145, 208, 380, 385.

triumph with Bryan, but with the return of the party of white supremacy the racial issue would surely be used again to obscure the demand for reform. Most of the southern Populists, therefore, and a few Midwestern leaders like Peffer and Donnelly, opposed fusion.

When the Populists assembled at St. Louis, the fusionists won the first victory by electing Senator Allen of Nebraska permanent chairman. Upon taking the chair, Allen immediately tried to impress his views on the convention. Insisting that he was not advocating Mr. Bryan's nomination, he went on to say:

If by putting a third ticket in the field you would defeat free coinage; defeat a withdrawal of the issue power of national banks; defeat government ownership of railroads, telephones and telegraphs; defeat an income tax and foist gold monometallism and high taxation upon the people for a generation to come, which would you do? It is for you to choose and not for me, but you should choose wisely, as doubtless you will.

Chiding the opponents of fusion, who called themselves "middle of the road" Populists, he said:

I do not want [my constituents] to say to me that the Populists have been advocates of reforms, when they could not be accomplished, but when the first ray of light appeared and the people were looking with expectancy and anxiety for relief the party was not equal to the occasion; that it was stupid; it was blind; it kept "in the middle of the road" and missed the golden opportunity.[24]

The convention then decided on the novel course of nominating the Vice-President first. Two reasons dictated this stratagem of the fusionists. In the first place, although many Populists advocated the nomination of Bryan, none advocated endorsing Sewall; there was general agreement that the party should put its own candidate in the field. In the second place, the fusionists feared that the middle-of-the-roaders would at any moment leave the convention if they were not appeased; to nominate a separate candidate for Vice-President would at least give the party an appearance of independence. The fusionists therefore allowed Thomas E. Watson, a strong opponent of fusion, to be nominated for Vice-President. Watson was not even present at the convention, refusing to take part in any attempt to return to the Democratic

[24] Bryan, *First Battle,* p. 270.

party, which, in his opinion, would be to "return as the hog did to his wallow."[25] Informed of his nomination, he declined it.

Watson, however, was urged that his acceptance would "harmonize all factions and prevent a split in the party." Still he refused. What finally swayed him was the illusion, fostered by the fusionists, that the Democrats had agreed to remove Sewall from the ticket if the Populists would endorse Bryan. Watson then accepted the Populist nomination, thinking that he was also assured of the Democratic nomination. Bryan had in fact declared that he would not accept the nomination of any convention which repudiated Sewall, but Allen withheld this information from the convention. Under the impression that Watson would be accepted by Bryan as his running mate, the middle-of the-road Populists then consented to the nomination of Bryan. The masterly machinations of Allen, which rivaled those of any machine politician, had secured the nomination of Bryan. The spectacle moved Henry Demarest Lloyd to write, "The new party, the Reform party, the People's party, [is] more boss-ridden, gang-ruled, gang-gangrened than the two old parties of monopoly."[26]

The opponents of fusion were bitterly disappointed. All their work of the last six years seemed to have been destroyed at one blow. Their hopes of reviving a two-party system in the South by organizing a genuine workingman's party which would cut across racial lines went up in thin air; clearly no help in that direction could be expected from the Democrats, no matter how ardently their leaders protested their devotion to reform. Many Populists had also hoped that the party would eventually attract the support of labor, and many urban reformers, who sympathized with the Populists in their hostility to land monopoly and in their demand for government ownership of public utilities, had already signified their willingness to co-operate. The silver issue meant little to them. Yet by fusing with the Democrats, the Populists had subordinated all issues to free silver. The wreckage of their platform was the greatest disappointment of all to the middle-of-the-road Populists, a disappointment shared by men like Lloyd, who wrote:

The Free Silver movement is a fake. Free silver is the cow-bird of the reform movement. It waited till the nest had been built by the sacrifices and

---

[25] C. Vann Woodward, *Tom Watson, Agrarian Rebel* (New York, 1938), p. 293.

[26] Lloyd, *Henry Demarest Lloyd*, I, 259.

labor of others, and then it laid its eggs in it, pushing out the others which it smashed on the ground. . . . The People's party has been betrayed. No party that does not lead its leaders will ever succeed.[27]

Most of the urban reformers deserted the party when it endorsed Bryan. Lloyd himself, who had done so much to promote an urban-agrarian coalition, voted the Socialist-Labor ticket headed by Daniel De Leon. Henry George and Eugene Debs, almost alone among urban radicals, voted for Bryan.[28]

In the summer of 1896 it seemed at times as though everyone who had an idea was organizing a separate party. Parties sprang up everywhere. In addition to the Democrats, the Republicans, the Populists, the Gold Democrats, and the Socialist-Labor party, the silver Republicans organized a National Silver party and endorsed Bryan, and even the Prohibitionists split into two groups—the regulars, who campaigned on the prohibition question alone, and the "broad gaugers," who added to temperance, silver, woman suffrage, and a sprinkling of other reforms. The structure of American politics seemed to be breaking down and parties reconstituting themselves along class lines—a prospect infinitely appalling to respectable middle-class citizens. "These leaders," Theodore Roosevelt was reported to have said, referring to Bryan and Altgeld, "are plotting a social revolution and the subversion of the American Republic." He intimated that civil war might follow and that he himself might soon meet Altgeld on the field of battle.[29] Others did not hope even for battle, but resigned themselves to the imminent victory of the Jacobins; a few made plans to leave the country. John Hay wrote to a friend, "And are you going to join the grand exodus

[27] *Ibid.,* I, 263–264.
[28] For the Populist convention and its aftermath, see Hicks, *Populist Revolt,* pp. 340–379; Woodward, *Watson,* pp. 294–301; Stanwood, *Presidency,* I, 550–555; Bryan, *First Battle,* pp. 259–281; Chester M. Destler, *American Radicalism, 1865–1900* (Connecticut College Monograph No. 3, New London, 1946), pp. 162–164; Howard H. Quint, *The Forging of American Socialism* (Columbia, S.C., 1953), pp. 210–246; Daniel Aaron, *Men of Good Hope* (New York, 1951), pp. 89, 129, 131, 164–168; Henry D. Lloyd, "The Populists at St. Louis," *Review of Reviews,* XIV (Aug., 1896), 298–303; Edward B. Mittleman, "Chicago Labor in Politics, 1877–1896," *Journal of Political Economy,* XXVIII (May, 1920), pp. 423–427; James Peterson, "The Trade Unions and the Populist Party," *Science and Society* (1944), pp. 143–160.
[29] Henry F. Pringle, *Theodore Roosevelt* (New York, 1931). p. 164. This story originated with Willis J. Abbott of the New York *Journal,* who quoted Roosevelt as having said these things in a conversation with him. Roosevelt subsequently denied the story.

from our wayward native land that is to occur when the Goldbugs are squashed under the heel of Silver's champion? Many of my friends are saving their money for the purchase of suitable residences in Paris. Shall we next meet on the Place de la République?"[30]

Meanwhile William Jennings Bryan, the center of so much adulation and denunciation, was making plans for an exhaustive campaign which would carry him to all parts of the land. Bryan was already a seasoned campaigner; he was not, as legend would have him, unknown to the country at the time of his nomination. Before 1896 he had won two elections to Congress in a rock-ribbed Republican district, and had spoken widely throughout the West. The *Review of Reviews* noted in August, 1896:

If, indeed, [his countrymen] had not heard of Mr. Bryan before, they had failed to follow closely the course of American politics in the past eight years. As a Democratic member of the Ways and Means Committee through two Congresses, Mr. Bryan was by all odds the ablest and strongest orator on the democratic side of the House. His subsequent canvass for the United States Senatorship in Nebraska was noteworthy and conspicuous on many accounts. He had been often mentioned as a presidential possibility among the Democrats of the West, but his youth had been considered a conclusive argument against his availability.[31]

Perhaps if his enemies had known Bryan better, they would have found him less terrifying. Certainly he was no wild-eyed radical, imbued with foreign ideologies and professing class conflict as his creed. His ideology was Jacksonian democracy, not socialism or anarchism, and his creed was that of the evangelical Christianity in which he had been raised. Born in Salem, Illinois, in 1860, in a family both sides of which had moved north from below Mason and Dixon's line, he was brought up in a strongly religious environment which was to give him, as his wife later wrote, "a source of tremendous strength . . . freedom from doubt." His father, Silas Bryan, who served eight years in the Illinois state senate and was twice elected judge in the second state circuit, was an old-fashioned Jacksonian Democrat who already, in 1869, was lamenting the drift toward centralization, warning his colleagues in the Illinois Constitutional Convention that "too much

30 In Beer, *Hanna,* p. 157.
31 *Review of Reviews,* XIV (Aug., 1896), 139; Josephus Daniels, *Editor in Politics* (Chapel Hill, 1941), pp. 163–164; Barnes, "Myths of the Bryan Campaign," pp. 380–382.

government in republics is the rock upon which they founder." Bryan never really departed from this simple proposition; later, when charged with socialism for advocating government ownership of the railroads, he answered that government ownership was a means of *avoiding* socialism. He took his stand on time-honored ground: "The Democratic party, if I understand its position, denies the economic as well as the political advantage of private monopoly and promises to oppose it wherever it manifests itself. It offers as an alternative competition where competition is possible, and public monopoly wherever circumstances are such as to prevent competition."[32]

Bryan's first ambition, according to his own account, was to be a Baptist minister; his second was "to be a farmer and raise pumpkins." His father, however, was a substantial citizen, and Bryan was enrolled in Illinois College in Jacksonville, where he distinguished himself in oratory and debate. Upon graduation he spent two years in Lyman Trumbull's law office in Chicago. Returning to Jacksonville, he married Mary Baird, the daughter of a prosperous storekeeper. For five years he practiced law with scant success and in 1887, in search of greater opportunity, moved west to Lincoln, Nebraska. In truth Bryan was never much interested in the law, which seemed to him dry and academic; he preferred the excitement of political campaigns. Elected to Congress in 1890, he was re-elected in 1892 and then defeated for senator in 1894 through the efforts of J. Sterling Morton's Democratic machine. For the next two years he served as editor of the Omaha *World-Herald,* a paper controlled by the silver interests. In Congress he had devoted his first speech to an exposition of the tariff, but he quickly discovered that the voters of Nebraska were more interested in free silver. As he confessed to an audience during the campaign of 1892, "I don't know anything about free silver. The people of Nebraska are for free silver and I am for free silver. I will look up the arguments later." This was not mere opportunism; it was a profession of faith in the ability of the people instinctively to know what was best for the country. If the voice of the people was the voice of God, as Bryan believed, a politician had no choice but to heed it.[33]

---

[32] Quoted in Richard Hofstadter, *The American Political Tradition* (Vintage ed., New York, 1954), p. 198; on Bryan's father see Paxton Hibben, *The Peerless Leader* (New York, 1929), pp. 22–43.

[33] Hofstadter, *American Political Tradition,* p. 190. For Bryan's early career, see Willis J. Abbott, "William Jennings Bryan—A Character Sketch," *Review*

Bryan was admirably suited for the politician's role as he conceived it, for he perfectly understood the popular mind and could speak in language at once eloquent and simple. He was not, however, a demagogue, much less a "slobbering demagogue" or a "political faker," as his enemies called him. His campaign was dignified and, considering the campaigns that had preceded it, unusually high-minded. He himself was courteous, earnest, and poised, as even eastern audiences were willing to admit. As the campaign wore on, indeed, Bryan's obvious sincerity, together with the fact that he was fighting against great odds, won him a certain respect and sympathy in unexpected quarters. Mrs. Henry Cabot Lodge, who was hardly attracted to his political views, nevertheless exclaimed at the end of the campaign:

The great fight is won . . . a fight conducted by trained and experienced and organized forces, with both hands full of money, with the power of the press—and of prestige—on one side; on the other, a disorganized mob, at first out of which burst into sight, hearing, and force—one man, but such a man! Alone, penniless, without backing, without money, with scarce a paper, without speakers, that man fought such a fight that even those in the East can call him a Crusader, an inspired fanatic—a prophet! It has been marvellous.[34]

There had never been a campaign like Bryan's; there was never to be another one like it until the days of radio. In three months Bryan traveled 18,000 miles in twenty-one states, made over 600 speeches, and addressed an estimated five million people.[35] He accomplished all this on a campaign fund of $300,000, most of it contributed by the silver and copper magnates Marcus Daly, F. Augustus Heinze, and William Clark, by their closely affiliated Senators Stewart and Jones of Nevada, and by William Randolph Hearst. The Republicans, on the other hand, had at their disposal the vast wealth of the nation's biggest corporations, mobilized by the indefatigable Mark Hanna. By preying on the fears of the rich, which he himself knew to be grossly exaggerated, Hanna emptied their pockets. From Standard Oil alone he collected $250,000—an amount almost as large as Bryan's entire campaign fund.[36] From J. P. Morgan he collected a like amount. The Chicago

---

of Reviews, XIV (Aug., 1896). 161–173; his wife's account in Bryan, First Battle, pp. 33–66; Wayne C. Williams, William Jennings Bryan (New York, 1936); M. R. Werner, Bryan (New York, 1929); Hibben, Peerless Leader, pp. 131–135.

[34] John A. Garraty, Henry Cabot Lodge (New York, 1953), p. 176.
[35] Josephson, Politicos, p. 688.
[36] Croly, Hanna, p. 220.

meat-packing houses were said to have given $400,000.[37] The life
insurance companies, as Croly says, were "liberal contributors." Since
"the customary method of voluntary contribution . . . was wholly
insufficient," according to Hanna's sympathetic biographer, funds had
to be raised by means of "systematic assessment according to the means
of the individual and institution," and regardless, it might be said, of
party affiliation. Banks were simply assessed a regular amount—about
a quarter of 1 per cent of their capital.[38] Businessmen were shocked at
such brazenness and afraid of the public reaction to it, but they contributed nonetheless. "I wish that Hanna would not talk so freely
about money," said one. "But I know that we are going to need
more."[39] By such means Hanna raised a campaign chest conservatively
estimated by Croly at $3,500,000, but estimated by others at $10 million or even more.[40]

Hanna not only raised more money than any political manager had
ever dreamed of raising; he made better use of it. Setting up two
campaign headquarters, one in New York under his own direction, the
other in Chicago under Henry C. Payne and Charles G. Dawes, he
proceeded to expose the public to a campaign of sustained propaganda
such as had never before been known. He sent out speakers by the
thousands. He distributed hundreds of thousands of pamphlets, tons of
copy to newspapers, carloads of cartoons and posters, and untold
quantities of campaign buttons.[41] He transported whole trainloads of
people to McKinley's home in Canton. Nothing was left to chance;

[37] Josephson, *Politicos,* p. 699.

[38] Croly, *Hanna,* p. 220.

[39] Beer, *Hanna,* p. 152.

[40] Croly, *Hanna,* p. 220. Croly's estimate derives from the amount that was
officially recorded. The total amount was certainly higher. Mrs. Lodge, in the
letter previously cited, wrote: "We acknowledge to 7 millions campaign fund."
Garraty, *Lodge,* p. 176. Some estimates ran as high as $16 million. Even the
minimum given by Croly, however, was unprecedented. In 1892 the Republican
campaign fund was recorded at $1,500,000.

[41] Republican campaign headquarters distributed a total of 120,000,000 documents (an average of twenty to every voter in the Middle West), of which the
most popular was William Allen White's famous editorial, "What's the Matter
with Kansas?" Hanna told White "that he had used it more widely than any
other circular in the campaign." *The Autobiography of William Allen White*
(New York, 1946), p. 284; Ellis, *Teller,* p. 281; W. B. Shaw, "Methods and
Tactics of the Campaign," *Review of Reviews,* XIV (Nov., 1896), 554–558.

Croly notes that "as the early hurrah for Bryan and free silver wore off, an
increasing demand was made for protectionist matter." Croly, *Hanna,* p. 217.

these famous front-porch appearances of the candidate, for instance, were planned in the most minute detail.

The general procedure [according to Croly] was something as follows: A letter would be sent to the National Committee or to Canton, stating that a delegation of farmers, railroad employees, cigar-makers, wholesale merchants, Presbyterians or what-not would, if convenient, call on Mr. McKinley on such a day. An answer would immediately be returned expressing pleasure at the idea, but requesting that the head of the delegation make a preliminary visit to the candidate. When he appeared, Mr. McKinley would greet him warmly and ask: "You are going to present the delegation and make some remarks. What are you going to say?" The reply would usually be: "Oh! I don't know. Anything that occurs to me." Then Mr. McKinley would point out the inconveniences of such a course and request that a copy of the address be sent to him in advance, and he usually warned his interlocutor that he might make certain suggestions looking towards the revision of the speech.

On occasion McKinley himself would write the delegate's speech and then answer it with an equally extemporaneous address of his own.[42] According to Oscar Amringer, a native of Canton who played in the local G.A.R. band and in that capacity heard every one of McKinley's front-porch speeches but one, Hanna's committee took pains to accompany each delegation from the railroad station to McKinley's house with music appropriate to the section of the country from which the delegates came. Before the appearance of the candidate, refreshments would be served on the lawn, and these also were made painstakingly appropriate to the occasion—hard or soft drinks, depending on whether the delegation was wet or dry. The refreshments not only served to put the delegates in a congenial frame of mind but gave McKinley's secretary, Joe Smith, time to look over the delegates' speeches (in case they had escaped previous scrutiny) and to make the necessary corrections in McKinley's remarks. Amringer remembered that the speeches of McKinley usually played on one of three themes— how the "Republican tariff had made Columbia the gem of the ocean," how a silver dollar would purchase only 53 cents worth of goods "in our sister republic across the Rio Grande," and how the Republican party, which had saved the Union in 1861, was now engaged in saving it again, this time from the greater menace of fiat money.[43]

[42] Croly, *Hanna,* pp. 209–227.
[43] Oscar Amringer, *If You Don't Weaken* (New York, 1940), pp. 153–155.

Against Hanna's superb machine of propaganda, the Democrats could pit only the oratory of Bryan. From New York, where he delivered his acceptance speech "in the heart of the enemy's country," as he put it, Bryan swung briefly through the Northeast, where he was received without great enthusiasm. His opening speech in Madison Square Garden was carefully prepared and somewhat laborious, and his failure to stir the audience as he had done at Chicago seems to have thrown him briefly off his stride. The real difficulty, however, was not Bryan's delivery, nor even his unfamiliarity with an urban audience, but the fact that he had nothing to offer the workingmen who came out in large numbers to hear him. To Bryan's demands for inflation the Republicans replied that inflation would impoverish the workingman, and the argument was convincing. Labor wanted not inflation but the prohibition of injunctions in strikes, the destruction of trusts, and better working conditions. The Democratic platform was admirably designed to meet these demands, but Bryan ignored most of the platform, concentrating, as sensitive observers had predicted he would, on the money question. At the beginning of the campaign McKinley had said, "I am a Tariff man standing on a Tariff platform. The money question is unduly prominent. In thirty days you won't hear anything about it." "In thirty days," replied Judge William R. Day, "you won't hear of anything else." But the apathy of city workers toward free silver and Hanna's skillful propaganda turned Bryan's emphasis on currency reform to the advantage of the Republicans. As Hanna said, "He's talking silver all the time, and that's where we've got him."[44]

In the West Bryan was more effective; there the result was in doubt until the very end. Not until late in October did Hanna return a campaign contribution sent by a friend with the words, "It is all over. Reports are satisfactory just where we wanted them most."[45] Even then his optimism doubtless seemed premature to some of his timid friends. When the ballots were counted, however, McKinley was found to have won by a safe margin, polling 7,104,779 votes to Bryan's 6,502,925.

[44] For the campaign in the East, see Barnes, "Myths of the Bryan Campaign," pp. 382–383; Bryan, *First Battle,* pp. 384, 600, which includes maps of his four major trips; Hibben, *Peerless Leader,* pp. 189–201; Josephson, *Politicos,* pp. 662–708. Charles S. Olcott, *The Life of William McKinley* (Boston, 1916), I, 321, reports the exchange between McKinley and Day.

[45] Beer, *Hanna,* p. 163.

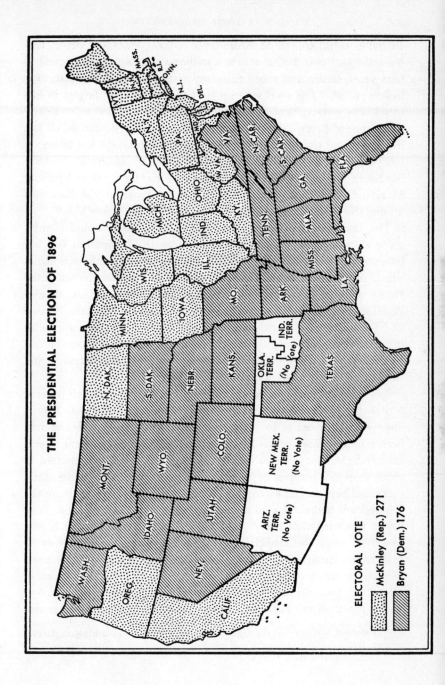

THE PRESIDENTIAL ELECTION OF 1896

ELECTORAL VOTE

McKinley (Rep.) 271

Bryan (Dem.) 176

In the electoral college McKinley received 271 votes and Bryan 176. Nevertheless Bryan polled almost a million votes more than Cleveland four years earlier and more than any victorious candidate had ever before polled. (The total vote up to that time was the largest in history.) The geographical distribution of the vote revealed more clearly the nature of Bryan's defeat. West of the Mississippi he carried all but five states, and two of those—Oregon and California—he lost by only a few votes. East of the Mississippi, however, he carried no states outside the South and lost even the border states of Kentucky, West Virginia, Maryland, and Delaware. In the industrial states of the East and around the Great Lakes, McKinley swept everything before him.[46]

The Bryan-Watson ticket polled only 222,600 popular and twenty-seven electoral votes, but that the full strength of Populism was not indicated by those figures was shown by the congressional elections, in which twenty-five Populists, silverites, or fusionists were elected to the House and six Populists to the Senate. State elections also showed Populist gains. In Kansas, Nebraska, South Dakota, Montana, Idaho, and Washington fusion tickets won control of the legislatures and of all important state offices. In North Carolina, Populists and Republicans combined to dominate the elections, and in Georgia, Alabama, and Texas they won over 40 per cent of the vote.[47]

Conservatism, nevertheless, had clearly triumphed, although opinion was sharply divided over the reasons for McKinley's election. Hostile observers attributed it to the unlimited resources which Hanna had been able to command, to the wide distribution of Republican literature and the harangues of innumerable orators. They also pointed to more unseemly features of the Republican campaign. In some states there had been actual corruption at the ballot box. In many more the Republicans had conducted a ruthless campaign of intimidation. Wall Street predicted that ruin would follow Bryan's election and hinted that ruin might be artificially induced if it failed spontaneously to materialize. Bankers wrote gold clauses into their loans. Manufacturers were given orders contingent upon the election of McKinley. Worst of all, factory owners informed their employees that a Democratic victory meant lower wages, half time, or even loss of a job. One employer said

---

[46] *Historical Statistics of the United States, 1789–1945* (Washington, 1949), p. 288; Robinson, *Presidential Vote*, pp. 4–7.
[47] Hicks, *Populist Revolt*, p. 377.

flatly, "Men, vote as you please, but if Bryan is elected tomorrow the whistle will not blow Wednesday morning."[48]

The effect of intimidation in determining the outcome cannot be measured, but even Republicans could not deny that it existed. William Allen White later wrote:

I do not believe, as the academicians have said, that McKinley won because Hanna spent so much money. Few votes were actually purchased in that campaign. McKinley won because the Republicans had persuaded the middle class, almost to a man, that a threat to the gold standard was a threat to their prosperity. Incidentally, labor as a class was persuaded to the point of coercion that if McKinley was defeated industry would shut down, and that if McKinley won prosperity would return because capital had confidence in the Republican party, and because the gold standard and the protective tariff as national policies would be established. The coercion was bald, unashamed, and effective. Hanna had more money than probably was ever spent in a campaign before. But Bryan had enough to present his case fairly to the people.[49]

Altgeld, however, denied that Bryan had even had a fair hearing. The Democratic party, he said,

was confronted by all the banks, all the trusts, all the syndicates, all the corporations, all the great papers. It was confronted by everything that money could buy, that boodle could debauch, or that fear or starvation could coerce. It was confronted by the disgust which the majority of the American people felt toward the national administration, for which they held us responsible. It was confronted by a combination of forces such as had never been united before and will probably never again be; and worse still the time was too short to educate the public.[50]

Some students have argued that an economic improvement in 1896 took the sting out of the Democratic campaign. It is true that gold from the new discoveries in Africa and Australia was beginning to flow into the channels of world trade, but not much of it had yet reached the United States. The amount of gold per capita in 1896 was $8.40; in 1891 it had been $10.10. Prices of agricultural commodities were no higher in October, 1896, than in the preceding months, if not lower. Business at the end of October, according to the *Commercial and*

---

[48] Williams, *Bryan,* p. 195; Barnes, "Myths of the Bryan Campaign," pp. 399–402.

[49] *Autobiography,* p. 285.

[50] John Peter Altgeld, *Live Questions* (Chicago, 1899), p. 691.

Financial Chronicle, was in "a half torpid state."[51] Wheat alone showed any advance in price, the result not of added circulation of gold or of any general economic improvement, but of reduced production in this country as well as in Australia, Russia, and India. Between July and November, wheat rose 13 or 14 cents on the Chicago exchange and from 18 to 20 cents at New York, but not all of this increase was passed on to the farmer. The government gave the average farm price of wheat per bushel as 72.6 cents on December 1, 1896, an increase of about 12 cents over the previous December. In any case, Bryan carried most of the wheat states.[52] Economic improvement does not seem to have been a factor in Bryan's defeat.

Nor did the Democrats lose, as some writers have maintained, because their platform was too radical, unless the radicalism of the platform frightened Republicans into unusually active efforts to win. Nor did they lose because they played on class divisions and hatred; the opposition far outdid them in vilification. The simple fact which shines out from the election returns is that Bryan failed to win the support of labor. The machines managed to turn out a large vote—nearly two-thirds of Bryan's votes, after all, came from states which he lost—but it was not large enough to overcome the Republican majorities. Yet workingmen were restive, and their numbers, if added to Bryan's majorities in agricultural states, might have swept the Democrats into office. The conclusion is inescapable that Bryan, by emphasizing to the exclusion of nearly everything else an issue which appealed only to farmers, drove away the support of labor, without which, given the hostility of the middle class, he could not hope to win.

To a degree not equaled perhaps at any other time in our history, the election of 1896 was primarily a revolt of the agrarians against industrialism and the large aggregations of economic power resulting from the industrial development. The chief exception was the silver miners who provided the funds for the Democratic campaign. In a sense the revolt was a protest of the old America against the new, and the evils of the new industrialism as it bore down on the farmer. It was, in truth, a political and economic revolt of major proportions. The Republicans, already attached to the new industrialism, were forced into a more conservative position. As the victory was followed by an upswing

[51] LXIII (Oct. 24, 1896), 730. See also Barnes, "Myths of the Bryan Campaign," 383–393.

[52] *Ibid.,* p. 389–394; *Yearbook of Agriculture, 1896,* p. 561.

of a new business cycle, the Republican position seemed justified and for the moment became secure. Its policies were to formulate the destinies of the nation as it moved into the fateful years of the new century.

Bryan had chosen to appear as the champion of an old and rapidly disappearing America. He had become almost deliberately the leader of a lost cause. Defeat, under such circumstances, was almost inevitable.

CHAPTER 10

The Drums of War

I N MARCH, 1897, William McKinley took office as President, and respectability breathed a sigh of relief. The republic was safe; the hosts of error had been put to rout. In his inaugural address McKinley dwelled on this good fortune, noting with pleasure signs that prosperity was returning to the land—presumably as a result of his recent victory. He made no reference to foreign affairs except to urge ratification of a recently signed treaty of arbitration with Great Britain and to say, "We want no wars of conquest; we must avoid the temptation of territorial aggression. War should never be entered upon until every agency of peace has failed; peace is preferable to war in almost every contingency."[1]

McKinley had good reason to go out of his way in order to assure his followers, as he said to Carl Schurz, that there would be no "jingo nonsense" under *his* administration.[2] There had been a good deal of jingo nonsense under the administration just leaving office. The foreign policy of the United States, in fact, had been growing progressively more truculent as the nation grew more populous and wealthy. Many people were arguing that the bigger and wealthier a nation became, the more important it was that it grow bigger and wealthier still. Notions of "manifest destiny," long dormant, were awakening in the public mind. By 1898 the population of the United States had grown to 76 million from only 31 million in 1860, and she did almost $2 billion worth of business every year with other countries. Surely such an im-

---

[1] John D. Richardson (ed.), *Messages and Papers of the Presidents* (Washington, 1911), VIII, 6241; *Congressional Record,* 55th Cong., (1897), 1st sess., pp. 2–5.

[2] Claude M. Fuess, *Carl Schurz* (New York, 1932), p. 349.

portant customer was entitled to the respect and admiration of the world. Surely she must conduct herself in a manner befitting her importance—build a navy, acquire colonies, and lord it over subject people. Such, at least, was the doctrine of the expansionists.

Expansionism in America had never completely disappeared, of course. Seward bought Alaska in 1867, and a few years later President Grant was obsessed with the desire to annex the republic of Santo Domingo. Expansionism was not pursued with any system, however, in the fifteen or twenty years following the Civil War. James G. Blaine was perhaps the first Secretary of State since the Polk administration to address himself vigorously to the problem of increasing America's influence in the rest of the world. It was Blaine who under the Garfield administration attempted to persuade England to abrogate the old Clayton-Bulwer Treaty, the first step toward building an isthmian canal. It was Blaine who wished to see the United States reassert her moral leadership over the Western Hemisphere and to that end invited the nations of Latin America to join the United States in abolishing war among them. Both these ventures failed, for the moment; Blaine was ahead of his time.

When Harrison was elected, however, Blaine returned to office brimming with enthusiasm. He presided over the first Inter-American Conference, which accomplished little, but at least set a precedent for other such gatherings in the future. When Canadian seal fishermen, by indiscriminately slaughtering herds in the Bering Sea, encroached on what Blaine considered, with some justice, "good public morals," he argued with Great Britain that American revenue cutters had a right to come to the seals' defense by seizing the Canadian ships. An international tribunal eventually decided against him. While the decision was still pending, the United States became involved with Italy over the lynching of eleven Italians in New Orleans, only three of whom were Italian nationals. When Blaine tried to explain to the Italian Minister that the state of Louisiana alone had jurisdiction over the case, Baron Fava continued to demand that the offenders be punished. Blaine burst out : "I do not recognize the right of any government to tell the United States what it should do. We have never received orders from any foreign power and we will not begin now." The Chicago *Tribune* cheered this "vigorous assertion of American rights." Blaine, the *Tribune* said, took away "the breath from the monkey and hand-organ man and he at once changed his tune." The United States eventually paid Italy $25,000.

The death of two American Navy sailors and the wounding of others in a brawl in Valparaiso, Chile, was an even more explicit threat to the national honor. The public reaction in the United States showed that jingoism was once again a force to be reckoned with, and that prudent statesmen would seek to avoid appealing to it if they wished to retain control of any given situation. President Harrison, however, talked loudly of vigorous action against Chile, and Blaine with difficulty restrained his ardor.

If Blaine was not a jingo, he was a more consistent expansionist than Harrison, and it was in this respect that his policies set the tone for what was shortly to follow. As early as 1881 he wrote to the American Minister in Honolulu that the United States could not permit either Cuba or Hawaii to be cut "adrift from the American system, whereto they both indispensably belong." During his second term of office he obtained the appointment of John L. Stevens, an exponent of annexation, as Minister to Hawaii. Nor was his interest in the Pacific limited to Hawaii. When Germany demanded control of the Samoan Islands, where the United States had a coaling station, Blaine negotiated with Bismarck in 1889 an agreement by which the United States, Britain, and Germany should jointly administer Samoa as a protectorate. Once again public opinion outran the judgment of diplomats; many papers clamored for some sort of retaliation against Germany. It was clear that the historical policy of isolationism was breaking down.[3]

For a time it seemed that the Cleveland administration would put an end to all this, for Cleveland was a convinced anti-imperialist. When he took office in 1893 he found a treaty of annexation with Hawaii already pending in the Senate. Cleveland, knowing that the treaty represented not the desires of the natives but of American residents who had fomented a rebellion with the aid of Stevens and the American Navy, withdrew it from the Senate and sent a special agent, James H. Blount, to Hawaii. Blount's investigations confirmed his

[3] For Blaine's policy, see Samuel F. Bemis, *A Diplomatic History of the United States* (3rd ed., New York, 1950), pp. 397–462; Thomas A. Bailey, *A Diplomatic History of the American People* (6th ed., New York, 1958), pp. 407–435; Samuel F. Bemis (ed.), *The American Secretaries of State and Their Diplomacy* (New York, 1927–1930); Alice Felt Tyler, *The Foreign Policy of James G. Blaine* (Minneapolis, 1927). For the rise of expansionist sentiment in this period, see Albert K. Weinberg, *Manifest Destiny* (Baltimore, 1935).

suspicions, and Cleveland proposed to re-establish the political *status quo ante* in Hawaii, provided the Queen would grant amnesty to the revolutionists. Neither the Queen nor the rebels would have anything to do with the idea. Cleveland then referred the matter to Congress, which sustained him. The House went on record as opposed to annexation or a protectorate. The Senate resolved that the United States should not intervene in Hawaiian affairs, at the same time warning other nations not to intervene. There the matter rested for a time.[4]

If Cleveland's refusal to consider Hawaiian annexation briefly silenced the adherents of a "large policy," his handling of the Venezuela boundary dispute gave them new encouragement. The dispute, on the face of it, was no concern of the United States. Venezuela and British Guiana had for some time been quarreling over their common frontier. Venezuela, after repeatedly demanding arbitration without success, severed relations with Great Britain and in 1887 appealed to the United States to intervene. Cleveland unhesitatingly took the side of Venezuela, perhaps out of sympathy for the underdog. In July, 1895, Olney, now Secretary of State, demanded on behalf of Venezuela that Great Britain submit the dispute to arbitration. Otherwise, he said, the United States would consider the Monroe Doctrine to have been violated, inasmuch as a refusal to arbitrate the matter "deprives Venezuela of her free agency and puts her under virtual duress." He further reminded the British that "today the United States is practically sovereign on this continent, and its fiat is law upon the subjects to which it confines its interposition."[5] It was a curious argument, worthy to stand with any of Olney's previous legal exercises. Lord Salisbury, after waiting four months, perhaps in the hope that Olney's temper would cool, replied that Britain could not possibly submit the dispute to arbitration and that the Monroe Doctrine had no standing in international law and in any event had no relevance to the dispute.[6]

Salisbury's note made President Cleveland "mad clear through," according to a friend.[7] He drafted an angry letter to Congress which he submitted on December 17, 1895. First he asked for an appropriation to enable him to set up a commission to study the boundary dispute.

---

[4] Julius W. Pratt, *Expansionists of 1898* (Baltimore, 1936), pp. 110–229; Allan Nevins, *Grover Cleveland* (New York, 1932), pp. 549–562.

[5] *Foreign Relations of the United States, 1895,* I, pp. 558, 561–562.

[6] *Ibid.*, pp. 563–576.

[7] Bailey, *Diplomatic History*, p. 443.

Then he practically informed Congress in advance what the results of the study would be. "When such report [of the commission] is made and accepted, it will, in my opinion, be the duty of the United States to resist by every means in its power . . . the appropriation by Great Britain of any lands or the exercise of any jurisdiction over any territory which after investigation we have determined of right belongs to Venezuela."[8] In other words, the United States was ready to go to war with Britain over the boundary of Venezuela.

Cleveland's message sent the country into paroxysms of patriotism. Theodore Roosevelt publicly declared that the country needed a war. "Canada would surely be conquered," he pointed out, "and once wrested from England it would never be restored."[9] Congress voted the appropriation with shouts of approval. Fortunately the commission never finished its inquiry, for Great Britain finally conceded to arbitrate the dispute, thereby enabling American orators to claim that it was the administration's boldness which had forced the British to give in. This illusion of success gave a powerful stimulus to the expansionist impulse.[10]

It was no coincidence that the rise of expansionist sentiment during the last two decades of the nineteenth century was accompanied by an increasingly intolerant exclusiveness. The same people who led the clamor for expansion were loudest in demanding that foreigners be kept out of the United States. Pressure from the West Coast three times forced Congress to pass bills suspending Chinese immigration, vetoed by Hayes and Arthur and finally signed by the latter. Senator Lodge of Massachusetts introduced a bill in 1897 prohibiting admission of anyone over sixteen who could not read and write, a measure clearly directed at the new immigrations from southern and eastern Europe. The House passed it by a large majority, the Senate by a vote of 34 to 31. Cleveland vetoed it.

Both expansionism and exclusionism fed upon social Darwinism, as expounded in this country by the philosopher John Fiske and the political scientist John W. Burgess. These men had no difficulty in

[8] Richardson, *Messages and Papers,* VIII, 6089; *Foreign Relations, 1895,* I, 545.

[9] New York *Evening Sun,* Dec. 23, 1895, quoted in Henry F. Pringle, *Theodore Roosevelt* (New York, 1931), p. 167.

[10] Nevins, *Cleveland,* pp. 629–648; Grover Cleveland, *Presidential Problems* (New York, 1904), pp. 173–281.

showing that Darwin's concept of "natural selection" as between biological species applied also to the "struggle for survival" between races. Nor did they find any reason to doubt that the Anglo-Saxon "race" was destined to expand, by virtue of its demonstrated ability in colonization, until it ruled the world. Such ideas were quickly seized upon by men like Lodge and Roosevelt, who developed them into a coherent rationale of expansion. The missionary churches also found them attractive, since they provided a convenient scientific justification for the conversion of heathens to Christianity. By a simple process the missionaries became expansionists predicting that the flag would follow the Bible. The Reverend Josiah Strong, a Congregational minister, prophesied as early as 1885: "This race of unequaled energy, with all the majesty of numbers and the might of wealth behind it—the representative, let us hope, of the largest liberty, the purest Christianity, the highest civilization . . . will move down upon Mexico, down upon central and South America, out upon the islands of the sea."[11]

No writer had more influence in shaping the ideology of expansionism than Captain Alfred Thayer Mahan. From his position on the faculty of the Naval War College at Newport, Rhode Island, Mahan launched a steady barrage of reading matter upon the public. Mahan referred only occasionally to Darwinian arguments. He was more interested in resurrecting the old mercantilist theory, which he expounded in book after book, that if a nation were to grow great it must expand both its trade and its territory and strengthen its navy to protect both. A nation like the United States, pending true greatness, must confine itself to the mere defense of its coast, which Mahan seemed to believe was in constant danger of attack. Meanwhile it must build ships as fast as possible.[12]

Although Mahan liked to think of himself as a prophet crying in the wilderness, his cherished goal of a bigger Navy was, in fact, being

[11] Quoted in Arthur M. Schlesinger, *The Rise of Modern America* (4th ed., New York, 1951), p. 171. John Fiske, "Manifest Destiny," *Harper's Magazine*, LXX (Mar., 1885), 578–590; John W. Burgess, *Political Science and Comparative Constitutional Law* (Boston, 1891), I, 30–38, 45; Josiah Strong, *Our Country* (New York, 1885), p. vii, and *Expansion under New Yorld Conditions* (New York, 1900), p. 295.

[12] Alfred Thayer Mahan, *The Interest of America in Sea Power, Present and Future* (Boston, 1897), and *The Influence of Sea Power on History* (Boston, 1890); William E. Livezey, *Mahan on Sea Power* (Norman, Okla., 1947; W. D. Puleston, *Mahan* (New Haven, 1939).

fulfilled at the time he was writing. At the end of the Civil War the American Navy had been the equal of any on the seas, but during the next fifteen years it had fallen into a state of decrepitude. Politicians saw no point in retaining the wartime Navy at full strength, and in any case more critical matters absorbed their attention. Not until 1884, when the Republican platform advocated naval reform, did either party take any official interest in the matter. What little money Congress appropriated for naval purposes was wasted in rebuilding old-fashioned ships at high contract prices. High-ranking naval officers understood that the Navy was "nearly worthless for war purposes," yet their own failure to profit from recent wartime experience, their jealousy of the engineering corps, and their incredible confidence in wooden sailing ships were partly to blame. By 1874 the Navy, in the opinion of the *Army and Navy Journal*, was little more than a "heterogeneous collection of naval trash."[13]

Beginning in the early eighties, the dawning realization that several South American countries actually owned navies which could easily destroy that of the United States introduced a note of alarm into discussions of the subject. A series of aggressive Secretaries of the Navy —William H. Hunt under Garfield, William E. Chandler under Arthur, and William C. Whitney under Cleveland—impressed on Congress the need for action, and the Treasury surplus made it possible to build ships without offending the thrifty. In 1883 Congress authorized the building of four new cruisers. These ships still carried sails, but they were equipped with steam power and steel-protected decks. Shortly afterward, under Whitney's leadership, Congress provided for the construction of thirty ships of various types, including two second-class battleships and one armored cruiser built of steel. That Congress was at last beginning to understand the full advantages of naval construction was shown by the stipulation in 1886 that ships must be made only with materials of "domestic manufacture." Under Secretaries Benjamin F. Tracy (1889–1893) and Hilary A. Herbert (1893–1897) new ships were regularly added, so that by 1897 the United States possessed a Navy which, while not the equal of the major European fleets, was adequate to protect the security of the country. Safe from the danger of unexpected foreign invasion and capable of holding her

[13] Mar. 21, 1874; quoted in George T. Davis, *A Navy Second to None* (New York, 1940), p. 16.

own against some of the lesser European powers, the United States was now in a position to embark on a more adventurous foreign policy.[14]

McKinley had said there would be no jingo nonsense while he was President. Cuba, however, the "Pearl of the Antilles," lay nearby, and Americans had always had a proprietary interest in Cuba. As early as 1854, Soulé, Mason, and Buchanan in the famous Ostend Manifesto had boldly declared that Cuba was "as necessary to the North American republic as any of its present members" and that the United States might "be justified in wresting it from Spain."[15] Four years later Stephen A. Douglas said, "It is our destiny to have Cuba and it is folly to debate the question. It naturally belongs to the American Continent."[16] After the Civil War, Seward and then Grant looked covetously at Cuba. The turbulence of Cuban politics was a constant temptation, as well as an excuse, to intervene; and when a ten-year rebellion broke out in Cuba in 1868, Grant flirted with the notion of recognizing the belligerency of the insurgents. He was finally dissuaded by his Secretary of State, Hamilton Fish, who reminded him that when England had recognized the belligerency of the Confederacy, the United States had protested vigorously. Twenty-five years later, however, a generation which remembered the Civil War only dimly found such arguments unconvincing.

There could be no doubt that Cuba suffered under Spanish rule, particularly from Spanish commercial regulations. From the deadening effects of those regulations the United States in 1890 provided some release in the form of the McKinley tariff, which admitted raw sugar free. A reciprocity treaty with Spain, signed the following year, reduced duties on a number of other items and further stimulated trade between the United States and Cuba. The Cuban economy began to revive, and talk of rebellion subsided.[17] Then in 1894 the Wilson-Gorman tariff imposed a 40 per cent ad valorem duty on sugar (one cent a pound) and put an end to the reciprocity treaty. Since at least

[14] Harold and Margaret Sprout, *The Rise of American Naval Power* (Princeton, 1939), pp. 165–222; Davis, *Navy Second to None*, pp. 3–100; Robert Seager II, "Ten Years before Mahan: The Unofficial Case for the New Navy, 1880–1890," *Mississippi Valley Historical Review*, XL (Dec., 1953), 491–512.

[15] Henry Steele Commager, *Documents of American History* (6th ed., New York, 1958), I, 333–335; Weinberg, *Manifest Destiny*, p. 205.

[16] Henry M. Flint, *Life of Stephen A. Douglas* (New York, 1860), p. 184.

[17] Russell H. Fitzgibbon, *Cuba and the United States* (Menasha, Wis., 1935), p. 14; F. W. Taussig, *The Tariff History of the United States* (7th ed., New York, 1923), pp. 275–279.

four-fifths of the wealth of Cuba was invested in sugar production, and since the growing beet-sugar industry of Europe had closed the European market to Cuba and had forced her increasingly to depend on the United States, the effects of the Wilson-Gorman tariff were immediately felt. A severe depression, added to conditions that were already intolerable—the corrupt, dictatorial government; the heavy taxation, nine-tenths of which went to support the army and the bureaucracy—provoked the Cubans once again to revolution.[18]

The insurrection which broke out in 1895, to a much greater degree than previous insurrections, was planned, financed, and instigated by exiles or emigrants from Cuba. Cuban juntos abounded throughout the Western Hemisphere and particularly in New York, the center of revolutionary activity and of funds. The Cuban patriots in New York played skillfully on the sympathy of Americans for the victims of oppression, disseminating stories of ghastly atrocities perpetrated by the Spaniards. They obtained funds both by such appeals to American idealism and, occasionally, by threatening to destroy American property in Cuba unless its owners contributed to the rebel cause.[19] They launched filibustering expeditions from the American coast, not all of which the authorities were able to divert. Thus they early entangled the United States both emotionally and financially in the civil war.

At the outset the patriot leaders, Salvador Cisneros Betancourt (President of the revolutionary republic), Máximo Gómez, and José Martí, could count on about a million dollars, mostly collected by Martí, with which to finance the revolt, and on arms and ammunition continually shipped by the juntos from neutral countries—a traffic exceedingly difficult for those countries to control.[20] In Cuba they received help from wealthy planters who had been ruined in the depression and by laborers who had been thrown out of work. How large an army they were able to recruit is difficult to estimate, but there is reason to believe that of the 180,000 men capable of bearing arms (out of a total population of between 1,500,000 and 1,800,000), no more than half were ever actively engaged on the rebel side. The Spanish put the number at 40,000, an estimate which was doubtless too conserva-

[18] Fitzgibbon, *Cuba,* pp. 14–15.

[19] Bailey, *Diplomatic History,* p. 452, n. 1.

[20] Fitzgibbon, *Cuba,* pp. 15–16; Elbert J. Benton, *International Law and Diplomacy of the Spanish-American War* (Baltimore, 1908), pp. 24–25; F. E. Chadwick, *The Relations of the United States and Spain* (3 vols., New York, 1909–1911), I, *Diplomacy,* pp. 406–407.

tive. They themselves were sufficiently concerned to send over 120,000 troops in the first thirteen months—a number which under ordinary circumstances should have been enough to suppress the rebellion.[21]

Against the tactics of the rebels, however, mere numerical superiority proved unavailing. Early in the war the rebel general, Gómez, attempted to starve and demoralize the enemy by forbidding "the introduction of articles of commerce, as well as beef and cattle, into the towns occupied by the enemy" and by ordering sugar plantations to "stop their labors." Anyone who violated the order by giving supplies to the Spanish would be "treated as a traitor," his sugar fields burned, and his houses demolished.[22] Faced with so fierce an antagonist, the Spanish authorities cultivated a ferocity of their own. They removed the soft-spoken Martínez de Campos and appointed a new Governor General, General Valeriano Weyler, whose answer to the rebels was a policy of "reconcentration."

If the aim of the rebels was to starve his troops, he would reply by starving the rebels, and to that end he ordered all the people of the countryside to come within eight days to the towns occupied by Spanish troops, or be considered rebels and "tried as such."[23] Most of the poorer peasants and almost all of the women, children, and old men submitted to this policy; the trouble was that the Spanish were unable to feed and house them properly, and much suffering ensued. Reconcentration was a cruel policy, but it was not more cruel than the merciless plundering and destruction of plantations and the burning of ungarrisoned towns. The alertness of the Cuban junto in the United States, however, prevented news of these rebel horrors from circulating, whereas the barbarities of the Spanish were given full play in the American press.[24]

The United States government had a better understanding of events in Cuba. Even before Gómez's proclamation formalized the rebel tactics, Olney accurately described the nature of the struggle to Depuy de Lôme, the Spanish Minister at Washington:

[21] Benton, *International Law*, pp. 26, 29–30; Woodford to Sherman, September 13, 1897, *Foreign Relations, 1898*, p. 564.

[22] Proclamation of July 1, 1895, quoted in Chadwick, *United States and Spain*, I, 408–409.

[23] Benton, *International Law*, pp. 27–34.

[24] Marcus W. Wilkerson, *Public Opinion and the Spanish American War* (Baton Rouge, 1932), pp. 29–53.

Spain still holds the seaports and most, if not all, of the large towns in the interior. Nevertheless, a vast area of the territory of the islands is in effect under the control of roving bands of insurgents, which, if driven from one place today by an exhibition of superior force, abandon it only to return tomorrow when that force has moved on for their dislodgment in other quarters.

The consequence of this state of things cannot be disguised. Outside of the towns still under Spanish rule, anarchy, lawlessness, and terrorism are rampant. The insurgents realize that the wholesale destruction of crops, factories, and machinery advances their cause in two ways. It cripples the resources of Spain on the one hand. On the other, it drives into their ranks the laborers who are thus thrown out of employment. The result is a systematic war upon the industries of the island and upon all the means by which they are carried on, and whereas the normal product of the islands is valued at something like eighty or a hundred millions, its value for the present year is estimated by competent authority as not exceeding twenty millions.

Bad as is this showing for the present year, it must be even worse for the next year and for every succeeding year during which the rebellion continues to live.

Entertaining no illusions about the rebels and professing no sympathy for them, Olney at the same time made it plain to de Lôme that the United States considered its interests in Cuba to be jeopardized by the continuation of the war. Hostilities, he said, were interrupting a flourishing commerce between the United States and Cuba, while "wholesale destruction of property on the island . . . is utterly destroying American investments that should be of commercial value, and is utterly impoverishing great numbers of American citizens." He did not suggest, however, how the conflict might be terminated.[25]

Olney estimated that trade between the United States and Cuba at the outbreak of the insurrection amounted to about $100 million a year and that American investments in Cuba were worth about $50 million —most of it in sugar plantations and iron plantations, some of it in mining, tobacco, railroads, and manufacturing.[26] Edwin F. Atkins, however, who owned one of the largest plantations on the island, estimated American investments at only $30 million.[27] Whatever the

[25] *Foreign Relations, 1897,* p. 542.

[26] *Foreign Relations, 1896,* p. lxxxv. The United States bought nine-tenths of her sugar from Cuba, in return for which she sold flour, meat, and manufactures. See *Foreign Relations, 1898,* pp. 560, 562, 563, 566, 574–575, 577–578.

[27] Edwin F. Atkins, *Sixty Years in Cuba* (Boston, 1926), p. 209. Cleona Lewis, *America's Stake in International Investments* (Washington, 1938), p.

precise figure, nobody in a position of responsibility suggested in 1896 and 1897 that America's economic stake in Cuba was high enough to justify going to war with Spain. Many Americans interested in Cuban trade and industry petitioned the government to intervene in order to bring hostilities to an end, but none of them suggested that it was necessary to go to war in order to restore peace. Both the Cleveland and McKinley administrations took the same position in negotiations with Spain.[28] As for the business community as a whole—as distinct from the small section of it which had interests in Cuba—it was profoundly hostile to the idea of war. Business was just beginning to recover from the depression; war might be a "material setback," as the *Banker and Tradesman* declared, "to the prosperous conditions which [have] just set in after five years of panic and depression.[29]

As late as the spring of 1898—and for that matter, even after the war began—business continued to oppose it. In April, 1898, Carl Schurz sent McKinley a report of a meeting of the New York Chamber of Commerce, "in which a resolution drawn by me was adopted commending your peace policy. It faithfully represents the feelings of the best part of the community."[30] Secretary Long of the Navy told McKinley that he was besieged with letters from State Street, all crying for peace. "As far as I can see," wrote one Boston businessman, "everybody is for the President's policy, and nobody really wants war."[31] The Boston Chamber of Commerce praised McKinley for his "splendid self-control and exalted courage" in resisting "the clamour [*sic*] of the press and of politicians."[32]

It was not to be expected that an administration so firmly committed to business interests would rush headlong into a war which they eagerly wanted to avoid. Other influences, however, were making a pacific policy increasingly difficult to follow. The expansionist clique— Lodge, Roosevelt, and Mahan, Whitelaw Reid of the New York

---

606, puts American investments in "Cuba and other West Indies" at $49 million in 1897.

[28] Pratt, *Expansionists*, pp. 250–251. For the general economic background, see Leland H. Jenks, *Our Cuban Colony* (New York, 1928), pp. 18–40.

[29] Quoted in Pratt, *Expansionists*, p. 239.

[30] Schurz to McKinley, April 8, 1898; Frederic Bancroft (ed.), *Speeches, Correspondence and Political Papers of Carl Schurz* (New York, 1913), V, 457.

[31] William Claflin to Long, April 3, 1898; Gardner Weld (ed.), *Papers of John Davis Long* (Massachusetts Historical Society Collections, 1939), p. 83.

[32] Joseph R. Leeson to Long, March 31, 1898; *ibid.*, p. 81.

Tribune, Albert Shaw of the *Review of Reviews*—was clamoring for bold action.[33] The religious press was in full cry.[34] Congress, sensitive to these pressures, grew increasingly restive; early in 1896 it passed a concurrent resolution advocating recognition of Cuban belligerency. Above all, the yellow journals, by deliberately cultivating war sentiment, were rapidly creating an atmosphere in which voices of reasonableness and sanity could no longer be heard. In New York, the *World,* the *Journal,* the *Sun,* and the *Herald* all sent special correspondents to Cuba, and their stories were distributed throughout the country by the wire services.[35] (All but the *Sun* were members of the Associated Press.) The ease with which the "exposures" of the New York dailies circulated among other papers created a uniformity of opinion absent in similar crises in the past. In 1893, for instance, when Harrison submitted his Hawaiian treaty of annexation to the Senate, some of the most important papers in the country opposed annexation. In New York, the *Sun* and *Tribune* favored it, but the *Times, World,* and *Evening Post* condemned it. In 1898, only Godkin's *Evening Post* opposed war and expansion.[36]

[33] Julius W. Pratt, "The Large Policy of 1898," *Mississippi Valley Historical Review,* XIX (Sept., 1932), 219–242, also mentions Senators Frye of Maine, Platt of Connecticut, Dolph of Oregon, Allen of Nebraska, and Hanley of Indiana.

[34] Pratt, *Expansionists,* pp. 279–316. Only the Unitarians and the Quakers consistently opposed war. For the influence of the religious argument on McKinley, see Charles S. Olcott, *The Life of William McKinley* (Boston, 1916), II, 109–111, quoted from the *Christian Advocate,* Jan. 22, 1903.

[35] Some of the best-known journalists of the country covered the Cuban crisis: Richard Harding Davis, Stephen Crane, Alfred Henry Lewis, James Creelman, Julian Hawthorne, Murat Halstead, and the artist Frederic Remington.

[36] Joseph E. Wisan, *The Cuban Crisis as Reflected in the New York Press* (New York, 1934), pp. 21–38; Wilkerson, *Public Opinion,* pp. 5–14. Charles W. Auxier, "Middle Western Newspapers and the Spanish-American War," *Mississippi Valley Historical Review,* XXVI (Mar., 1940), pp. 523–534, believes that the influence of Midwestern journalism in bringing about the Spanish-American War came not from sensational journalism, but rather from editorial comment stressing "the fundamental interests of the United States in the Caribbean, Spanish violation of these interests, the propaganda activities of the Cuban *Junta,* and the implications of the Cuban question in the domestic politics of the United States." Ray A. Billington, "The Origins of Middle Western Isolationism," *Political Science Quarterly,* LX (Mar. 1945), notes that "the West's first reaction to the Cuban struggle was true to the section's humanitarian traditions; westerners viewed the conflict as one between autocracy and self-rule which deserved their unwavering support."

In the bitter rivalry between Pulitzer's *World* and Hearst's *Journal,*
Cuba simply provided "convenient ammunition."[37] Hearst and Pulitzer
seized upon every incident calculated to shock, horrify, titillate, or
disgust their readers and blew it up to fantastic proportions. When a
Spanish gunboat fired on an American ship, the *Alliance,* under the
misapprehension that it was engaged in filibustering expeditions to
Cuba, Hearst and Pulitzer screamed for vengeance; when Spanish
authorities captured the American *Competitor,* a ship that actually was
engaged in filibustering, and sentenced two Americans to death, they
were beside themselves with righteous indignation.[38] But these early
stories were tame compared with those which followed the coming of
Weyler and his policy of reconcentration. Stories of suffering, cruelty,
rape, and murder daily filled the papers; even Richard Harding Davis,
who sympathized entirely with the insurgents, warned newspaper readers not to believe everything they read, since many of the atrocity
stories were manufactured by the rebels.[39]

The *Journal* and the *World,* however, threw all caution, all thought
of accuracy (except when they were trying to embarrass each other),
to the winds. Thus the *Journal* reported the searching of three Cuban
women on a ship flying an American flag under the headline "Does
Our Flag Protect Women?" and illustrated it with a drawing by
Frederic Remington showing villainous Spanish officials disrobing a
woman in her cabin. The *World,* after diligent research, piously reported that the story was false; that the women had been searched by
an elderly matron.[40] At the same time, however, the *World* was printing dispatches from its correspondents which claimed to be reports of
the news, but which could only be classified as poetry of a rather
macabre variety:

No man's life, no man's property is safe. American citizens are imprisoned or
slain without cause. American property is destroyed on all sides. There is no
pretense at protecting it. . . . Millions and millions of dollars worth of
American sugar cane, buildings and machinery have already been lost. This
year alone the war will strike $68,000,000 from the commerce of the U.S.
. . . Wounded soldiers can be found begging in the streets of Havana. . . .

[37] Walter Millis, *The Martial Spirit* (New York, 1931), p. 68.
[38] *Ibid.,* pp. 27–29, 53; Wisan, *Cuban Crisis,* pp. 69–87; Wilkerson, *Public Opinion,* pp. 15–28.
[39] Wisan, *Cuban Crisis,* pp. 187–236; Wilkerson, *Public Opinion,* pp. 29–53.
[40] Bailey, *Diplomatic History,* p. 453.

Cuba will soon be a wilderness of blackened ruins. This year there is little to live upon. Next year there will be nothing. The horrors of a barbarous struggle for the extermination of the native population are witnessed in all parts of the country. Blood on the roadsides, blood on the fields, blood on the doorsteps, blood, blood, blood! The old, the young, the weak, the crippled— all are butchered without mercy. There is scarcely a hamlet that has not witnessed the dreadful work. Is there no nation wise enough, brave enough to aid this blood-smitten land?[41]

Perhaps the most sensational of all the war stories was the *Journal's* rescue of Evangelina Cisneros. Miss Cisneros' uncle, the President of the insurgent republic, had been captured by the Spanish and imprisoned on the Isle of Pines, where she was permitted to join him. The Spanish subsequently charged her with having been an accomplice in the murder of Colonel Berris, Military Governor of the Isle of Pines and nephew of the Prime Minister of Spain, and sent her to prison in Havana. The *Journal,* however, claimed that Colonel Berris had offered to protect Miss Cisneros' father at the price of her honor, that she had "turned from the brute in horror and told her friends," and that her outraged friends had then planned his murder. The *Journal* enlisted the aid of hundreds of prominent women on behalf of Miss Cisneros, including Mrs. Jefferson Davis, who petitioned the Queen Regent of Spain to release the prisoner, and Julia Ward Howe, who solicited assistance from Pope Leo XIII. The Pope, convinced that Miss Cisneros's safety was a matter of international concern, interceded with the Queen Regent, who ordered Weyler to remove the girl to a convent. Weyler, supported by de Lôme, denied the truth of the *Journal's* story and refused to release her.[42] Hearst then sent one of his reporters, Karl Decker, to Havana with orders to get Miss Cisneros out of jail. Decker climbed onto the roof of a house next to the jail, pulled out a rotting bar from the window of her cell, and neatly effected her escape. He then smuggled her out of Cuba aboard an American ship. Hearst arranged a monster reception to greet her in New York; in Washington she and Decker visited the President. The *Journal* was showered with congratulations, one governor, perhaps with a hint of

[41] New York *World,* May 17, 1896; quoted in Wilkerson, *Public Opinion,* p. 32.
[42] Fitzhugh Lee, American Consul at Havana, also criticized the *Journal's* sensational misrepresentations.

irony, suggesting that Hearst send five hundred reporters to free Cuba.[43]

If the Cisneros rescue was the most sensational of the *Journal's* scoops, the disclosure of the de Lôme letter probably had a more shattering impact on American relations with Spain. Shortly after President McKinley's annual message to Congress in December, 1897, de Lôme communicated his reaction to the message in a private letter to the editor of the Madrid *Herald,* at that time in Cuba. The letter was stolen by a clerk in the Havana post office, a spy in the service of the insurgents, and it eventually found its way, as all such communications seemed to do, to the offices of the *Journal.* Hearst printed it on February 9, 1898. In it, de Lôme wrote of McKinley's message:

Besides the ingrained and inevitable bluntness [*groseria*] with which is repeated all that the press and public opinion in Spain have said about Weyler, it once more shows what McKinley is, weak and a bidder for the admiration of the crowd, besides being a would-be politician [*politicastro*] who tries to leave a door open behind himself while keeping on good terms with the jingoes of his party.

Worse still, de Lôme wrote in another paragraph,

It would be advantageous to take up, even if only for effect, the question of commercial relations, and to have a man of some prominence sent hither in order that I may make use of him here to carry on propaganda among the Senators and others in opposition to the junta and to try to win over the refugees.

De Lôme, learning that the letter would be released, immediately telegraphed his resignation, which was at once accepted. The Spanish government "with entire sincerity lamented the incident."[44] The damage, however, had been done—not so much in arousing public resentment against Spanish arrogance as in removing from the scene the patient, skillful, and tireless de Lôme, whose efforts in Washington had neutralized the anti-Spanish propaganda of the jingo press and whose dispatches to Madrid had sought to explain the complexity of

---

[43] Evangelina Cisneros, *The Story of Evangelina Cisneros . . . Told by Herself* (New York, 1898); Wisan, *Cuban Crisis,* pp. 324–332; Millis, *Martial Spirit,* pp. 82–84.

[44] *Foreign Relations, 1898,* pp. 677, 1007–1008, 1015; Chadwick, *United States and Spain,* I, 538–541.

the American attitude toward the struggle and to persuade his government to proceed with patience.[45]

By the beginning of 1898 the jingo press had brought the nation to the edge of war. Yet the press could not have created war sentiment out of nothing; it could not have persuaded the public that war was desirable if the public had not wanted to be persuaded of it. The country was in a receptive mood. Americans in 1897 and 1898 had grown weary of four years of depression and of endless and bitter political controversy. The election of 1896, with its alarming overtones of class and sectional conflict, had frightened the country and made many people on both sides of the conflict long for a moratorium on all political discussion. Nor was it an accident that war spirit was particularly intense in the regions where agrarian radicalism had lately flourished or that many Populists and silverites, including Bryan himself, welcomed the prospect of war. The agrarians, defeated and discouraged in their struggle for reform, happily embraced the chance to carry their crusading ardor to other, more distant, battlefields.[46]

Nor could the press have driven the country to war in the absence of a clear-cut threat, real or imagined, to the security and prestige of the United States. Hearst and Pulitzer tried to create a sense of imminent danger by dwelling on America's economic interests in Cuba, but they never succeeded in convincing their readers that those interests were important enough to justify war. Failing in that, they were forced to rely on the sentimental argument that the United States should enter the war simply to save a valiant and oppressed people from destruction. Something more tangible, however, was necessary to provoke a nation of 76 million people into war, some consummate outrage, some intolerable affront to the national honor. The sinking of the *Maine*, six days after the publication of the de Lôme letter, accomplished what the *World* and the *Journal*, for all their ingenuity, had

[45] The disclosure of the de Lôme letter would in itself not have led to war, for the administration declined to make it a *casus belli*. As Assistant Secretary of State Day said, "The publication of the letter created a good deal of feeling among Americans, and but for the fact that it was a private letter, surreptitiously if not criminally obtained, it might have raised considerable difficulty in dealing with it diplomatically." The fact that it was written in privacy, however, made the situation less serious. "If a rupture between the countries must come, it should not be upon any such personal and comparatively unimportant matter." *Foreign Relations, 1898*, pp. 680–681.

[46] Richard Hofstadter, "Manifest Destiny and the Philippines," in Daniel Aaron (ed.), *America in Crisis* (New York, 1952), pp. 173–200.

failed to accomplish. After that, talk of peace became almost immediately outmoded and archaic.

The United States had kept the Atlantic fleet in the North Atlantic for two years, in deference to Spanish fears that its presence in the Caribbean might lead to an incident, but early in the winter of 1897–98 the Navy decided to send it south for training. On January 12, 1898, a riot broke out in Havana and the American Consul, Fitzhugh Lee, nervously cabled the State Department that ships might be necessary to protect Americans and their interests, "but not now," he added.[47] Nevertheless, on January 24 McKinley ordered the battleship *Maine* detached from the fleet and sent to Havana, at the same time explaining to de Lôme that the visit was merely a courtesy call. De Lôme notified Madrid that the order was "a mark of friendship" and "an act of friendly courtesy."[48] The Spanish authorities were not impressed by these protestations of friendship. McKinley's action caused them "increasing anxiety," for it might, through some mischance, bring about a conflict. "We are trying to avoid it at any cost," they said, "making heroic efforts to maintain ourselves in the severest rectitude."[49]

The *Maine* lay in Havana harbor for three weeks. The riot that had so alarmed Consul Lee had long since subsided. There was no evidence of anti-American feeling either during the riot or afterward. Then on the evening of February 15 a terrific explosion rocked the *Maine,* which sank to the bottom of the harbor with the loss of 250 men. The Spanish government, when notified of the disaster, expressed its profound regret and condolence and allowed the *Maine* dead to be buried in Cuba on land given to the United States.[50] How the disaster occurred, whether by accident or intent, no one knows. The least probable of all the causes was any official connection with the Spanish government, whose primary interest was to avoid war. The disaster could have occurred within the *Maine;* it could have been caused by the insurgents, whose hope of success had declined, by a Spanish

[47] *Foreign Relations, 1898,* p. 1025.

[48] De Lôme to Gullón, January 24, 1898, *Spanish Diplomatic Correspondence and Documents, 1896–1900* (Washington, 1905), p. 68; *Foreign Relations, 1898,* pp. 1028–1029.

[49] Gullón to Spain's European ambassadors, February 8, 1898, *Spanish Correspondence,* p. 80.

[50] Charles D. Sigsbee, *The Maine* (New York, 1899), p. 110; *Foreign Relations, 1898,* pp. 1029–1035.

sympathizer, or by simple accident. The United States government sent four naval officers to investigate, none of whom were experts on such a problem, and refused Spanish co-operation. The "court of inquiry" reported that the *Maine* was destroyed "by a submarine mine which caused the partial explosion of two or more of the forward magazines."[51] A Spanish commission investigating at the same time attributed the disaster to an internal explosion.[52] In 1911 a second group of investigators raised the *Maine*, examined her, and then towed her out to sea and sunk her. It also believed that destruction came from "a low form of explosive exterior to the ship."[53] But no positive evidence exists that a mine even existed, or how the explosion occurred.[54]

The American press, however, declared without reservation that "the *Maine* was destroyed by treachery," as the *Journal* screamed in eight-column headlines. Said Theodore Roosevelt, "the *Maine* was sunk by an act of dirty treachery on the part of the Spaniards. . . ." When Captain Sigsbee of the *Maine* reported the disaster to Washington, he added, "Public opinion should be suspended until further report"; that is, until the wreck should have been investigated.[55] To expect that the American public would suspend judgment on the explosion after having been subjected for months to the propaganda of the yellow press was to expect a miracle. Only the *Journal* and the *World* could perform miracles. The *Journal* offered $50,000 for the detection of the culprits who sank the *Maine;* the *World* sent a special tug equipped with deep-sea divers and the inevitable correspondents. (To Pulitzer's humiliation, the authorities would not permit his men to examine the wreck.) Both papers worked feverishly to prevent the "war fever," which Hearst announced had "thrilled" the nation on the day after the explosion, from abating.[56] On March 28, the report of the American "court of inquiry," which seemed to support the contention of the press that Spanish agents had sunk the *Maine,* removed all trace of doubt or reservation in the public mind. Spain had sunk the *Maine,* and Spain must be punished.

[51] 55th Cong., 2nd sess., *Senate Document 207;* Sigsbee, *The Maine,* Appendix C.
[52] *Foreign Relations, 1898*, pp. 1044–1045; Sigsbee, *The Maine,* Appendix F.
[53] "Final Report on Removing Wreck of Battleship 'Maine' from Harbor of Havana, Cuba," 63rd Cong., 2nd sess., *House Document No. 480*, pp. 26–28.
[54] Millis, *Martial Spirit,* pp. 127–129.
[55] A facsimile of this telegram is in Sigsbee, *The Maine,* Appendix, p. 76.
[56] Wisan, *Cuban Crisis,* pp. 384–399; Wilkerson, *Public Opinion,* pp. 98–107.

The State Department had been working all this time on its own solution of the difficulties in Cuba, which was quite different from the solution advocated in other quarters. The State Department wished simply to restore peace in Cuba as quickly as possible, if for no other reason than to make it impossible for the press and the pulpit to continue demanding intervention. In April, 1896, Olney had offered to Spain his good offices in bringing peace and a measure of home rule to Cuba. Spain declined the offer.[57] Stewart L. Woodford, the new Minister to Spain under the McKinley administration, repeated the offer immediately upon assuming his duties; in October, 1897, Spain again declined, but promised autonomy to Cuba.[58] In November a new and more liberal Spanish ministry recalled General Weyler, modified his reconcentration policy, and made a formal offer of autonomy to the Cubans provided they would lay down their arms. The insurgents, wanting nothing less than complete independence and hoping for American intervention on their side, refused these terms. McKinley was more patient; in his December message, which de Lôme was for some reason to find so unsatisfactory, he asked Congress that Spain "be given a reasonable chance to realize her expectations."[59]

The sinking of the *Maine* did not ruin these negotiations, as one might have supposed it would. Instead it made the Spanish more willing to embrace the American position. On March 27, just before the American report on the *Maine* was made public, Day instructed Woodford to find out (1) whether Spain would grant a six months' armistice to the insurgents; (2) whether she would revoke the *reconcentrado* order at once, allow the Cubans to return to their farms, and co-operate with the United States in furnishing them with provisions and supplies; and (3) whether Spain would "if possible" allow the United States to be the final arbiter between Spain and the insurgents if they were unable to make peace by October 1, when the armistice was to expire.[60] Ignoring the last of these demands, which the United States was not prepared to insist on in any event, Spain agreed to revoke the reconcentration order, at least in the western parts of Cuba. An armistice, however, she could not grant—unless, of course, the rebels asked for it. Woodford hopefully cabled to McKinley:

[57] *Foreign Relations, 1897,* pp. 540–548; Nevins, *Cleveland,* pp. 703–710.
[58] *Foreign Relations, 1898,* pp. 568–573, 581–591.
[59] *Ibid., 1897,* p. xx.
[60] *Ibid., 1898,* pp. 711–712.

I believe the ministry are ready to go as far and as fast as they can and still save the dynasty here in Spain. They know that Cuba is lost. Public opinion in Spain has moved steadily toward peace. No Spanish ministry would have dared to do one month ago what this ministry has proposed to-day.[61]

On April 3 he again cabled, "I know that the Queen and her present ministry sincerely desire peace, and if you can still give me time, and reasonable liberty of action I will get for you the peace you desire so much and for which you have labored so hard."[62] Two days later Spain revoked the reconcentration policy throughout Cuba.

On April 6 the American representatives of Great Britain, Germany, Austria-Hungary, France, Russia, and Italy waited on the President and appealed to his feelings of "humanity and moderation." On April 9 Spain at last agreed to suspend hostilities in Cuba "for such length of time as [the Governor General] may think prudent."[63] The American demands had been met in substance; diplomacy had triumphed and war appeared unnecessary. Secretary Long wrote to a friend in Boston:

Do you realize that the President has succeeded in obtaining from Spain a concession upon every ground which he asked; that Spain has yielded everything up to the present time except the last item of Cuban independence; that she has released every American prisoner; recalled Weyler; recalled de Lôme; changed her reconcentration order; agreed to furnish food; and ordered an armistice? . . . If the country and Congress had been content to leave the matter in his hands, independence would have come without a drop of bloodshed, as naturally as an apple falls from a tree.[64]

Congress, however, would not leave the matter in the President's hands. Congress wanted war, and McKinley was not the man to resist. Knowing that, if he turned the whole matter over to Congress, it would declare war, McKinley proceeded to do just that. On April 11 he asked Congress to "empower the President to take measures to secure a full and final termination of hostilities . . . to secure in the island the establishment of a stable government . . . and to use the

[61] *Ibid.*, p. 724.

[62] *Ibid.*, p. 732.

[63] *Ibid.*, pp. 740–741; Orestes Ferrara, *The Last Spanish War* (New York, 1937), pp. 65–78; L. B. Shippee, "Germany and the Spanish American War," *American Historical Review*, XXX (July, 1925), 754–777.

[64] Lawrence S. Mayo (ed.), *America of Yesterday as Reflected in the Journal of John Davis Long* (Boston, 1923), pp. 179–180.

military and naval forces of the United States as may be necessary for these purposes." "The issue is now with Congress," he concluded. "I have exhausted every effort to relieve the intolerable condition of affairs which is at our doors. Prepared to execute every obligation imposed upon me by the Constitution and the law, I await your action." He added, as a kind of footnote, that the day before, and previous to "the preparation of the foregoing message," he had received word that the Queen of Spain had directed Blanco "to proclaim a suspension of hostilities, the duration and details of which have not yet been communicated to me. . . . If this measure attains a successful result, then our aspirations as a Christian, peace-loving people will be realized. If it fails, it will be only another justification for our contemplated action."[65]

Congress was in no mood to wait to see whether the measure attained a "successful result." In a joint declaration, April 19, 1898, Congress declared Cuba free and independent, demanded the withdrawal of Spain from the island, and directed and empowered the President to use the armed forces of the United States to secure these ends. To this declaration was added the Teller amendment, which was to prove so embarrassing to subsequent administrations:

That the United States hereby disclaims any disposition or intention to exercise sovereignty, jurisdiction, or control over said island, except for the pacification thereof and asserts its determination when that is accomplished to leave the government and control of the island to its people.

On the following day McKinley sent the resolution to Madrid and gave the Spanish government until noon of April 23 to "relinquish its authority and government of the island." On April 21 Spain broke off diplomatic relations with the United States, and on April 25 Congress declared that a state of war had existed since that day.[66]

The United States thus went to war with Spain in order to secure ends which had already been secured by diplomacy; it rushed into battle with an enemy which had already conceded all she had been asked to concede. Nor was the country oblivious to these facts. Senator Spooner, writing to a friend a few days after the declaration of war, accurately expressed not only the circumstances which had impelled the nation into war but the mood of many intelligent people on the eve

[65] *Foreign Relations, 1898*, pp. 759–760.
[66] *Ibid.*, pp. 762–774.

of battle. Spooner wrote laconically, "I think . . . possibly the President could have worked out the business without a war, but the current was too strong, the demagogues too numerous, and the fall elections too near."[67]

[67] Spooner to C. W. Porter, May 2, 1898; Spooner Papers, Library of Congress.

CHAPTER II

The War with Spain

ON APRIL 30, 1898, five days after Congress officially declared that a state of war existed between the United States and Spain, Theodore Roosevelt telegraphed to Brooks Brothers for a "blue cravenette regular Lieutenant-Colonel's uniform without yellow on the collar and with leggings."[1] A week later he resigned his position as Assistant Secretary of the Navy and, impeccably attired, set off to war. In Nebraska, William Jennings Bryan assumed command of the Third Nebraska Regiment. All over the country, in the hills of Vermont, in the black belt of the South, on the plains of Kansas where farmers had lately listened to the impassioned rhetoric of Mary Ellen Lease and "Sockless" Jerry Simpson, young men flocked to the colors. The country was united as it had not been united since the time of Jackson. Southerner and Northerner, silverite and gold bug, joined their voices in a common hymn of praise to the flag, to the President, to the gallant heroes of the *Maine*. It was a heartwarming spectacle; it was glorious; it was splendid; it was, as Roosevelt so aptly summed it up, "bully."

Not many Americans had the faintest notion of the actual strength of the American and Spanish forces; not many ever knew how fortunate it was for this country that the war was largely fought on sea. Spain's regular troops in Cuba were estimated at 155,000 veterans of many months of warfare under the most exacting conditions, and their arms and equipment were far superior to anything the United States could provide. The regular Army of the United States numbered only 28,000 troops scattered throughout the nation, experienced only in small-scale Indian wars. After war was declared, Congress increased

[1] Henry F. Pringle, *Theodore Roosevelt* (New York, 1931), p. 183.

the regular Army to 61,000. There was no lack of volunteers: 125,000 responded to McKinley's first call on April 22, 75,000 to a second call late in May. By the end of November more than 223,000 men had enlisted, of whom, however, only 87,000 ever left the country.[2] But to clothe, feed, and equip such an army with modern weapons was a problem which the country was not prepared to solve. There was endless confusion in assembling and quartering the men. Sanitary and medical services remained inadequate. In the five months from the end of April to the end of September, 2,565 men died from disease or from causes other than battle wounds—more than seven times the number, 345, who died in battle. This ratio was higher even than that of the Civil War, when disease had swept off appalling numbers of men.[3]

The American Navy, however, was three times as large as Spain's. The United States owned four first-class battleships and one second-class battleship; Spain owned a single first-class battleship, and that was laid up and never saw service. Her cruisers and other ships were inadequately equipped, out of repair, and poorly manned; those of the United States were in excellent condition and the morale of the men was high. The American Navy was capable of annihilating the Spanish fleet and of imposing a strict blockade of Cuba; the United States could probably have won the war without an invasion of Cuba. The strength of the American Navy, together with Spain's political instability, the chronic inefficiency of her government, and her distance from the scene of the war, tipped the scales in America's favor. In the end victory came easily, but few Americans had bothered to consider the possibility that it might not. When Bismarck observed that there was a special providence for drunkards, fools, and the United States of America, he must have had the war with Spain specifically in mind.[4]

Utter confusion reigned in the War Department. There were not enough rifles to go around, nor enough khaki cloth, nor even, it seemed,

[2] F. E. Chadwick, *The Relations of the United States and Spain: The Spanish American War* (New York, 1911), I, 46–54; R. A. Alger, *The Spanish-American War* (New York, 1901), pp. 6–28.

[3] According to Alger, *Spanish-American War*, p. 454, this ratio was lower than that for a comparable period during the Civil War, although it is doubtful if conditions were comparable at any time during the two wars. The ratio for the Civil War as a whole was lower.

[4] Chadwick, *Spanish-American War*, I, 28–46; Harold and Margaret Sprout, *The Rise of American Naval Power, 1776–1918* (Princeton, 1939), pp. 223–249; John D. Long, *The New American Navy* (New York, 1903), I, *passim*.

enough food; soldiers claimed that they were fed on "embalmed beef." General Miles wrote of conditions at Tampa, where the regulars were encamped:

Several of the volunteer regiments came here without uniforms; several came without arms, and some without blankets, tents, or camp equipage. The thirty-second Michigan, which is among the best, came without arms. General Guy V. Henry reports that five regiments under his command are not fit to go into the field. There are over 300 cars loaded with war material along the roads about Tampa. . . . To illustrate the embarrassment, 15 cars loaded with uniforms were side-tracked twenty-five miles away from Tampa, and remained there for weeks while the troops were suffering for clothing. Five thousand rifles, which were discovered yesterday, were needed by several regiments. Also, the different parts of the siege train and ammunition for the same, which will be required immediately on landing, are scattered through hundreds of cars on the side-tracks of the railroads.[5]

Over this chaotic empire presided the genial Russell A. Alger, politician, governor of Michigan, lumber magnate. Alger was not without war experience; he had risen during the Civil War from private to the rank of brevet major general. Later he served as commander in chief of the Grand Army of the Republic; his appointment as Secretary of War, in fact, was designed to please the veterans. If his earlier military career had prepared him for the management of the War Department, there was little evidence to show it. His failings, however, were not peculiar to himself; his impatience with detail, his easygoing optimism, and his tendency to assume that difficult problems would solve themselves were characteristics which he shared with the majority of his countrymen.

Alger had for some time regarded war with Spain as inevitable, but had done nothing to prepare for it. When asked by McKinley about a month before the war, "How soon can you put an army into Cuba?" Alger answered blithely, "Forty thousand men there in ten days."[6] It took seven weeks to get 17,000 men to Cuba, and then only after frantic exertions. But although Alger made a convenient scapegoat, he was no more to blame for any of this than Congress, the executive, the

---

[5] *Correspondence, War with Spain* (Washington, 1903), I, 24–25. Alger, *Spanish-American War*, pp. 67–68; *Investigation of the War Department in the Conduct of the War Department in the War with Spain* (Washington, 1900), II, 888. See also Walter Millis, *The Martial Spirit* (Boston, 1931).

[6] Quoted in Millis, *Martial Spirit*, p. 127.

Army, or the people. Congress had neglected the Army for years. The War Department had long been manned by "elderly incompetents," as Roosevelt called them, without the "slightest conception of preparing the army for war."[7] The Army itself was rusty from disuse. That there had been no occasion to use it was nobody's fault in particular; yet the fact that the country had been at peace for thirty years, more than anything else, explained why going to war proved baffling in 1898. The American tradition of unpreparedness was rooted in historical experience. And perhaps, as Alger pointed out in his own defense, it was something of an achievement that in all the confusion an expedition did manage to sail from San Francisco for the Philippines within five weeks of McKinley's first call and that the first troops reached Santiago in seven weeks. Nobody could take particular pride in such information, but neither was it necessary to hang one's head in shame.[8]

Since the United States had presumably gone to war to rescue the Cubans from their brutal Spanish overlords, it was something of a surprise when the first crash of arms took place 6,000 miles away in the Philippine Islands. Most Americans, according to Mr. Dooley, did not even know "whether they were islands or canned goods," much less colonies of Spain and therefore liable to attack in case of war. The expansionists, however, had long regarded the Philippines with unusual interest. They realized that, with the Spanish fleet stationed at Manila, war with Spain would afford an excellent opportunity for seizing the Philippines on the grounds of national defense. On April 27, only two days after war was declared and four days before Dewey's victory in Manila Bay, Albert J. Beveridge announced before an audience at the Middlesex Club of Boston, "The Philippines are logically our first target."[9] Roosevelt, sharing the same sentiments, first influenced the appointment of Dewey as commander of the Asiatic squadron and then sent him the following cable:

Washington, February 25, '98

Dewey, Hong Kong:

Order the squadron, except the Monacacy, to Hong Kong. Keep full of coal. In the event of declaration of war Spain, your duty will be to see that

[7] Theodore Roosevelt, *An Autobiography* (New York, 1913), p. 244.

[8] Alger, *Spanish-American War,* p. 28. Even Roosevelt admitted that "it was impossible to avoid the great bulk of all the trouble that occurred . . . during the Spanish War." *Autobiography* (New York, 1913), p. 244.

[9] Albert J. Beveridge, *The Meaning of the Times and Other Speeches* (Indianapolis, 1908), p. 45.

the Spanish squadron does not leave the Asiatic coast, and then offensive operations in the Philippine Islands. Keep Olympia until further orders.

ROOSEVELT [10]

Since Secretary Long was away from the office when Roosevelt sent this famous cable, it has often been assumed that McKinley and Long were oblivious to what was going on, and that the eventual annexation of the Philippines can therefore be attributed purely to the dark machinations of an imperialist clique within the government. That there was an annexationist group cannot be doubted; but it was hardly working in secrecy to undo the policy of the administration. Secretary Long learned of Roosevelt's order to Dewey on the day after it was sent and in fact rebuked Roosevelt for sending it. He did not, however, revoke the order, as he would surely have done if he had disapproved of the contents and not merely of the manner in which it was sent.[11] The fact is that military necessity dictated the destruction of the Spanish fleet, and one Spanish fleet was stationed at Manila. No sensible strategist could have ignored the necessity of naval operations in Manila Bay.[12]

It was not the decision to attack the Spanish fleet in Manila which eventually led to the acquisition of the Philippines. As McKinley later regretfully said, "If old Dewey had just sailed away when he smashed the Spanish fleet, what a lot of trouble he would have saved us." The fateful decision was the one to land troops on the islands and to take possession of them, and it was McKinley himself who willingly approved this step even before official reports of Dewey's victory had been received. McKinley later insisted, "I didn't want the Philippines, and . . . they came to us, as a gift from the gods," but there is evidence to suggest that as early as June he wanted at least Manila. Even earlier, on May 24, Lodge told Roosevelt that he believed "in absolute certainty, that the Administration is grasping the whole policy at last" and that unless he was "utterly and profoundly mistaken," the President was "now fully committed to the large policy that we both desire."

[10] *Autobiography*, p. 234.

[11] Lawrence S. Mayo (ed.), *America of Yesterday as Reflected in the Journal of John Davis Long* (Boston, 1923), p. 169.

[12] For this episode, see also Henry Cabot Lodge, *Selections from the Correspondence of Theodore Roosevelt and Henry Cabot Lodge* (New York, 1925), I, 303–305; *Autobiography of George Dewey* (New York, 1913), pp. 167–170, 179; A. Whitney Griswold, *The Far Eastern Policy of the United States* (New York, 1938), pp. 12–13; Pringle, *Roosevelt*, p. 178.

Far from an unwitting agent of the "large policy," McKinley seems to have been one of the first converts to it.[13]

Five days before the declaration of war Dewey's fleet lay off Manila Bay. At daybreak of May 1 he entered the bay. Five times the American fleet steamed past the assembled maritime antiquities of the enemy, pouring upon them a deadly fire and leaving them in smoking ruin. Then Dewey efficiently silenced the Spanish batteries on shore. Of 1,743 Americans engaged in this notable action, eight men were slightly wounded by splinters; 381 Spaniards were dead or wounded and the entire fleet destroyed.[14] In the words of an English writer, the battle was "a military execution rather than a real contest."[15]

After blocking Manila, Dewey awaited the American troops, which did not arrive until the end of June. Between June 30 and July 31 four contingents were landed, under the command of General Wesley Merritt. The Spanish offered little resistance; by the middle of August the Americans, in conjunction with Filipinos in revolt against Spain, had captured Manila and were extending their control inland. A source of greater uneasiness to the American commanders was the conduct of Vice-Admiral Otto von Diederichs, who commanded a squadron of five German ships in Manila Bay—a squadron as powerful as Dewey's. During the three months in which the port was under blockade, ships of various flags entered the harbor to observe conditions or to care for their nationals. All of them scrupulously observed the terms of the blockade except Germany.

Early in July, however, when Filipino insurgents attacked a Spanish force at Subic Bay, Diederichs sent one of his ships to evacuate noncombatants. Dewey ordered two American ships to follow it, and they passed it on its way back from the scene of combat. Both the British and the Americans believed that Germany had designs on the Philippines, of which they interpreted Diederichs' movements as proof. The trivial incidents at Manila later gave rise to the myth that Germany had actually tried to destroy the American fleet and that Captain

[13] Foster Rhea Dulles, *America's Rise to World Power* (New American Nation Series, New York, 1954), pp. 49–51; Griswold, *Far Eastern Policy*, pp. 13–14; H. H. Kohlsaat, *From McKinley to Harding* (New York, 1923), p. 68; Lodge, *Correspondence of Roosevelt and Lodge*, I, 299–300.

[14] Chawick, *Spanish-American War*, I, 204–205.

[15] Herbert W. Wilson, *The Downfall of Spain* (London, 1900), p. 152, quoted in Chadwick, *Spanish-American War*, I, 207.

Edward Chichester, the British commander, had by intervening two of his ships saved Dewey from disaster. But Chichester's movement of his ships to a position between the German and American fleets during the bombardment of Manila on August 13 was nothing more than an effort to observe the bombardment. That Germany hoped to acquire

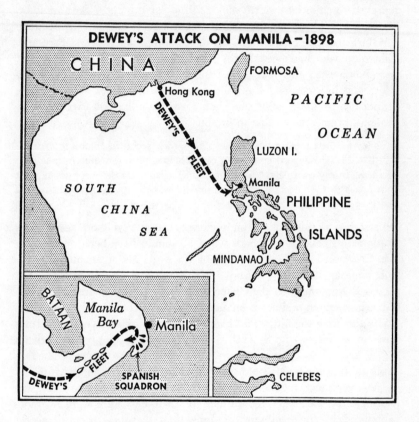

DEWEY'S ATTACK ON MANILA – 1898

territory in the Far East as a result of the defeat of Spain and that Britain wished to prevent her from doing so can hardly be denied, but neither Britain nor Germany was ready to go to war for those ends. The United States, however, genuinely feared German intervention in the summer of 1898, and this fear may have influenced the decision to take over the Philippines instead of setting them free.[16]

[16] T. A. Bailey, "Dewey and the Germans at Manila Bay," *American His-*

Naval operations in the Caribbean were by no means so clear-cut and decisive as those of Dewey at Manila. The Spanish Admiral, Cervera, left the Cape Verde Islands on April 29 and headed westward. The United States, assuming that he was sailing for either Puerto Rico or Cuba, divided her fleet into two squadrons and searched for him both north and south of those islands. Days went by and still he did not appear. Wild rumors spread that he was heading for the American coast. Panic broke out. Men like Senators Frye and Chandler, who had been loudly demanding war a few weeks before, now bombarded the War Department with demands for protection. Men who had opposed the building of naval ships for years wanted frantically to know why the country did not have a larger Navy. Roosevelt remembered that in Boston

so many business men of the city . . . took their securities inland to Worcester that the safe deposit companies of Worcester proved unable to take care of them. In my own neighborhood on Long Island, clauses were gravely put into leases to the effect that if the property was destroyed by the Spaniards the lease should lapse.[17]

In response to this panic, Commodore Schley's "Flying Squadron" was stationed off Hampton Roads when he should have been out looking for Cervera. Thus Cervera was able to elude his opponents and slip into Santiago Harbor on May 19, unable to go any further for lack of coal. Not until ten days later did Schley discover him there. The American search had not been an unqualified success.[18]

By this time the Navy had come to the conclusion that it could not risk an attack on the Spanish fleet but would have to wait until an army arrived to attack the city. The state of the Army seemed to indicate that the wait would be a long one. Half the regular Army and a few volunteer regiments had been stationed at Tampa since the outbreak of war, but preparations for their departure were no more advanced by the beginning of June than they had been six weeks before. The volunteers included the Rough Riders, recently arrived from their training camp in San Antonio and commanded by Colonel Leonard Wood and by Roosevelt, now a lieutenant colonel. Composed

torical Review, XLV (Oct., 1939), 59–81; L. B. Shippee, "Germany and the Spanish-American War," ibid., XXX (July, 1925), 754–777.

[17] Autobiography, p. 235.

[18] Chadwick, Spanish-American War, I, 214–307; Winfred S. Schley, Forty-Five Years under the Flag (New York, 1904), pp. 256–285.

largely of cowboys, college athletes, and the sons of wealthy men, they were armed with the best equipment available and spoiling for a fight; their only fear was that the war would be over before they embarked.[19] Finally, on June 7, orders came from Washington to embark.

Merely transporting the troops to the waterside proved to be a major undertaking. According to Roosevelt:

When we were finally informed that [the expedition] was to leave next morning, we were ordered to go to a certain track to meet a train. We went to the track, but the train never came. Then we were sent to another track to meet another train. Again it never came. However, we found a coal train, of which we took possession, and the conductor, partly under duress and partly in a spirit of friendly helpfulness, took us down to the quay.[20]

When the Rough Riders reached the wharf, they found to their consternation that the U.S.S. *Yucatan,* on which they were to sail, had through some mistake been assigned to two other regiments.

When they reached the wharf, it was largely the problem of the officers literally to capture a ship and get their troops aboard. As far as the Rough Riders were concerned, Wood and Roosevelt managed to hold a gangplank to the discomfiture of a regiment made up of volunteers and regulars until they had got their own troops aboard.[21] By late afternoon most of the men were on shipboard and the fleet ready to sail, when General William R. Shafter in command of the Cuban expeditionary army received orders from the War Department, "Wait until you get further orders before you sail." Whereupon the loaded ships lay in Port Tampa harbor for a week while the Navy searched the St. Nicholas Channel (along the northern coast of Cuba) to check a report that a Spanish cruiser and torpedo-boat destroyer were still out at sea. Having satisfied itself that the rumor was false, the Navy sent its convoy to protect and direct the troopships to Cuba. The expedition—17,000 officers and enlisted men, including eighteen regular infantry and two volunteer infantry regiments (the 71st New York and the 2nd Massachusetts) and six cavalry regiments—sailed on June 14.

[19] While Wood was recruiting his Rough Riders at San Antonio, Texas, the governor of Nebraska made Bryan colonel of the Third Nebraska regiment. But this was a war run by Republicans, and Bryan and his troops were left to rot away in the Florida swamps.

[20] Roosevelt, *Autobiography,* p. 254.

[21] *Ibid.*

On June 20 they reached Admiral Sampson's fleet off Santiago. Sampson hoped that Shafter would attack Santiago from the entrance of the harbor, but Shafter preferred to surround the city. Sampson and Shafter went ashore to confer with the rebel general Calixto García, who advised them to put the troops ashore at Daiquiri, a village eighteen miles east of Santiago. On June 22, after a thirty-five-minute bombardment of the shore, the Army landed amid scenes of uproarious confusion. Two men drowned. The horses were thrown overboard to swim to shore, with buglers blowing cavalry calls from shore. The few hundred Spaniards who were guarding the shore, perhaps unnerved by the spectacle, offered no resistance. Hardly had the landing been accomplished when orders came to push on to Siboney, eight miles further west. There the rest of the American Army disembarked and set up a base of operations.[22]

Shafter had not yet left his ship. For the general, in fact, the whole adventure was rapidly becoming a personal ordeal. He was sixty years old and, since he weighed 300 pounds, suffered intensely from the heat. He later said of his days in Cuba: "I was nearly prostrated . . . when I would sit up it would make me dizzy. . . . I had a beastly attack of gout so that I could not wear a boot for a week, and had to wear a gunny sack on my foot, and I could not climb my horse, and would have to build a platform to climb up on."[23]

From his ship Shafter dispatched General Henry W. Lawton to Siboney with instructions to take up a strong defensive position before making any preparations to advance, but Joseph Wheeler, a former Confederate officer and a volunteer major general of the cavalry, ignored Shafter's orders and on June 24 advanced toward Santiago with squadrons of the First and Tenth Cavalry and the Rough Riders. At Los Guásimas they encountered Spanish defenses atop a commanding hill and sent back for reinforcements. Just as they arrived the Spanish left the hill to the advancing Americans. The incident was unnecessarily hazardous; it cost the Americans sixteen dead and fifty-two wounded.[24]

[22] Chadwick, *Spanish-American War,* II, 3–39; Herbert H. Sargent, *The Campaign of Santiago de Cuba* (Chicago, 1907), II, 1–44; John D. Miley, *In Cuba with Shafter* (New York, 1899), pp. 1–81.

[23] Quoted in Pringle, *Roosevelt,* pp. 192–193.

[24] Millis, *Martial Spirit,* pp. 269–276; Chadwick, *Spanish-American War,* II, 48–58; Sargent, *Campaign of Santiago,* II, 45–82; Joseph Wheeler, *The San-*

With all troops finally ashore and supplies brought up in a confusion reminiscent of Tampa, Shafter moved his headquarters to El Pozo, seven miles northwest of Siboney. Calling his division commanders together on June 30, he directed them to make an attack on the following morning against the fortified village of El Caney and against San Juan Hill. General Lawton with 6,600 men was to attack El Caney; General Jacob F. Kent with 8,000, San Juan. By capturing El Caney, Shafter hoped not only to prevent reinforcements from reaching the defenders of Santiago and to cut off the city's water supply, but to protect his own attack on San Juan Hill. The capture of the latter would then open the road to Santiago.

At 6:30 the next morning Lawton moved upon El Caney. The Spanish numbered only 500, but they were stationed behind formidable breastworks and used smokeless Mauser rifles to conceal their position. Shafter supposed that Lawton would expel the enemy within two hours, but not until 6:30 that evening, after twelve hours of heavy fighting, did the Spanish withdraw. The Americans lost 81 men killed and 360 wounded. Not until noon of the next day did Lawton reach San Juan Heights, where he was to join forces with Kent.

Kent, meanwhile, had waited for Lawton to drive the Spanish from El Caney before launching his attack. After waiting for two hours, Grimes' battery, set up near El Paso, opened up with fire which accomplished little except to indicate his position to the Spanish. After forty-five minutes of pointless artillery fire Kent ordered an advance, which was led by Wheeler's dismounted cavalry division (there had been room on the transports for enough horses to equip only one cavalry squadron; the rest went horseless) and followed by his own infantry division. General S. S. Sumner, who commanded Wheeler's division that morning, was ordered to deploy his men in front of Kettle Hill; Kent would take up a position at the foot of the nearby San Juan Hill. The greatest obstacle to the success of these maneuvers was the difficulty of getting some 8,000 troops moving along a road—the so-called Santiago road—which in places was no more than a trail through a jungle of trees and underbrush. The discovery of another trail by a Signal Corps balloon only slightly relieved the congestion. Unfortunately the balloon also revealed the Americans to the Spaniards, who poured a deadly fire upon them.

tiago Campaign, 1898 (Boston, 1898), pp. 13–38; Richard Harding Davis, *The Cuban and Porto Rican Campaigns* (New York, 1898), pp. 120–172.

It was noon before the troops drew up before the heights. There they hesitated, exposed to the full fire of the enemy, awaiting definite orders. Finally the word came: "The heights must be taken at all hazards. A retreat now would be a disastrous defeat." Sumner ordered part of his division to attack Kettle Hill, the rest under General Hawkins to attack San Juan Hill. Roosevelt found himself at the foot of Kettle Hill surrounded by Rough Riders and colored troops from other cavalry regiments. "I waved my hand," he remembered many years

THE SANTIAGO CAMPAIGN – 1898

later, "and we went up the hill with a rush."[25] By the time they reached the top, the Spanish had evacuated it and fled to San Juan Hill. Sumner and Roosevelt collected their troops and hurried on, but the enemy was in full flight by the time they reached San Juan Hill; Kent's infantry, Hawkins's dismounted cavalry, and three batteries of artillery had routed the enemy.[26] Later Roosevelt liked to recount the affair at such length and with such conspicuous omissions of all but his

[25] *Autobiography*, p. 242.

[26] Chadwick, *Spanish-American War*, II, 61–113; Sargent, *Campaign of Santiago*, II, 83–166; Millis, *Martial Spirit*, pp. 269–292; Miley, *In Cuba with Shafter*, pp. 101–128; Alger, *Spanish-American War*, pp. 83–296; Wheeler, *Santiago Campaign*, pp. 39–196; Davis, *Cuban and Porto Rican Campaign*, pp. 173–295.

own part in it that Mr. Dooley, on reading his *The Rough Riders,* was driven to say to Mr. Hennessy:

"I haven't time f'r to tell ye the wurruk Tiddy did in ar-rmin' an' equippin' himself, how he fed himself, how he steadied himself in battles an' encouraged himself with a few well-chosen worruds whin th' sky was darkest. Ye'll have to take a squint into the book ye'erself to l'arn thim things."

"I won't do it," said Mr. Hennessy. "I think Tiddy Rosenfelt is all r-right an' if he wants to blow his horn lave him do it."

"Thrue f'r ye," said Mr. Dooley. . . . "But if I was him I'd call th' book 'Alone in Cubia.' " [27]

In all the engagements between July 1 and July 3 the Americans had lost 225 dead and 1,384 wounded—10 per cent of the men engaged. Shafter was downcast; convinced that he could not capture Santiago without reinforcements and believing that the Navy was not giving adequate support to his attack, he considered a retreat and notified Washington to that effect. Roosevelt on July 3 expressed the mood of the Army when he wrote to Lodge, ". . . we are within measurable distance of a terrible military disaster; we *must* have help. . . ."[28] In reality it was the Spanish who were faced with disaster. Surrounded on one side, blockaded on the other, their food and water running low, they were already doomed when Shafter, persuaded by more hopeful advisers that victory was not far off, demanded on July 3 that the city surrender. On the same day Sampson and Schley destroyed the Spanish fleet, thus effectively ending the war.

Admiral Cervera had already reached the melancholy conclusion that his fleet was lost—lost, he said, "ever since it left Cape Verde." He was faced with two alternatives, either to scuttle the ships when Santiago was captured or to attempt to escape, a maneuver which would probably draw him into battle against a fleet "four times superior to his own," thereby "sacrificing to vanity the majority of [his] crews and depriving Santiago of their cooperation." Governor General Blanco sternly ordered the latter course. Cervera, believing that the physical conformation of the harbor and the American searchlights rendered a night escape impossible, determined to make the attempt by day. Slowly his fleet—four cruisers and two destroyers—moved out of the narrow harbor in single line and turned westward. The American fleet discerned the movement almost immediately and

---

[27] Elmer Ellis (ed.), *Mr. Dooley at His Best* (New York, 1938), pp. 102–103.
[28] *Correspondence of Roosevelt and Lodge,* I, 317.

set out in pursuit. One of the Spanish destroyers ran on the rocks and blew up; the other soon surrendered. Three of the four cruisers, including the flagship *Maria Theresa*, caught fire or suffered heavy damage from explosions and headed for shore. The *Cristobal Colón* managed to elude her pursuers, but at one o'clock her engines faltered from the inferior coal which they were burning and she hauled down her colors and ran aground on the beach fifty miles from Santiago. The Spanish fleet was destroyed. Three hundred men had been killed in the action, 151 wounded, and the rest captured. One American had been killed and one wounded.[29]

In less than four hours the power of the Spanish empire had been utterly broken. "When I gave the order to fire," said Captain Concas of the Spanish flagship, "it was the signal that the history of four centuries of grandeur was at an end and that Spain was becoming a nation of the fourth class."[30] Two weeks later Santiago formally surrendered. On August 12 Spain signed a preliminary peace in which she agreed to relinquish Cuba; to cede one of the Ladrones Islands to the United States as an indemnity; to permit American occupation of "the city, bay and harbor of Manila pending the conclusion of a treaty of peace which shall determine the control, disposition and government of the Philippines"; and to cede Puerto Rico, which had been overrun without difficulty by General Miles, to the United States. In signing these terms the Spanish representative said, "This demand strips us of the very last memory of a glorious past and expels us . . . from the Western Hemisphere, which became peopled and civilized through the proud deeds of our ancestors."[31]

America, however, rejoiced. "It has been a splendid little war," wrote John Hay; "begun with the highest motives, carried on with magnificent intelligence and spirit, favored by that Fortune which loves the brave."[32] In the orgy of self-congratulation which followed victory, the only discordant note was the suggestion in some quarters that the war had not been prosecuted as efficiently as it might have

[29] Since some of the Spaniards may have escaped to shore, the number of dead is not certain. Chadwick, *Spanish-American War*, II, 176–177; Sargent, *Campaign of Santiago*, II, 167–236; John D. Long, *The New American Navy* (New York, 1903), II, 1–50.

[30] Concas y Palau, *The Squadron of Admiral Cervera* (trans. by the Navy Department, Washington, 1900), p. 74.

[31] *Foreign Relations, 1898,* p. 824.

[32] Hay to Roosevelt, July 27, 1898, quoted by William R. Thayer, *The Life and Letters of John Hay* (2 vols., Boston, 1915), II, 337.

been. Critics, most of them Democrats, pointed out that the Army had been totally unprepared for the war, that military equipment of every kind had proved inadequate, that operations in Cuba had been bungled, and that victory had been far more costly than necessary. One authority went so far as to say:

The marvelous thing is that General Shafter should have succeeded. Indeed, his success was little short of the miraculous. Had the Spaniards then at Santiago been properly handled, they could easily have prevented his landing at Daiquiri and Siboney; or failing to attempt that, could have crushed him at Los Guasimas or defeated him at San Juan Hill.[33]

The War Department was the favorite target for criticism. So bitter were the attacks on Secretary Alger that in September, 1898, he asked the President to appoint a board to investigate his conduct of the war. The results of the inquiry, which were not published until 1900, disappointed those who wished to embarrass the administration. Although the board considered the Quartermaster's Department "not as efficient as it should have been" and charged both the Medical Department and the Ordnance Department with having been unprepared for the emergency, it exonerated the War Department of the most serious charge against it, that of having served "embalmed beef" to the troops. General Miles, among others, had charged that his men had been fed on such fare. He testified to that effect before the board of investigation, but mysteriously refused to swear an oath. The board concluded that "after careful consideration we find that canned meat, as issued to the troops, was generally of good quality, was properly prepared, and contained no deleterious substance."[34] During the campaign of 1900 a heckler once reminded Roosevelt of the "embalmed beef." "I ate it," he snapped. "That was only one of many slanders put forth for political purposes."[35]

Other aspects of the war effort also met with criticism. Incessant rivalry between the Army and the Navy had hampered the Cuban campaign. Sampson, for instance, had allowed Shafter to do the hard and bloody work of surrounding Santiago while his ships waited safely

---

[33] Sargent, *Campaign of Santiago de Cuba*, II, 162.

[34] *Investigation of the Conduct of the War Department in the War with Spain* (Washington, 1900), I, 120–122, 124, 147, 166, 188, 199–200; Alger, *Spanish-American War*, pp. 376–410.

[35] Arthur W. Dunn, *From Harrison to Harding* (2 vols., New York, 1922), I, 262.

outside the harbor to prevent the possible exodus of Cervera. After his heavy losses on July 1 Shafter had urged Sampson "immediately to force the entrance" of the harbor, declaring, "You can now operate with less loss of life than I can." When Sampson refused, Shafter replied, "I am at a loss to see why the Navy cannot work under a destructive fire as well as the army."[36] Sampson was on his way to confer with Shafter on July 3 when Cervera made his dash out of the harbor, hotly pursued by the rest of the American fleet. Sampson in his flagship had to turn about and set out after his own ships, and the battle was over before he caught up with them. Sampson, notwithstanding his absence from the scene of battle, refused to give Schley credit for winning it. When the country learned the details of the operations in Santiago Bay, people were outraged at such "bureaucratic" ingratitude in the Navy and demanded an investigation. A court of inquiry upheld Sampson.

In the uproar over the victories in Cuba the annexation of Hawaii went almost unnoticed. On July 7 McKinley signed a joint resolution of Congress incorporating Hawaii into the territory of the United States. Thus ended the long agitation for the annexation of that island.[37] In the debate on the measure the only argument in favor of annexation which had not already been advanced again and again was that Hawaii was needed in the war against Spain—a spurious contention, since Cervera had been defeated before the resolution passed the Senate. Otherwise the old arguments were simply repeated: that Hawaii would benefit commercially and, presumably, spiritually from our supervision; that it would serve as a naval base; that its acquisition was in any case dictated by our manifest destiny.[38] Advanced a few months before, these ideas had seemed unconvincing; in the flush of victory they suddenly acquired the force of divine revelation. Only when the Philippine question came up did many senators who had voted for Hawaiian annexation realize that in doing so they had set a dangerous precedent.

[36] Millis, *Martial Spirit*, pp. 295–296.

[37] See above, pp. 250–251; Julius W. Pratt, *Expansionists of 1898* (Baltimore, 1936), pp. 146–229.

[38] The resolution passed largely by a party vote in the House of 209 to 91, in the Senate by 42 to 21, receiving particular support from the Northwest, North Central, and Pacific representatives. Barbara A. Morin, "The Reaction of Congress to the Annexation of Alaska and the Hawaiian Islands" (M.A. thesis, Smith College, 1944), exhaustively treats this subject.

The case of Hawaii, to be sure, was not precisely analogous to that of the Philippines. With the former, the United States had long been so closely associated that McKinley was able to argue plausibly that "annexation is not change; it is consummation," and John Sherman could say that it was "a destined culmination of the progressive policies and dependent associations of seventy years."[39] Senator Hoar, who shortly denounced annexation of the Philippines as "ruffianism and tyranny," argued that Hawaii, on the other hand, fell into America's economic and strategic orbit.[40] Such fine distinctions, however, were lost on the public.

After the annexation of Hawaii the expansionist tide ran more swiftly. Whitelaw Reid's New York *Tribune*—a respectable paper, not to be confused with the *World* or the *Journal*—came out for retention of the Philippines. "Having once freed them from the Spanish yoke," Reid said, "we cannot honorably require them to go back under it again. That would be to put us in an attitude of nauseating national hypocrisy. . . ."[41] The religious press cried that it would be unchristian to allow the Filipinos (many of whom, incidentally, were Catholics) to fall back into heathenism.[42] Even businessmen were beginning to advocate annexation. By August, Captain Mahan was happily observing that "the *mere* opportunist, the *mere* dollar and cents view, the *mere* appeal to comfort and well being as distinct from righteousness and foresight, in a word *mere* selfishness and regard for present ease, are being rapidly dropped behind, and nobler, if somewhat crude and even vainglorious, feelings are taking possession of the people."[43]

President McKinley, always sensitive to the rhythm of public opinion, took note of these developments. When the time came to negotiate a permanent peace with Spain, he packed the peace commission with expansionists. Senators William P. Frye of Maine and Cushman K. Davis of Minnesota both favored annexing at least some of the Philippine Islands. Whitelaw Reid's views were known. Secretary of State Day, who resigned in order to sit on the commission, was uncertain but could no doubt be converted. Only one member of the

[39] Albert K. Weinberg, *Manifest Destiny* (Baltimore, 1935), p. 262.
[40] George F. Hoar, *The Lust of Empire* (New York, 1900), p. 129; Foster Rhea Dulles, *America in the Pacific* (Boston, 1938), p. 195.
[41] Whitelaw Reid, *Problems of Expansion* (New York, 1900), pp. 11–12.
[42] Pratt, *Expansionists*, pp. 279–316.
[43] W. D. Puleston, *Mahan* (New Haven, 1939), pp. 200–201.

commission, Senator George Gray of Delaware, was a Democrat and an outspoken anti-imperialist. The President's mind was made up; on September 16 he instructed the commission that the "United States cannot accept less than the full right and sovereignty of the island of Luzon."[44] On October 26 he went further and said, "The cession must be the whole archipelago or none. The latter is wholly inadmissible, and the former must therefore be required."[45] Spain had no choice except to acquiesce. The Americans, after consenting to pay $20 million for her possessions, signed the treaty on December 10.[46]

The responsibility for this fateful step rested on McKinley, who chose the peace commission. In his choice of commissioners he listened, as usual, to the wrong advice. He listened to the imperialists, to the churches, to those businessmen who now saw in the Philippines the gateway to the China market, and to the audiences who greeted his expansionist speeches in the Middle West with shouts of enthusiasm. He later stressed the need "to educate the Filipinos, and uplift and civilize and Christianize them, and by God's grace to do the best we could for them as our fellow men for whom Christ died," and he doubtless meant what he said, but the process by which he arrived at the decision to keep the Philippines was by no means as painful as he claimed. Having prayed for guidance, he said, he discovered with the help of the Almighty that the United States could neither hand the islands back to Spain nor turn them over to France or Germany nor let them go, for they were "unfit for self-government."[47] Even assuming that the Filipinos were incapable of governing themselves, however, it was not necessary to have held them as a colony. The more prudent policy would have been to hold them as a protectorate; this, at least, might have provided the United States with an avenue of escape from responsibilities which later became too burdensome to exercise. The fact is that McKinley had been beguiled by the arguments of the expansionists—among them, the vision, just beyond the Philippines (which proved to be a mirage), of the glittering wealth of Asia.

Throughout the negotiations leading to the treaty nobody seems to have given much thought to the feelings of the Filipinos, who had

---

[44] *Foreign Relations, 1898,* p. 908.

[45] *Ibid.,* p. 935.

[46] *Ibid.,* pp. 949, 996.

[47] Charles S. Olcott, *William McKinley* (Boston, 1916), II, 110–111, quoted from the *Christian Advocate,* June 22, 1903.

initially looked upon the Americans as deliverers from the tyranny of Spain. The peace commission held hearings in Paris on the subject, but deliberately selected witnesses sympathetic to its point of view. All the witnesses, most of whom were majors and generals, agreed that the Filipinos, conscious of their backwardness in the art of self-government, wanted nothing more than to be governed by the United States. For the most part the witnesses merely echoed the suggestions of the commissioners:

The CHAIRMAN. If the United States should say that we shall take this country and govern it in our own way, do you think they would submit to it?

General MERRITT. Yes, sir.

The CHAIRMAN. What they desire is a government for their benefit, maintained and paid for by us?

General MERRITT. Yes, sir.[48]

These observations soon proved to be entirely without foundation. When the terms of the treaty were made known in the Philippines, the natives rebelled against American rule as they had rebelled against Spain. For three years the United States was forced to fight a guerrilla war in the islands. Having intervened in the name of humanity to save the Cubans from Spain, the United States within a few months found herself in precisely the same position as the Spanish had been: all too happy to quit. The circle of intervention was complete.[49]

In the Senate the treaty was accepted only after long and bitter debate. Opposition to annexation had been developing for some time. On June 15 a group of prominent Bostonians met at Faneuil Hall and denounced imperialism "in the name of all the past glories of Massachusetts."[50] On November 19 an Anti-Imperialist League was organized in Boston with George S. Boutwell as president. Grover Cleveland, George F. Edmunds, John Sherman, Carl Schurz, Samuel Gompers, John G. Carlisle, Andrew Carnegie, and Charles Francis Adams were among the League's forty-one vice-presidents—a distinguished if heterogeneous collection. Most of these men, however, lent little to the cause but their names, for the activities of the League were mainly literary. Doubtless because it raised a clear-cut moral issue, anti-impe-

[48] 55th Congress, 3rd sess. (1899), *Senate Document 62*, pp. 368–369.

[49] During the negotiations Spain tried to shift the Cuban debt to Cuba or the United States. She was finally compelled to assume it herself.

[50] Boston *Transcript*, June 2, 1898 (from Gamaliel Bradford's announcement of the meeting).

rialism appealed to a great number of intellectuals and writers—William James, Hermann E. von Holst, William Graham Sumner, William Vaughn Moody, Thomas Bailey Aldrich, William Dean Howells, Mark Twain. Moody's lines are justly celebrated:

> Ah no!
> We have not fallen so.
> We are our fathers' sons: let those who lead us know!
> 'Twas only yesterday sick Cuba's cry
> Came up the tropic wind, "Now help us, for we die!" . . .
> And at the lifting of a hand sprang forth,
> East, west, and south, and north,
> Beautiful armies. Oh, by the sweet blood and young
> Shed on the awful hill slope at San Juan . . .
> We charge you, ye who lead us,
> Breathe on their chivalry no hint of stain!
> Turn not their new-world victories to gain![51]

Mark Twain bitterly advised the nation to explain to the "Person Sitting in Darkness" the facts of the case:

. . . . We should say to him:

. . . . There have been lies, yes, but they were told in a good cause. We have been treacherous, but that was only in order that real good might come out of apparent evil. True, we have crushed a deceived and confiding people; we have turned against the weak and the friendless who trusted us; we have stamped out a just and intelligent and well-ordered republic; we have stabbed an ally in the back and slapped the face of a guest . . . but each detail was for the best. We know this. The Head of every State and Sovereignty in Christendom . . . including our Congress and our fifty state legislatures, are members not only of the church but also of the Blessings-of-Civilization Trust. This world-girdling accumulation of trained morals, high principles, and justice cannot do an unright thing, an unfair thing, an ungenerous thing, an unclean thing. It knows what it is about. Give yourself no uneasiness; it is all right.[52]

Finley Peter Dunne observed satirically, "They'se wan consolation; an' that is, if th' American people can govern thimsilves, they can govern anything that walks."[53]

[51] "An Ode in Time of Hesitation," *Poems of William Vaughn Moody* (Boston, 1901), pp. 19–20.

[52] Bernard DeVoto (ed.), *The Viking Portable Mark Twain* (New York, 1946), pp. 611–612.

[53] Ellis, *Mr. Dooley*, pp. 45–66. On the Anti-Imperialist League, see Fred H.

The Anti-Imperialist League circulated petitions, distributed innumerable pamphlets, and, between the signing of the peace treaty and the election of 1900, which they hoped to make a referendum on imperialism, kept up a ceaseless agitation. The anti-imperialist argument was simply: for the United States to govern a people without their consent violated the cardinal principle of American democracy. Some labor leaders, who feared the competition of cheap labor, contributed a less idealistic argument to the movement, and a few agricultural interests —tobacco and beet sugar, for instance—objected to certain economic aspects of annexation.[54] Most anti-imperialists regarded these arguments as sordid and avoided them; what absorbed them was the fear that the United States, by turning her back on the Declaration of Independence and entering upon a course of imperialism, was about to go the way of Europe and of Rome. They predicted that liberty, stamped out abroad, would disappear at home and that the United States would fall under the yoke of tyranny. In support of this last contention they cited the administration's censorship of news from the Philippines in order to conceal from the public the real nature of the rebellion against American rule.

The administration claimed that the Filipinos had started the war by launching an unprovoked attack on American troops on February 5, 1899. A number of correspondents, however, wrote home that American soldiers had fired first. For several months the administration carefully censored these reports, until finally the correspondents filed an angry protest which, slipping the censors, appeared in the papers on July 17:

We believe that owing to official dispatches from Manila made public in Washington, the people of the United States have not received a correct impression of the situation in the Philippines. . . . The censorship has compelled us to participate in these misrepresentations by exercising or altering uncontroverted statements of fact. . . .[55]

Harrington, "The Anti-Imperialist Movement in the United States, 1898–1900," *Mississippi Valley Historical Review,* XXII (Sept., 1935), 211–230, and "Literary Aspects of American Anti-Imperialism," *New England Quarterly,* X (Dec., 1937); Maria C. Lanzar, "The Anti-Imperialist League," *Philippine Social Science Review,* III (Aug., 1930). See also William Graham Sumner, "The Conquest of the United States by Spain," *War and Other Essays* (New Haven, 1911), pp. 303–305.

[54] American Federation of Labor, *Report of Proceedings, 1898,* pp. 26–27.

[55] Moorfield Storey and Marcial P. Lichauco, *The Conquest of the Philippines by the United States* (New York, 1928), p. 98.

An Associated Press correspondent said that he had been told by one of the censors, "My instructions are to shut off everything that could hurt McKinley's administration."[56]

The most dramatic case of censorship was that of Edward Atkinson of Boston, a prominent cotton magnate and mugwump, who compiled three pamphlets in which he attempted to demonstrate the enormous burden which imperialism placed on the taxpayer. Curious to see how far the government would go in interfering with freedom of opinion, he decided to send copies of his pamphlets to American officials in the Philippines. He wrote to the War Department asking permission, enclosing copies of the pamphlets. Receiving no reply, he sent the propaganda anyway. Alger turned his copies of the pamphlets over to Postmaster General Charles E. Smith, who thumbed through them, discovered they were "seditious," and ordered the authorities at San Francisco to stop their passage through the mails.[57] Even the imperialist press came to Atkinson's defense. The Boston *Journal* declared, "If the United States Government knew Edward Atkinson in the same way that we know him here in Boston, and knew him as well, it would lay its hand upon neither him nor his pamphlet."[58] The Springfield *Republican* wrote, "If Mr. Atkinson's act of sending his pamphlets to a few officials at Manila is seditious, then the person who sends to any soldier there, or officer, the copy of any speech delivered in or out of Congress against imperialism, or the copy of any newspaper containing anti-imperialist material, or the copy of any article criticising the course of the Administration, commits an act of sedition." Such were "the despotic tendencies of the imperialist policy," according to the *Republican*. "The mailed hand of the rule of blood and war is being gradually disclosed, which will next fall heavily upon freedom of speech within the old borders of the United States. It is impossible that a national career of conquest can be persisted in without the impairment of that most cherished privilege under the constitution."[59]

In the Senate, more than a third of the members at first seemed unfavorably disposed to the treaty—more than enough to defeat it. "I confess I am utterly disheartened and cast down at the thought that the

[56] *Ibid.*, p. 99.
[57] Boston *Transcript*, May 6, 1899. Harold F. Williamson, *Edward Atkinson* (Boston, 1934), pp. 227–229.
[58] Quoted *ibid.*
[59] Quoted *ibid.*, May 6, 1899.

treaty is in such serious danger," Roosevelt wrote to Lodge.[60] Opinion was divided without regard to party lines. Hoar, Hale, and Pettigrew among the Republicans and Gorman, Tillman, and McLaurin among the Democrats led the attack on the treaty, rehearsing the arguments against annexation—that annexation was contrary to the Declaration and the Constitution; that Filipinos would immigrate to the United States and debase the American standard of living; that Filipino goods would flood the American market; that free nations could not govern subject provinces without becoming despotisms; that the acquisition of the Philippines would embroil the United States in Far Eastern politics without bringing any comparable advantages in trade; that Christianity could not be advanced by subjecting other peoples to tyranny.[61] The expansionists argued in reply that the Constitution set no limits to expansion. They pointed to the lucrative commercial opportunities of the Far East. They appealed to manifest destiny, to duty, to conscience, and above all to the unquestionable rectitude of their own motives. "[We] have no purpose to enslave the people of the Philippine Islands," said Knute Nelson of Minnesota. ". . . . We come as ministerial angels, not as despots."[62] "Providence," said Orville H. Platt, "has put [this duty] upon us."[63]

In the middle of December, 1898, William Jennings Bryan appeared in Washington. Bryan opposed annexation; he had left the Army, he said, because of his opposition to the use to which the administration was putting the war.[64] Nevertheless, he urged upon his followers in the Senate the necessity of ratifying the treaty in order that it might be submitted to the electorate in 1900. "It will be easier, I think, to end the war at once by ratifying the treaty, and then deal with the subject in our own way."[65] It was a strange argument and a strategic blunder of the first magnitude, for the treaty, once ratified, became a *fait accompli* which could not be undone even by the oratory of Bryan. Whether Bryan actually changed the result, however, is doubtful. Senator Hoar somewhat extravagantly claimed that he had changed

[60] January 26, 1899. Elting E. Morison (ed.), *The Letters of Theodore Roosevelt* (Cambridge, 1951), II, 923.

[61] Pratt, *Expansionists*, pp. 345–354.

[62] *Congressional Record,* 55th Cong., 3rd sess. (1899), p. 838.

[63] *Ibid.,* p. 503.

[64] William Jennings Bryan and Mary Baird Bryan, *The Memoirs of William Jennings Bryan* (Philadelphia, 1925), p. 120.

[65] *Outlook,* LX (Dec. 24, 1898), 996.

seventeen votes; Carnegie gave the number as seven; Boutwell said merely that Bryan had "induced his friends to vote for the ratification of the treaty . . . which otherwise would have been defeated."[66] The very people whom Bryan might be expected to have convinced, however—men like Pettigrew of South Dakota and Jones of Arkansas—denied that he had changed any votes at all.[67]

On February 6, 1899, the treaty was ratified by a vote of 57 to 27—one vote more than the necessary two-thirds. Eight days later, Senator August O. Bacon, supported by Bryan, offered an amendment promising independence to the Filipinos when they established a stable government. Bryan thus salved his conscience; years later he was able to say, "I have never regretted the position taken; on the contrary I never showed more statesmanship than I did when I insisted on the termination of war and the making of the promise embodied in the Bacon resolution."[68] The Bacon amendment, which was defeated by the casting vote of Vice-President Hobart, was a mere gesture so far as the practical issue was concerned, for the treaty was already ratified, but it did expose the hypocrisy of the imperialists' contention that annexation was necessary because the Filipinos could not govern themselves. If the United States intended to administer the Philippines merely in order to instruct them in self-government, the imperialists should have been willing to agree to let them go once the instruction was complete. By defeating the Bacon amendment the imperialists showed that they did not mean what they said. Their real reason for wanting to keep the Philippines was the belief that they would be of value to the United States.

In itself this belief was not morally reprehensible. The only trouble

[66] George F. Hoar, *Autobiography of Seventy Years* (New York, 1903), I, 322; Andrew Carnegie, *Autobiography* (Boston, 1920), p. 364; George S. Boutwell, *Party or Country* (Boston, 1900), p. 13; Merle E. Curti, "Bryan and World Peace," *Smith College Studies in History*, XVI (Northampton, 1931), 119–132; William Jennings Bryan, *The Second Battle* (Chicago, 1900), pp. 87–140, 153–159.

[67] Erving Winslow, secretary of the Anti-Imperialist League, said, "Senator Allen of Nebraska and Senator Jones of Nevada may have been gained to the Administration side by the 'tribune of the people,' though Senator Jones of Arkansas maintained to the last that Mr. Bryan had not caused the change of a vote." *Independent*, LI (May 18, 1899), 1349. See also Richard Franklin Pettigrew, *Imperial Washington* (Chicago, 1922), p. 270.

[68] *The Memoirs of William Jennings Bryan* (Philadelphia, 1925), p. 121; *Congressional Record*, 55th Cong., 3d sess. (1899), pp. 1845–1846.

with it was that it was based on a set of illusions about the direction of American trade, about Far Eastern politics, and about the value of colonies generally. It was not very long before the expansionists of 1898 realized their mistake; by 1907 Roosevelt was referring to the Philippines as America's "Achilles heel" and wishing that he could get rid of them. By that time, of course, it was too late. The nation had accepted a new policy of political and economic imperialism, concerning which it lacked experience, and in a distant area of which it knew little. Then followed a half century of frustrating and unsuccessful diplomacy, a war with Japan, and a situation more difficult than any in its history. The mistake of annexing the Philippines was finally redressed, but the decision was too late to be of much value in a rapidly changing world.

CHAPTER 12

End of a Decade

A MERICANS remembered the administration of William McKinley as a singularly propitious time. The Spanish-American War
dazzled the country and flattered the national vanity. The return of
prosperity dulled the sharp edge of class conflict. The President himself seemed to embody the genial mood. Handsome, engaging, modest,
courteous, and sincere, McKinley was the ideal man to preside over a
nation seeking to forget its troubles. McKinley was everybody's friend
at a time when everybody needed a friend. He seemed to have no
enemies, and the country was tired of Presidents who made too many
enemies.

Of Scotch-Irish descent, McKinley was born at Niles, Ohio, in 1843,
the son of a small steel and iron producer. Local schools and a short
period at Allegheny College in Pennsylvania completed his early formal
education. In 1861 he enlisted as a private in the 23rd Ohio Volunteer
Infantry, later commanded by Rutherford B. Hayes; fought in many
battles; and was mustered out of the Army in 1865 as a brevet major.
After two years of preparation in a law office and at the Albany Law
School, he was admitted to the bar and began a successful practice
which continued until his election to Congress in 1876. Except for a
short time near the end of the Forty-eighth Congress, when his election
(which he won by eight votes) was contested and he was unseated, he
served continuously until 1890. A gerrymander of his district in that
year, together with the unpopularity of the tariff which bore his name,
defeated him. In 1891, however, he was elected governor of Ohio and
served two terms until his election to the Presidency.[1]

[1] Charles S. Olcott, *The Life of William McKinley* (Boston, 1916), I, 82–85,
gives maps showing the gerrymandering of McKinley's district.

A man of deep religious convictions, McKinley scorned the offers of easy money so frequently available to politicians and lived on his modest salaries. As a result he suffered occasional financial hardship. When he endorsed notes of a friend who went bankrupt, his finances became precarious, and his friends Herman Kohlsaat, Mark Hanna, and Myron T. Herrick had to come to his rescue.[2] The episode also shows his warmth and generosity, feelings which were not always tempered by cool judgment. As President the same characteristics were a source both of strength and of weakness. Tactful and cordial, he could refuse patronage without giving offense, and through personal contact he enjoyed amicable relations with Congress. At the same time, as de Lôme correctly pointed out, he was quite unable to resist pressure from his friends or from the country; he had none of Cleveland's ability to defend an unpopular cause. Slow to commit himself, and with his political ear always close to the ground, he was a follower rather than a leader. It did not occur to him to exploit the vast resources of presidential power.

In 1880, four years after he entered Congress, McKinley was appointed to the House Ways and Means Committee. From that time on he was a leader of the protectionist cause; by 1890 no member of the Republican party, except perhaps Thomas B. Reed, knew more about the tariff. It was the tariff (and Mark Hanna) which made McKinley a national figure in 1890 and which enabled him to become permanent chairman of the Republican convention in 1892 and to receive 182 votes for the presidential nomination that year. He had staked his political career on the proposition that the first duty of government was to aid business enterprise. It was appropriate that he should have been elected in 1896 as the "advance agent of Prosperity," for he had always frankly considered himself the agent of businessmen, who, he believed, created prosperity.[3]

His selection of a cabinet reflected these views. He would have liked to appoint Hanna to the cabinet, and twice offered him a position, but Hanna wanted to be senator from Ohio. McKinley then appointed John Sherman as Secretary of State so that Hanna could fill his term

[2] Herman H. Kohlsaat, *From McKinley to Harding* (New York, 1923), pp. 10–17; Herbert Croly, *Marcus Alonzo Hanna* (New York, 1923), pp. 169–170; Olcott, *McKinley*, I, 288–292.

[3] Olcott, *McKinley*, I, 298.

in the Senate.[4] Sherman had few qualifications for the State Department, and his appointment was severely criticized. Seventy-four years old, his powers were rapidly declining, a fact McKinley refused to admit. Sherman, however, had the reputation of a statesman; he had served as Secretary of the Treasury under Hayes; and since 1883 he had been a member of the Senate Committee on Foreign Relations. His impressive record and his conservatism convinced McKinley that in making a place for Hanna in the Senate he was also doing the country a service.[5] In any case most of the work of the State Department was conducted by the Assistant Secretary, McKinley's old friend William R. Day. When Sherman resigned in April, 1898, Day succeeded him. Day himself resigned in September to sit on the peace commission and John Hay became Secretary. Five years later Roosevelt appointed Day to the Supreme Court.[6]

Except for the appointment of Alger as Secretary of War, McKinley's other appointments were more fortunate. He named Lyman J. Gage, a prominent banker of Chicago and formerly a supporter of Grover Cleveland, Secretary of the Treasury after Nelson Dingley declined.[7] John D. Long, formerly a congressman and governor of Massachusetts, served well in the Navy Department. Joseph McKenna, a California politician, appointed a circuit judge by Harrison in 1892, became Attorney General. Within a year McKinley elevated him to the Supreme Court and appointed John W. Griggs, former governor of New Jersey, and, still later, Philander C. Knox, as Attorney General. Cornelius N. Bliss of New York, treasurer of the Republican National Committee, was made Secretary of the Interior; James A. Gary of

[4] McKinley used his influence to secure Hanna's appointment by Governor Asa Bushnell of Ohio, who disliked Hanna. Bushnell appointed him to succeed Sherman in February, 1897. The next winter the legislature elected him for a full term.

[5] Louis M. Sears, "John Sherman," in S. F. Bemis (ed.), *The American Secretaries of State and Their Diplomacy* (New York, 1927–1929), IX, 8–23; Joseph B. Foraker, *Notes on a Busy Life* (Cincinnati, 1917), I, 507–509; Winfield S. Kerr, *John Sherman* (Mansfield, Ohio, 1902), II, 395–396; Champ Clark, *My Quarter Century of American Politics* (New York, 1920), I, 411–417.

[6] Olcott, *McKinley*, I, 327–339; James Ford Rhodes, *The McKinley and Roosevelt Administrations* (New York, 1923), pp. 30–35.

[7] E. N. Dingley, *The Life and Times of Nelson Dingley, Jr.* (Kalamazoo, 1902), pp. 412–414; Moses P. Handy, "Lyman J. Gage: A Character Sketch," *Review of Reviews,* XV (Mar., 1897), 289–300.

Maryland, Postmaster General; and James Wilson of Iowa, Secretary of Agriculture, a position he was to hold for sixteen years.[8]

If the business interests of the country had elected McKinley in the understanding that he would watch faithfully over their security and well-being, they could not have wished a cabinet better suited to the purpose. Many of the cabinet members were themselves wealthy men; all of them were conservatives. No silverites sat in this select circle, no representative of labor, no one who could possibly be said to have any leanings in the direction of reform. The cabinet, to a man, profoundly believed that the world of 1897 represented the pinnacle of human progress and that any attempt to change it, any "absurd attempt to make the world over," as William Sumner once put it, would be not only futile but pointless. The cabinet, in fact, was more uncompromisingly conservative than McKinley himself. Whereas the cabinet was filled mostly with gold men, McKinley himself was a bimetallist both out of conviction and out of expediency. In his inaugural address he characteristically skirted the money question; many goldbugs found the message disappointing for that reason. He said merely that he would give his "early and earnest attention" to the question of an international agreement to secure a double standard and that in the meantime silver coin would be maintained at a par with gold. McKinley was fully alive to the silver sentiment in the Senate, which indeed shortly resolved that the principal and interest of government bonds should be paid in gold or silver at the option of the government. He wanted no repetition of Cleveland's disastrous brush with Congress over the Sherman Act.

The rest of his message was equally cautious except for his promise to call a special session of Congress to revise the tariff in such a way as to end the Treasury deficit and help to pull the country out of the depression. Since little had been said about the tariff during the campaign, this commitment seemed unnecessary to many of McKinley's friends. But they could endorse his promise to redeem the party's campaign pledge of "opposition to all combinations of capital organized in trusts, or otherwise to control arbitrarily the condition of trade among our citizens," knowing that he had no intention of acting upon it. Few could take violent exception to his request for better immigra-

---

[8] Bliss was followed in 1898 by Ethan A. Hitchcock of Missouri and Gary by Charles E. Smith of Pennsylvania.

tion laws, civil-service reform, the "restoration of our merchant marine," and ratification of a recently signed arbitration treaty with Great Britain.[9]

Little came of any of these promises. As expected, McKinley maintained Richard Olney's policy of nonenforcement of the Sherman Antitrust Act. During his administration only three cases, all in equity, were filed by the Justice Department.[10] Congress debated a bill to subsidize the merchant marine, strongly supported by Hanna, but the manufacturing and agricultural interests, who for once found themselves in agreement, combined to defeat it.[11] No immigration legislation of any importance was passed until 1907. The arbitration treaty with Great Britain failed to pass the Senate in 1897.[12] As for the civil service, the administration's record was mediocre at best. McKinley's subordinates used every known device to get rid of classified employees. McKinley himself issued an order in 1899 removing 4,000 positions from the classified lists. The civil-service reformers were not happy; William Dudley Foulke noted that this order was "the first considerable reduction in the area of the merit system since the civil service law was enacted in 1883 . . . a step," he added, "which the President had promised not to make."[13] As if to make amends McKinley then extended the merit system to the Philippine Islands. Since the Philippines did not vote in American elections, there was nothing very daring in this action.

The administration departed only twice from its policy of evasion and avoidance—a policy, it need hardly be said, designed to advance the interests of those who had elected McKinley to power. In the case of tariff legislation and of the gold standard, McKinley did conclude that positive action was required in order to safeguard the welfare of Wall Street. In both these instances he acted with a good deal of energy. The tariff, of course, was for McKinley an *idée fixe*. The Wilson-Gorman tariff of 1894 was high enough for most protectionists, and there was no great demand for change. It was not high enough, however, to suit McKinley; and, as he had promised in his inaugural,

[9] *Congressoinal Record,* 55th Cong., 1st sess. (1897), pp. 2–5.

[10] Walton Hamilton and Irene Till, *Antitrust in Action* (TNEC Monograph No. 15, Washington, 1941), p. 135.

[11] Paul M. Zeis, *American Shipping Policy* (Princeton, 1938), pp. 39–53.

[12] John B. Moore, *A Digest of International Law* (Washington, 1906), VII, 74–78; *Tribune Almanac* (New York, 1898), X, 84.

[13] William Dudley Foulke, *Fighting the Spoilsmen* (New York, 1919), p. 123.

he promptly called a special session to advance the rates still further. Such a bill had already been drawn up by Nelson Dingley in the previous Congress. When the special session convened, Dingley introduced his measure in the House, which passed it within two weeks. The Senate, as usual, was more deliberate. A special committee took it up item by item and added 872 amendments. As finally patched up, it passed both houses on July 24, 1897.

Defenders of the bill argued that it was designed to bring in more revenue by shifting the duty on raw sugar from a 40 per cent ad valorem rate to a specific rate and by raising the general level of rates. Revenue did indeed increase, but the general improvement in economic conditions, not the provisions of the Dingley bill, was doubtless responsible. During its first year of operation the Dingley tariff yielded less revenue than the Wilson-Gorman Act yielded in either of its two years.[14] The new law removed raw wool from the free list in order to win the support of western senators for the bill, and raised duties on manufactured woolens to compensate the manufacturing interests for this hardship. The effect of these changes was to raise the price of wool and to allow the woolen industry to expand under a tariff so high as to perpetuate its dependence on protection.

The Dingley bill also raised duties on flax, cotton bagging, silks, and linens, probably without effect on those industries, which were already able to compete on even terms with foreign textiles; by 1897 the United States imported only high-grade specialties. Hides, which had been admitted free since 1872, were subjected to a 15 per cent duty— another sop to the senators from the West. No changes were made in the metal schedules except for increased duties on lead and on some finished products, nor were they necessary, for the American metal industry was the largest in the world and had nothing to fear from foreign competition. There were a few minor reductions, but the Dingley duties as a whole averaged 52 per cent.[15] Thus the downward trend of the Wilson-Gorman Act, almost imperceptible to begin with, was abruptly reversed.[16]

[14] Frank W. Taussig, *Tariff History of the United States* (7th ed., New York, 1923), pp. 358–360; Edward Stanwood, *American Tariff Controversies in the Nineteenth Century* (Boston, 1903), II, 390–394.

[15] Mr. Dooley has comments on a later effort to reduce the Dingley tariff. Elmer Ellis, *Mr. Dooley at His Best* (New York, 1938), pp. 86–92.

[16] U.S. Tariff Commission, "Tariff History of the United States," in *Dictionary of Tariff Information* (Washington, 1924), p. 756; Taussig, *Tariff*

During the debate on the Dingley tariff, there were few signs of the sectionalism which had alarmed the country in the recent election. The problem of financing the Spanish-American War, however, briefly revived sectional antagonism. The agrarians wanted the war to be financed by heavier taxation rather than by loans—by imposition of such income taxes as were permitted under the Supreme Court decision of 1895; by inheritance taxes, already widely used in Europe; and by taxation of corporate earnings. They demanded also, as they had demanded five years before, that the government coin the silver seigniorage in the Treasury. Finally, they asked for the further issue of greenbacks.

Such a program was anathema to men like Aldrich and Dingley, who succeeded in beating down this latest threat to sound money. On a number of points, however, they had to compromise. They avoided an income tax but agreed to a tax on legacies, from which, however, all estates under $10,000 and all property passing from husband to wife were exempted. Estates over $10,000 were taxed progressively, the tax ranging from .75 per cent on legacies to direct heirs to 15 per cent on bequests of more than $1 million to distant relatives or others. Aldrich also made a gesture in the direction of a corporation tax; a tax of 1 per cent was to be levied on all receipts over $200,000 of companies engaged in refining oil or sugar. None of these taxes was large enough to be of any importance. The corporation tax was merely a concession to the outcry against Rockefeller's Standard Oil and Havemeyer's sugar trust. The tax act of 1898 made a number of other changes in the tax structure. It doubled excise taxes on tobacco, beer, and fermented spirits; levied special taxes on banks, brokers, theaters, bowling alleys, and poolrooms; and levied a stamp tax on checks and drafts, stocks and bonds, insurance policies, commercial and legal documents, patent medicines, and toilet articles. Of these the taxes on tobacco and alcohol provided the best part of the new revenue.

Taxation, however, was not the only source of war revenue. The same act authorized the Secretary of the Treasury to issue $100 million in certificates of indebtedness, to coin one and a half million silver dollars every month from the bullion in the Treasury (purchased in accordance with the Act of 1890), and to borrow up to $400 million

History, pp. 321–360, and *Some Aspects of the Tariff Question* (Cambridge, 1915), pp. 342–365; Stanwood, *Tariff Controversies*, II, 360–390; Dingley, *Nelson Dingley*, pp. 414–419.

in 3 per cent ten- to twenty-year bonds.[17] Of these bonds $200 million were sold to 300,000 subscribers for a total of $1,400,000,000. The tremendous success of this "popular loan" reflected both the popularity of the war and the desire of national banks to increase their bank-note circulation. The government had hoped that "the dissemination of government securities among the people would attach the holders thereof by closer bonds of sympathy to the government," but within a short time 116,000 subscribers had sold their bonds at a small profit, and the bonds eventually found their way into the hands of a few wealthy persons or corporations. By floating a popular loan instead of selling the bonds at competitive bidding, the government probably sacrificed about $5 million.[18]

The total cost of the Spanish-American War is difficult to estimate. The immediate cost can be estimated by comparing the expenditures of the Army and Navy for the years 1894–1897—$328 million—and for the years 1898–1901—$842 million. The difference between them—something over $500 million—is a fair indication of the cost of the war. But this figure includes not only the pacification of the Philippines, which cost nearly two-thirds as much as the war with Spain, but also the Boxer expedition as well. Fiscally the war with Spain was a minor, almost a trivial, episode.

One other measure of the Fifty-fifth Congress should be mentioned— the act authorizing appointment of a "nonpartisan commission to collect information and . . . recommend legislation to meet the problems presented by labor, agriculture, and capital." The result of this law was the creation of the Industrial Commission. Its famous nineteen-volume report, published in 1900–1902, has served historians and economists as a mirror of economic conditions at the end of the century.[19]

Throughout the first two years of McKinley's term the Republican had a clear majority in the House but an extremely narrow one in the Senate—a situation which explains why McKinley avoided raising the

[17] 30 U.S. Statutes at Large 448 (1898).

[18] Sidney Ratner, *American Taxation* (New York, 1942), pp. 228–246; Davis R. Dewey, *Financial History of the United States* (10th ed., New York, 1922), pp. 465–466; *Report of the Secretary of the Treasury, 1898*, pp. xxiv, xciii–xcvii; *ibid., 1899*, pp. vii, xxxiii; Lyman J. Gage, *Memoirs* (New York, 1937), pp. 127–139.

[19] 30 U.S. Statutes at Large 476 (1898).

question of the gold standard.[20] The mid-term elections, however, brought aid and comfort to sound-money men. Although the Republican membership in the House declined from 207 to 186 while that of the Democrats increased from 122 to 162, the Republicans still controlled the lower chamber. Moreover, Populist strength ebbed from twenty-one to seven, and most of the new Democrats favored the gold standard. In the Senate the results were even more comforting; eight silver men were replaced with goldbugs.

Throughout the country Populism was clearly on the wane. In North Carolina the Populists were swept out of power; in Georgia and Alabama they polled only 30 per cent of the vote; in Florida, Mississippi, and Louisiana they had almost ceased to exist. Only in Texas did Populists maintain their position in the South. In the West, fusion tickets were overwhelmed everywhere except in South Dakota and Minnesota, where fusion governors were elected, and in Nebraska, where they won all the state offices and elected six congressmen. Even there they lost the legislature. Surveying the results of the elections, the *Review of Reviews* gloated: "For the present and for some years to come the cause of free silver in the United States is thoroughly and hopelessly defeated. Surely there can be no transcendent virtue in stubbornly denying a fact that is as patent as the rising of the sun."[21] *The Nation* also regarded the horizon with deepest satisfaction: "For the first time in twenty years the silver menace is cleared away from the financial horizon. . . . The silver lining no longer adorns the Western sky."[22]

The declining strength of agrarian radicalism indicated not so much the triumph of conservatism as the waning of the issues which had given the agrarian crusade its purpose and meaning. In the East, for instance, many Democrats "actually declined to disclose their opinions" on the currency question, refusing to reopen old wounds.[23] The gradual return of prosperity to the countryside sapped the vigor of agrarian

[20] The Fifty-fifth Congress was composed of 46 Republicans, 34 Democrats, 5 Populists, 3 Independents, and 2 silverites in the Senate; and 202 Republicans, 130 Democrats, 21 Populists, 3 silverites, and 1 fusionist in the House. Edward Stanwood, *A History of the Presidency from 1897 to 1916* (New York, 1916), p. 2. By the end of the session Republican strength in the House had slightly increased. *Ibid.*, p. 29.
[21] XVIII (Dec., 1898), 628.
[22] LXIX (Nov., 1898), 361.
[23] *Review of Reviews*, XVIII (Dec., 1898), 628.

reform. In 1897 the wheat crop in Europe was 30 per cent smaller than usual, while that of the United States was unusually large. American farmers exported 150 million bushels of wheat that year, almost twice as much as they had exported in 1896. Prices began to rise. The whole economy was reviving. Total exports in 1897 reached the billion-dollar mark for the second time in history. More important, exports, industrial as well as agricultural, considerably exceeded imports—in 1898 by as much as $615 million. For the first time since 1891, gold flowed freely into the country. Almost simultaneously gold was discovered in Australia and in the Klondike, and a few years later in South Africa; within a few years gold production doubled. The development of the cyanide process for extracting gold from ore further increased production. The price of gold fell and with it the price of money; the inflation for which the agrarians had been crying for years suddenly became a reality. In the long run all prices, not just those of farm commodities, turned upward, and the farmer was often the first to benefit.[24]

The renewed influx of capital and gold created in the country an excess of free capital which quickly found its way into industrial expansion, particularly in transportation. The demand for new and heavier rails, for bridges, for steel frames for larger city buildings, set off a boom in the basic iron and steel industry. The war stimulated some industries. An increase in immigration brought new laborers and new customers to the country. Business regained confidence in the future, and the country entered upon another frantic period of expansion and speculation. Farmers lost interest in reform and businessmen lost interest in fighting it.

The disintegration of the Populist party, as distinct from the Populist impulse in general, was clearly related to the return of prosperity and the disappearance of the silver issue. The party suffered, however, from other weaknesses as well. Ever since the ill-starred St. Louis convention of 1896, internal dissension had troubled the party. Fusion with the Democrats had almost destroyed its identity; the bitter recriminations of the antifusionists completed the process. By 1900 the Populists were so badly split that the fusionists and the middle-of-the-roaders held

[24] Alexander D. Noyes, *Forty Years of American Finance* (New York, 1909), pp. 267–270; Harold U. Faulkner, *The Decline of Laissez Faire* (New York, 1951), pp. 22–26; William L. Thorp, *Business Annals* (New York, 1926), pp. 137–138.

separate conventions. The Populist party had become a pair of insignificant, feuding factions. In the South the dissolution of Populism had a peculiarly sinister aspect. The case of North Carolina is enlightening. There, it will be recalled, the Populists fused with the Republicans and carried not only all the state offices but many local offices in 1896. In some counties the bulk of Republican voters happened to be Negroes; Negro voters not surprisingly elected Negro officers. The result could have been predicted; before the bogey of Negro domination, even some of the Populists fled in terror. In 1898 the party of white supremacy was returned to power. Thus ended the most promising experiment in interracial co-operation in politics in the history of the South.[25]

Whatever the long-range implications of the elections, their immediate result was to enable the Congress to pass the Gold Standard Act of 1900, a measure for which the advocates of honest money had long been hoping. Not that there was any overwhelming demand for currency legislation; the elections showed that the country had grown indifferent to it. Nor was there any particular need for legislation to protect gold. About $100 million in gold had been added to the Treasury since 1897, and the gold standard was safe. The only real interest in the problem of currency now centered, not around the gold standard, but around the problem of national bank notes, which, because they were secured on government bonds, circulated according to the indebtedness of the government, not according to the real currency needs of the country. A convention meeting in Indianapolis in 1897 recommended that bank notes be based on commercial assets instead of on government bonds, and guaranteed by the banks which joined in issuing them. Congress, however, showed no interest in this proposal until the approach of the presidential election reminded the Republicans of their promise to reform the nation's currency. Then they passed only a hasty, inadequate measure.[26]

In his annual message of 1899, McKinley stressed banking and currency, and in response to this suggestion Congress took up the matter at its next session. To control and speed action, the Republican machine took the bill out of the hands of the House Banking and

[25] John D. Hicks, *The Populist Revolt* (Minneapolis, 1931), p. 410.
[26] The "Indianapolis movement" represents the origin of the agitation which eventually led to the Federal Reserve Act. Henry P. Willis, *The Federal Reserve System* (New York, 1923), pp. 9–13.

Currency Committee and allowed it to be framed by a small caucus of party leaders. The House passed it in January. The Senate evolved a separate measure and the two bills were sent to a conference committee, where agreement was reached early in March. The bill, which passed the House by a majority of 46 and the Senate by a vote of 44 to 26, in both cases by a party vote, was signed by McKinley on March 14, 1900.[27]

The main concern of the legislators was to perpetuate the gold standard. They declared that henceforth the gold dollar was to be the sole standard of currency and that all other forms of money were to be maintained at a parity with gold. In order to avoid the embarrassing incidents of recent years, they raised the gold-reserve limit to $150 million and separated it from the general Treasury balance; it was not to be drawn on to meet normal expenses. If the gold reserve should drop below $150 million through the redemption of treasury notes, the redeemed notes were to be held in the Treasury, not reissued; thus Cleveland's "endless chain" of demands for gold would, it was hoped, be broken. But if the gold reserve should drop below $100 million, it was to be restored by the sale of short-term bonds—the kind Cleveland had wanted to issue and which Congress had forbidden him to issue. The Act of 1900 was designed specifically to preclude the recurrence of any such episode as had terrified the business world in the dark days of 1893.

A second section of the act attempted to make bank-note currency more elastic and to encourage the establishment of national banks in smaller towns. It reduced to $25,000 the capitalization requirement for national banks in towns smaller than 3,000. It provided that notes might now be issued at the full face value of the bonds on which they were secured, instead of at 90 per cent as before. Finally, in order to induce banks to buy bonds and thus to increase their note circulation, the act invited them to exchange their old bonds for new ones. Those who bought new bonds in order to increase note circulation were taxed on the circulation of their notes at the rate of only ½ per cent instead of the usual 1 per cent.[28] This advantage was enough to encourage

[27] *Congressional Record*, 56th Cong., 1st sess. (1900), pp. 2821–2864.

[28] Under the National Bank Act of 1863, the government had allowed banks to issue money in order to induce them to buy bonds. The government was now allowing banks to buy bonds at an advantage in order to induce them to issue money. Such are the intricate ironies of high finance.

enthusiastic co-operation, and within a year more than half of the bonds outstanding had been refunded. Partly as a result of these provisions of the Act of 1900, national bank-note circulation increased from $223 million in 1898 to $433 million in 1904. Within a year and a half, over 500 new national banks with less than $50,000 capital were organized. These developments helped to relieve the money stringency in rural areas. The real weakness of the banking system, the dependence of bank-note circulation on the bonded indebtedness of the government, went untouched.[29]

Having redeemed their campaign promises, the Republicans could face the national elections with equanimity. If their prospects were bright, however, it was not because of the Gold Standard Act but because of the prosperity of the country. The nomination of McKinley, as the advance agent of that prosperity, was clearly in order. Quite as certain was the nomination of Bryan by the Democrats, in the absence of any other candidate with even an outside chance to win. Bryan was nominated without enthusiasm. Silver was dead, and the charm of the Boy Orator was already wearing off.

If both parties were practically unanimous in their choice of presidential candidates, neither seemed able to settle on a Vice-President. The Republicans were particularly contentious. McKinley and Hanna preferred Senator Allison or Cornelius N. Bliss, but both of them declined to run. McKinley then refused to back anyone, and the decision was thrown into the lap of the party managers. They settled eventually on Theodore Roosevelt, whom neither McKinley nor Hanna wanted, and who himself repeatedly protested that he did not want to be Vice-President because it would end his political future. That, in fact, seemed to be the hope of Boss Platt of New York and Boss Quay of Pennsylvania, Platt particularly desiring to remove Roosevelt from the governorship. It was the convention, however, not Quay and Platt, which nominated Roosevelt, and nominated him unanimously.[30] The Democrats, meanwhile, nominated Adlai E. Stevenson of Illinois in preference to Hill of New York or Charles A. Towne of Minnesota.

The two Populist conventions had a distinctly funereal air. The

[29] 31 U.S. Statutes at Large 45 (1900).
[30] Croly, *Hanna,* pp. 302–318; Olcott, *McKinley,* II, 267–284; Louis J. Lang (ed.), *The Autobiography of Thomas Collier Platt* (New York, 1910), pp. 383–397; Theodore Roosevelt, *Autobiography* (New York, 1927), pp. 308–309.

fusionists, as in 1896, nominated Bryan and their own vice-presidential candidate, Towne of Minnesota. The middle-of-the-roaders nominated Wharton Barker of Pennsylvania and Ignatius Donnelly. "That the People's Party is passing must be evident to all observers," admitted Senator Peffer. "*Why* it is going, and *where*, are obviously questions of present public concern."[31] Why it was going was as evident as the fact of its going. Where it was going was less clear. Most of the Populists returned to oblivion. A few of them, however, joined the rapidly growing Socialist movement.

Marxian socialism had reached America as early as the 1850's. Its early followers had been mostly German immigrants, with a scattering of Jews, Poles, Bohemians, and Italians. From its early center in the Middle West it spread to other parts of the country and gained followers among native Americans. The first political party to call itself Socialist was the Socialist Labor party, founded in 1877. In 1892 and 1896 this party nominated presidential candidates; in 1896 it polled 30,000 votes. By that time it had fallen under the leadership of Daniel De Leon, whose failure either to convert the Knights of Labor or the A.F. of L. to socialism or to weaken the latter by his organization of the Socialist and Labor Alliance as a rival union stirred up a revolt against him. Led by Morris Hillquit, many German and Jewish labor leaders who had won important places in the unions which De Leon was now turning against organized their own party, which they insisted on calling the Socialist Labor party. De Leon maintained that *his* party was the Socialist Labor party, and the courts upheld him. The Hillquit faction then held its own convention at Rochester early in 1900 and made known its willingness to merge with other Socialist groups, particularly with the Social Democratic party founded some years earlier in Milwaukee by Victor Berger. The Social Democrats accepted the invitation, and the new party, calling itself by that name, nominated Eugene V. Debs for President and Job Harriman as his running mate.[32]

[31] "People's Party," in *Harper's Encyclopaedia of United States History* (New York, 1902), VII.

[32] The next year they changed their name to the Socialist party. Ira Kipnis, *The American Socialist Movement, 1897–1912* (New York, 1952), pp. 13–106; Nathan Fine, *Labor and Farmer Parties in the United States, 1828–1898* (New York, 1928), pp. 184–213; David A. Shannon, *The Socialist Party of America* (New York, 1955), pp. 1–55; Howard H. Quint, *The Forging of American Socialism* (Columbia, S.C., 1953), pp. 319–394.

The Republican platform contained no surprising or novel suggestions. It dwelt with pride on the prosperity of the past three years; defended McKinley's foreign policy; and pledged the party to a gold standard, a protective tariff, and an isthmian canal. Although they had done little or nothing to eliminate monopoly, to subsidize shipping, or to reform the civil service, the Republicans favored such action in their platform. The Democratic platform, on the other hand, was an able and progressive document. Insisting that imperialism was the "paramount issue," it declared "that no nation can long endure half republic and half empire, and . . . that imperialism abroad will lead quickly and inevitably to despotism at home." It denounced monopoly as "indefensible and intolerable." It advocated an end to government by injunction, enlargement of the powers of the Interstate Commerce Commission, and the direct election of United States senators, a reform advocated by the Populists. It favored a Nicaraguan canal. The platform was marred only by Bryan's insistence that the party once again declare for free silver.

At the outset of the campaign Bryan tried halfheartedly to make imperialism the paramount issue. Finding his audiences, particularly in the West, unresponsive, he shifted to the issue of monopoly and special privilege. He was perfectly willing to campaign on the currency question, and the Republicans were eager to join him on that ground, but the public was not interested in the old battles. Roosevelt wrote to Lodge from New York: "The apathy which you speak of is very marked here. There is not the slightest enthusiasm for Bryan and there is no enthusiasm for us and there seems to be no fear of Bryan. The wage earner is no longer interested in free silver and cannot be frightened by the discussion of it."[33] It was all very puzzling.

In view of the confusion as to what the main issue was, it is difficult to know what the outcome of the election signified, if anything. Certainly imperialism was not the issue. With only a few exceptions, all

---

Other parties in the field in the election of 1900 were the Prohibition party, which nominated John G. Woolley and Henry B. Metcalf on the traditional platform and in the election ran third to the two major parties; the Union Reform party, which hoped to eliminate bossism by eliminating the major parties, and which advocated the initiative and referendum; and the United Christian party, which favored reforms consistent with Christian principles. Stanwood, *Presidency*, pp. 32–72; *Tribune Almanac, 1901*, pp. 58–73; Kirk H. Porter, *National Party Platforms* (New York, 1924), pp. 210–243.

[33] Roosevelt to Lodge, August 22, 1900, in H. C. Lodge (ed.), *Correspondence of Theodore Roosevelt and Henry Cabot Lodge* (New York, 1925), I, 474.

anti-imperialists who believed at the same time in sound money threw over their anti-imperialism and voted for McKinley. Silver men, on the other hand, voted for Bryan even though they approved of the administration's foreign policy. This is not to say that silver was the most important issue. The mass of voters showed little interest either in silver or in the abstract and legalistic debate over imperialism. They probably voted for McKinley as a kindly, warmhearted man who had presided over the revival of prosperity. Bryan himself believed that prosperity was the Republicans' most effective argument, and Mark Hanna said, "There is only one issue in this campaign, my friends, and that is, let well enough alone."[34]

Hanna once again ran McKinley's campaign as chairman of the Republican National Committee. Without difficulty he raised $2,500,-000, more than five times the amount raised by the Democrats. As in 1896, he concentrated his efforts on the Middle West and Northwest, assuming that the East was safe for McKinley. McKinley, as usual, did not make an active campaign; but in order to counter the influence of the "talking candidate" of the Democrats, as Hanna called him, the Republicans sent Theodore Roosevelt on the circuit to hypnotize the war enthusiasts of the West. Hanna himself also toured the country, with considerable success. Western audiences were surprised to find that his vest was not covered with dollar signs, as cartoonists insisted it was. "But he don't look like he ought to, Billy!" an old Populist said to his son.[35] Hanna's tour doubtless reconciled some of the western states to the party which they had angrily left in the early nineties.

In spite of the reported indifference of the voters to the issues of the campaign, the vote was as large as it had been in 1896—13,973,-071. McKinley polled 7,219,525 of these votes and Bryan 6,358,737.[36] In the electoral college McKinley polled 292 votes and Bryan 155. In 1896 McKinley had won only 7,104,779 popular votes against Bryan's 6,502,925 and 271 electoral votes against Bryan's 176; his victory in 1900, therefore, was somewhat greater. Bryan in 1900 polled

[34] Thomas A. Bailey, "Was the Presidential Election of 1900 a Mandate for Imperialism?" *Mississippi Valley Historical Review*, XXIV (June, 1937), 43–52; W. J. Bryan, "The Election of 1900," *North American Review*, CLXXI (Dec., 1900), 789; *Review of Reviews*, XXII (Dec., 1900), 657.

[35] Thomas Beer, *Hanna* (New York, 1929), p. 232.

[36] Woolley, the Prohibition candidate, received 209,157 votes; Debs, 94,864; Barker, 50,599; and Joseph Mallory (Socialist Labor), 33,432. The vote of the other two candidates was negligible. Stanwood, *Presidency*, pp. 30–32.

a higher vote in New England, in New York, and in Maryland than he had four years before, and he carried Kentucky, which the Gold Democrats had thrown into the Republican column in 1896. These gains represented not an increase in silver sentiment in those states but simply the return of normally Democratic votes—another indication that the silver issue was no longer decisive. In the heart of the silver country Bryan made a poor showing, losing Kansas, Nebraska, South Dakota, Utah, and Wyoming.[37] Conservatism was again triumphant. The history of the next two decades, however, was to show that the demand for reform had by no means abated. It had merely become respectable. One by one the reforms advocated by the Populists were taken up by the very people who had denounced the Populists as socialists, anarchists, and Jacobins; Theodore Roosevelt, elevated to the Presidency by the bullet of a real anarchist, became a leader of at least mild reform.

What was there about the decade of the nineties which distinguished it from other decades? No line unmistakably divided it either from the 1880's or from the first years of the twentieth century. Turner declared in 1893 that the disappearance of the frontier line marked "the closing of a great historic movement," but in reality population continued to move westward and new areas to be settled for some time thereafter. Other students found the distinctive character of the period in territorial expansion, but expansion had been a persistent feature of American history and "manifest destiny" dated at least from the 1840's. The rise of the city likewise was a development of long standing, and cities had grown more rapidly in the previous decade than in the nineties. Immigration was also larger in the eighties, and the shift of its source from northwestern to southeastern Europe had begun early in that decade.

Nevertheless it was in the nineties that Americans first became acutely conscious of the significance of these changes. It was in the nineties that they began to see the importance of the frontier in their history and to sense the greater importance of its imminent disappearance. It was in the nineties that the historic expansionist impulse drove

[37] Stanwood, *Presidency*, pp. 72–76; Croly, *Hanna*, pp. 319–341; Rhodes, *McKinley and Roosevelt Administrations*, pp. 138–144; Hicks, *Populist Revolt*, pp. 396–403; Paxton Hibben, *The Peerless Leader* (New York, 1929), pp. 224–235; *Review of Reviews*, XXII (Dec., 1900), 654–659.

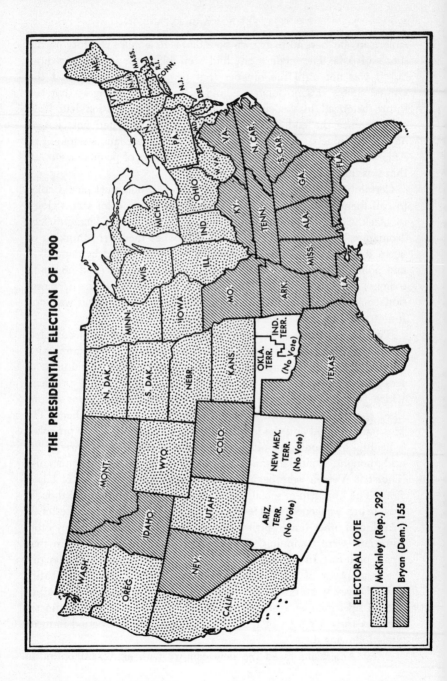

THE PRESIDENTIAL ELECTION OF 1900

ELECTORAL VOTE

McKinley (Rep.) 292

Bryan (Dem.) 155

Americans far beyond their own boundaries to acquire territory on the shores of Asia. The modern city had been taking shape for some time, but it was not until the nineties that people began to see that the United States was no longer a land of farms and villages; that the future belonged to the city. And if the new immigration had been evident since the end of the Civil War, its impact had not; it was only in the nineties that men began to ponder the changes wrought in American life by the introduction of vast numbers of people new to all that was familiar to American experience.

Certainly the nineties were not "gay"; nor, if one must pick a color to call them, were they "mauve"; the predominant color seems closer to black. Some writers have referred to the period as "naughty" or "romantic," but it is difficult to imagine what they were thinking of when they used such words to describe years dominated by depression and political controversy, unless it was the extravagant (and no doubt tedious) festivities of the "Four Hundred" as pictured in the sensational press. The World's Fair might have been "gay," but it was soon forgotten in the hard times which followed.

The strange thing is that the nineties were not a time of complete despair, as one might imagine them to have been from an examination of statistics of unemployment, farm mortgages, business failures, or tenement-house conditions. The novelty and difficulty of the problems which beset the country in this period, however, are no more striking than the confidence with which the country confronted them. The passing of the old and the familiar caused anxiety, but it also provoked a healthy questioning of old beliefs which invigorated all parts of life and thought. Politicians and students of politics and economics like Thorstein Veblen were beginning to question the supremacy of laissez faire. The iron grip of social Darwinism on social and political thought was being weakened by Henry George, Edward Bellamy, Lester F. Ward, and other brave spirits. Turner, Henry Adams, and many other historians were beginning to understand that history was more than "past politics." In philosophy William James was already challenging the assumptions of Kantian and Hegelian philosophy, and in education John Dewey was arguing for the abandonment of the old formalism. On all sides men were advocating change and innovation; the nineties were as truly a period of reform as the "progressive" period immediately following it.

Most Americans faced the new century with exuberant optimism.

The victory over Spain and the acquisition of Puerto Rico, Hawaii, and the Philippines; the return of prosperity; the unprecedented material growth of the country in the past thirty-five years—all heralded America's coming of age. Every observer dwelt on it; the words "power," "strength," and "supremacy" suddenly became indispensable to discussion of any aspect of the American scene. At the same time a note of melancholy and apprehension could be heard in all this talk of greatness. Even Captain Mahan, who contributed his share to it, spoke occasionally with something like nostalgia of the world he had helped to destroy: "The jocund youth of our people now passes away never to return; the cares and anxieties of manhood's years henceforth are ours."[38] Pride in America's new-found power was sometimes tempered by misgivings as to the uses to which she would put it, and for many people the magnificence of the new world vied in their affections with the safety and familiarity of the old. Brooks Adams, in a letter to his brother after a trip to the West Coast in 1901, caught this mood:

I came home straight, and sat most of the time in an observation car. It is no use for the world to kick, the stream is too strong, nothing can resist it. Beginning on the crest of the rockies the tide flows down into the Mississippi valley, and then across to the eastern mountains in an ever increasing flood, with an ever heightening velocity. At last you come to the lakes and Buffalo. There, I take it, modern civilization reaches its focus. No movement can keep pace with the demand; no power can be found vast enough . . . . No one who has watched that torrent from its source on the Divide to its discharge in New York Bay can, I think, help feeling the hour of the old world has struck.[39]

Most Americans, however, gave only momentary thoughts to the world that was passing. Skeptics who suggested that it was a better world than their children might know were held in utter disregard. Success, progress, and prosperity were the dominant notes; the future was bright, and to many the new century held dreams of greatness and glory beyond any yet achieved.

[38] W. D. Puleston, *Mahan* (New Haven, 1939), p. 201.
[39] Quoted in Daniel Aaron, *Men of Good Hope* (New York, 1951), p. 269.

Bibliography

Although bibliographies are soon out of date, certain standard bibliographical works should be mentioned. One useful aid is H. P. Beers, *Bibliographies in American History: Guide to Materials for Research* (New York, 1942). Annual volumes sponsored by the American Historical Association, prepared by Grace G. Griffin *et al.*, *Writings of American History*, cover the years 1906–40 and 1948. Also important are Samuel F. Bemis and G. G. Griffin, *Guide to the Diplomatic History of the United States, 1775–1921* (Washington, 1935), and the *Harvard Guide to American History* (Cambridge, Mass., 1954), compiled by Oscar Handlin, Arthur M. Schlesinger, Samuel Eliot Morison, Frederick Merk, Arthur M. Schlesinger, Jr., and Paul M. Buck. A short cut to the sources and secondary works on biography at the time of publication will be found in Allen Johnson and Dumas Malone (eds.), *Dictionary of American Biography* (22 vols., New York, 1928–58). More rewarding are the bibliographies in the specialized volumes covering the period, which will be later mentioned.

PERIODICALS AND NEWSPAPERS

For the historian certain periodicals stand out as particuarly valuable for the nineties. *The Arena* (1889–1909), edited by Benjamin C. Flower, John Clark Ridpath, and others, has been described as the "original muckraking magazine," and contained much on the problems of the decade, as did *The Forum* (1886–1930). Nor should the more conservative *North American Review* (1815–1940) be neglected. The *Political Science Quarterly* (1886——), beginning in 1889, furnished a semiannual record of political events, and the *Review of Reviews* (1890–1937) carried comments and articles on current events. The *Literary Digest* (1890–1937) presented symposiums of press opinions, as did *Public Opinion* (1886–1903). The outstanding weekly was *The Nation* (1865——), edited by the independent Edwin L. Godkin, whose opinions on matters of politics and economics were expressed with forthrightness and often with brilliance. Competitors were *The Independent* (1848–1928) and *The Outlook* (1870–1935), the latter specializing on religious news, and *Harper's Weekly* (1851–1916), useful for editorial comment, cartoons, and pictures.

Among the outstanding newspapers of the decade were the New York *World, Tribune, American, Herald,* and *Sun,* the Chicago *Daily Tribune,* St. Louis *Post-Dispatch,* Baltimore *Sun,* Springfield *Republican,* Louisville *Courier-Journal,* and the Kansas City *Star.* The new popular magazines, *McClure's* (1893–1929), *Cosmopolitan* (1886–1925), *Collier's* (1888–1956), and the *American* (1876–1956), later so famous for their muckraking articles, had reached closer to the common man by lower prices and larger sales, but had not yet entered the area of reform. *Life* (1883–1936), *Puck* (1877–1918), and *Judge* (1881–1939) throw light on the humor and social aspects of the period.

For detailed economic history the weekly *Commercial and Financial Chronicle,* published under that name since 1896, with its "Annual Summary," is essential. Other journals, published quarterly, contain articles on economic history relative to the period. They include the *American Economic Review* since 1911 (superseding the *Economic Bulletin* and the *Economic Association Quarterly*); the *Quarterly Journal of Economics,* Harvard University (1887——); *Political Science Quarterly,* Columbia University (1886——); *Journal of Political Economy,* University of Chicago (1892——); and *Journal of the American Statistical Association* (1889——), published before 1922 under other names. Also useful are many numbers of the *Annals* of the American Academy of Political and Social Sciences (Philadelphia, 1890——). Articles touching on the nineties can be found in *Agricultural History* (1927——), published by the Agricultural History Society, and in *Journal of Economic History* (1941——), published with annual supplements. *The American Federationist* (1894——) will keep the student abreast of the policies and philosophy of the American Federation of Labor.

Of the professional historical magazines the most rewarding for the nineties is the *Mississippi Valley Historical Review* (1914——). An occasional article can be found in the *American Historical Review* (1895——). Material can also be found in the journals of many of the state historical societies.

GENERAL HISTORIES

James Ford Rhodes, *History of the United States from the Compromise of 1850* (published from 1893 to 1922, new ed., 9 vols., New York, 1928), has covered the nineties in Vol. VIII, *History of the United States from Hayes to McKinley 1877–1896* (New York, 1919), and in Vol. IX, *The McKinley and Roosevelt Administrations 1897–1909* (New York, 1922). They are conventional and lack the power, research, and authority of Rhodes' earlier volumes. More compact, scholarly, forthright, but at the same time more biased than Rhodes, is the last volume of Ellis Paxson Oberholtzer, *A History of the United States since the Civil War* (5 vols., New York, 1917–37). Both Rhodes and Oberholtzer write an essentially political story. Harry Thurston Peck's popular and readable *Twenty Years of the Republic, 1885–1905* (New York, 1907) conveys the spirit of two decades. In his first volume, Mark Sullivan, *Our Times* (6 vols., New York, 1926–1935), dips into various aspects of the nineties.

The social history of the decade is covered in Arthur M. Schlesinger, *The Rise of the City* (New York, 1933), and Harold U. Faulkner, *The Quest for Social Justice* (New York, 1931), Vols. X, XI in Arthur M. Schlesinger and Dixon Ryan Fox (eds.), *History of American Life* (13 vols., New York, 1927–48). Grace M. Mayer, *Once Upon a City* (New York, 1958), is a description of the New York of 1890 to 1910 through 200 excellent photographs.

Agricultural history from 1860 to 1897 is expertly handled in Fred A. Shannon, *The Farmer's Last Frontier* (New York, 1945), and the general economic history of the last three years of the decade is covered in Harold U. Faulkner, *The Decline of Laissez Faire* (New York, 1951), Vols V, VII in Henry David, Harold U. Faulkner, Louis M. Hacker, Curtis P. Nettels, and Fred A. Shannon (eds.), *The Economic History of the United States* (New York, 1945——). Joseph Dorfman, *The Economic Mind in American Civilization* (3 vols., New York, 1946–49), discusses in Vol. III the development of economic thought in the decade.

Three recent books covering the reform movement and thought of the decade are Russell B. Nye, *Midwestern Progressive Politics* (East Lansing, Mich., 1951); Eric F. Goldman, *Rendezvous with Destiny* (New York, 1952); and Henry Steele Commager, *The American Mind* (New Haven, 1950). See also Arthur Mann, *Yankee Reformers* (Cambridge, Mass., 1954). Van Wyck Brooks, *The Confident Years, 1885–1915* (New York, 1952), surveys the literature of the period, while Merle Curti, *The Growth of American Thought* (New York, 1943), and Vol. III of V. L. Parrington, *Main Currents of American Thought* (3 vols., New York, 1927–30), develop the intellectual trends. Richard Hofstadter, *Social Darwinism in America* (Boston, 1955), and Stow Persons (ed.), *Evolutionary Thought in America* (New Haven, 1950), cover this area well.

MANUSCRIPT MATERIAL

A large amount of manuscript material pertaining to Benjamin Harrison is in the Division of Manuscripts, Library of Congress; the second largest collection is in the Indiana State Library. The papers of his Vice-President, Levi P. Morton, are in the New York Public Library. An enormous collection of the Cleveland papers is in the Library of Congress, and a much smaller collection of McKinley, who left no private papers of importance. There is also much Bryan material there.

Manuscript and other material of prominent public figures of the nineties may be found as follows:

Nelson W. Aldrich (custody of Winthrop Aldrich, New York City)

William B. Allison (Historical, Memorial and Art Department of Iowa, Des Moines)

William E. Curtis (Library of Congress)

Joseph B. Foraker (Historical and Philosophical Society of Ohio, Cincinnati)

Walter Q. Gresham (Library of Congress)

Daniel S. Lamont (Library of Congress)

Justin S. Morrill (Library of Congress)

Richard Olney (Library of Congress)

Orville H. Platt (Connecticut State Library, Hartford)

Theodore Roosevelt (Library of Congress and the Roosevelt Memorial Association)

John Sherman (Library of Congress)

William F. Vilas (Wisconsin Historical Society)

Henry Watterson (Library of Congress)

William C. Whitney (Library of Congress)

BIOGRAPHIES AND AUTOBIOGRAPHIES—POLITICAL

No one has yet written a first-class volume on Benjamin Harrison, but the best of the campaign biographies is that of Lew Wallace, *Life of Gen. Ben Harrison* (Philadelphia, 1888). Harrison, however, gave his views on many public questions in speeches during and after his Presidency and in such compilations as *This Country of Ours* (New York, 1897), a series of revised articles in the *Ladies' Home Journal,* and in Mary L. Harrison (comp.), *Views of an Ex-President* (Indianapolis, 1901). William Allen White, *Masks in a Pageant* (New York, 1928), appraises the three Presidents of the 1890's as well as other political figures.

Cleveland, alone of the three Presidents of the nineties, has been adequately studied. Robert M. McElroy, *Grover Cleveland, the Man and the Statesman* (2 vols., New York, 1923), is well written but eulogistic; Allan Nevins, *Grover Cleveland, A Study in Courage* (New York, 1932), is better balanced, more discriminating and complete, and one of the best biographies that has been done on an American President. Eugene T. Chamberlain's campaign biography (Chicago, 1884) was read and corrected by Cleveland. Cleveland himself wrote *Presidential Problems* (New York, 1904). Among the more valuable appraisals of Cleveland are Dennis T. Lynch, *Grover*

Cleveland, A Man Four Square (New York, 1932); George F. Parker, *Recollections of Grover Cleveland* (New York, 1909); and Horace Samuel Merrill, *Bourbon Leader: Grover Cleveland and the Democratic Party* (Boston, 1957).

Charles S. Olcott, *The Life of William McKinley* (2 vols., Boston, 1916), offers but a slight contribution except in various items of McKinley's private life. The best of the campaign biographies is Robert P. Porter, *Life of William McKinley, Soldier, Lawyer, Statesman* (Cleveland, 1896).

For Harrison's Vice-President, see Robert M. McElroy, *Levi Parsons Morton, Banker, Diplomat and Statesman* (New York, 1930); for Cleveland's, J. W. Cook, "The Life and Labors of Hon. Adlai Ewing Stevenson," *Journal of the Illinois State Historical Society* VIII (July, 1915), 209–231, and J. S. Ewing, "Mr. Stevenson, the Democratic Candidate for Vice President," *Review of Reviews*, XXII (Oct., 1900), 420–424; and for McKinley's (first term), David Magie, *Life of Garrett Augustus Hobart* (New York, 1910).

Biographies of five Secretaries of State of the nineties are available in the following volumes: David S. Muzzey, *James G. Blaine* (New York, 1934); Edward Stanwood, *James Gillespie Blaine* (Boston, 1905); Charles Edward Russell, *Blaine of Maine* (New York, 1931), a critical picture; Henry James, *Richard Olney* (New York, 1923); Matilda Gresham, *Life of Walter Quinton Gresham* (2 vols., Chicago, 1919); T. E. Burton, *John Sherman* (Boston, 1906); and Tyler Dennett, *John Hay: From Poetry to Politics* (New York, 1933). The Muzzey and Dennett volumes are particularly good. See also briefer biographies of Blaine, Foster, Gresham, Olney, Sherman, Day, and Hay in S. F. Bemis (ed.), *The American Secretaries of State and Their Diplomacy* (10 vols., New York, 1927–29), Vols. VIII and IX.

Other volumes of significance on cabinet members include Alice Felt Tyler, *The Foreign Policy of James G. Blaine* (Minneapolis, 1927); John Sherman, *Recollections of Forty Years* (2 vols., Chicago, 1895); James A. Barnes, *John G. Carlisle, Financial Statesman* (New York, 1931), an excellent biography of Cleveland's Secretary of the Treasury; and Mark D. Hirsch, *William C. Whitney, Modern Warwick* (New York, 1948), particularly good on the political life of Cleveland's Secretary of the Navy during the first term and his most influential backer for the nomination and election of 1892. See also F. P. Summers (ed.), *The Cabinet Diary of William L. Wilson* (Chapel Hill, 1957), and James C. Olson, *J. Sterling Morton* (Lincoln, Neb., 1942).

Fortunately, one of the best biographies of leading personalities of this period is that of Herbert Croly, *Marcus Alonzo Hanna* (New York, 1912), the Warwick of McKinley. Thomas Beer, *Hanna* (New York, 1929), is a more intimate picture by a relative. No full-length or competent biography of Bryan has yet been done. Paxton Hibben, *The Peerless Leader: William Jennings Bryan* (New York, 1929), and Morris R. Werner, *Bryan* (New York, 1929), are popular and mildly satirical; John C. Long, *Bryan, The Great*

Commoner (New York, 1928), and Wayne C. Williams, *William Jennings Bryan* (New York, 1936), are more appreciative. Mary Baird Bryan and William Jennings Bryan, *The Memoirs of William Jennings Bryan* (Chicago, 1925), is the nearest we have to an autobiography. For the pre-presidential years, Roosevelt's *Autobiography* (New York, 1913), and Joseph B. Bishop, *Theodore Roosevelt and His Times Shown in His Own Letters* (2 vols., New York, 1920), an official biography, have material. Far more judicious and realistic is Henry Pringle, *Theodore Roosevelt* (New York, 1931). The almost innumerable books on Roosevelt are mostly dominated by hero worship and concentrate chiefly on the years after 1900. The Roosevelt bibliography, however, has been greatly improved in recent years by John M. Blum's realistic interpretation, *The Republican Roosevelt* (Cambridge, 1954); by Elting E. Morison (ed.), *The Letters of Theodore Roosevelt* (8 vols., Cambridge, 1951–1954); and by the first of three projected volumes by Carleton Putnam, *Theodore Roosevelt, The Formative Years, 1858–1886* (New York, 1958).

Of the lesser politicians at least one has had two excellent biographies: Samuel W. McCall, *The Life of Thomas B. Reed* (Boston, 1914), and William A. Robinson, *Thomas B. Reed, Parliamentarian* (New York, 1930). The same is true of Frederick H. Gillett, *George Frisbie Hoar* (Boston, 1934). See also George F. Hoar, *Autobiography of Seventy Years* (2 vols., New York, 1903). Biographies of other national political figures include Lee B. Richardson, *William E. Chandler* (New York, 1940); Louis A. Coolidge, *An Old-Fashioned Senator, Orville H. Platt* (New York, 1910); William H. Smith, *The Life and Speeches of Hon. Charles Warren Fairbanks* (Indianapolis, 1904), a campaign biography; Nathaniel W. Stephenson, *Nelson W. Aldrich* (New York, 1930); James E. McGarren, *Bourke Cochran* (New York, 1948); Francis B. Simkins, *Pitchfork Ben Tillman* (Baton Rouge, 1944); Blair Bolles, *Tyrant from Illinois: Uncle Joe Cannon's Experiment with Personal Power* (New York, 1951); L. White Busbey, *Uncle Joe Cannon* (New York, 1927); Edward N. Dingley, *The Life and Times of Nelson Dingley, Jr.* (Kalamazoo, 1902); John R. Lambert, *Arthur Pue Gorman* (Baton Rouge, 1953); and Horace S. Merrill, *William Freeman Vilas, Doctrinaire Democrat* (Madison, Wis., 1954).

Altgeld never was elected to a federal office, but he became a powerful influence in the Democratic party. Two readable biographies discuss his career: Waldo R. Browne, *Altgeld of Illinois* (New York, 1924), and Harry Barnard, *"Eagle Forgotten," The Life of John Peter Altgeld* (Indianapolis, 1938). See also Jean B. Kern, "The Political Career of Horace Boies," *Iowa Journal of History*, XLVII (July, 1949), 215–246, and Claude M. Fuess, *Carl Schurz, Reformer* (New York, 1932). Elmer Ellis, *Henry Moore Teller*

(Caldwell, Idaho, 1941), is the life of a silver advocate who followed the silver cause from the Republican to the Democratic tickets.

On the third-party figures, two important volumes are Fred E. Haynes, *James Baird Weaver* (Iowa City, 1919); and C. Vann Woodward, *Tom Watson, Agrarian Rebel* (New York, 1938). See also Thomas E. Watson, *Life and Speeches of Thomas E. Watson* (Nashville, Tenn., 1908), a campaign biography. Briefer sketches are John D. Hicks, "The Political Career of Ignatius Donnelly," *Mississippi Valley Historical Review,* VIII (June–Sept., 1928), 80–132; Albert Shaw, "William V. Allen: Populist," *Review of Reviews,* X (July, 1894), 30–42; Carl Snyder, "Marion Butler," *Review of Reviews,* XIV (Oct., 1896), 427–435; Annie L. Diggs, "The Farmers Alliance and Some of Its Leaders," *Arena,* V (Apr., 1892), 590–604; and Hamlin Garland, "The Alliance Wedge in Congress," *ibid.* (Mar., 1892), 447–457. For Debs, who first ran for the Presidency in 1900, the best study is Ray Ginger, *The Bending Cross* (New Brunswick, N.J., 1949), but McAlister Coleman, *Eugene V. Debs* (New York, 1930), also gives a spirited picture of the Socialist leader.

Of varying value but essential for an understanding of the decade are the following reminiscences: Shelby M. Cullom, *Fifty Years of Public Service* (Chicago, 1911); Champ Clark, *My Quarter Century of American Politics* (New York, 1910); Thomas C. Platt, *Autobiography of Thomas Collier Platt* (New York, 1910); Richard F. Pettigrew, *Imperial Washington* (Chicago, 1922); Robert La Follette, *Autobiography* (Madison, Wis., 1913); Belle and Fola La Follette, *Robert M. La Follette* (New York, 1953); John Benson Foraker, *Notes of a Busy Life* (Cincinnati, 1917); and George R. Brown (ed.), *Reminiscences of William M. Stewart of Nevada* (New York, 1908).

POLITICS

The campaign handbooks of the major parties give their platforms, positions, and leading arguments. The platforms are in Kirk H. Porter (comp.), *National Party Platforms* (New York, 1924). There is also much political information in the *World Almanac* (New York, 1886——) and the *Tribune Almanac* (New York, 1838–1914). Edgar E. Robinson, *The Presidential Vote, 1896–1932* (Stanford University, 1934), has a distribution of votes by sections, states, and counties. Matthew Josephson, *The Politicos 1865–1896* (New York, 1938), is a popular and sometimes penetrating account of politics and political leaders. Useful and judicious is Edward Stanwood, *A History of the Presidency* (2 vols., Boston, 1898–1912), which emphasizes the campaigns and gives the platforms, but also contains brief discussions of the administrations as a background. Two general and popular but competent histories are Frank R. Kent, *The Democratic Party, A History* (New York, 1928), and William S. Meyers, *The Republican Party, A History* (rev. ed., New York,

1931). Francis Curtis, *The Republican Party* (2 vols., New York, 1904), covering the years 1854–1904, is factual, with many quotations, including platforms, but is neither objective nor interpretative. Horace S. Merrill, *The Bourbon Democracy of the Middle West, 1865–1896* (Baton Rouge, 1953), discusses the conservative democracy of this section. George H. Knoles, *The Presidential Campaign of 1892* (Stanford University, 1942), is the most thorough study of that campaign.

William J. Bryan, *The First Battle* (Chicago, 1897), is the most convenient source for important information on the Democratic aspects of the 1896 campaign, but his *The Second Battle* (Chicago, 1900) is of little value, except for its access to many speeches reprinted in it. Francis B. Simkins, *The Tillman Movement in South Carolina* (Durham, S.C., 1926), is a study of a prominent Democratic politician, as is Daniel M. Robinson, *Bob Tyler and the Agrarian Revolt in Tennessee* (Chapel Hill, 1935). Useful is Harvey Wish, "John P. Altgeld and the Background of the Campaign of 1896," *Mississippi Valley Historical Review,* XXIV (Mar., 1938), 303–578.

In addition to the biographies and reminiscences of political figures already noted, glimpses of many politicians can be found in such books as Arthur W. Dunn, *From Harrison to Harding* (2 vols., New York, 1922); David S. Barry, *Forty Years in Washington* (Boston, 1924), Charles W. Thompson, *Party Leaders of the Time* (New York, 1906), chatty descriptions of legislators, cabinet members, and others; and O. O. Staley, *Twenty Years in the Press Gallery* (New York, 1906), brief summaries of the legislative histories of the Forty-eighth to the Fifty-eighth Congresses, followed by brief accounts of more than seventy-five senators or congressmen.

The repeal of the Silver Purchase Act is discussed in Jeannette P. Nichols, "The Politics and Personalities of Silver Repeal in the United States Senate, *American Historical Review,* XLI (Oct., 1935), 26–53. See also Fred Wellborn, "The Influence of the Silver-Republican Senators, 1889–1891," *Mississippi Valley Historical Review,* XIV (Mar., 1928), 462–480, and James A. Barnes, "The Gold Standard Democrats and the Party Conflict," *ibid.,* XVII (Dec., 1930), 422–450.

THIRD PARTIES

The history of the most important third party of the nineties has been ably done in John D. Hicks, *The Populist Revolt* (Minneapolis, 1931). It has extensive bibliographies. Able interpretations of Populism are in Richard Hofstadter, *The Age of Reform* (New York, 1955), chs. II and III. Joseph C. Manning, *The Fadeout of Populism* (New York, 1928), contains the reminiscences of a prominent Populist. Frank L. McVey, *The Populist Movement* (New York, 1896), is bitterly anti-Populist. More specialized are Alex M. Arnett, *The Populist Movement in Georgia* (New York, 1922); John B.

Clark, *Populism in Alabama* (Auburn, Ala., 1927); and William D. Sheldon, *Populism in the Old Dominion* (Princeton, 1935). In James Baird Weaver, *A Call to Action* (Des Moines, 1892), are the Populist arguments, by their first presidential candidate. The same type of material is in Thomas E. Watson, *Not a Revolt, It Is a Revolution, The People's Party Campaign Book* (Washington, 1892). See also T. C. Jory, *What Is Populism? An Exposition of the Principles of the Omaha Platform, Adopted by the People's Party* (Salem, Ore., 1895); William Peffer, *The Farmer's Side, His Troubles and Their Remedy* (New York, 1891); F. G. Blood, *Handbook and History of the National Farmer's Alliance and Industrial Union* (Washington, 1893); and J. E. Bryan, *The Farmers' Alliance: Its Origin, Progress and Purposes* (Fayette, Ark., 1891).

Articles concerning the party or its program include Marion Butler, "The People's Party," *Forum*, XXVIII (Feb., 1900), 658–662; William A. Peffer, "The Mission of the Populist Party," *North American Review*, CLVII (Dec., 1893), 665–678, and CLXVI (Jan., 1898), 12–23; Henry Demarest Lloyd, "The Populists at St. Louis," *Review of Reviews*, XIV (Sept., 1896), 293–303; Herman C. Nixon, "The Cleavage within the Farmers' Alliance Movement," *Mississippi Valley Historical Review*, XV (June, 1828), 22–33; Ernest D. Stewart, "The Populist Party in Indiana," *Indiana Magazine of History*, XIV (Dec., 1918), 332–367, and XV (Mar., 1919), 53–74; James A. Woodburn, "Western Radicalism in Western Politics," *Mississippi Valley Historical Review*, XIII (Sept., 1926), 143–168; and John D. Hicks, "The Third Party Tradition in American Politics," *ibid.*, XX (June, 1933), 3–28. See also James C. Malin, "Notes on the Literature of Populism," *Kansas Historical Quarterly*, I (Feb., 1932), 160–164, and Alan Weston, "The Supreme Court the Populist Movement and the Campaign of 1896," *Journal of Politics*, XV (Feb., 1953), 3–41.

The problems of other third parties are discussed in Nathan Fine, *Labor and Farmer Parties in the United States* (New York, 1928); Fred E. Haynes, *Third Party Movements since the Civil War* (Iowa City, 1916), and his *Social Politics in the United States* (Boston, 1894); Morris Hillquit, *History of Socialism in the United States* (New York, 1903), and his *Loose Leaves from a Busy Life* (New York, 1934); Harry W. Laidler, *Social Economic Movements* (New York, 1946); Howard H. Quint, *The Forging of American Socialism* (New York, 1953); David A. Shannon, *The Socialist Party of America* (New York, 1955); and Ira Kipnis, *The Socialist Movement, 1897–1912* (New York, 1952).

AGRICULTURE

Much of the source material on agriculture will be found in the publications of the Department of Agriculture, notably the annual *Yearbooks* since

1894, as well as in the *Department Bulletins,* the *Technical Bulletins,* the *Miscellaneous Publications,* and the *History Series.* Particuarly valuable is the *Yearbook of the Department of Agriculture* (Washington, 1940), devoted largely to history. This volume contains Everett E. Edwards, "American Agriculture—the First 300 Years," the best brief history of American agriculture. Two notable historical studies sponsored by the Department are Alfred C. True, *A History of Agricultural Experimentation and Research in the United States, 1607–1925, including a History of the United States Department of Agriculture* (Miscellaneous Publication No. 251, Washington, 1937), and his *History of Agricultural Education in the United States* (Miscellaneous Publication No. 36, Washington, 1929). Nor should the publications of the various state departments of agriculture and articles in *Agricultural History* (1927——) be neglected.

Although the Carnegie Institution sponsored excellent studies of American agriculture in the period before 1860, there is no full-length single volume covering the whole period of our agricultural history. Vols. V and VII in the *Economic History of the United States* series by Shannon and Faulkner, already noted, cover agriculture in the nineties. The volume of Harold Barger and Hans H. Landsberg, *American Agriculture, 1899–1939* (New York, 1942), a product of the National Bureau of Economic Research, is largely quantitative and statistical, but it gives data for the later nineties. Much useful information can be found in Liberty Hyde Bailey (ed.), *Cyclopedia of American Agriculture* (3rd ed., 4 vols., New York, 1910). The *Final Report of the Industrial Commission* (Washington, 1902) gives the Commission's reactions to its study of agriculture and agricultural labor at the end of the century, material for which is found in Vol. X, published in 1901.

Some information on rural population, its movements and trends, is available in Warren S. Thompson and Pascal K. Whelpton, *Population Trends in the United States* (New York, 1922); C. Warren Thornthwaite, *Internal Migration in the United States* (Philadelphia, 1934); and P. K. Whelpton, "Occupational Groups in the United States, 1820–1920, *"Journal of the American Statistical Association,* XXI (Sept., 1926), 335–343. Special aspects of agricultural history for this period are noted in Edwin G. Nourse, *American Agriculture and the European Market* (New York, 1924); T. Swann Harding, *Two Blades of Grass* (Norman, Okla., 1947), a popular history of the scientific efforts of the Department of Agriculture; Leland O. Howard, *Fighting the Insects* (New York, 1933); David G. Fairchild, *Exploring for Plants* (New York, 1930), and his *The World Was My Garden* (New York, 1938); Joseph C. Bailey, *Seaman A. Knapp* (New York, 1945), a scientist who aided southern agriculture; and Harvey W. Wiley, *An Autobiography* (Indianapolis, 1930), a pioneer for pure food. More popular is Paul H. de Kruif, *Hunger Fighters* (New York, 1928).

Other useful books or articles are Henry C. Taylor, *Outline of Agricultural Economics* (rev. ed., New York, 1931); Gordon S. Watkins, "Cooperation," University of Illinois *Bulletin,* XVIII (Mar., 1921); Oscar B. Jesness and William H. Kerr, *Cooperative Purchasing and Marketing Organizations among Farmers in the United States,* Department of Agriculture, Department Bulletin No. 547 (Washington, 1917); William J. Spellman and Emanuel A. Goldenweiser, "Farm Tenantry in the United States," *Yearbook of the Department of Agriculture* (Washington, 1916); Goldenweiser and Leon E. Trusdell, *Farm Tenancy in the United States,* Census Monograph IV (Washington, 1924); L. C. Gray *et al.,* "Farm Ownership and Tenancy," *Department of Agriculture Yearbook* (Washington, 1923), pp. 507–600; and Lawanda F. Cox, "Tenancy in the United States, 1865–1900," *Agricultural History,* XVIII (July, 1944), 97–105. The problem of farm credit going back to this period is discussed in Carl W. Thompson, *Costs and Sources of Farm-Mortgage Loans in the United States,* Department of Agriculture, Department Bulletin No. 384 (Washington, 1916).

THE FRONTIER

On the frontier of the nineties, including the last rancher's frontier, Walter P. Webb, *The Great Plains* (Boston, 1931), is the best for an over-all picture, as is Ernest S. Osgood, *The Day of the Cattleman* (Minneapolis, 1929), for the crash of the cattle industry in the Northwest. Other important volumes are Edward E. Dale, *The Range Cattle Industry* (Norman, Okla., 1930), and his *Cow Country* (Norman, Okla., 1942); Louis Pelzer, *The Cattlemen's Frontier* (Glendale, Calif., 1936); O. B. Peake, *The Colorado Range Cattle Industry* (Glendale, Calif., 1939); Everett Dick, *The Sod House Frontier* (New York, 1937); and Merrill G. Burlingame, *The Montana Frontier* (Helena, 1942). The *Mississippi Valley Historical Review* has many articles on the last frontier, including E. E. Dale, "The Ranchman's Last Frontier," X (June, 1923), 34–46; R. S. Fletcher, "End of the Open Range in Eastern Montana," XIV (Sept., 1929), 188–211; Louis Pelzer, "A Cattleman's Commonwealth on the Western Range," XIII (June, 1926), 30–49; and Harold Briggs, "The Development and Decline of Open Range Ranching in the Northwest," XX (Mar., 1934), 521–536.

On the area which showed the greatest expansion in the nineties, see the excellent histories of Oklahoma by Grant Foreman, *A History of Oklahoma* (Norman, Okla., 1942), and Roy Gittinger, *The Formation of the State of Oklahoma* (Berkeley, Calif., 1917). See also Carl C. Rister, *Land Hunger: David L. Payne and the Oklahoma Boomers* (Norman, Okla., 1942), and Gerald Forbes, *Guthrie, Oklahoma's First Capital* (Norman, Okla., 1932).

The later distribution of the public domain is covered in Benjamin H. Hibbard, *A History of the Public Land Policies* (New York, 1924); Ray M.

Robbins, *Our Landed Heritage: The Public Domain, 1776–1936* (Princeton, 1942), and Robbins, "The Public Domain in an Era of Exploitation, 1862–1901," *Agricultural History,* XIII (Apr., 1939), 97–118. See also Paul W. Gates, "The Homestead Act in an Incongruous Land System," *American Historical Review,* XLI (July, 1936), 652–681. How the railroads contributed to the settlement may be seen in James B. Hedges, "Promotion of Immigration to the Pacific Northwest by the Railroads," *Mississippi Valley Historical Review,* XV (Sept., 1928), 183–203, and "The Colonization Work of the Northern Pacific Railroad," *ibid.,* XIII (Dec., 1926), 312–342. Richard C. Overton, *Burlington West* (Cambridge, 1941), describes the work of the Chicago, Burlington and Quincy Railroad, and Edwin M. Parker of the Southern Pacific in "The Southern Pacific Railroad and the Settlement of Southern California," *Pacific Historical Review,* VI (June, 1937), 103–119.

DECLINE AND REVIVAL OF AGRICULTURE

The most useful volume on the decline and partial recovery of agriculture in New England is Harold F. Wilson, *The Hill Country of Northern New England* (New York, 1936), but the annual reports of the New Hampshire Board of Agriculture, the Maine Board of Agriculture, and the Vermont Department of Agriculture are rich mines of information. Also helpful are such contemporary articles as Charles C. Nott, "A Good Farm for Nothing," *The Nation,* XLIX (Nov. 21, 1889), 406–408, and Walter C. Frost, "Desolate Farm Sites in New England," *ibid.* (Nov. 28), p. 431. Information on agriculture in the South may be found in such books as William D. Kelley, *The Old South and the New* (New York, 1888); Philip A. Bruce, *The Rise of the New South,* Vol. XVII in G. C. Lee and F. N. Thorpe (eds.), *The History of North America* (20 vols., Philadelphia, 1903–10); and C. Vann Woodward, *Origins of the New South* (Baton Rouge, 1951). The battle between costs and prices is studied in Willet M. Hayes and Edward C. Parker, "The Cost of Producing Farm Products," U.S. Department of Agriculture, Bureau of Statistics, *Bulletin,* No. 48 (Washington, 1906). A general survey by an economist is C. F. Emerick, "An Analysis of Agricultural Discontent in the United States," *Political Science Quarterly,* II (Sept., Dec., 1896; Mar., 1897). Gerald T. White, "Economic Recovery and the Wheat Crop of 1897," *Agricultural History,* XIII (June, 1939), gives information regarding improved conditions, at least in the trans-Mississippi West, during the last years of the decade. But some light is thrown (despite recovery) on the real condition of American farmers in Fred A. Shannon, "The Status of the Midwestern Farmer in 1900," *Mississippi Valley Historical Review,* XXXVII (Dec., 1950), 491–510.

THE AGRARIAN REVOLT

Besides Hicks, the standard volume on Populism, mentioned under "Politics," see also his first chapter, "The Region of Discontent," in Theodore Saloutos and John D. Hicks, *Agricultural Discontent in the Middle West, 1900–1939* (Madison, Wis., 1951). The story from the Greenback party and the Grangers to Populism is well but briefly told in Solon J. Buck, *The Agrarian Crusade* (Chronicles of America, New Haven, 1921). In much greater detail on the whole movement is Carl C. Taylor, *The Farmers' Movement, 1620–1920* (Cincinnati, 1953), heavily documented.

The causes and history of Populism are discussed in Ralph Smith, "The Farmers' Alliance in Texas, 1875–1900," *Southern Historical Quarterly*, XLVIII (Jan., 1945); William A. Peffer, "The Farmers' Defensive Movement," *Forum*, VIII (Dec., 1889), 464–473; Hallie Farmer, "The Economic Background of Frontier Populism," *Mississippi Valley Historical Review*, X (Mar., 1924), 406–427; Raymond C. Miller, "The Background of Populism in Kansas," *ibid.*, XI (Mar., 1925), 469–489; John D. Barnhart, "Rainfall and the Populist Party in Nebraska," *American Political Science Review*, XIX (Aug., 1925), 527–540; Hallie Farmer, "The Railroads and Frontier Populism," *Mississippi Valley Historical Review*, XIII (Dec., 1926), 389–397; J. Martin Klotsche, "The United Front Populists," *Wisconsin Magazine of History*, XX (June, 1937); and Herman C. Nixon, "The Economic Basis of the Populist Movement in Iowa," *Iowa Journal of History and Politics*, XXI (July, 1923), 373–396.

Certain local studies include Homer Clevinger, "The Farmers' Alliance in Missouri," *Missouri Historical Review*, XXXIX (Oct., 1944), 22–44; Paul R. Fossum, *The Agrarian Movement in North Dakota* (Baltimore, 1925); Herman C. Nixon, "The Populist Movement in Iowa," *Iowa Journal of History and Politics*, XXIV (Jan., 1926), 3–107; E. D. Stewart, "The Populist Party in Indiana," *Indiana Magazine of History*, XIV, XV (Dec., 1918; Mar., 1919), 332–367, 53–74; Leon W. Fuller, "Colorado's Revolt against Capitalism," *Mississippi Valley Historical Review*, XXI (Dec., 1934), 343–360; Melvin J. White, "Populism in Louisiana during the Nineties," *ibid.*, V (June, 1918), 3–19; Charles M. Destler, "Consummation of a Labor-Populist Alliance in Illinois, 1894," *ibid.*, XXVII (Mar., 1941), 589–602; and Lucia E. Daniel, "The Louisiana People's Party," *Louisiana Historical Quarterly*, XVI (Oct., 1943), 1055–1149. A full treatment of a strong Populist area is given in Roscoe C. Martin, *The People's Party in Texas* (Austin, 1933). See also Harold F. Taggart, "California and the Silver Question in 1895," *Pacific Historical Review*, VI (Sept., 1937), 249–269; Carroll H. Woody, "Populism in Washington: A Study of the Legislature in 1897," *Washington Historical Quarterly*, XXI (April, 1930), 103–119. Arthur F. Bentley, *The Condition of the Western Farmer as Illustrated by the Economic History of a Nebraska*

Township (Baltimore, 1893), and W. A. Russ, Jr., "Godkin Looks at Western Agrarianism: A Case Study," *Agricultural History*, XIX (Oct., 1945), 233-242.

Fuller biographies on the agricultural revolt are given in Ray Allen Billington, *Westward Expansion* (New York, 1949), in Hicks, and in the footnotes of Taylor.

FOREIGN TRADE

Government publications are essential for any detailed knowledge of the subject. During these years the *Foreign Commerce and Navigation of the United States* was published annually (since 1820) by the Bureau of Statistics of the Treasury Department, the *Monthly Summary of Commerce and Finance* (since 1896) by the same bureau, and the *Statistical Abstract of the United States* as an annual (since 1878). All these eventually came under the Department of Commerce. A short cut to statistical material on foreign commerce as well as many other economic aspects is the *Historical Statistics of the United States, 1789–1945, a Supplement to the Statistical Abstract of the United States* (1949), prepared by the Bureau of Census with the co-operation of the Social Science Research Council. A continuation of this volume to 1952 was published in 1954. The State Department's official *Papers Relating to the Foreign Relations of the United States and Treaties, Conventions, International Acts, Protocols and Agreements between the United States and Other Powers* (4 vols., Washington, 1910–38) contain material on international economic problems.

Of the secondary material, Vol. II of Thurman W. Van Metre, Grover G. Huebner, and David S. Hanchett, *History of Domestic and Foreign Commerce of the United States* (2 vols., Washington, 1915), covers the nineties. Frank W. Taussig, *Tariff History of the United States* (7th ed., New York, 1923), deals thoroughly with the tariffs of 1890, 1894, and 1897. With more political background the same is done by Edward Stanwood, *American Tariff Controversies in the Nineteenth Century* (2 vols., Boston, 1903). See also Sidney Ratner, *American Taxation* (New York, 1942). Frank W. Taussig, *Some Aspects of the Tariff Question* (Cambridge, 1915); Chester W. Wright, *Wool Growing and the Tariff: A Study in the Economic History of the United States* (Cambridge, 1910); and Arthur H. Cole, *The American Wool Industry* (Cambridge, 1926), all deal with one or more protected industries. Agricultural exports and their history are clearly handled in Edwin G. Nourse, *Agriculture and the European Market* (New York, 1924). On the promotion of foreign trade, see John B. Osborne, "The Work of the Reciprocity Commission," *Forum*, XXX (Dec., 1900), 394–411, and George B. Cortelyou, "Some Agencies for Extension of Our Domestic and Foreign Trade," American Academy of Political and Social Science, *Annals*, XXIV (July, 1904).

On the 1894 tariff, Festus P. Summers, *William L. Wilson and Tariff Reform* (New Brunswick, N.J., 1953), and Roger Q. Mills, "The Wilson Bill," *North American Review,* CLVIII (Feb., 1894), 235–244, are useful.

BUSINESS CYCLES, CURRENCY, AND FINANCE CAPITALISM

The general financial story of the decade can be found in Davis R. Dewey, *Financial History of the United States* (10th ed., New York, 1928), and in William J. Shultz and M. R. Caine, *Financial Development of the United States* (New York, 1937). Particularly useful is Alexander D. Noyes, *Forty Years of American Finance, 1865–1907* (New York, 1909). Also of value are Henry Clews, *Fifty Years in Wall Street* (New York, 1908), the reminiscences of a Wall Street broker; Margaret G. Meyers *et al., The New York Money Market* (4 vols., New York, 1931–32); and George W. Edwards, *The Evolution of Finance Capitalism* (New York, 1938). Henry Parker Willis, *The Federal Reserve System* (New York, 1923), develops the background into the nineties. Burton J. Hendrick, *The Story of Life Insurance* (New York, 1907), is based on the exposures of the Armstrong investigation of the New York legislature printed in the *Report of the Joint Committee of the State and Assembly of the State of New York Appointed to Investigate Affairs of Life Insurance Companies* (Albany, 1907).

The most useful study of the depression following the panic of 1893 is Charles Hoffman's unpublished doctor's thesis at Columbia, "The Depression of the Nineties—An Economic History" (1954). See also his "Depression of the Nineties," *Journal of Economic History,* XVII (June, 1956), 137–164, and the footnotes in the article. W. Jett Lauck, *The Causes of the Panic of 1893* (Boston, 1907), stresses the causes, emphasizes money and banking, but does little on the depression. The same emphasis is true of C. M. W. Sprague, *History of Crises under the National Banking System* (Washington, 1910). Joseph A. Schumpeter, *Business Cycles* (New York, 1939), touches briefly on this panic. See also Wesley C. Mitchell, *Business Cycles and Their Causes* (Berkeley, Calif., 1941), and Willard L. Thorp, *Business Annals* (New York, 1926). References to contemporary opinions regarding the depression will be found in the footnotes of Chapter 7. Some social history is covered in the excellent article of Samuel Resneck, "Unemployment, Unrest, and Relief in the United States during the Depression of 1893–1897," *Journal of Political Economy,* LXI (Aug., 1953), 324–345.

The best known and probably the most effective propaganda for free silver were two small books by William H. Harvey, *Coin's Financial School* (Chicago, 1894), and *Up to Date, Coin's Financial School Continued* (Chicago, 1895). More scholarly was E. Benjamin Andrews, *An Honest Dollar* (Hartford, 1894), by a bimetallist. Ignatius Donnelly, *The American People's Money* (Chicago, 1895), is a plea for silver. J. Lawrence Laughlin, *The His-*

tory of Bimetallism in the United States (New York, 1892), and his Facts about Money (Chicago, 1895), uphold the gold standard, the latter book being largely an answer to "Coin" Harvey. Francis A. Walker, International Bimetallism (New York, 1896), and his "The Free Coinage of Silver," Journal of Political Economy, I (Mar., 1893), 163–178, are warnings against silver monometallism. Frank W. Taussig, The Silver Situation in the United States (Publications of the American Economic Association, 1892), VII, 1–118, is a cool and detached survey. Willard C. Fisher appraises Harvey and his critics in "Coin and His Critics," Quarterly Journal of Economics, X (Jan., 1896), 187–208. Alonzo B. Hepburn, History of Currency in the United States (New York, 1915), puts the conflict of the nineties in chronological perspective, and James A. Barnes, John G. Carlisle (New York, 1931), is the most detached account of the repeal of the Sherman Silver Purchase Act.

Finance capitalism developed most rapidly after the turn of the century, but it was well under way before 1900. The technique and results are well told in Louis D. Brandeis, Other People's Money and How the Bankers Use It (New York, 1913), and in the Report of Committee Appointed Pursuant to H.R. 429 and 504 . . . , 62nd Cong., 3rd sess. (Washington, 1913), generally known as the Pujo Committee. But material on the nineties is available in such volumes as John Moody, The Truth about the Trusts (New York, 1904), and his Masters of Capital (Chronicles of America, New Haven, 1921); Frederick L. Allen, The Lords of Creation (New York, 1935), and his The Great Pierpont Morgan (New York, 1949); Lewis Corey, The House of Morgan (New York, 1930); Stanley H. Holbrook, The Age of the Moguls (Garden City, N.Y., 1953; Matthew Josephson, The Robber Barons (New York, 1934); and the various lives of the important capitalists of the nineties.

TRANSPORTATION

Important and accessible material on railroads is found in the Interstate Commerce Commission Annual Reports and Statistics of Railways in the United States, published annually since 1888. The Annual Reports note the important problems faced by the I.C.C. and also summarize the transportation cases in the federal courts and the decisions of the Commission. An important source is the Industrial Commission, Report, Vol. IV (1900). Of the private sources, Henry V. Poor, Manual of the Railroads of the United States, annually since 1868, gives the financial history and structure of the individual railroad companies and is invaluable for these years.

Secondary material includes Slason Thompson, A Short History of American Railroads (New York, 1925), and the two volumes by William Z. Ripley, Railroads: Rates and Regulations (New York, 1912), and Railroads: Finance and Organization (New York, 1915), scholarly and objective studies, with useful illustrative material. Special phases are dealt with in Edward G. Campbell, *The Reorganization of the American Railroad System, 1893–1900* (New York, 1938); Balthasar M. Mayer, *A History of the Northern Securities Case,* University of Wisconsin, Bulletin No. 142 (Madison, 1906); Jules I. Bogen, *The Anthracite Railroads* (New York, 1927); Charles A. Prouty, "National Regulation of Railroads," *American Economic Association Publications,* 3rd series, Vol. IV, No. 1 (Feb., 1903); Solomon Huebner, "The Distribution of Stockholdings in American Railroads," American Academy of Political and Social Science, *Annals,* XXII (Dec., 1903). The raid of financiers on the Chicago and Alton is told objectively in Ripley and defended in George Kennan, *E. H. Harriman* (2 vols., Boston, 1922).

The volumes of I. L. Sharfman, *The Interstate Commerce Commission* (5 vols., New York, 1931–37), are exhaustive and valuable. Other studies and interpretations of value on various aspects are D. Philip Locklin, *Economics of Transportation* (Chicago, 1938); I. L. Sharfman, *The American Railroad Problem* (New York, 1921); James C. Bonbright, *Railroad Capitalization* (New York, 1920); and Frank H. Dixon, *Railroads and Government* (New York, 1922). John Moody, *Railroad Builders* (New Haven, 1921), a Chronicles of America volume, is bright and popular, with material on the nineties and earlier.

A well-written popular account of street railways is John Anderson Miller, *Fares, Please* (New York, 1941). Statistics and some history are in U.S. Bureau of Census, *Street and Electric Railways, 1902* (Washington, 1905). Their later development and difficulties are developed in the *Proceedings of the Federal Electric Railways Commission* (3 vols., Washington, 1920) and in Delos F. Wilcox, *Analysis of the Electric Railway Problem* (New York, 1921). Brief accounts of early developments are in Herbert H. Vreeland in Vol. I of C. M. Depew (ed.), *One Hundred Years of American Commerce* (2 vols., New York, 1895); in Frank J. Sprague, "The Electric Railway," *Century Magazine,* LXX (July, Aug., 1905), 435–451, 512–527; and in H. C. Passer, "Frank Julian Sprague," in William Miller (ed.), *Men in Business* (Cambridge, 1952). Three articles by Burton J. Hendrick, "Great American Fortunes in the Making," *McClure's Magazine,* XXX (Nov., 1907–Jan., 1908), touch on the financing of early street railways. Edward S. Mason, *The Street Railway in Massachusetts* (Cambridge, 1932), tells of the rise and decline of this form of transportation in a single state.

Federal studies of inland waterways which throw light on the period before 1900 include *Report of the Commissioner of Corporations on Transportation by Water in the United States* (4 pts., Washington, 1909–13); *Preliminary Report of the Inland Waterways Commission,* 60th Cong., 1st Sess., Senate Document No. 325; and the *Final Report of the National Waterways Commission,* 62nd Cong., 2nd Sess., Senate Document No. 469. Such individual histories of canals as Walter S. Sunderlin, *The Great National Project, A History of the Chesapeake and Ohio Canal,* Johns Hopkins Studies, LXIV, No. 1 (Baltimore, 1946); Chester L. Jones, *The Economic History of the Anthracite-Tidewater Canals,* University of Pennsylvania Series on Political Economy and Public Law, No. 22 (Philadelphia, 1908); and Noble E. Whitford, *History of the Barge Canal of New York State,* Supplement to the Annual Report of the State Engineer and Surveyor for the Year Ended June 30, 1921 (Albany, 1922), include the declining years of the eighties and nineties.

The American Merchant Marine and its decline by the nineties are covered in the *Report of the Merchant Marine Commission,* Senate Document No. 2,755, 58th Cong., 3rd Sess. (3 vols., Washington, 1904–5), and *Development of the American Merchant Marine and American Commerce,* Senate Report No. 10, 59th Cong., 1st Sess. Early studies of subsidies include Walter T. Dunmore, *Ship Subsidies* (Boston, 1907), and Royal Meeker, *History of Shipping Subsidies,* American Economic Association, 3 Series, *Publications,* Vol. VI (1905). More recent surveys are Paul M. Zeis, *American Shipping Policy* (Princeton, 1938), and John C. B. Hutchins, *The American Maritime Industries and Public Policy, 1789–1914* (Cambridge, 1941).

Bibliography on the early years of the automobile industry will be found under "Manufacturing." An extremely helpful study of the development of centralized highway control is the Bureau of Public Roads, U.S. Department of Agriculture, and Connecticut State Highway Department, *Report of a Survey of Transportation on the State Highway System of Connecticut* (Washington, 1926). Its history is typical of many states. Charles L. Dearing, *American Highway Policy* (Washington, 1941), is the best general history, but John F. Brindley, *Highway Administration and Finance* (New York, 1927), may be found useful. On city roadways, see Nelson P. Lewis, "Modern City Roadways," *Popular Science Monthly,* LVI (Mar., 1900), 524–539; and on country roads, Nathaniel S. Shaler, "The Common Roads," *Scribner's Magazine,* VI (Oct., 1889), 473–483. The influence of rural free delivery on country roads is well described in Wayne E. Fuller, "Good Roads and Rural Free Delivery of Mail," *Mississippi Valley Historical Review,* XLII (June, 1955), 67–83.

MANUFACTURING

Important statistically and historically is the Census of Manufacturing as published in the regular censuses of 1890 and 1900. For the period under study, the *Report of the Industrial Commission* (19 vols., Washington, 1900–1902) is essential for any study of the economic life of the nineties. The excellent volumes of the National Bureau of Economic Research, Inc., are largely statistical and quantitative and generally begin with 1899 or thereafter. At least two of them reach back earlier, the study of Harold Barger, *The Transportation Industry, 1889–1946* (New York, 1951), and of Arthur F. Burns, *Production Trends in the United States since 1870* (New York, 1934).

Victor Clark, *History of Manufactures* (3 vols., New York, 1949), covers the period to 1914. Also concerned in the economic problems of American industry is Evon B. Alderfer and Herman E. Michl, *Economics of American Industry* (New York, 1942). Three excellent chapters, by Louis C. Hunter on the iron industry, by Samuel Resneck on mass production, and by Charles B. Kuhlmann on the processing of agricultural products, are in Harold F. Williamson (ed.), *The Growth of American Economy* (2nd ed., New York, 1951). A contemporaneous picture of many industries is in Chauncey M. Depew (ed.), *One Hundred Years of American Commerce* (2 vols., New York, 1895).

The bibliography of American industrial history has gradually grown, helped by a few industries which have opened their archives. Among the most useful are Melvin T. Copeland, *The Cotton Manufacturing Industry in the United States* (Cambridge, 1912); Arthur H. Cole, *The American Wool Manufacture* (2 vols., Cambridge, 1928); Arthur H. Cole and Harold F. Williamson, *The American Carpet Manufacture* (Cambridge, 1941); Charles B. Kuhlmann, *The Development of the Flour-Milling Industry in the United States* (Boston, 1929); Rudolph A. Clemen, *The American Livestock and Meat Industry* (New York, 1923); K. O. Backert (ed.), *The ABC of Iron and Steel* (4th ed., Cleveland, 1923); Howard and Ralph Wolf, *Rubber: A Story of Glory and Greed* (New York, 1936); and Joel Seidman, *The Needle Trades* (New York, 1936). Allan Nevins, *Ford, the Times, the Man, the Company* (New York, 1954), has much to say of the early years of the automobile industry as a whole. The Ford archives are now open to students. The general books on the industry are Lawrence H. Seltzer, *A Financial History of the American Automobile Industry* (Boston, 1928); Ralph C. Epstein, *The Automobile Industry* (Chicago, 1928), both emphasizing the financial and commercial aspects; and Edward E. Kennedy, *The Automobile Industry* (New York, 1941), more general and popular.

CONSOLIDATION OF BUSINESS

The *Report of the Industrial Commission* (already noted) has much material on trusts at the end of the century. The Bureau of Corporations, after the organization of the Department of Commerce and Labor in 1903, published several studies on industries, some of which go back into the nineties and are involved in antitrust legislation. Among them were studies on the *Beef Industry* (1905), *Freight Rates in Connection with the Oil Industry* (1906), *Petroleum Industry* (2 vols., 1907), *Prices of Tobacco* (1909), etc. Other useful government publications include Willard L. Thorp, *The Integration of Industrial Operation,* U.S. Bureau of the Census, Census Monograph III (Washington, 1924); Walton Hamilton, *Patents and Free Enterprise,* Temporary National Economic Committee Investigations of the Concentration of Economic Power, Monograph No. 31 (Washington, 1941), and his *Antitrust in Action,* Monograph No. 16 (Washington, 1941).

The textbooks on this problem are unusually good on the early period: Henry R. Seager and Charles A. Gulick, Jr., *Trust and Corporation Problems* (New York, 1929); Jeremiah W. Jenks and Walter E. Clark, *The Trust Problem* (5th ed., New York, 1920); and Eliot Jones, *The Trust Problem in the United States* (New York, 1924). Arthur S. Dewing, *Corporate Promotions and Reorganizations* (Cambridge, 1914), contains the early history of many consolidations. Similar material is in Henry R. Seager, "The Recent Trust Decisions," *Political Science Quarterly,* XXVI (Dec., 1911), 581–614; in William S. Stevens, "A Group of Trusts and Combinations," *Quarterly Journal of Economics,* XXVI (Aug., 1912), 593–643, and his "A Classification of Pools and Associations Based on American Experience," *American Economic Review,* III (Sept., 1913), 545–575. Other studies of early consolidations include A. Bergland, "The United States Steel Corporation," *Columbia University Studies in History, Economics and Public Law,* XXVII, No. 2 (1907); Meyer Jacobstein, "The Tobacco Industry," *ibid.,* XXVI, No. 3 (1907); Henry R. Mussey, "Combination in the Mining Industry: A Study of Concentration in Lake Superior Iron Ore Production," *ibid.,* XXIII, No. 3 (1905); and Eliot Jones, *The Anthracite Coal Combination in the United States* (Cambridge, 1914). Allan Nevins, *Study in Power: John D. Rockefeller, Industrialist and Philanthropist* (New York, 1953), tells the story of the early oil mergers, as does Ida M. Tarbell, *History of the Standard Oil Company* (2 vols., New York, 1904). Two efforts to deal statistically at the opening of the new century are Luther Conant, "Industrial Consolidation in the United States," *Publications of the American Statistical Association,* VII, n.s., No. 53 (March, 1901), and John Moody, *The Truth about the Trusts* (New York, 1904), an extremely valuable contribution.

LABOR

Primary sources for pre-1900 are in the *Annual Reports* of the Bureau of Labor, beginning 1886; of the Department of Labor, 1888–1903; and in the *Special Reports* and particularly the bimonthly *Bulletins.* Also important is the material on labor in *Report of the Industrial Commission* (already cited). Statistical material on strikes is given in the U.S. Commission of Labor, *Twenty-first Annual Report, 1906* (Washington, 1907), and analyzed in George G. Groat, *Organized Labor in America* (New York, 1916). Essential for the Pullman strike is United States Strike Commission, *Report of the*

Chicago Strike of June–July, 1894 (Washington, 1895), which is interpreted and fitted into the general picture in Almont Lindsey, *The Pullman Strike* (Chicago, 1942). The most complete study of the march of the unemployed on Washington is Donald L. McMurry, *Coxey's Army* (Boston, 1929), but also see Henry Vincent, *The Story of the Commonweal* (Chicago, 1894). Ray Ginger, *Altgeld's America* (New York, 1958), gives an excellent picture of Chicago in the 1890's.

Important for any study of organized labor are the reports of the annual sessions of the Federation of Organized Trades and Labor Unions of the United States and Canada (1881–86) and of the American Federation of Labor (1886——), and the *American Federationist* (1894——), the monthly journal of the A.F. of L. There are, of course, the publications of the various state bureaus of labor statistics and of the many unions in the A.F. of L. and of the four Railroad Brotherhoods.

The best known of the secondary volumes on labor history are those of John R. Commons *et al., History of Labor in the United States* (4 vols., New York, 1918–35); Vol. II carries the story of organization to 1896 and Vol. IV, by Selig Perlman and Philip Taft, continues it to 1932. Lewis Lorwin, *The American Federation of Labor* (Washington, 1933), is standard on that organization to the date of publication. Samuel Gompers, *Seventy Years of Life and Labor* (2 vols., New York, 1925), is both an autobiography and a history of the A.F. of L. Other useful volumes covering this period in part are Selig Perlman, *A History of Trade Unionism in the United States* (New York, 1922); Leo Wolman, *The Growth of American Trade Unions* (New York, 1924); George G. Groat (already cited); Rowland H. Harvey, *Samuel Gompers, Champion of the Toiling Masses* (Stanford University, 1935); John Mitchell, *Organized Labor* (Philadelphia, 1903); Elsie Glück, *John Mitchell* (New York, 1929); Charles H. Wesley, *Negro Labor in the United States* (New York, 1927); and Lorenzo J. Greene and Carter G. Woodson, *The Negro Wage Earner* (Washington, 1930).

Special studies on philosophy, tactics, and relations with the government include Harry W. Laidler, *Boycotts and the Labor Struggle* (New York, 1913); Leo Wolman, *The Boycott in American Trade Unions* (Baltimore, 1916); Edward Berman, *Labor Disputes and the Presidents of the United States* (New York, 1924); Edwin Witte, *Government in Labor Disputes* (New York, 1932); Louis I. Reed, *The Labor Philosophy of Samuel Gompers* (New York, 1930); Clarence Darrow, *The Story of My Life* (New York, 1932); Industrial Relations Research Association, *Interpreting the Labor Movement* (Madison, Wis., 1952); and Lloyd Ulman, *The Rise of the National Trade.Union* (Cambridge, Mass., 1955). See also Edward B. Mittleman, "Chicago Labor in Politics, 1877–1896," *Journal of Political Economy,* XXVIII (May, 1920), 407–427; James Peterson, "The Trade Unions and the Populist Party," *Science and Society,* VIII (1944), 143–160; and Howard L. Hurwitz, *Theodore Roosevelt and Labor in New York State 1880–1900* (New York, 1943).

The literature on the general condition of labor, particularly after 1900, as distinguished from the history of trade unionism, is fairly voluminous. The general picture can best be obtained in Don D. Lescohier and Elizabeth Brandies, *History of Labor in the United States, 1896–1932* (New York, 1935), Vol. III in the well-known Commons *et al., History of Labor.* Its bibliographies in footnotes and elsewhere are unusually complete for this period. A much briefer survey is ch. XI in Faulkner, *Decline of Laissez Faire.* On wages and their relation to hours and cost of living, see the publications of the Department of Labor, particularly *Bulletin of the Department of Labor,* No. 18 (Sept., 1898), and the *Nineteenth Annual Report of the Commissioner of Labor, 1904* (Washington, 1905). See also the Twelfth Census of the U.S., Special Report by Davis R. Dewey, *Employees and Wages* (Washington, 1903). Other important studies are Paul H. Douglas, *Real Wages in the United States, 1890–1926* (Boston, 1930); Paul F. Brissenden, *Earnings of Factory Workers, 1897–1917,* Census Monograph X (Washington, 1929); and Whitney Coombs, *The Wages of Unskilled Labor in Manufacturing Industries in the United States, 1890–1924* (New York, 1926).

Income, wealth, and its distribution are discussed in C. D. Spahr, *The Present Distribution of Wealth in the United States* (New York, 1926); Willford I. King, *The Wealth and Income of the People of the United States* (New York, 1915); and Sidney Ratner, *New Light on the History of Great American Fortunes* (New York, 1953), a reprinting of lists of millionaires made by the New York *Tribune* in 1892 and the *World Almanac* in 1902. Articles of interest are Thomas C. Shearman, "The Owners of the United States," *Forum,* VIII (Sept., 1889), 262–273; G. P. Watkins, "The Growth of Large American Fortunes," *Publications of the American Economic Association,* 3rd series, VIII (1907), 735–904; and George K. Holmes, "The Concentration of Wealth," *Political Science Quarterly,* VIII (Dec., 1893), 589–600.

EXPANSION AND THE SPANISH-AMERICAN WAR

The general background for expansion is understood by reading the volume of Foster R. Dulles, *America's Rise to World Power, 1898–1954* (New York, 1955); Albert K. Weinberg, *Manifest Destiny* (Baltimore, 1935); Julius W. Pratt, *Expansionists of 1898* (Baltimore, 1936), and his "The Large Policy of 1898," *Mississippi Valley Historical Review,* XIX (Sept., 1932), 219–242; Richard Hofstadter, "Manifest Destiny and the Philippines," in Daniel Aaron (ed.), *America in Crisis* (New York, 1952); and the writings of such advocates of manifest destiny as John W. Burgess, Joseph Strong, Alfred T.

Mahan, Henry Cabot Lodge, and Theodore Roosevelt, as given in footnote references to Chapter 10. Backgrounds of policy may be found in Samuel F. Bemis, *The Latin American Policy of the United States* (New Haven, 1943), and A. Whitney Griswold, *The Far Eastern Policy of the United States* (New York, 1938).

Some light on the economic background is given in Cleona Lewis, *America's Stake in International Investments* (Washington, 1938); Nathaniel T. Bacon, "American International Indebtedness," *Yale Review,* IX (Nov., 1900), 265–285; and Charles F. Speare,. "Foreign Investments of the Nations," *North American Review,* CXC (July, 1909), 82–92. See also Pratt, *Expansionists of 1898.*

On the role of the newspapers in precipitating the war, the following give much information: Marcus W. Wilkerson, *Public Opinion and the Spanish-American War* (Baton Rouge, 1932); Charles W. Auxier, "Middle Western Newspapers and the Spanish-American War," *Mississippi Valley Historical Review,* XXVI (Mar., 1940), 523–534; and particularly Joseph E. Wisan, *The Cuban Crisis as Reflected in the New York Press* (New York, 1934). See also Ray A. Billington, "The Origins of Middle Western Isolationism," *Political Science Quarterly,* LX (Mar., 1945), 44–64. On the immediate Cuban background, see Russell H. Fitzgibbon, *Cuba and the United States* (Menasha, Wis., 1935); Leland H. Jenks, *Our Cuban Colony* (New York, 1928); and Edwin F. Atkins, *Sixty Years in Cuba* (Boston, 1926).

In following the diplomacy with Spain preceding the war, the annual volumes, *Papers Relating to the Foreign Relations of the United States,* during the administration of Cleveland and McKinley, are the most important sources. This story is developed with authority in French E. Chadwick, *Diplomacy,* Vol. I of *The Relations of the United States and Spain* (3 vols., New York, 1909–1911), and from a different angle in Elbert J. Benton, *International Law and Diplomacy of the Spanish-American War* (Baltimore, 1908). Also important is the translation of the *Spanish Diplomatic Correspondence and Documents, 1896–1900* (Washington, 1905). On the attitude of other nations, see Orestes Ferrara, *The Last Spanish War* (New York, 1937); Bertha A. Reuter, *Anglo-American Relations during the Spanish-American War* (New York, 1924); and L. B. Shippee, "Germany and the Spanish-American War," *American Historical Review,* XXX (July, 1925), 754–777. The official American explanation of the *Maine* catastrophe is given in 55th Cong., 2nd Sess., *Senate Document No. 207,* and in the "Final Report on Removing Wreck of Battleship 'Maine' from Harbor of Havana, Cuba," 63rd Cong., 2nd Sess., *House Document No. 480.* See also account of Charles D. Sigsbee, *The Maine* (New York, 1899).

The chief mine of material on the war is the *Report of the Commission Appointed by the President to Investigate the Conduct of the War Depart-*

ment in the War with Spain, printed in 8 vols. as *Senate Document No. 221,* 56th Cong., 1st Sess. The most detailed and authoritative history of the war itself is in the last two volumes of Admiral French E. Chadwick's *Relations,* already cited. Popular, well written, essentially sound, but touched with humor and sometimes satiric exaggeration, is Walter Millis, *The Martial Spirit* (New York, 1931). Described by Chadwick as the "best naval history of the war" is Herbert W. Wilson, *The Downfall of Spain* (Boston, 1900). The most interesting and exciting book on the war is Frank Freidel, *The Splendid Little War* (Boston, 1958), told largely in the words of those who were there and illustrated with 300 pictures. See also Hubert H. Sargent, *The Campaign of Santiago de Cuba* (3 vols., Chicago, 1907), a detailed account, and Richard H. Titherington, *A History of the Spanish-American War* (New York, 1900). Three useful books are Russell A. Alger, *The Spanish-American War* (New York, 1901), a defense of his Department by the Secretary of War; Lawrence S. Mayo (ed.), *America of Yesterday as Reflected in the Journal of John Davis Long* (Boston, 1923), the Secretary of the Navy; and John D. Long, *The New American* (2 vols., New York, 1903). Other widely read books in the years after the war include: *Autobiography of George Dewey* (New York, 1913); Joseph Wheeler, *The Santiago Campaign* (Boston, 1899); Richmond P. Hobson, *The Sinking of the Merrimac* (New York, 1899); John B. Atkins, *The War in Cuba* (London, 1899), by an English correspondent; Richard Harding Davis, *The Cuban and Porto Rican Campaigns* (New York, 1898); and Theodore Roosevelt, *The Rough Riders* (New York, 1899).

Opposition to territorial expansion is evident in such articles as John G. Carlisle, "Our Future Policy," *Harper's Magazine,* XCVII (Oct., 1898), 720–728; Richard Olney, "Growth of our Foreign Policy," *Atlantic Monthly* (Mar., 1900), 289–301; Carl Schurz, "Manifest Destiny," *Harper's Magazine,* LXXXVII (Oct., 1893), 737–746; William G. Sumner, "The Fallacy of Territorial Extension," *Forum,* XXI (June, 1896), 414–419, and his "The Conquest of the United States by Spain," reprinted in *War and Other Essays* (New Haven, 1911). The history of one phase of this opposition is in Fred H. Harrington, "The Anti-Imperialist Movement in the United States, 1898–1900," *Mississippi Valley Historical Review,* XXII (Sept., 1935), 211–230; his "Literary Aspects of American Anti-Imperialism, 1898–1902," *New England Quarterly,* X (Dec., 1937), 650–667; and Erving Winslow, "The Anti-Imperialist League," *Independent,* LI (May 18, 1899), 1347–1350.

For the campaign of 1900, see Thomas A. Bailey, "Was the Presidential Election of 1900 a Mandate for Imperialism?" *Mississippi Valley Historical Review,* XXIV (June, 1937), 43–52, and W. J. Bryan, "The Election of 1900," *North American Review,* CLXXI (Dec., 1900), 789.

Index

Abbott, Grace, 30
Adams, Brooks, 1; quoted, 279
Adams, Charles F., 253
Adams, Henry, quoted, 1, 126; theory of history, 17; *History of the United States,* 17; on the panic, 143, 144, 278
Adams, Henry C., 15
Addams, Jane, social reformer, 19; quoted, 25; founding of Hull House, 29, 30
Agriculture, westward movement, 49; movement of farmers to cities, 49; declining rural population, 50; in New England, 50–51; in the South, 51–52; in the West, 52–54; decline of morale, 55–60; influence of railroads, 56–57; decline of prices, 57–60; improvement after 1897, 60–62; agricultural education, 63–64; agricultural science, 64–66; agricultural exports, 84–86
Aldrich, Nelson, 10, 150, 159, 266
Aldrich, Thomas Bailey, 254
Alger, Russell A., Secretary of War, 237–238
Allen, Frederick Lewis, 156
Allen, William V., 150, 160, 198, 199
Allison, William B., 150, 159, 272
Altgeld, John Peter, biography, 179; conflict with Cleveland, 179–180; promotes silver, 192, 193; endorsed Bryan, 196; Roosevelt's opinion of Altgeld, 200; causes of Bryan's defeat, 209
American Economic Association, 15

American Federation of Labor, 87–91, 174
American Historical Association, 18
American Railway Union, 169, 170, 173–177
American Sugar Refining Co., 159–160, 184
Amringer, Oscar, quoted, 205
Anti-Imperialist League, 253–255
Apperson, Elmer and Edgar, 81
Arena, The, 19
Arnold, J. W., 177
Art museums, 44
Ashford, Bailey K., 64–65
Associated Press, 20
Atchison, Topeka and Santa Fe Railroad, 76, 141
Atkinson, Edward, 256
Atlantic, quoted, 151
Atwater, Wilbur O., 65
Australian ballot, 136–137
Automobiles, early years of, 80–82

Bacon, August O., Bacon amendment, 258
Bacon, Robert, 155
Baker, Ray Stannard, quoted, 60–61, 163, 168
Banker's Magazine, quoted, 142
Baring Brothers, 146
Beard, Charles A., 18
Bellamy, Edward, 278
Belmont, August, 36, 147, 155–157
Bemis, Edward W., 19
Berger, Victor, 273
Berkman, Alexander, 132
Betancourt, Salvador C., 220

Revised March, 1964

hARPER ✦ TORChBOOkS

HUMANITIES AND SOCIAL SCIENCES

American Studies

JOHN R. ALDEN: The American Revolution, 1775-1783.† Illus.   TB/3011

RAY STANNARD BAKER: Following the Color Line: An Account of Negro Citizenship in the American Democracy.‡ Illus. Introduction by Dewey Grantham, Jr.   TB/3053

RAY A. BILLINGTON: The Far Western Frontier, 1830-1860.† Illus.   TB/3012

JOSEPH L. BLAU, Ed.: Cornerstones of Religious Freedom in America. Selected Basic Documents, Court Decisions and Public Statements. Enlarged and revised edition with new Intro. by Editor   TB/118

RANDOLPH S. BOURNE: War and the Intellectuals: Collected Essays, 1915-1919.‡ Edited with an Introduction by Carl Resek   TB/3043

A. RUSSELL BUCHANAN: The United States and World War II. † Illus.   Volume I TB/3044
                                                    Volume II TB/3045

ABRAHAM CAHAN: The Rise of David Levinsky: a novel. Introduction by John Higham   TB/1028

JOSEPH CHARLES: The Origins of the American Party System   TB/1049

T. C. COCHRAN & WILLIAM MILLER: The Age of Enterprise: A Social History of Industrial America   TB/1054

FOSTER RHEA DULLES: America's Rise to World Power, 1898-1954.† Illus.   TB/3021

W. A. DUNNING: Reconstruction, Political and Economic, 1865-1877   TB/1073

CLEMENT EATON: The Growth of Southern Civilization, 1790-1860.† Illus.   TB/3040

HAROLD U. FAULKNER: Politics, Reform and Expansion, 1890-1900.† Illus.   TB/3020

LOUIS FILLER: The Crusade against Slavery, 1830-1860.† Illus.   TB/3029

EDITORS OF FORTUNE: America in the Sixties: the Economy and the Society. Two-color charts TB/1015

LAWRENCE HENRY GIPSON: The Coming of the Revolution, 1763-1775.† Illus.   TB/3007

FRANCIS J. GRUND: Aristocracy in America: Jacksonian Democracy   TB/1001

OSCAR HANDLIN, Editor: This Was America: As Recorded by European Travelers to the Western Shore in the Eighteenth, Nineteenth, and Twentieth Centuries. Illus.   TB/1119

MARCUS LEE HANSEN: The Atlantic Migration: 1607-1860. Edited by Arthur M. Schlesinger; Introduction by Oscar Handlin   TB/1052

MARCUS LEE HANSEN: The Immigrant in American History. Edited with a Foreword by Arthur Schlesinger, Sr.   TB/1120

JOHN D. HICKS: Republican Ascendancy, 1921-1933.† Illus.   TB/3041

JOHN HIGHAM, Ed.: The Reconstruction of American History   TB/1068

ROBERT H. JACKSON: The Supreme Court in the American System of Government   TB/1106

THOMAS JEFFERSON: Notes on the State of Virginia.‡ Introduction by Thomas Perkins Abernethy   TB/3052

WILLIAM E. LEUCHTENBURG: Franklin D. Roosevelt and the New Deal, 1932-1940.† Illus.   TB/3025

LEONARD W. LEVY: Freedom of Speech and Press in Early American History: Legacy of Suppression   TB/1109

ARTHUR S. LINK: Woodrow Wilson and the Progressive Era, 1910-1917.† Illus.   TB/3023

BERNARD MAYO: Myths and Men: Patrick Henry, George Washington, Thomas Jefferson   TB/1108

JOHN C. MILLER: The Federalist Era, 1789-1801.† Illus.   TB/3027

PERRY MILLER & T. H. JOHNSON, Editors: The Puritans: A Sourcebook of Their Writings
                                                    Volume I TB/1093
                                                    Volume II TB/1094

GEORGE E. MOWRY: The Era of Theodore Roosevelt and the Birth of Modern America, 1900-1912.† Illus.   TB/3022

WALLACE NOTESTEIN: The English People on the Eve of Colonization, 1603-1630.† Illus.   TB/3006

RUSSEL BLAINE NYE: The Cultural Life of the New Nation, 1776-1801.† Illus.   TB/3026

GEORGE E. PROBST, Ed.: The Happy Republic: A Reader in Tocqueville's America   TB/1060

FRANK THISTLETHWAITE: America and the Atlantic Community: Anglo-American Aspects, 1790-1850   TB/1107

---

† The New American Nation Series, edited by Henry Steele Commager and Richard B. Morris.

‡ American Perspectives series, edited by Bernard Wishy and William E. Leuchtenburg.

* The Rise of Modern Europe series, edited by William L. Langer.

** Researches in the Social, Cultural, and Behavioral Sciences, edited by Benjamin Nelson

§ The Library of Religion and Culture, edited by Benjamin Nelson.

Σ Harper Modern Science Series, edited by James R. Newman.

⁰ Not for sale in Canada.

Anthropology & Sociology

Art and Art History

Business, Economics & Economic History